STUDENT COUNSELLING SERVICE

Psychodynamics, Training, and Outcome in Brief Psychotherapy

Psychodynamics, Training, and Outcome in Brief Psychotherapy

David Malan DM, FRCPsych
Formerly Consultant Psychiatrist, Tavistock Clinic

and

Ferruccio Osimo MD
Assistant Psychiatrist for Milan Health Authority
Formerly Clinical Associate, Tavistock Clinic

Editorial Work by David Malan

Follow-up Interviews by Ferruccio Osimo

Butterworth-Heinemann Ltd
Linacre House, Jordan Hill, Oxford OX2 8DP

 PART OF REED INTERNATIONAL BOOKS

OXFORD LONDON BOSTON
MUNICH NEW DELHI SINGAPORE SYDNEY
TOKYO TORONTO WELLINGTON

First published 1992

British Library Cataloguing in Publication Data
A catalogue record for this book is available
from the British Library

Library of Congress Cataloguing in Publication Data
A catalogue record for this book is available
from the Library of Congress

ISBN 0 7506 1545 1

Composition by Scribe Design, Gillingham, Kent
Printed and bound in Great Britain by Billings & Sons Ltd, Worcester

What this book is about

In this book we describe 24 brief therapies conducted by trainees under supervision at the Tavistock Clinic, representing a continuous series as far as the availability of follow-up allowed. All 24 are described in detail, from initial assessment, through therapy, to follow-up many years later. Because the patients were selected for *clear pathology* and *ability to interact dynamically,* they illustrate many aspects of dynamic psychotherapy with great clarity, including:

1 selection criteria;
2 the principles of therapeutic technique;
3 the way in which events of therapy lead unmistakably to an understanding of neurosis;
4 the factors leading to therapeutic effects, and
5 the types of change that are found at final follow-up.

In spite of the absence of a control sample, the evidence that improvements were caused by therapy rather than by spontaneous remission is very strong, and the results – with certain reservations – are distinctly encouraging. In consequence of all this the book is much more than simply an account of a particular follow-up study, but it has become both a series of engrossing (though sometimes tragic) human stories, and a mine of information about many aspects of the science of psychodynamics – a term which by now should need little justification. We believe that the book will be of interest to anyone, at whatever stage in relation to psychotherapy, who wishes to gain further experience of actual patients, or who holds the efficiency or the validity of psychotherapy to be important issues.

In our approach we have made a bid to reverse what has been described as the 'flight into process' in psychotherapy research, since in the later chapters we concentrate more on outcome than on technique. The penultimate section of the book consists of a detailed analysis of the types of change that may follow from dynamic psychotherapy, a kind of study which to our knowledge has not been carried out before. These changes include such subtle but crucial aspects of an individual's life as the freeing of creativeness, the ability to 'be oneself', and the discovery of constructive self-assertion, which do not appear in the literature as criteria by which outcome is usually assessed. There is a surprising uniformity in the changes that appeared in some of these patients, an observation that is of very considerable interest. In addition there were a number of patients whose improvements were clearly due to various kinds of false solution – such as withdrawal from the anxiety-provoking situation – the evidence for which is both fascinating and compelling. This is a type of result which needs to be looked for and taken into account by all researchers seeking to study the effectiveness of psychotherapy of any kind.

Of course there were poor results as well, some of them due to serious clinical mistakes, which emphasises the need for constant vigilance, particularly at initial assessment. Much can be learnt from these, and their description can perhaps help to reduce the incidence of similar mistakes by other workers.

The kind of therapy described here was highly skilled, and the therapists, even though they were trainees, possessed a considerable degree of psychodynamic sophistication. Nevertheless they were trainees, and our study has therefore allayed a fear which many of us shared, namely that only experienced therapists can carry out this kind of work effectively. Moreover, the lower limit for effective work in terms of skill and experience has not been explored, so that the degree of sophistication shown by these trainees may not be a necessary condition for success. We do believe, however, that experienced supervision is an essential factor. Therefore where supervisors of the right quality are available, the evidence suggests that brief therapy by trainees can provide an important resource, particularly for psychotherapeutic centres faced – as so often – with demands for therapy that are impossible to meet.

Acknowledgments

We wish to express our deep gratitude to those patients who have given permission for their material to be published. Should any other readers recognise themselves, may we say that we have tried to disguise their material in such a way that others will not recognise them; that it is published with sympathy and respect; and that the ultimate aim is for brief psychotherapy to be better understood and more generally accepted, and hence for more people to be helped by it.

We are greatly indebted to the following colleagues for clinical material: Janette Albrecht, Austin Case, Cecilia Clementel-Jones, Barbara Cottman, Philip Crockatt, Graham Davies, Laraine El-Jazairi, Andreas Giannakoulas, Alberto Hahn, David Heath, Christopher Holland, Jill Leonard, Remy Meyer, Marilyn Miller-Pietroni, Samuel Packer, Susan Phillips, Andrea Pound, Gustav Schulman, Rafael Springman, Arturo Varchevker, and Kenneth Wright.

We should also like to give our grateful thanks to Mrs Jocelyn Gamble for her dedicated work as research assistant in this study.

Contents

Part One

Introduction to the Present Study

1

Beginning at the end

The Nurse Mourning her Fiancé

Interviewer (FO, one of the present authors): Can you tell me how you feel now that you're here for this follow-up interview?

Patient (now aged 39): I got out of the car and I felt very nervous. It reminded me of the first time I came. I remember sitting here, and then I was crying a lot while going home. When I first got the letter from Dr Malan asking me to come for follow-up, those days didn't seem part of my life any more. It was as if they never happened.

Interviewer: Can you tell me what feelings you can recall from that first session 6 years ago?

Patient: It didn't seem real somehow. It seems so different now for the last 3 of 4 years that it seems impossible I was in such a state.

Interviewer: Can you tell me what it is that's different?

Patient: Well, I am quite happy now. I do get upset, but it's not a lasting feeling. Then, I just didn't feel anything.

Interviewer: So now you do feel something?

Patient: Yes ... for instance, a few days ago when I heard of the soldiers killed in the Falklands, I was moved and cried. Six years ago, when I first came, I wouldn't have cried. I would have been shut off. Last August, my stepmother was very ill, in hospital, and I did become very upset. But it seemed to be just normal upset, I was able to get over it. Crying made me feel better afterwards. And you can see the opposite feeling as well – in those days I didn't laugh any more.

Interviewer: So now you are participating in both happy and sad events?

Patient: Yes, in everything somehow. I was just existing for 4 years. It seemed perfectly normal to me at the time. But, looking back ... then, I couldn't care less about anything, really.

Interviewer: Can you say at all how this change took place?

Patient: I can't really pinpoint it to anything. Not that everything was better at once, but gradually things began to fall into place.

Interviewer: Can you say what things, and what you mean by 'falling into place?'

Patient: I think, after I left here, I didn't immediately feel I was better, but I feel now that I am. I don't know how it happened. It is difficult to put into words. With my stepmother last year ... it was pneumonia, and some friends were blaming somebody else for giving her the initial cold. I thought I was possibly the one, and I told my husband. I felt it was my fault. I was very upset, but we talked

3

it over and then I was better. Before, I would have shut it inside without saying anything to anybody, and felt awful.

Interviewer: So you were able to talk it over with him?

Patient: Yes. It was a bit difficult to begin talking – I suppose I still have got the ability to shut things off, but I deliberately try not to.

Interviewer: Why is that?

Patient: Because it makes me feel better.

Interviewer: Why couldn't you do it before?

Patient: Because I thought it would be too painful to do it.

Interviewer: What made you change your mind?

Patient: I don't know. The first time when I was crying, it was the initial feeling of relief.

Interviewer: You didn't cry at all before that first session?

Patient: Not for years.

Interviewer: What made you cry?

Patient: I suppose it made me feel something. I was worried about coming here. It was a relief when I saw I could get through the hour.

Interviewer: What were you afraid of before coming?

Patient: I was afraid she was going to ask me all those questions I was trying to forget about.

Interviewer: Can you try and say why you came back for the second session?

Patient: Well, I came back for more relief.

Interviewer: So there was a difference between the doctor you expected and the real one. Can you say what?

Patient: Yes, I suspect . . . She didn't ask direct questions that I couldn't avoid answering. So I suppose I felt . . . sort of safer, because she wasn't threatening me directly . . . .

Interviewer: Was she like that subsequently?

Patient: Yes, occasionally she asked things but not often. Most of the time I can't really remember what happened. The first time I particularly remember, the rest of it I don't remember anything really.

. . .

Interviewer: Now can you perhaps tell me about your engagement and your marriage? As I understand it, you didn't think it possible ever again to become close to a man.

Patient: I thought I must try and let myself get really involved. I had boy-friends but I would never get really close to them. There was a long time when I couldn't allow myself to think what it had been like with my fiancé. Then I started thinking about what happened before his death. I remember I was talking to a girl-friend, and saying I wish there was someone I really cared about – a two-way relationship, security. It wasn't enough just to go out with different men. I felt I had missed out. There had been a time when I started relying on a man and I provoked great rows. I did it on purpose so that it would come to an end.

Interviewer: Why didn't you do the same with your future husband?

Patient: I felt too strongly that the relation with him was worth risking.

. . .

Interviewer: Do you sometimes get angry?

Patient: Yeah!

Interviewer: Can you give me an example?

Patient: With my husband sometimes. It doesn't last long. I feel more irritated than angry.

Interviewer: What about with other people?

Patient: The other day, when the pupils went out for an excursion, two boys had been to a pub and came back to the school a bit drunk and caused a disturbance [the patient is a qualified nurse who works as matron in a mixed boarding school]. I was furious, I shouted at them, I really did shout and tried to make them feel as awkward as possible.

Interviewer: Were you successful?

Patient: Yes, with one of them anyhow.

. . .

These extracts from the follow-up of a 31-session therapy, 5½ years since termination, illustrate many features which will form important themes in the pages to follow.

The first issue is concerned with the validity of dynamic psychotherapy. Perhaps we may start by saying that the patient should really be called 'the Nurse who *couldn't* mourn her Fiancé', because the point of her story is that after her fiancé's sudden death in an accident 4 years before she came to us, she had not only been unable to cry, but had virtually lost the power to feel anything. The process of putting her in touch with her feelings began in the very first session. This is powerful evidence that her recovery was really due to her therapy, and that therefore it is justifiable to speak of 'therapeutic results' rather than the non-committal 'changes that were found at follow-up' – for it is very difficult to maintain that a disturbance lasting for several years should 'just happen' to begin to remit spontaneously within 1 hour of starting treatment.

The evidence for one of the important therapeutic factors is also highly suggestive. Surely it is clear that the patient's ability to cry, after the lapse of as many as 4 years, could not possibly have been caused by nothing more than the relief of managing to survive the session, and that the therapist must have done much more than simply refrain from asking awkward questions; for the patient really implied that she found in her therapist a 'holding' atmosphere in which she felt that she now dared to face her pain. It was certainly the therapist's aim to create this atmosphere. Her account of the session included not only many sympathetic interventions but also the following: 'At one point I was thinking that very often the only way to help people in grief is to sit silently by their side' – an example of the sensitivity and maturity possessed by many of these trainee therapists, which will be illustrated repeatedly in the following pages.

This story also illustrates the features of a *complete* therapeutic result. Although of course the evidence is much more extensive than in these brief extracts, much of it can be found there: in addition to the lifting of depression, the patient's new-found ability to experience appropriate feelings within the situation that caused them, the relief that followed, the entirely changed attitude to feelings of all kinds, the abandonment of the determination never again to become involved with a man, the closeness that she achieved with her husband, the clear evidence that this relation is not idealised, and the ability to feel anger and to assert herself. Therapeutic results possessing such completeness are rare in any form of therapy, but we can state unequivocally that they do occur.

Also illustrated is the fact that for many patients their therapy is like a dream, which sinks into unconsciousness when the dreamer enters the waking state. This patient remembered little other than silence from the first session (and indeed there was much silence), but in fact – as mentioned above – the therapist made many interventions, and towards the end the patient reached a crucial piece of insight: that during the silences she was thinking irrelevant thoughts in order to stop herself from thinking painful ones; but this device no longer worked, and that was why she was depressed. It was in fact this moment of insight that brought on her tears, which began to come at that point in the session, and not afterwards as she remembered. The rest of therapy also contained much interaction and was sometimes quite dramatic.

Yet, although she remembered little of what actually happened, she clearly possessed complete insight into the basic pathological mechanism involved in her difficulties: namely, her defences (mainly emotional withdrawal), why they were needed (to avoid almost unbearable pain), and what she was defending herself against (overwhelming grief) – or in other words the three corners of the *triangle of conflict*, which consists of *defence*, *anxiety*, and *underlying feeling*, and which represents a fundamental concept in the science of psychodynamics. Moreover, evidence for the therapeutic effectiveness of this insight is conclusive, for the patient clearly described using it *to prevent the pathological mechanism from coming into action again and thus leading to similar difficulties* – one of the major aims of dynamic psychotherapy of any kind.

We may now turn to another patient, with whom insight into the therapist's role and a clear memory of the events of therapy featured much more strongly.

The Girl (now aged 32) and the Mountain Tarn

(She had opened her initial interview with a story of how her father refused to come with her to climb up to a mountain tarn, which epitomised her lifelong disappointment in him.)

Part of the account of the 7-year follow-up interview, which was carried out by an experienced psychologist, reads as follows:

> She had felt more intelligent than her previous therapist and hadn't respected him, but this one was shrewder than she'd initially given him credit for. She tested him out in lots of ways and he wasn't stupid. She remembers one incident particularly. A colleague from work used to pick her up in his car after her sessions. In one session she spent the entire time resisting everything, and when she got into her friend's car she 'had hysterics', screaming and yelling and bashing her head on the dashboard. Her friend apparently lifted her up bodily, carried her back into the Clinic, and escorted her to her therapist's room. It was very important that her therapist had taken her back in, and particularly that his other patients would have to wait. She apparently sat on the floor and just stayed there for half an hour. Nothing shocked her therapist, he accepted her, and he wasn't cross, threatening, or rejecting. She spoke of the importance for her of a solid structure – meaning, on this occasion, both the therapist and the floor she was sitting on.

This was a situation in which many therapists, however experienced, might well have found themselves in difficulties, but our trainee evidently passed the test. Once more we receive evidence about the 'holding' quality of the therapist as an important therapeutic factor.

However, this book is not only concerned with successes, as the following two extracts will show.

The Miner's Daughter

Patient (now 34): It's strange to be here again.
Interviewer (FO): How does it feel?
Patient: I sort of put it all in the past. I started thinking of it again after getting the letter.
Interviewer: How was it to think of it again?
Patient: It made me feel it wasn't very good, whereas then I wouldn't have allowed myself these criticisms.
Interviewer: Can you tell me more about your criticisms?
Patient: I came and saw Dr —— for about 6 months 8 years ago – I had completely forgotten her name before seeing the letter. Then she left the Clinic, and it really was terrible. It was wrong to be abandoned when I wasn't ready, I felt very rejected. I thought treatment was something helpful and she let me down, even though she suggested I could see somebody else. But I felt it would be disloyal to her and she didn't make it clear, as though assuming that I didn't need further treatment. I was really upset, I never felt I could talk about it then, but I can talk to you now. I was attached to her and it was really bad that she was going. I felt hurt. I didn't feel I wanted to see someone else.
Interviewer: How did you feel about Dr ——'s behaviour?
Patient: Not resentment.
Interviewer: If it's not resentment, what is it?
Patient: I suppose it *is* resentment really.

It is clear from the above extract that there was some improvement at follow-up, namely her new-found ability to speak of her real feelings; but in fact there was little else, and we could wish that these feelings had not included intense un-resolved resentment against her therapist.

It is also clear that in spite of much effort on the therapist's part, this patient had been unable to work through her feelings about the bereavement caused by termination, and who thus was probably selected wrongly for brief psychotherapy. This is a danger requiring constant vigilance, and yet it is difficult to see how such patients can be recognised at the beginning.

The Borderline Graduate Clerk

This also was a patient wrongly selected for brief psychotherapy, since the true depth of his disturbance only became clear in the third session.

The following are extracts from the account of the 5-year follow-up, which was carried out by an experienced psychiatrist:

> I asked him if he could tell me anything about his therapy. He replied that he felt extremely resentful about the tests that he was initially given here and about the 'author-itarian system' that operated within the Clinic.
> I asked him what he felt he had got out of his therapy. He said, 'I suppose a kind of confidence with some people to some extent. What happened was that we developed a fiction of me as a person with a lot of rage which had to be kept down in order for me

to be an agreeable person who could have love relationships. Therapy was more support-ing and reassuring than investigative. The therapist [a male psychiatrist] would make a suggestion and then he would reinforce it, making some little lesson that I was supposed to have learnt. I definitely feel there was a lack of exploring my real feelings and a suggestion that I should suppress rage and try to be more agreeable.'

I asked him about discussion of his relationship with the therapist – transference – to which he said, 'No, it was never touched on.'

This is an example of the extraordinary distortion that one may find in follow-up work. The truth is as follows: therapy was extremely intense and highly (and exclu-sively) interpretative; transference interpretation was used extensively (the super-visor's criticism was that it was used too much); the patient admitted his rage and expressed it on numerous occasions; much work was done on 'paranoid projec-tion' (a mechanism by which people perceive their own aggression in the outside world, which thus becomes sinister and threatening) as a result of which this deep-seated and primitive mechanism was temporarily reversed; and the origin of the patient's rage in his jealousy of his younger brother's relation with his mother emerged with the utmost clarity.

Perhaps the following extracts will serve to illustrate this.

The patient had spoken many times of his male rivals, whom he saw as 'wise guys' – a phrase that was tinged with paranoid feelings – and with whom rivalry was always unsuccessful. There had been a particular 'wise guy' who had kissed a girl by whom he, the patient, had been attracted.

The patient opened Session 11 with: 'I was more choleric last week. I felt rage. My friends rejected me, or I thought they had.' He then got stuck and became silent. The therapist, recognising that this resistance lay in the transference, related the anger to himself and interpreted that the patient saw his own anger in other people (paranoid projection). The patient said, 'I doubt the projection theory. I resent it. It's all too much in one go.' The therapist related the patient's anger to various events in the transference, particularly to the fact that the patient had seen him talking to a colleague in the corridor (a situation of jealousy), and to the coming Christmas holiday in which three sessions would be missed (a situation of rejection).

Now, this bringing out of anger in the transference produced a series of major shifts within the patient's psyche, consisting first of the partial undoing of the paranoid mechanism. For the first time he envisaged the possibility of overcom-ing the 'wise guys', saying that if *he* got the girl then *they* would feel the rejection that he felt. Then, contradicting his earlier statement of doubt, he openly admit-ted his projection: 'Maybe the wise guys weren't that vicious. It could be that my feelings have been put on them all along. The truth may be that a trivial event is over-blown.'

The next effect of the patient's open expression of his feelings in the transfer-ence consisted of a sudden freeing of his unconscious, for the traumatic situation in his background now emerged with the utmost clarity. Subsequent events are described in the therapist's words:

The patient told a story about how his mother and her friends used to laugh at him. I [the therapist] commented on how left out and isolated he must have felt and said that the anger over it must have been intense.

His next association was that his mother liked silly juvenile girls. He added that she herself was a 'good time girl' at heart. 'She's the type who likes to be with the wise guys.' [Suddenly we learn that the wise guys were rivals for his mother.]

I commented that his mother was possessed by his father as well as by the wise guys. [This was an attempt to focus the patient's attention on the Oedipal situation, but this time it wasn't his father of whom the patient was jealous, as will be seen.] The patient interrupted and said that his mother rejected his father in some ways too. With some pressure of speech he went on to say that the wise guy who kissed the girl that he wanted was viewed as an attractive boy by his mother. The next association was, 'My younger brother is married and settled down, but my mother said that no woman would ever have *me*.' [Thus we learn that the original wise guy was his brother.]

I interpreted his keen sensitivity to anger over his mother's cruel statement, and that the most hurtful part was that his mother loved the wise-guy younger brother rather than him and laughed at him. I went on to say that he sees himself as a mild chap, but with rage inside, just as he had described his father. He then sees the rage in all the wise guys about him, making it impossible to feel accepted.

Thus the therapist once more interpreted the mechanism of paranoid projection, now linking it with the past. This time there was an even more striking response, for the patient responded by 'taking the anger back into himself' and expressing it openly. The therapist's account continues:

The patient reacted to this interpretation with vigour and described how he made fun of his brother, taking his anger out on him in many ways. We agreed on how his wise-guy brother possessed the good-time-girl part of his mother, and how angry, abandoned, and helpless he felt about this.

There could hardly be a greater contrast between this account and that of the patient, who said that therapy was largely supportive, that his rage was a 'fiction', and that neither his real feelings nor his relationship with the therapist were ever explored.

Let us finally turn to some of the events of therapy in another successful case.

The Librarian who Sought Suffering

When this 30-year-old patient first came to us she was almost entirely unaware of anger, and she defended herself against her unacceptable feelings by turning them into the opposite. In particular, she dealt with her intense jealousy by actively promoting an affair between her husband and a woman called Denise. The therapist was a woman social worker.

The following is an account of the events covering Sessions 13 and 14.

The patient said that she had been anxious to let her husband be free enough to have time with Denise, but he was tied to feeding some new puppies. The therapist said that this promoting of her husband's affair must be a way of expressing guilt about her anger at his rejecting her. The patient then told of a half-waking dream in which she found the puppies thin and dead, and her husband and Denise also dead in bed together, Denise having stabbed him and taken an overdose. The therapist interpreted the obvious hostile impulses towards the man, the woman, and rival children (represented by the puppies), and linked this with the patient's father, mother, and siblings. The therapist wrote in her account that at this point she began to feel a sense of withdrawal, expressed as sleepiness; and she felt that this must indicate she was sensing that the patient was angry with her, which she tentatively interpreted without knowing its cause. The patient said that it had to do with the therapist's small stature, which linked with the small stature of other people who were a cause of jealousy – her GP's wife, her grandmother, and her younger sister. She said that her sister was preferred to her, and that she herself was humiliated by her father for growing into a 'big strapping girl'.

She then said, 'I feel you are stopping me from going forward. I came in here happy and now it's all gone.' The therapist wrote: 'I suggested that she saw me, as she saw her sister in the past and now Denise, as coming between her and the man she wants – myself with her GP, her sister with her father, and Denise with her husband – and that she feels guilty about her anger with all three of us.' Thus the therapist linked the *transference* with both the *past* and with the *current* situation – the *triangle of person* – a type of interpretation which, according to strong evidence, is often crucial in dynamic psychotherapy.

The day after this session the therapist received a phone call from the patient, of which the following is the therapist's description: 'She wanted to tell me that she was very angry with me yesterday for connecting things with her childhood. But suddenly things have fallen into place. She realises that the guilt she feels towards Denise is in fact connected with her parents. She is afraid that Denise will die and that is what she felt about her parents – she was very fond of them in one way but hated their guts in another.'

The events of this last paragraph represent a second illustration of sudden freeing of the unconcious, a phenomenon that is similar to Davanloo's description (1990) of 'unlocking' (the first example was described above in the case of the Graduate Clerk). This occurs particularly when a patient both experiences and expresses anger at a therapist's correct interventions. Here, anger at the link being made between transference and past led to the de-repression of crucial feelings about the past.

The therapist's account continues:

> The patient opened the next session by saying that it was strange that she should feel so much better after realising that her guilt about Denise was linked with her anger and guilt about her parents. She has come to realise that she has a *monster of violent anger* within her. She is glad that she no longer feels guilty about her anger towards Denise for wanting her husband. She realises that she wasn't allowed to express even small amounts of anger to her parents, which made her anxious about her aggression and afraid that they would die.

At 6-year follow-up she spoke as follows: 'When I was only offered 30 sessions I was very angry, but I feel that I worked through a tremendous amount in that time. I was able to have feelings which I regarded as wicked, but it didn't make me into a wicked person, so that I learned not to be afraid of my feelings. Talking with my therapist enabled me to disentangle what belonged to my father and what belonged to my husband.'

The extracts from this therapy illustrate one of the crucial issues in brief psychotherapy: they completely contradict the *conservative* view of technique, according to which therapists should keep their interpretations superficial, should deal only with the current situation and not link it with the past, and should avoid the transference – a view which was conclusively disproved in the work reported in *A Study of Brief Psychotherapy* and two subsequent books (Malan, 1963, 1976a, 1976b). It was in response to these findings that the therapists in the present study were encouraged not to flinch from using the full range of interpretations called for by the patient's material. This is an example of a rarely observed phenomenon, the influence of research on clinical practice.

Conclusion

We hope that these extracts will have given a foretaste of the kinds of issue with which this book will be concerned. Of course we could wish that all our results were like those given by three of the patients described above; and yet, putting sympathy for suffering patients aside, psychodynamic material is so rich that sometimes it is as fascinating to write about failure as about success.

2

The present study: background, aims, methods

Balint's Workshop

In 1955 Michael Balint founded his Brief Psychotherapy Workshop at the Tavistock Clinic. This consisted of a small group of experienced and gifted psychotherapists setting out to explore the efficacy and limits of brief psychotherapy. Only 9 years had passed since the publication of the book *Psychoanalytic Therapy* by Alexander and French (1946) describing pioneering work on brief psychotherapy in Chicago. The passionately hostile and entirely unfair reactions provoked among psychoanalysts by this work may be illustrated by two quotations.

The first consists of the closing remarks of a review by Ernest Jones in the *International Journal of Psychoanalysis* (1946): 'The word "unconscious" is not mentioned in the index, nor have we been able to find it in the text itself. Perhaps indeed it is not germane to the content of the book.'

The second is from a long review article by Eissler in the *Journal of General Psychology* (1950, p. 150; the italics have been supplied): 'Alexander reverts to *magical treatment* couched in psychoanalytic phraseology ... This does not mean that magical therapy is ill-advised; it only means that a physician using magical therapy should know that he is outside the bounds of psychoanalysis.'

One of the main reasons for hostility to Alexander and French was that they dared to claim deep-seated therapeutic results without protracted working through of the transference neurosis as in psychoanalysis. A consequence was the crystallisation of two opposite and incompatible viewpoints concerning brief psychotherapy, which may be defined as conservative and radical respectively (see Malan, 1963).

Those who held the conservative view regarded brief psychotherapy as the appropriate treatment only for mild conditions of recent onset, advocated a restricted technique in which interpretations were kept superficial and avoided referring to the distant past or to the transference, and assumed (without examining the empirical evidence) that the results could be no more than palliative.

The radical view, on the other hand, held that far-reaching dynamic changes could be brought about by brief psychotherapy alone, even in certain patients with relatively deep-seated and long-standing disturbances; and that, as long as the technique involved the *active* pursuit of a chosen theme (later to be called the focus) it could contain the complete range of interpretations as used in full-scale psychoanalysis.

One of the main aims of Balint's Workshop was to obtain evidence that enabled a choice to be made between these two opposing views.

The results of this work were published in the three books mentioned at the end of Chapter 1 (Malan, 1963, 1976a, 1976b). Sixty patients were treated in all, and follow-ups mostly of 5–10 years were obtained on 45 (75%). All the case histories of the patients successfully followed up were published in some detail.

As mentioned in Chapter 1, the conservative view was conclusively disproved. It became clear that with appropriately selected patients, ambitious therapeutic aims could be achieved in 12–40 sessions, by the use of radical techniques, in certain patients with relatively severe and long-standing disorders. Moreover, the more radical the technique the more apparently deep-seated were the therapeutic results. A particular example of this last finding was that when the link between *transference* and *distant past* was made meaningfully, the therapy was more likely to be successful.

The results from Balint's Workshop were therefore highly encouraging. An important feature of this work, however, was that it was carried out by experienced clinicians, who were supervising each other in an enthusiastic research group led by a charismatic personality. The question was whether anything comparable could be achieved within a less ideal context. It would obviously be a finding of great practical importance if similar results could be obtained when the therapists were trainees.

Malan's Brief Psychotherapy Workshop

A clinical approach to this problem was begun in the mid 1960s in a weekly supervision seminar, which will be referred to as Malan's Workshop.

The therapists

The therapists were trainee psychiatrists, psychologists, or social workers, and were mostly full-time employees of the National Health Service at the Tavistock Clinic undertaking the Four-year Course in Psychotherapy, but they also included some visiting associates attending for shorter periods. It was made a requirement of the Four-year Course that a trainee should attend the Workshop for a year and treat at least one patient. A detailed description of the experience of the therapists is given in Chapter 4.

Selection of patients

Patients were selected according to the criteria that had emerged from Balint's Workshop, as follows.

First of all, patients who were obviously unsuitable were rejected. The main criteria for this were:

1 Extreme vulnerability, including:
   a excessive dependence;
   b severe inability to cope with stress;
   c the potential for depressive or psychotic breakdown.

2 Poor impulse control, as represented by sociopathic tendencies or addiction to alcohol or drugs.

Once these patients had been rejected, the criteria on which patients were selected were as follows:

1 The psychodynamics were understood, and on this basis it was possible to formulate a feasible theme or focus for the therapist's interpretations.
2 The patient had responded to interpretations on this focus in the initial assessment period.
3 Motivation appeared adequate.
4 Possible dangers of giving interpretative brief psychotherapy had been considered, and they could either be discounted or foreseen and overcome.

Technique

All patients were seen face-to-face and once a week. The technique consisted of the active use of all the basic types of interpretation found in psychoanalysis. The therapist actively interacted with the patient, using interpretations as his sole therapeutic tool, and at least in the initial stages trying to guide the patient towards a previously chosen theme or focus. In his interpretations he constantly made use of the two therapeutic triangles – the *triangle of conflict,* consisting of defence, anxiety, and underlying feeling or impulse; and the *triangle of person,* consisting of current relationships, the transference, and distant past relationships, together with the links between them. (These two concepts will be described in greater detail in Chapter 4.) Supervision was in a group setting and based on pre-circulated accounts of each session, dictated from memory. It was our policy to set each patient a time limit in advance. This was given in the form of a termination date, allowing for roughly 30 sessions.

Follow-up

Although several of these patients were given follow-up interviews by their therapists a few months after termination, no systematic long-term follow-up had been undertaken (with two exceptions to be mentioned below) and it was high time this work was properly evaluated.

Previous follow-up studies at the Tavistock Clinic

The present work could be based on experience gained from a number of previous follow-up studies carried out at the Tavistock Clinic. The three relevant studies were as follows. The first was the study of patients from Balint's Workshop, in which, as mentioned above, results were encouraging.

In 1977 a small study (unpublished) of male patients from Malan's Workshop, who were diagnosed as suffering from Oedipal problems, was undertaken by Dr Gary Rodin, a visiting psychiatrist from Canada. The results were moderate. Several of these patients are included in the present work.

The third was a study of 84 patients given individual psychotherapy of any length, which included some brief therapy patients from Malan's Workshop. This was undertaken by a team consisting of one of the present authors (DM), together with Peter Hildebrand, John Wilson, and Cecilia Clementel-Jones (Clementel-Jones and Malan, 1988; Clementel-Jones, Malan, and Trauer, 1990). It will be referred to in the following pages as the 'Individual Study' and the team as the 'Individual Team'. Several of these patients are included in the present work; but, by chance, the Individual Study did not pick up any of those who gave the best results. In consequence the main observation was discouraging for brief psychotherapy, namely that most major improvements were shown by patients who had had relatively long-term therapy, i.e. over 200 sessions.

These two last studies constitute the exceptions to the lack of systematic follow-up of patients from Malan's Workshop mentioned above.

Assessing outcome in previous follow-up studies

The method of assessing outcome in all these studies was basically the same. A team of four clinicians was given the initial assessment material, which they read independently. The team then met together and prepared a list of all the patient's known disturbances, together with the relevant history; a simple dynamic hypothesis of the patient's central problem; and a list of criteria, which – if fulfilled – would indicate that the patient's disturbances had not merely *disappeared* but had been *replaced by something positive*.

The patient was then interviewed by a member of the team, and an account of the interview was submitted to the other members. Each member independently gave a score for 'dynamic improvement' on a scale extending from +4 to –2, with half-points allowed. (The reason for the discrepancy between the maximum positive and maximum negative scores is that we have always found it much more difficult to make a dynamic assessment of a deterioration than an improvement – please see p. 22 for a discussion of this.)

The team then met to work out a consensus formulation of the changes, but were not allowed to alter their original scores. The final score for outcome was taken as the mean of those given by the four independent judges.

A detailed discussion of this method is given in Chapter 3.

Method of working in the present study

In 1982 the authors began an attempt to obtain follow-up information on all patients who began therapy under the auspices of Malan's Workshop in the years 1970 to 1978 inclusive. Patients not already followed up by either Rodin or the Individual Team were interviewed by FO, one of the present authors.

The method of working was the same as that described above, except for the following:

1 There were two judges (DM and FO) instead of four.
2 Both judges had access to the accounts of therapy and previous follow-ups, in addition to the initial assessment material.
3 Scores for outcome were given independently, but *after* discussion of the follow-up material, rather than before.

A more recent article describing this work was published by one of us (Osimo, 1984).

Aims and characteristics of the present study

We can now summarise these as follows: the aim of the study is to evaluate the long-term results of brief psychotherapy carried out by trainees, using interpretation as their sole therapeutic tool and supervised in a workshop setting.

Its important characteristics are that:

1 It is a study of a continuous series as far as availability for follow-up will allow.
2 The outcome criteria are firmly grounded in psychodynamics.
3 Clinical details are published on initial assessment, therapy, and outcome of all cases successfully followed up, so that the reader can both gain a true impression of the quality of each individual result and relate this to the events of therapy.
4 The follow-up period is long enough for a proper evaluation of the effects of therapy to be made (in all cases except one the length of follow-up exceeded 3½ years since termination, the longest being over 8 years).

Of course it must be added that there was no control series, which leaves the possibility that the observed improvements were due to no more than normal maturation and life experience (spontaneous remission). However, as touched on in Chapter 1, there is very considerable evidence that most of the improvements were in fact due to therapy. (For a detailed presentation of the evidence, please see Chapter 30.)

Previous work by other authors

A search of the literature has failed to reveal any previously published study of brief psychotherapy by trainees, from which it is possible to gain a true impression of the kinds of patient treated, the technique used, and the kinds of change that were found at follow-up. However, it is extremely important to mention the work of Davanloo, described below.

The work of Davanloo

Descriptions of this work have been published in two books (Davanloo, 1978, 1980) and in numerous articles in the *International Journal of Short-term Psychotherapy* (1986 to the present), a number of which have been collected together in a third book (Davanloo, 1990). However, more important than any of these has been the author's world-wide presentation of audiovisual recordings of his own initial assessments, therapeutic sessions, and follow-up interviews, from which the viewer can obtain first-hand evidence about his method and its effectiveness.

In summary, his technique involves *systematic challenge to the patient's defences* and *minute attention to manifestations of transference*. It is capable of breaking through the defences of even the most resistant patients in a single interview, and enabling them to experience and express transference feelings directly. This in turn results in an 'unlocking' of the unconscious, which is followed by direct access to the hitherto repressed feelings about the past that have led to the patient's neurosis.

In the least resistant patients this is enough; in those who are more resistant the length of therapy varies up to 40 sessions. The regularly observed result is *total resolution* of the patient's neurosis, confirmed at follow-up of many years. All this has been demonstrated unequivocally by videotapes, shown time and again at international symposia and workshops. Thus the effectiveness of the method, in the hands of Davanloo himself, can be in no doubt.

For the purpose of the present work, however, the most important observation is that the technique is capable of being transmitted to trainees, who have achieved some similar and spectacular results under Davanloo's supervision. These also have been shown on videotape. One of the present authors, FO, is currently attending a training course which Davanloo is running in regular visits to Europe.

Further comments on the significance of this work and its impact on the field of brief psychotherapy will be deferred till the final summing up at the end of Chapter 37.

3

Measuring outcome

Introduction

Since in the following pages the outcome in these therapies will be both described in words and scored numerically, it is important to give an account of the principles on which the scores were given.

These are best illustrated by means of an actual example, for which purpose we will use the following patient, whose therapy is described in Chapter 5.

The Sculptress with Nightmares

The patient was a woman of 36, separated from her husband for 2 years. The immediate cause of the break-up of her marriage was her husband's sterility and his unsympathetic attitude to her desperate wish to have a child. Her disturbances can be listed as follows:

A Recent disturbances

Since her husband left her 2 years ago she has suffered from:

1 Manifest depression: early waking, self-reproach, loss of confidence.
2 Physical symptoms: skin rashes and allergic rhinitis.
3 Drinking: she reacts to stress by drinking heavily.
4 Over-activity: she can keep her depression at bay by 'rushing around to friends and to the pub'.
5 Promiscuity: she 'sleeps around' and gets involved with a new man almost every week.
6 Loss of creativity.

B Disturbances of long standing

1 Problems with men: apart from the relation with her husband, which lasted for 7 years, she has never been able to sustain a relation with a man for long. She broke four engagements before her marriage.
2 Difficulties over self-assertion: she reacts to situations of conflict with other people by ineffective, histrionic behaviour.

Brief dynamic hypothesis used as a focus for therapy

Clearly her recent disturbances are concerned with the loss of her husband. Behind this, however, there appear to be highly ambivalent feelings about men in general. These are almost certainly derived from the loss of the close relation with her father, who had profoundly disappointed her in her teens.

Criteria for resolution of her neurotic problems

Here the fundamental principle is that any inappropriate or maladaptive reaction in terms of behaviour or feeling should not merely disappear, but should be replaced by the corresponding appropriate or adaptive reaction.

In this patient the criteria are very easy to formulate, as follows:

A 1 Loss of depressive symptoms, with replacement by a 'normal' mood and self-confidence.
 2 Loss of physical symptoms.
 3 Ability to cope with stress effectively without resorting to alcohol.
 4 Much calmer behaviour.
 5 Restoration of creativity.

B 1 The ability to commit herself to a man with whom she can achieve a close and intimate long-term relationship.
 2 The ability to cope with losses by normal mourning and without serious depression or other pathological reactions.
 3 The replacement of histrionic behaviour in response to conflict by the ability to assert herself constructively and effectively.

If, at long-term follow-up, all these criteria were fulfilled, then we could make the *empirical* statement that no trace of her original disturbances could now be found. This would lead to the tentative *theoretical* judgment that her neurosis had been resolved.

These are the criteria for a total therapeutic result, with which the actual changes found need to be compared.

Changes found at follow-up

The changes actually found at 5½-year follow-up were as shown below:

A 1 *Depression:* She said, 'I am never depressed for a long time.' However, she suffered an attack of depression after the severe stress of losing two pregnancies. For this she received nine sessions of psychotherapy and she is now recovered.
 2 *Physical symptoms:* Her rhinitis is much better but she still suffers from eczema.
 3 *Alcohol:* She said, 'I don't drink any more' (but see below for a qualification of this statement).
 4 *Over-activity:* She said she is 'much calmer and happier.'
 5 *Creativeness:* She said that her latest sculpture is the best she has ever done and that her creativeness 'no longer depends on having a man at my side'.

B 1 *Relations with men:* It is here that there is both great improvement and residual disturbance. She is no longer promiscuous, and she stayed for 5 years with a man whom she met during therapy. While he was with her the relation was close and warm; but he never moved in with her permanently – he always had to go away after a few weeks – and it became clear that he had a severe problem over final commitment. After this relation ended she took up with another man who had a similar problem.

2 *Reaction to loss:* The relation with this second man has also broken up. She described how he started treating her badly, to which she reacted by behaving calmly and realistically and *'didn't drink until she had sorted out all she felt'*. It is therefore important to note that the tendency to react to stress by drinking seems to be still present, though it is now controllable – and moreover, whereas previously she would have got drunk, on this occasion she apparently did not. Her depression in response to the loss of her second pregnancy has been mentioned above.

3 *Coping with conflict in relation to other people:* Here we wish to make a crucial general comment. Although the terms 'inappropriate' or 'maladaptive', and 'appropriate' or 'adaptive' may seem to be highly subjective, this is not always so. On the one hand there are certain forms of behaviour which are quite clearly and objectively both destructive and self-destructive; while on the other hand there are other forms which are equally clearly constructive and represent expressions of enlightened self-interest. Both aspects are shown with extraordinary clarity by the following incident, here told in detail in the patient's own words, because it is important to illustrate the kind of raw data on which our assessments of outcome were based:

> Eighteen months ago I was very distressed because my place of work was amalgamated with another. I felt de-motivated, there was a new man who was extremely difficult to get on with, and I was now excluded from the main meetings. My reaction was to start abusing everybody.

On unmistakable criteria, this was a maladaptive reaction – destructive to everyone around her, and most of all to herself. Her account continues:

> Then I received a letter from a colleague saying that if I went on like this I'd lose my job. I began to look at it in a more positive way. I first organised an exhibition and then a meal for the whole staff in the canteen. Since then it's been all right.

On equally unmistakable criteria, this was an adaptive reaction, an example of constructive behaviour and enlightened self-interest.

Summary of changes found at follow-up

We can therefore summarise her final position as follows. Symptomatically she is almost recovered; her depression has disappeared, though it did return in response to severe stress; she has recovered her creativity and has developed it further; she no longer seriously resorts to alcohol, and – with certain reservations – she can cope with situations of stress and conflict by appropriate action; in relation to men she has given up promiscuity and has attained a close long-term relation, but she apparently continues to express her difficulty over commitment by taking up with men who suffer from a similar problem.

Scoring

The next question is, how are we to score this numerically? Here we use the following principles:

1 The state at initial assessment is taken as the base line.
2 The actual changes are compared with the criteria for total resolution, and weighted according to the importance attached to them.
3 The score is an intuitive judgment of the degree to which there has been overall resolution, combined with a judgment about the adaptiveness of the patient's present position.

This score is thus essentially a *proportion,* and it could be expressed in any kind of scale, e.g. a percentage. We have always chosen to use a simple scale, namely 0 to 4 with half-points allowed.

With the above patient there has been improvement in so many areas that it is easiest to start from the highest possible score of 4, and to consider by how much this should be reduced in view of the criteria that have *not* been met. The most important of these is the residual difficulty over commitment to a man, but there are also traces of other disturbances still present – depression, perhaps drinking, and inappropriate behaviour in response to some kinds of stress.

There are now many questions to ask, the answers to which have to be given even though they can only be a matter of opinion:

1 How much importance do we attach to her residual difficulty in relation to men? From a *psychodynamic* point of view, presumably it means that unresolved feelings about men are still present. From the point of view of the patient's *adaptation,* will it seriously interfere with her future happiness? Here perhaps we can add: from a *sociological* point of view, is it reasonable or necessary, in western civilisation in the late 20th century, to expect someone to be able to commit herself (or himself) to a long-term relation with the opposite sex?
2 How much importance do we attach to the signs that she still has a tendency to react to stress and conflict with inappropriate behaviour, which may possibly include drinking?
3 Should we discount the temporary depression in response to the very severe stress of losing a second pregnancy, when she so desperately wanted to bear a child?
4 The eczema apparently originally came on in response to stress, and it is still present. Do we regard this as a symptom still expressing unresolved conflict, or as a condition that has become established and essentially somatic?

These are all problems on which we had to make a decision in order to give a score.

Two of the principles that we use are: to lay greatest emphasis on our judgment of the underlying psychodynamics, and to attach great importance to the relation with the opposite sex.

There is overwhelming evidence that disturbances in relation to the opposite sex are the most difficult problems of all to resolve; and therefore, if there are serious problems in this area and they remain entirely unchanged, we lay it down that the patient cannot score more than the half-way mark of 2. The above patient has made great gains, but we think that, psychodynamically speaking, considerable disturbance is still present. This suggests a score of 3 and no greater. If we discount the evidence for residual disturbance in other areas, then 3 is the correct score. If we attach some importance to these other disturbances, then 2.5 is probably the correct score. In the end, one judge scored 3.0 and the other 2.5, giving a mean of 2.75.

It is important to note that our scoring represents the proportion of the original disturbance that appears to be resolved *regardless of the initial severity* – it is not a 'before and after' scale, in which a score is given for the degree of original disturbance and the degree of disturbance found at follow-up. This represents a disadvantage that has to be accepted; but, if the scores are used for statistical purposes, it also has certain advantages, a discussion of which is beyond the scope of this book.

The scoring of 'false solutions'

The above patient will have to suffice as a detailed example of our method of assessing outcome. In Chapter 12 we discuss the problem of giving a score when the patient has adopted a 'false solution', i.e. there has been apparent improvement but this is largely because the main conflict has been in some way avoided. Here the patient may be given a limited positive score, which is based on the degree of adaptiveness of the solution and the quality of life that has resulted from it.

Patients who are worse

In this situation we have always found the scoring more difficult, for the following reason: whereas an improvement usually indicates some degree of true resolution, in most cases a deterioration appears to be simply the result of an increased *manifestation* of the underlying neurotic disturbance rather than an increase in the disturbance itself. Therefore it could be argued that the score should remain at zero. But, as with false solutions, we need also to take into account the change in adaptiveness of the patient's position; which means that for patients whose position is *less* adaptive we need negative scores. However, because we usually do not believe that the underlying disturbance has changed, we have not felt the need for the full range of four negative points and have settled for two only, –1 (worse) and –2 (very much worse), with half-points allowed.

As a typical example of this kind of problem we may consider the Borderline Graduate Clerk already mentioned in Chapter 1 (a full account is given in Chapter 18). His case can be summarised very easily. When he first came to us he was in a state of extreme generalised tension and anxiety, which was present in all situations and particularly in his relations with people of both sexes. At 5-year follow-up he had coped with his anxiety by a position of almost total withdrawal. Put succinctly, when he first came to us he was full of anxiety but was still trying; at follow-up he had given up trying.

Here we may suppose that the underlying pathology has not changed, but his position is certainly much less adaptive, and he clearly must be regarded as worse. In fact there was complete consensus among the members of the Individual Team, all of whom gave a score of –1.0.

Conclusion

We hope that these considerations will have given an impression both of the reasoning, and of the problems, lying behind our method of representing the complexity of psychodynamic change on a single scale. Perhaps it is worth mentioning that the method is extremely easy to teach, and that experienced clinicians attain a high degree of reliability after practising with only two or three cases. In the study on the patients from Balint's Workshop reported in *Toward the Validation of Dynamic Psychotherapy* (Malan, 1976b), the inter-rater reliability varied from $r = +0.67$ to $+0.82$, with a mean of $+0.76$. In a study of group patients (Malan *et al.*, 1976) the corresponding figures were $r = +0.73$ to $+0.83$, mean $+0.80$. For judgments of such complexity we regard this as highly satisfactory.

In our working on this case material we did in fact lay down criteria in advance and compare the findings at follow-up with them, as has been described above. From a scientific point of view this is the correct way to proceed. However, in the following pages we have not laboriously gone through this procedure, but have regarded the criteria as basically self-evident. We hope the result will be that these human stories, every one of which is of the greatest interest, will be more like brief biographies and easier to read.

4

Overview of the present study and its results

Introduction

Our work began early in 1982 with an attempt to obtain follow-up information on all patients treated in Malan's Workshop, a total of 57, who were first seen at the Clinic in the years 1970 to 1978 inclusive. Since most therapies lasted for about 6 months, this allowed for a follow-up period of at least 2½ years since termination, which in our opinion is about the minimum needed for a meaningful assessment of outcome.

We found that 3 patients had entered further treatment either immediately after, or very soon after, attempted termination. Since, with these patients, it was impossible to determine the long-term effects of their brief therapy, we made no attempt to interview them.

We therefore tried to trace and interview the remaining 54 patients.

The return rate

In the end we succeeded in obtaining adequate follow-up information on 31 of the 54, a return rate of 57%. This is obviously not as high as we would have wished, but it must be remembered that (with one exception) the length of follow-up ranged from nearly 4 to over 8 years, with a median of 5 years 8 months. In the Individual Study, it was only with the help of a full-time research assistant, and with members of the team willing to travel to any part of Britain to interview patients in their homes, that we managed to raise an initial return rate of only 25% to a final value of 75%. In the present study we did not have the resources to do this.

Eligibility for the study

The basic criteria for eligibility were that:

1 Therapy had consisted of no more than 40 sessions.
2 The follow-up was by direct interview not less than 2 years after termination of brief therapy.
3 At the time of follow-up the patient should have had no further treatment; or if there had been further individual treatment, then the total (including the original brief therapy) was no more than 40 sessions.

There were two exceptions to these criteria, the Anorexic Museum Assistant (follow-up 1 year) and the Borderline Graduate Clerk (50 sessions). The reasons are made clear on pp. 165–6 and 186 respectively.

Over-all results

The quantitative data are given in Table 4.1 and the data concerning the 24 eligible patients in Table 4.2.

Table 4.1 Quantitative data

Period covered	Patients first seen 1970-1978
Total number of patients treated in Malan's Workshop during this period	57
Number of patients not followed up because they were known to have entered further treatment either immediately or very soon after attempted termination	3
Number of patients for whom follow-up was attempted	54
Number of patients successfully followed up	31 (57% of 54)
Number of patients eligible for the study	24

The ages of patients in the study

These covered a very narrow range, from 22 to 38, which reflects the policy of the Clinic at the time to reject patients over 40 for psychotherapy of any length – on the assumption that their neurotic patterns would be too well established for therapy to be effective. By now it is realised that this policy is quite mistaken, and patients are seen up to the age of 70 and beyond. It is clear that many such patients are suitable for brief psychotherapy (e.g. see Gutmann, 1980).

Therapeutic aims

As described in *The Frontier of Brief Psychotherapy* (Malan, 1976a, p. 297), there is a spectrum between 'trying to do a lot with a good patient', at one extreme, and 'trying to do a little with a bad patient' at the other. All these therapies *started* with aims of the first type. However, there were two patients, the Girl with Eye Problems and the Borderline Graduate Clerk, who turned out early in therapy to be much more disturbed than was detected originally; and with the former of these (though not with the latter) the aim had to be changed to the second type.

Where the aim is of the first type, then the desired outcome is 'total resolution' of the neurosis. The aim is that the patient's nuclear problem should be effectively worked through so that the way is cleared for the beneficial effects of further maturation and life experience, with the final result that at long-term follow-up no residual neurotic disturbances can be detected. That this is not an unrealistic dream is illustrated, in previous work, by such patients as the Railway Solicitor (see Malan, 1963, 1976b), or the Indian Scientist or Almoner (see Malan, 1976a), or in the present work by the Nurse Mourning her Fiancé, who was described in Chapter 1.

Table 4.2 Eligible patients

Sex	Age	Pseudonym	Occupation (marital status)	No. of sessions	Follow-up years	Follow-up months	Outcome scores				Mean
Major resolution											
F	33	Nurse Mourning her Fiancé	School matron (S)	31	5	6	4.0	3.5			3.75
M	30	Pacifist Conductor	Orchestra manager (S)	16	6	6	3.0	3.0			3.0
F	30	Librarian who Sought Suffering	Assistant librarian (M)	30	5	10	3.0	3.0	2.5	3.0*	2.875
M	26	Car Battery Man	Minicab driver (S)	29	8	3	2.5	3.0			2.75
F	36	Sculptress with Nightmares	Sculptress (Sep.)	30	5	8	2.5	3.0			2.75
M	25	Betrayed Son	Delicatessen manager (M)	30	4	1	2.5	2.0			2.25
F	25	Girl and the Mountain Tarn	Civil servant (Sep.)	25	5	9	2.5	1.5	1.0.	3.0*	2.0
Limited resolution and false solutions											
F	32	Rebellious Script Writer	Script writer (Cohab.)	29	6	6	1.5	2.0			1.75
F	22	Allergic Receptionist	Medical receptionist (S)	30	5	1	1.5	2.0			1.75
M	24	Concert-goer in an Acute Panic	Lecturer (S)	26	5	11	2.5	1.0	2.0	1.0*	1.625
F	26	Mother or Teenage Daughter	Telephonist (Div.)	30	3	10	1.5	1.5			1.5
M	28	Hypomanic Advertising Executive	Advertising executive (M)	26	5	1	1.0	1.0	1.0	2.5*	1.375
F	34	Secretary in a State of Nirvana	Secretary to an architect (S)	29	4	4	1.0	1.0			1.0
M	21	Self-driving Physicist	Research physicist (S)	28	3	9	1.0	1.0	1.0	1.0*	1.0
Minimal improvement											
F	22	Acting-out Accounts Clerk	Accounts clerk (S)	13	7	10	0.5	0.5			0.5
F	33	Actress with Elocution Problems	Actress (S)	30	4	8	0.0	0.5			0.25
F	25	Miner's Daughter	Lathe operator (S)	22	8	2	0.0	0.5	0.0	0.5*	0.25
No improvement											
F	25	Anorexic Museum Assistant	Museum assistant (S)	34	1	2	0.0	0.0			0.0
F	25	Psychiatric Nurse	Staff nurse in mental hospital (S)	31	4	1	0.0	0.0			0.0
Deterioration											
F	26	Girl with Eye Problems	Housewife (M)	20	6	10	0.0	-1.0	0.0	-1.0*	-0.5
M	28	Borderline Graduate Clerk	Clerk (S)	38	5	3	-1.0	-1.0			-1.0
M	24	Robot Man	Patents officer (S)	24	5	0	-1.0	-1.0			-1.0
F	33	Victimised Telephonist	Telephonist (S)	12	3	9	-1.0	-1.0			-1.0
F	28	Acutely Suicidal Receptionist	Receptionist (S)	9	0	0	Suicide				No score

*Scores given by the 4 members of the 'Individual Team'.

Patients who had subsequent treatment

In view of the therapeutic aims described in the previous section, if a patient returns for further treatment at any time after termination of brief therapy, the result must be regarded as at least a partial failure. Moreover, if the patient is unimproved or worse even at final follow-up, then both the brief therapy and the subsequent treatment must be regarded as failures.

Of course the fact of having subsequent treatment does not necessarily mean that brief therapy was of no benefit – but in order to give an outcome score for the original brief therapy it is necessary to know the patient's exact status at the beginning of the later treatment; and since at this time the evaluation will usually have been carried out by other clinicians for routine rather than research purposes, the information is almost always inadequate, and no exact score can be given.

However, with certain patients who had subsequent treatment, evidence can be obtained indicating that the original brief therapy did have significant therapeutic effects. This applied in particular to a patient who had had 18 months of group treatment in the follow-up period. She was followed up by the Individual Team, who gave her a mean outcome score of 2.875. It is worth giving some details here.

The Divorced Mother

This patient bore a remarkable resemblance to the Librarian who Sought Suffering, who was mentioned in Chapter 1 and will be described fully in Chapter 8, both in her symptomatology and in the underlying pathology that emerged. She was a young woman complaining of depression, who – like the Librarian – suffered from a series of self-destructive character defences, which included presenting herself as immature and helpless, being very passive and quite unable to assert herself, and allowing herself to be exploited and misused in many kinds of situation. As with the Librarian, brief therapy put her in touch with intense angry and jealous feelings of which she had been totally unaware. It emerged, for instance, that when she was small she had made some kind of attempt on the life of her younger brother soon after he was born. (Very remarkably, it is possible that the Librarian also – unconsciously – made an attempt on the life of her younger brother, though this is not certain.) Therapy was terminated after 39 sessions, with considerable improvement. However, 2½ years later she returned to the Tavistock Clinic because of further periods of depression and was given 18 months of group treatment. At 6-year follow-up she was no longer depressed, the character defences had largely disappeared, she was able to be constructively self-assertive, she had made good use of her opportunities, and she had established a close long-term relation with a man. Some members of the Individual Team had doubts about the depth of these changes, which is why the mean score is no higher than 2.875 out of a maximum of 4. At follow-up she spoke more positively of her group treatment than of her brief individual therapy, but she nevertheless made clear that there had been a steady progression towards her present much improved position from the beginning of her brief therapy to the present.

Another moderately good therapeutic result in an ineligible patient

It is also worth describing one further patient because, together with the Divorced Mother, he indicates the occurrence of at least some major improvements among the patients not included in the present series. The follow-up was only by letter, since he had moved out of range of London.

The Public Speaker

This 22-year-old married student complained of claustrophobic anxiety, manifesting itself as deep sighing respiration, in situations from which he could not escape without embarrassment. His two other main disturbances were passivity and difficulty in asserting himself, particularly with people in authority; and sado-masochistic impulses, which included a fascination for pornography, and sexual fantasies of being beaten by a governess with a cane. His wife suffered from a chronic illness which interfered with their sex life. The principal feature of his background was the combination of an extremely dominating mother and an ineffective father.

He was treated for 31 sessions by a male psychiatrist. The focus was twofold: guilt about surpassing his father, and resentment about his mother's domination.

When he was contacted 18 months after termination he had moved out of range of London so that he could not be interviewed; but he wrote an extremely honest and helpful letter, from which it was obvious that he had considerably improved. His work now involved much public speaking, which often included debate and argument with other speakers. This is one of the situations which formerly would have brought on his claustrophobic symptoms, and moreover it requires a considerable degree of self-assertion. His letter illustrates the remarkable degree to which some patients understand the issues involved in their neurosis, and hence also the issues involved in follow-up work, since it covers many of the questions that an interviewer would have wished to ask him.

> I do believe that the understanding which I obtained through therapy was at the very least reassuring and at the most positively instrumental in effecting my recovery. During treatment I expressed concern to Dr —— that the claustrophobia would impair my performance in public speaking. In fact I have found that talking and thinking on my feet have been good therapy. Nevertheless I do admit that very occasionally during a long session of speaking in an enclosed and crowded hall, I experience a recurrence of the old symptoms. But so rare are these occasions now that I do not regard the condition as a significant disability, especially as I have already achieved a moderate success in my work.
>
> Sexual problems still trouble me – in particular a mildly obsessive interest in pornography and a tendency to voyeurism generally. But the sexual problems which accompanied my wife's illness are being resolved now that she has recovered, and we appear to be moving back into a fuller and more satisfactory sexual relationship.
>
> In conclusion, I would make one general remark. Even the educated public seems doubtful about the value of psychotherapy and the theories on which it is based. I do not know, but I think that my relationship with Dr —— was certainly helpful in guiding me to an understanding of my problems; and I think there was a definite connection between that understanding and the relief of symptoms.

This patient would probably be given a score for outcome in the region of 2.0 or 2.5.

Definition and scientific status of the present study

The result of all the above considerations is that the study becomes one of *all patients followed up who had brief individual therapy by trainees and nothing else.*

Perhaps we should emphasise that the study is more *clinical* than *scientific*. For instance, the numerical scoring is a convenient way of summarising the outcome of these therapies, but it has not been used statistically in any way. On the other hand, any study of process and outcome can be used scientifically, and the present study has provided a number of research results of great importance – particularly concerning the validity of dynamic psychotherapy. These results form the subject of Part Four.

5

The therapists

It is clearly essential to give some description of the trainee therapists who carried out this work, so that the nature and degree of their experience can be compared with those of therapists available in other settings.

As mentioned in Chapter 2, the therapists were psychiatrists, psychologists, or social workers, most of whom were employed full time by the National Health Service at the Tavistock Clinic, and were undertaking the Four-Year Course in Psychotherapy. However, there were also some clinical associates, mostly from abroad, who attended parts of the training course and stayed for shorter periods.

The existence of the extremely thorough Four-Year Course enabled the Clinic to choose very able trainees from among many applicants. Their degree of previous psychotherapeutic experience varied widely. In order to illustrate this, we present the answers to a questionnaire given to five of the therapists, presented in order of increasing experience. Therapist A was one of the least experienced among the 17 therapists involved, while Therapist E was probably the most experienced of all.

The answers refer to their experience at the point of starting their brief therapy patient. Where supervision at the Tavistock Clinic is mentioned this was always by senior staff, all of whom were experienced analysts.

It was a condition of employment at the Clinic that all full time trainees should be under at least three-times-a-week personal analysis.

Therapist A (the woman psychiatrist who treated the Rebellious Script Writer)

Before coming to the Clinic: I attended the Introductory Psychotherapy Courses both at the Portman Clinic [a dynamically oriented forensic outpatient clinic] and the Tavistock Clinic for 2 years. During this time I treated three once-a-week patients and brought sessions for supervision to the seminars from time to time.
At the Clinic: I had been at the Clinic for 5 months and had started three once-a-week patients and one three-times-a-week patient during this time, supervised individually.
Personal therapy: 10 months at three times a week.
Psychoanalytic or Jungian training: None.

Therapist B (the woman psychologist who treated the Sculptress with Nightmares)

Before coming to the Clinic: Apart from a number of unsupervised patients as a student and staff psychologist at the Maudsley Hospital, I treated one once-a-week adult patient for 2 years, and two children over a similar period. These patients were supervised by senior staff from the Tavistock Clinic.

At the Clinic: I had been at the Clinic for 4 months, and had started several once-a-week, one twice-a-week, and one three-times-a-week patient, all supervised.

Personal therapy: 2 years at once a week before coming to the Clinic, going up to three times a week soon after.

Psychoanalytic or Jungian training: None.

Therapist C (the male psychiatrist from abroad who treated the Girl with Eye Problems)

Before coming to the Clinic: I had recently completed my MD and psychiatric training in my home country. During this time I had seen various once-a-week patients and one three-times-a-week patient for about 2 years, with two weekly supervisions.

At the Clinic: I had been at the Clinic for 9 months and was seeing about five once-a-week patients, two twice-a-week, and one three-times-a-week. I had three weekly supervisions.

Personal therapy: 6 months of five-times-a-week analysis.

Psychoanalytic or Jungian training: I settled in England and was accepted for psychoanalytic training during the treatment of my brief therapy patient, but I had not yet started lectures and seminars.

Therapist D (the woman social worker who treated the Librarian who Sought Suffering)

Before coming to the Clinic: Starting 9 years before I came to the Clinic:

2 years' family casework with a Family Service Unit, individually supervised.
1 year individual counselling or therapy for the Richmond Fellowship [an organisation which runs residential hostels for people with psychiatric problems], with group supervision.
1 year mental health course at London School of Economics.
5 months' adult individual therapy at the Maudsley Hospital, individually supervised.
5 months at a Child Guidance Clinic, mostly working with parents, individually supervised.
6 months' individual in-patient therapy at a mental hospital, with group supervision.

At the Clinic: I had been nearly 2 years at the Clinic, during which time I had treated several once-a-week patients, some twice-a-week, and probably two three-times-a-week. I had individual supervision two or three times a week during this period.

Personal therapy: One year four-times-a-week Jungian analysis, with 6 months at once a week before that.

Psychoanalytic or Jungian training: I had just applied for Jungian training and started during the next year.

Therapist E (the male psychiatrist who treated the Borderline Graduate Clerk)

Before coming to the Clinic: As a psychiatric resident in the USA I undertook 10 hours a week out-patient psychotherapy, with two weekly supervisions, for a total of 3 years. My supervisors were psychiatrists but not analysts.

I was then in unsupervised private psychotherapeutic practice for 8 years, treating patients at 1–4 times a week.

At the Clinic: 2 years treating patients under supervision at one to two-times-a-week.

Personal therapy: 2 years at four-times-a-week, followed by 2 years at five-times a week.

Psychoanalytic or Jungian training: I had attended lectures and seminars at the British Institute of Psychoanalysis for one academic year. I qualified as a psychoanalyst 3 years later.

Comment

Of course a formal account of previous experience tells nothing about a therapist's true ability. Our own view is that these therapists were of very high quality. None of them made elementary mistakes or needed instruction in basic principles. Their quality is confirmed by the fact that, at the time of publication, eight of the 17 therapists in this study have been accepted for psychoanalytic or Jungian training, and six of these have now qualified as analysts. However, an interest in analysis was not necessarily an advantage in the conduct of brief therapy, since one of the supervisor's recurrent criticisms was that therapists were 'too psychoanalytical' in their approach, which applied particularly to the compulsive use of transference interpretations.

We hope the reader will be able to judge the quality of these therapists from the descriptions of their work, which make up the major portion of this book.

6

Therapeutic technique and the two therapeutic triangles

A summary of the essential characteristics of the technique used with these patients has been given in Chapter 2, p. 14.

The focal technique and focal patients

A question that is often asked is how it is possible to keep interpretations focal. We always found this a difficult question until we realised that the answer lies more with *selection* than with *technique*. As described in Chapter 2, the first two criteria which led to the selection of a patient for brief psychotherapy were: that the psychopathology was understood, and on this basis a feasible focus could be formulated; and that the patient had responded positively to interpretations relevant to this focus. If these two criteria are fulfilled, two inferences can be made: that the patient consciously or unconsciously recognises the focus as an important issue; and that, since there has been a response to interpretations on this focus in the initial assessment period, there will continue to be a response during therapy. Consequently, even though the patient is allowed complete freedom to choose how to start a session, it is probable that the material will soon become relevant to the focus, either spontaneously, or as a result of directed comments, questions, or interpretations from the therapist. Then, provided the initial formulation is correct, work on the focus can begin.

Of course it is impossible, with every patient, to work out a complete and accurate formulation of the psychopathology, and consequently the initial focus may either be incorrect, or correct but not what the patient needs to work with. Nevertheless, provided the patient has been accurately chosen as someone who can respond to interpretative therapy, a focus will quickly crystallise, and therapy can proceed from there. As an example, this happened in the case of the Pacifist Conductor (see Chapter 7), where the initial focus was thought to be failure to mourn his parents, but the focus that crystallised within the first few sessions consisted of his defences against anger and aggression.

A third kind of situation occurs when the initial focus is correct but incomplete, and therefore the therapy needs to deal with other issues as well. This occurred in the case of the Sculptress with Nightmares (see Chapter 7), where the initial focus was formulated as her highly ambivalent feelings for her father, which indeed played a major part in her therapy, but where several other issues were later dealt with in depth, particularly the whole theme of the integration of good and evil. A very important empirical observation is that with a highly responsive patient it is not necessary for therapists to feel compelled to stick to a single focus, but that they can freely work on any other issues that play an important part in the patient's neurosis.

The two therapeutic triangles

Throughout the accounts of therapy in Part Three of this book there will be repeated use of two concepts, each of which may be represented diagrammatically by a triangle. The first is the *triangle of conflict*, which refers to one of the corner-stones of psychodynamic theory, namely that neurosis arises from *defences* against *feelings* or *impulses* which are made intolerable by the *anxiety, guilt,* or *pain* with which they are associated, and which therefore become unconscious or 'hidden'.

This first triangle is related to the second, the *triangle of person*, by an almost universal empirical observation in dynamic psychotherapy, namely that the intol-erable feelings were originally experienced in relation to family members in the *distant past*, have been repeated in relation to people in the patient's *current* (or recent past) life, and during the course of therapy become directed towards the *therapist* (*transference*).

These two triangles are shown in Figure 6.1.

The most deeply unconscious of the elements represented by the two triangles usually consists of the *hidden feeling* in relation to the *past*, which is why these two elements are placed underneath the others, with each triangle standing on an apex. This also means that in practice the conflict in relation to the past can usually only be reached via the same conflict in current life and in the transference.

The importance of the two triangles is that between them they can be used to represent almost every interpretation that a therapist makes. Much of a therapist's skill consists of knowing which elements of which triangle to include in an inter-pretation at any given moment.

These concepts have been used in teaching psychotherapy for many years, but the comment has often been made that if the two triangles are kept separate as

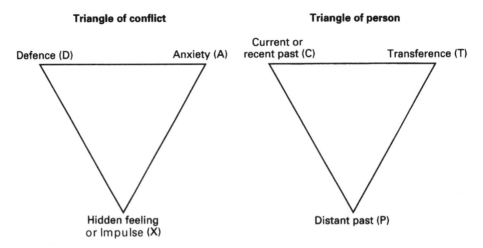

Fig 6.1

in the diagram, it is not easy to grasp the relation between them. We have therefore devised a single composite diagram, as shown in Figure 6.2. This builds on some clear thinking by a colleague, Angela Molnos, who has published two articles on the subject, the first of which was entitled 'The two triangles are four' (see Molnos, 1984, 1986). Figure 6.2 represents a considerable simplification of her diagram, but like hers it takes account of the fact that there are really three *triangles of conflict*, one in relation to each of the corners of the *triangle of person*, thus making four triangles in all. In this diagram the large triangle represents the triangle of person, and in each corner there is a small triangle representing the conflict in relation to each of the three categories of person, current, transference, and past.

An idealised course of dynamic psychotherapy can now be represented as follows. The therapist starts in the middle of the large triangle shown in Figure 6.2, ready to proceed towards any of the three corners, according to the material that the patient brings. Usually this will concern a conflict in relation to people in the patient's current life (C), and the therapist's aim will be to reach the hidden feeling in this area. This is represented in the diagram by X, the 'unknown', following a creative idea by Molnos. However, any attempt to go straight for X will raise the patient's anxiety (A) – which includes the fear of experiencing pain or guilt – and will therefore intensify the Defences (D); so that the therapist will encounter the patient's *resistance*, represented by the line D–A, standing in the way. Resistance can be defined as *defences appearing in the therapeutic session*. It will then be necessary to clarify the triangle of conflict in relation to C, pointing out the nature of the defence, *why* it is being used (i.e. the nature of the anxiety) and *what* the patient is defending against (i.e. the nature of X). In practice, of course, the therapist will usually carry out this process in stages, working on each element of the triangle in turn, perhaps over several sessions, and only proceeding to the

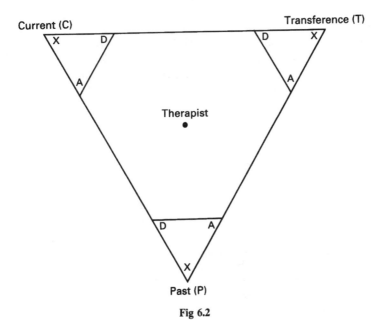

Fig 6.2

next element when there has been positive response. As a general rule, however, it is the defence that should be dealt with first.

As therapy proceeds, it is almost universally observed that the feelings represented by X will begin to be directed towards the therapist, and that these will raise the same anxiety and be defended against in the same way as in the area C. The therapist must therefore proceed towards the right hand upper corner of the triangle; and, meeting a new form of resistance, now in the *transference,* represented by a second line D–A, must interpret defence and anxiety as well as X in the area T. As Davanloo has repeatedly shown, the direct experience of X in relation to T has the effect of *unlocking* the patient's unconscious. Moreover, since the triangle of conflict in relation to C has already been clarified, it is now possible to point out the similarities between the conflicts in the two areas, thus making the transference–current or TC link, represented in the diagram by the line T–C.

At some point in this process material relevant to the past will have emerged, and now the therapist is armed to proceed to the bottom corner of the main triangle, pointing out the parallels between the triangles of conflict in the areas C and T, on the one hand, and the triangle of conflict in the area P on the other – i.e. making the TP and CP links. An interpretation which links all three areas can be described as a *TCP* interpretation; and often this is the most powerful kind of intervention of all, leading to the true experience of X in relation to P, and the beginning of therapeutic effects.

In summary, the therapist's aim is to reach X in relation to both current and distant past, and to link the two; but this can only be done by clarifying defence and anxiety first, and usually it is necessary to proceed via the same conflict in the transference.

Four general principles, which can be used to answer the question of which element of which triangle to interpret at any given moment, are as follows:

1 The therapist chooses the area suggested as currently most important by the patient's material, aiming to clarify the triangle of conflict in this area, and starting with the defence.
2 In interpreting the hidden feeling, X, it is very important to make clear the defences that are being used against it.
3 If possible the anxiety, A, should be interpreted at the same time; but often the nature of A may be self-evident (e.g. fear of experiencing the pain of grief), or alternatively it may be unknown, and therefore will not be mentioned.
4 Only when the triangle of conflict has been clarified in one area is the link made to another area.

It seems to be true that, for therapeutic effects to be permanent, both a cognitive and an affective element must usually be present. In other words the patient must both *experience* X and *understand* the nature of the defences, in relation to C and P; must also understand the similarities between the two areas; and (as described above) this can usually only be done via the same kind of experience and understanding in the transference.

Of course such a scheme is in no way rigid, and in practice there are many variations on the order described; but in most successsful therapies – whatever the order – all these elements will be found to have been present at one time or another. Also, the whole process usually has to be repeated many times, which is known as working through.

The best illustrative example of the use of the two triangles in the present work is probably Session 10 of the Hypomanic Advertising Executive, which is analysed in these terms on pp. 107–8.

Part Two

Clinical Material

7

The conservative and radical techniques: two patients with favourable outcome

Introduction

We have divided the patients in our series into six categories according to outcome:

1 Favourable outcome (7 patients, with scores 3.75 to 2.0).
2 False solutions (5 patients, scores varying from 1.75 to 1.0).
3 Moderate outcome (2 patients, scores 1.75 and 1.5 – overlapping with the scores for false solutions).
4 Minimal improvement (3 patients, scores 0.5 to 0.25).
5 No improvement (2 patients with a score of 0).
6 Deterioration (5 patients with negative scores).

We begin the clinical material with two favourable therapies, chosen because they lie towards the opposite ends of the conservative/radical spectrum of technique, and therefore are very suitable for the purpose of illustrating the range of work carried out by these trainees. Both therapists were in their first half-year at the Clinic and had had only limited supervised psychotherapeutic experience before that.

As will be discussed more fully at the end of this chapter, the first patient represents the most favourable – and unfortunately also the rarest – category of those suitable for brief psychotherapy, namely one whose feelings are very close beneath the surface and need little more than a touch to become freed and lead to major therapeutic effects. With this patient a very simple non-transference focus was used, namely his defences against his aggression and the link with his upbringing. The therapist was the woman psychiatrist who had treated the Nurse Mourning her Fiancé, and we may therefore note that she was responsible for the two best therapeutic results. Here her work showed both her great strength, which was to create an atmosphere of calm acceptance and then say the right thing at the right time, and her weakness at this stage of her career, which was to make a number of interpretations 'out of the book' that were of questionable relevance.

The second patient was the Sculptress, already described in Chapter 3, who showed severe pathological behaviour patterns. She was treated by a woman psychologist. Here the work was both complex and of very considerable depth. It involved extensive use of the transference, the link between the transference and the past, and work on the depressive position – the integration of good and evil, love and hate.

Notes on the case histories

In compressing the account of each of these 24 therapies into a few pages we have of course had to be highly selective. However, although much has had to be *omitted,* we do not believe that our accounts are in any way *distorted.*

In Part Three of this book, which is devoted to a discussion of the changes that took place in these patients, there are many interesting detailed accounts of individual incidents reported by each patient, illustrating the evidence on which our judgments of outcome were made. These supplement the follow-up material given in each case history in Part Two.

Finally we need to make clear that the length of follow-up is always measured from the date of termination rather than the date when the patient was first seen.

The Pacifist Conductor

Age 30, single, orchestra manager, 16 sessions, score 3.0.

Initial disturbances

The patient describes periods of 'weariness and depression' in which he may go to bed and sleep for a whole week-end. At other times he suffers severely from a difficulty in getting to sleep. In addition he may wake up as many as four times in the night; and in the morning he finds that in his semi-conscious state he has eaten 'such absurd things as whole tins of cold rice pudding, half a pound of biscuits, or great hunks of cheese – anything I could put my hands on'. At other times he suffers periods of moderate elation. He is not suicidal.

One of the manifestations of his depression has been a serious loss of creativeness. Although well qualified in music, he has given up his chosen career as a conductor and is at present working as manager of an orchestra.

He has suffered from asthma since the age of 2, and still takes preventive medication, but he has not had a serious attack since his mid-teens.

His pattern with girl-friends has been for relations to last for 2 or 3 years, but he then terminates the relation because 'sexual boredom sets in'.

Background

He was an only child, the son of a vicar. He had great respect and admiration for both his parents, and considered his childhood had been happy. His father died when the patient was 18, from hypertension and arteriosclerosis. There had been progressive mental and physical deterioration, but the patient had great admiration for the strength and faith with which his father faced his death. The patient had stayed at home for 1 year to help his mother get over her loss. His father had been her whole life. Four years ago his mother had gone into a diabetic coma, followed by strokes. Since then, she had slowly deteriorated and suffered from dementia, much to the patient's grief, while he was living alone with her. When she eventually went to hospital, he visited her frequently until she died. This was 2 years ago.

Events of initial interview

The interviewer was the woman psychiatrist who eventually took him on for treatment. The patient was quite unaware of any precipitating cause for his symptoms, but the therapist eventually established – after considerable resistance – that their onset coincided with his mother's death, and when she pointed this out he immediately recognised the connection, saying, 'Of course, that was the starting point'. She questioned him closely about his reaction to the death of both parents. Although he had been distressed, and he said that the funeral services had been a support and comfort to him, there was considerable evidence that he had used the need to organise his parents' affairs as a way of avoiding a true mourning process. The therapist suggested that his mourning had not been properly worked through. He agreed that this was a great problem but said it was not the whole problem. He mentioned his asthma, and the therapist said that there was evidence that asthma was connected with unexpressed anger. To this he said that he is 'notorious for not getting angry', that his father was a pacifist, and that he cannot recall any instance in which either of his parents was angry with him. Later he added that he is incapable of feeling jealousy, and indeed he had previously mentioned not feeling jealous when he found a girl-friend with another man.

Reasons for acceptance for brief psychotherapy

He was taken on because of his clear response to interpretation and his potential for insight, and because of the obvious therapeutic focus provided by his incomplete mourning for both parents.

Course of therapy (16 sessions)

Initial resistance, easily penetrated

In contrast to the patient's ready cooperativeness in the initial interview, he arrived for Session 1 in a state of high resistance, remaining silent for a long period. He then said, with an undertone of defiance, 'I might sit silent for an hour. Silence was regarded as a virtue in my pacifist upbringing.' Instead of meeting his resistance head-on, the therapist decided to adopt an accepting attitude, and merely said, 'So your parents were pacifists ... ' A further 10 minutes' silence followed, and this time the therapist broke it with another accepting comment, saying: 'Perhaps you are trying to convey that silence is a more meaningful communication than words.'

It is interesting that at follow-up, over 6 years later, when the patient was asked what he remembered about his therapist, he replied: 'Her not judging and her asking the right questions', and he spoke with appreciation of her remark about his pacifist upbringing mentioned above.

This approach in the first session enabled the patient to start talking, and it was here that the shadows emerged of a cluster of unexpressed feelings towards his dead parents:

1 The shadow of love for his father: In his last months of life, his father had been writing an essay on faith and pacifism. The last few pages were gibberish, and the patient had re-written them, and the essay was published.
2 The shadow of hostile feelings against his father and manic defence against grief: Soon after his father's death he took a temporary job as a gravedigger. He said he 'liked those men making jokes all the time about corpses, and dancing on the coffins.' He added that this helped him to get over his father's death.
3 The shadow of love towards his mother: He again mentioned that after his father's death he decided to stay with his mother for a year, to look after her and sustain her.
4 The shadow of hostile feelings towards his mother: When he went to University, he would be 'almost cruel' to his mother, not writing to her for a whole term, and not going home very often.
5 The shadow of transference: At the very end he asked 'if this was the way he was supposed to be behaving', to which the therapist made no comment.

Aggression and defences against it

After this session the supervisor commented that he was almost sure the patient's main problem was his inability to be angry with his highly moral and upright parents. From then on the main theme of the therapist's interventions consisted of pointing out the patient's anxieties about his own aggression and his defences against it. Although these interventions never led to any direct feelings of anger towards the parents, they nevertheless seem to have been the key to unlocking not only aggression but many other feelings as well.

In Session 3 the patient told of the following relatively recent sequence of events:

1 He was abruptly fired by a male employer.
2 He had a quarrel with his then current girl-friend, Susan.
3 She had become highly emotional, while
4 He remained cool, but verbally vicious.
5 She had smashed some things in the house.
6 At this point he had become completely immobile and unable to speak for an hour.

The therapist interpreted that he might have felt angry with Susan for not giving him support about being fired, and perhaps he wanted to hit her, but that he didn't trust himself to stop there and might have murdered her. He laughed and said it might be true. Thus in this incident there became clear both the patient's anxiety about aggression, and two of his defences, one of which was to remain calm while everybody around him expressed the aggression for him, and – when this failed – the other was to become paralysed.

In this same session the therapist also made the comment, 'I get the feeling of a lonely person', to which the patient said, 'It's not loneliness, it's independence'. Here once more the patient showed his capacity for insight, for he now suddenly realised that his independence was a defence and that he was incapable of forming a lasting relation with a woman.

In Session 4 the patient reported another incident in which he had used his standard defence against his own aggression. His present Indian girl-friend had

had a hysterical outburst, to which he reacted by becoming cool and verbally hurtful. He said that when he was very angry he felt as though he were another person, looking at himself. This time, instead of pointing out the defence of detachment, the therapist made a 'superego' interpretation, that it was as though his father were present, telling him to be cool and not let himself go. The patient responded immediately with memories, not of aggression, but of grief. He spoke of sitting with his dying father in hospital, in a state of despair at not being able to express his feelings and thus get close to him. He added that something similar had happened with his mother.

Insight into defences against feeling

This kind of work led to a breakthrough in Session 5, indicating how close the patient had been to his capacity to feel and to reaching insight about his defences. He spoke excitedly about what had happened to him in the last few days, and how extraordinary it was in connection with what they had been talking about, namely his difficulty in handling his own feelings. In fact he had just been offered a job as a conductor again, which he had accepted. He said he felt that the reason why he had given up being a conductor and had become an orchestra manager was that he had the right personality for it: while everyone else would get emotional and irrational, he would be the one who would always be calm, and could deal with people coming into the office shouting. The therapist offered an interpretation of the defence of projection, that he could watch with satisfaction the emotional turmoil in other people as a part of himself that was being acted out by them. The patient responded by saying that he entirely agreed, and he went on to say that something was missing from this kind of satisfaction, namely creativeness. Furthermore, he felt that his doubts about getting back to conducting were concerned with the fact that a conductor had to give something of himself emotionally to the performers.

Later in this session the therapist suggested, in connection with aggressive feelings, that there was an intermediate position between, on the one hand, being utterly unreasonable and bursting into a rage without provocation, and on the other hand being incapable of expressing feelings at all. The patient was able to understand this and accept it.

Breakthrough of feeling

The first clear ability to express anger was reported in the following session, number 6. The patient told how incensed he had felt about an unfavourable review of the opera he was managing. He wrote an angry letter to the paper concerned, saying in the session that he got 'over-emotional' about it. However, he then added the important insight that being upset in this way was the price to be paid if one didn't want to act as a robot all the time.

Another – much less desirable – effect of giving up his defences against anger was reported in Session 8. He now went to the other extreme and started hitting his Indian girl-friend. This was in the context of a discussion in which she reminded him of his offer to marry her to solve her problems over a work permit. He said she was becoming over-dependent on him, and the therapist interpreted this as meaning that he was mothering her, and that this was a way of trying to compensate for his own deprivation as a child. The patient took up this theme of childhood deprivation again in Session 9, now adding that he had been prevented from rebelling against his parents by their premature deaths. He then quoted a highly significant and insightful remark that his previous girl-friend, Susan, had made: 'In your family there was a lot of care and respect, but little love.'

Therapeutic effects

In Session 10 the patient reported that he had gone back to conducting, after a gap of 5 years. He was in fact working on a modern opera, whose main character said that it was as if she was living in a glass box, she was frozen. At some point she mentioned being able to cry, and the patient changed this to *not* being able to cry, with which the composer agreed. The therapist enquired about the patient's own inability to cry, and he said that this inability started 4 years ago, when he heard that his mother was ill. He added that he was now able to sleep, because he was doing something that satisfied him.

In Session 11 he reported an event which turned out to represent a major therapeutic effect: he had had a violent argument with the director of the opera he was setting up, and had shouted at him in public. He was 'incoherent with rage' – something that had never happened before in his life. This might have been regarded as a disaster, but in fact it was the opposite, for he eventually got his own way without residual bitterness. Moreover, two composers who were present at a rehearsal were clearly impressed by his new-found personality and his capacity to interpret the music, and told him they would like him to conduct their compositions. He was thus making the discovery of *constructive self-assertion*, the results being entirely positive rather than destructive.

In Session 12 there was an example of a similar therapeutic effect, in which self-assertion and creativeness were combined. An orchestra had been dissatisfied with another conductor's interpretation of a piece of music, and when this conductor went on holiday he took her place and changed the interpretation to a style of his own. The composer told him he was very satisfied with the change.

End of therapy

Therapy continued for a further four sessions, with the therapist showing a problem often seen in trainees strongly influenced by psychoanalysis, namely having difficulty in allowing a patient's improvements to be genuine and therefore trying to interpret them as if they represented a 'flight into health'. The patient then himself suggested termination, and under pressure from the supervisor the therapist accepted this.

First follow-up, with the therapist, 6 months since termination

The following important features emerged:

1 He has continued conducting, with very considerable success.
2 He gave clear evidence of an ability to communicate inner feelings and of a realisation of the importance of this.
3 On the other hand, there were alarming developments in his relation with his girl-friend. He wants to get rid of her but feels unable to because she has no work permit and has nowhere to go. He feels the only way the relationship could

finish is if he kills her. She deliberately provokes him and if he does not respond she hits him, and he then becomes violent with her – at which point, he said, he sees a glow of satisfaction in her eyes. 'She thinks I enjoy it. I do not. I think she enjoys it.' He said that sex is 'always satisfactory and often gentle – in our relation we seem to oscillate between physical violence and physical intimacy.'

4 He has not been depressed at any time. 'I have rows instead.'

5 In contrast to his earlier pathological pattern of waking up several times a night and stuffing himself with food, he now wakes up once a night and eats a few biscuits. He said it doesn't worry him.

Final follow-up (6 years 6 months since termination)

The important event is that he married his Indian girl-friend. This seems to have begun as a way of getting her a work permit, but has turned into a much more genuine commitment. He spent 1 year in India with her after getting a grant to study Indian music. He conveyed the feeling that India meant to him a profound emotional contact, which has enabled him to understand his wife better and to get much closer to her. However, he is still doubtful about having children, saying that this 'would mean a final commitment'. The episodes of violence still occur, but far less frequently.

He was *invited* to become conductor for a large music organisation and is doing very well there. He said, 'Yes, therapy worked. I got faith in my creative ability.'

It seems that anger and self-assertion are no longer problems for him. 'I find it easier to be angry – and then (he snapped his fingers) it just passes.'

He said that in general he is much less afraid of showing emotions.

He is no longer depressed and his episodes of elation seem no more than normal. He now gets up twice in the night and eats biscuits but he said again that it doesn't worry him. He still takes medication for his asthma, but said that his anxiety about having an attack is continuing to improve.

He described his therapy as a turning point in his life, and said that he still tries to work on his feelings for an hour a day.

He was given a score of 3.0 out of a maximum of 4 by both judges, mainly because of residual doubts about the relation with his wife.

The Sculptress with Nightmares

Age 36, separated, sculptress, 30 sessions, score 2.75.

Disturbances

These have already been described in Chapter 3.

Background

The family is of French extraction. The patient is the eldest of four daughters. In her early childhood her father owned a ladies' dress shop. She described the atmosphere at this time as idyllic and said that her father was devoted to his family and he and she were very close. She has remained close to her mother, but the relation with her father went wrong as described below.

Early in their marriage her parents became passionately vegetarian, and a family dream took shape that her father would run a vegetarian restaurant in the Channel Islands and his wife and daughters would help him and enjoy the sun and sea in their spare time. This led to tragedy and trauma. When the patient was 14 the dream became a reality, but with a difference. Instead of playing his full part in running the restaurant, her father left all the work to the women, who slaved in the kitchen while he spent his time mixing with the customers and enjoying the women's admiration. When the patient was at school she was expected to come home in her lunch hour and serve at table, and to rush home after school to prepare the evening meal.

Events of two initial assessment interviews

The interviews were carried out by the woman psychologist who later took her on for treatment (Therapist B in Chapter 5). We shall pick out three significant passages:

1 Early in the first interview the patient spoke of her most recent relationship with a man (since the break-up of her marriage), saying that it was very strange because she knew he was going away from the very beginning. Yet the violence of her reaction to his final decision to leave had surprised her – 'it was like being taken over by an evil spirit.' This theme of good and evil was to play a prominent part in her therapy.
2 After she had described the events of her childhood mentioned above, the therapist said that 'the contrast between her contented childhood and her becoming Cinderella in her own house must have been a severe blow to her.' Amazingly, the patient replied that she had never realised that her difficulties might be related to this. The therapist said that it sounded as if everyone was still very angry with the patient's father, to which the patient said, 'Yes, we are, and we can still be very nasty to him.' She went on to describe fairly severe disturbances in two of her sisters, one of whom seemed to be suffering from a conflict between anger and rebellion on the one hand, and a strong sense of guilt on the other. She had run away from home at 17, got into bad company, and eventually had to be put on probation; but then had returned home and worked in the restaurant for many years, even after her marriage. The patient herself had also spent many years working in the restaurant, with the feeling that she was trying to make up for her own angry behaviour as an adolescent.
3 In the second interview the therapist said that the dream of the restaurant had come true for the patient's father, but at a terrible cost to her mother and herself. The patient responded by talking bitterly about her father's need for praise and reassurance from everybody around.

Reasons for acceptance for brief psychotherapy

The interviewer made very good contact with her, and there was an excellent response to interpretation. The focus was obvious and consisted of the patient's feelings about the trauma of her childhood, with special reference to her highly ambivalent relation with her father.

Course of therapy (30 sessions)

Preliminary work on the family situation

In the first few sessions the patient's pattern became clear of forming apparently passionate but evanescent relations with men who were unable or unwilling to commit themselves. The beginning of insight into the defensive nature of this appeared when she wondered if she might be 'just playing a part'. In Session 4 the therapist suggested that she was seeking some perfect relation which would make up for the pain she experienced with her father when she was 14, and would get her back to the happy relation she had with him in childhood. She responded by saying that this relation was 'all too perfect to be true', thus beginning to see through her own idealisation, and she went on to speak of how everyone including herself thought he was marvellous. She then came out with a major communication about the effect of the family situation on her sister Sylvie. Sylvie, apparently driven by guilt, had worked for her father for years and 'had got into a terrible state and was becoming quite evil and horrible' (thus the theme becomes clear of 'good' as an over-compensating defence against 'evil'). On one relatively recent occasion Sylvie overheard the patient telling her parents about a holiday in France and came rushing into the room 'screaming awful things to her' – having been overcome by envy of the patient and anger at her own imprisonment. This incident had eventually led to the patient's persuading her parents to close the restaurant.

Talking about her sister's anger seems to have touched off her own anger, which was revealed in the next session (number 5). She reported having had a violent row with her father over the phone, telling him that many of her problems were the result of his setting up the restaurant. She then spoke of the other side of her feeling, namely her guilt and remorse. After all, the restaurant had been his life's work, and moreover he now has a heart condition and she was afraid that she might upset him so much that he would die. She then added a story which revealed something malignant in the relation between her father and his own father, which may throw light on her father's and the family's pathology. This was that her father, after having done a great deal for his parents and having helped his father out of his debts, by some legal oversight had been left out of his father's will. The patient said that he had felt very unloved. The therapist gave an interpretation of the family problem, that her father had denied his anger with his own father and tried to get rid of the bad feeling by vegetarianism and good works, but that it had rebounded in a destructive way upon them.

The nightmares and the dawning acceptance of hitherto projected aggression

In Session 7 the patient spoke of her current man as cold and unfeeling, and the therapist said that this must remind her of her father after he opened the restaurant. In response the patient recalled the first of five nightmares which were reported in the next few sessions. The first three contained identical themes, namely that she was forced to watch something sadistic and bloody done to an animal. This first dream was about rabbits having their heads cut off. In retrospect one can see in this a very rich cluster of implications and meanings, not all of which were seen by either therapist or supervisor at the time, and which it is useful to number as below:

1 Sadism to animals is obviously a complete negation of the vegetarian ideals with which she had been brought up, thus once more revealing 'evil' under 'good'.
2 There are presumably transference messages: (a) that the therapist is forcing her to look at violent and sadistic feelings in herself, and (b) possibly that in therapy she feels that she is being subjected to some sadistic assault.
3 The question is, where did the violent and sadistic feelings come from? In view of what emerged later it seems that these feelings belonged both (a) to her father and (b) to her.
4 If they belonged to her, against whom were they directed? Again, speaking with hindsight, it seems that they were directed against everyone close to her – (a) her father, (b) her mother, (c) her sisters, and (d) the therapist.
5 Finally in two of the later nightmares there was clear evidence of fantisied attacks both on babies in her mother's womb – obviously referring to her sisters – and on women's fertility. These attacks were probably linked with the patient's severe reaction to her own failure to have children.

The first interpretation given by the therapist in Session 7 was essentially a combination of 2b and 3a above, namely that she feels exposed and cut in pieces by the therapist as she did by her father in her adolescence. The patient agreed that she feels very helpless here, but there was no greater response than this.

Session 8, on the other hand, represented a major breakthrough, as the patient began to recognise some of the violence in herself. She opened by saying that her latest man had become worried about her being too involved with him and had broken with her. She had immediately replaced him with a new man, called Gerald. A significant detail is that Gerald was living with another woman who was about to have a baby. Later the patient spoke of writing to her sister about her angry feelings for her father, and she then remembered that she used to treat her sister with the same kind of deliberate indifference as her father showed to her, which used to 'drive her sister crazy'. This was a hint of interpretation 4c above, made by the patient herself, and was the first time that she acknowledged cruel feelings in herself as opposed to simple anger. She went on to say that someone had told her that when she spoke about her father she sounded so angry that it was frightening. The therapist suggested that she might be angry with her (the therapist) because of all the disturbing feelings aroused by the therapy (interpretation 4d). The patient said that she did feel very upset by coming. She then said that the dreams reminded her of an actual incident in childhood exactly repeating the same theme, in which a man who knew she was a vegetarian had deliberately pulled off a chick's head in front of her. 'He was actually quite kind but he just didn't realise it upset me so much.' The therapist linked this with the transference and then went on to give interpretation 3b, saying that perhaps in the first dream described above the patient was also the one doing the cutting. In response the patient remembered that she had once tried to stab her sister with a knife – 'it hadn't caused much harm but it could have done.'

In Session 10 her association to a second nightmare was a picture of a female rabbit full of embryos. This brought in interpretation 5, namely her envy of her mother's fertility and relation with the patient's father, who lost interest in the patient just when she was turning into a woman, at 14, but continued to give her mother babies. In response the patient herself made the link between past and current, speaking of the tension she feels when Gerald goes home to his pregnant girl-friend.

In Session 11 there was a third dream, which included a new detail. It took place in a slaughterhouse and a blood-stained man grabbed her. Someone said that he had always fancied her. This was probably a reference to her father, an interpretation which the therapist seems to have missed. The patient's association led to telling how Gerald's baby had now been born and a friend had severely criticised the patient for coming between him and his wife. Later in the session the theme of women's fertility appeared again when the patient mentioned that her mother had had a hysterectomy.

In the previous session the therapist had begun interpreting the patient's hectic relations with men as a defence against true involvement. In the present session she continued this by pointing out that drinking, travelling, and entertaining were ways of avoiding her real feelings.

In Session 12 a fourth dream appeared, in which the aggression came much nearer to being in the patient: she was 'supposed' to shoot some people in the Underground, but only fired in the general direction of the train. She next told of a woman friend who had had a breakdown in which she believed that she was the devil incarnate. This continued the theme of being taken over by evil, and the therapist made an interpretation about the patient's destructive feelings. This led eventually to the following story: a friend had had a baby and had called it Sarah – a name which the patient wanted to keep for a daughter that she might have. She had been furious about this and had to admit an element of pleasure when the friend had a second child which died. She also spoke of an impulse to kick pregnant women in the belly.

The triangular relation involving the patient and her parents

In Session 13 there was a fifth dream which eventually led back to the link between her current triangular situation and the triangular situation involving herself and her father and mother (a current–past or CP link). She was huddled up with Gerald in a hut, trying to protect herself from an avalanche of stones. She then said that recently she had got the feeling of being spied upon, as if someone was waiting to catch her in some crime. She was lying in bed and could see her shadow on the wall seeming to move on its own.

The therapist now gave a highly creative series of interpretations. First: 'The avalanche is like the stones that were to be used against the woman taken in adultery, so that being with Gerald is both the cause of the punishment and a comforting refuge from it.' Then, an interpretation of the patient and her shadow as a description of her splitting herself into two parts, one of which was her punitive superego: 'In her room she herself is the one who is watching and judging. The guilty part of her would not let her rest, although when she is actually with Gerald she manages to split it off and not to know about it.' In answer to a question about Gerald the patient said that he hadn't stated his position in relation to her or the other woman. The therapist said: 'I am reminded of how your father managed not to know what he was doing to them all, so that he could continue to feel he was a loving father while actually behaving quite destructively.' The patient said that she is afraid of how angry she is with her parents (plural). The therapist pointed out that this was the first time she had included her mother in her anger. She now spoke of her mother's inability to stand up to the father either for her own sake or for theirs – he was so attractive and charming to women that he always got his own way. She went on to speak of her overtly erotic relation to him: how intensely attracted to him she herself was when she was young, and that it was particularly powerful because she was the favourite daughter and he was very proud of her and still is. She remembered once getting very drunk at a party and flaunting herself at him. The therapist said that the patient may have been quite frightened that her mother could not defend herself. The patient said that that might be right, as her mother had always been so loving and generous and had never taken anything for herself.

In Session 14 she reported that she had finally managed to end the relationship with Gerald. She had then met him again, but he had proceeded to ignore her for another woman. It was the first indication of a therapeutic effect that she had not been devastated by this and had managed to do a lot of sculpture in spite of it.

In Session 15 she said she had been disappointed that the therapist had not expressed pleasure about the end of the relationship with Gerald. The therapist now made the link between the transference and the situation in her background (a transference–past or TP link): 'It is as if I was your mother and you are saying to me, "Look what I've given up. Father finds me very exciting and attractive. I could have him if I wished, but I have given him up because I love you and I don't want to hurt you", and your mother doesn't realise what a sacrifice you have made, because in her naiveté she does not understand the sexual feeling between you and your father.' The patient, who usually kept up an incessant flood of talk, was silent for a very long time. Eventually she said, 'It's a strange thought, but it could be like that.' The therapist reinforced her interpretation by saying that the patient seemed to feel she was required to give the man up and that this pattern of giving up the man was built into all her relationships from the very beginning. The patient's only response was, 'I feel you want me to try to be alone.'

In Session 17 she revealed that Sylvie's husband had once tried to rape her (the patient) and that a previous boy-friend had tried to murder her. The therapist said that on the face of it these men were very different from her father, but perhaps both sisters were aware of violence in their father, which they found exciting, but which he tried to cover up with vegetarianism. The patient said she was not sure about this, but quickly went on to tell of having got involved in yet another triangular situation, namely that she had just discovered that her latest man was still seeing a previous girl-friend.

A phase of resistance

In Session 18 she said that last session was the first in which she had left without a headache. However, this began a period of several sessions in which the material appeared confusing and neither therapist nor supervisor was able to see clearly what was happening, though certainly the transference to the therapist as a woman seemed to be an important issue. For instance, in Session 19 the patient mentioned having lost her temper with a woman for the first time that she could remember, but attempts to link this with the transference did not produce any clear response. In Session 22 she reported a dream in which the therapist was about to reveal personal details to her, but was prevented by a third person. Her feeling was of great disappointment. Again, the true significance of this did not become clear. The therapist raised the question of what the patient really wanted from therapy, both pointing out the 'compulsion to repeat' and making the current–past or CP link, saying that the patient was still caught up in a repetitive cycle of setting up situations in which she becomes the loser in matters of love just as she lost out with her father. This eventually led to the information that the trouble between the patient and her husband had started before the issue of babies arose between them, when she had found it difficult to bear his repeated absences. She had come to hate his work and everything to do with it, but the therapist pointed out that she had chosen him knowing that his work would create this situation – was her husband's work his 'restaurant'? This was another interpretation of both the CP link and the compulsion to repeat.

In Session 24 she reported taking up with a new man, an Irishman named Patrick, who plays an important part in the subsequent story. It is an indication of the total lack of reality in her relationships that he was already talking of moving in with her and giving her a baby.

Evidence of therapeutic effects

In this session, however, she also reported three therapeutic effects:

1 She is working creatively and not drinking nearly so much.
2 Her husband, with whom she is still in touch, says that her recent sculptures are the best she has ever done.
3 Her mother has recently said that the patient is now much more understanding and aware of what she is doing.

Important independent information about her childhood

During this period the patient began to ask her mother about her childhood. She learned that she had been very jealous and possessive of her father, and at the age of 9 (which was long before they started the restaurant) she had been extremely hostile to her mother, saying that she wasn't her real mother. After the move to the restaurant all the children had reacted to the family situation by deliberately destructive behaviour, e.g. shouting and swearing in the kitchen so that the customers could hear. She and her next sister had persecuted Sylvie (who was 4 years younger than the patient) so badly that a hut had to be built for her in the garden where she could lock herself in.

Later in Session 24 the therapist tried to make a transference–past (TP) interpretation of the resistance, saying that the patient seemed to be deeply disappointed in her mother – perhaps because she could not control the patient's destructiveness – and was keeping her, the therapist, at a distance so as not to suffer the same feelings in the transference. There was no clear response to this, but soon afterwards the patient mentioned the following incident: she had visited a friend who was also a sculptress. The friend had put some clay figures resembling babies into a kiln, and they had made a strange noise while they were being fired, making the patient fear that they had been damaged. The therapist made an interpretation about babies inside her mother being damaged by her attacks. At this the patient became considerably upset and spoke of how destructive she had been to her mother, adding that it is too late now and cannot be made up to her.

In Session 26 she reported having broken with Patrick and taken up with a 'lovely, lovely man' named Charles. The therapist interpreted that as soon as important feelings concerning her mother began to come up in the therapy, the patient as usual rushes into a new relationship which sweeps these feelings aside and puts them out of her mind. This led her to return to her childhood and say that her father almost seemed to enjoy the way she was treating her mother and sisters. The therapist said that in a similar way her father also encouraged her seduction of him, to which the patient said, 'Yes, and I seem to keep repeating it with other men. I always feel I have to do the chasing – it's not exciting and it's too easy. With father I always felt I had to amuse and interest him in special ways.' She then said that in her childhood she did not know how other fathers behaved except the man who had pulled the chick's head off, by whom she was rather fascinated. The therapist said that perhaps this man represented the bad side of her father.

A healing experience and the integration of good and evil

In Session 27 the theme of good and evil, which had recurred so many times in the patient's life, appeared once more in the most vivid form. Moreover, towards the end of the session the patient gave evidence of having begun to reach the 'depressive position', in which good can exist side by side with evil and survive.

Evil materialised in the shape of Patrick the Irishman, who laid an atavistic curse on her, saying that she would come back to him after beginning to hate Charles and behave destructively towards him. She had been extremely upset by this and told a friend. Good then appeared in the shape of a man whom this friend knew, who claimed to be a white witch. The patient recounted the following strange experience in a tone of childlike wonder.

This man secretly prepared a room full of white flowers, and just before midnight phoned her and asked her to come over. In this room he went through an elaborate ceremony of purification for her. She described how moved she was by the love and concern shown to her.

The therapist affirmed to the patient that this seemed to mean that darkness could be overcome by light. She remarked in her notes that the patient related to her more warmly and genuinely in this session than she had ever done before.

The therapist then said that it seemed Patrick was trying to get the patient to do his hating for him, and added that this reminded her of the father's behaviour in the family. The patient confirmed this CP interpretation by saying that when her father had wanted to carry on a quarrel with someone outside, he would often use her as a messenger.

Later in the session she made another crucial communication about good being able to exist side by side with evil and survive. This was that, in spite of all the bitterness between her and her husband, she felt each of them took away something valuable that they had learned from each other – she took away her capacity to be creative, while he took away a new capacity for passion. This was probably an indirect communication about her hope of being able to take away something valuable from therapy, which the therapist indirectly made use of later in this session and the next.

The issue of termination; therapeutic effects

She then spoke of feeling slowed down, calmer, more contained. The therapist asked whether she attributed this to the relation with Charles rather than to therapy, saying that she might find it easier to attribute the improvement to a man rather than to a woman. The patient said she definitely attributed it to therapy.

The therapist then made an implied TP interpretation: that up till now the patient had envied and devalued her mother's care and felt that only her father was valued and admired, but that there must have been good experiences with her mother, who perhaps gave her vitality and inner strength. The patient said that she knows her mother was a very warm mother, and that is why she feels so terrible about what she did to her in childhood.

In Session 28 the patient spoke of how much she had gained from therapy, and the therapist linked the theme of the previous session with the issue of termination, raising the question of whether the patient could preserve an image of her therapist as someone who has cared for her and understood her, or will she devalue her like the image of her mother?

In the last two sessions the patient spoke of many encouraging signs: when she is no longer coming, she wants to use the time of her appointments for creative work, because therapy is too valuable to be forgotten. She has got rid of a number of sculptures expressing the most disturbed sides of her, because she wants to put this behind her. Finally she said that Charles is quite different from the other men – loving, attentive, and reliable.

She thanked the therapist very warmly.

Follow-up (3 months, 1 year 11 months, and 5 years 6 months since termination)

The follow-up on this patient was described in outline in Chapter 3. Here we will add some further detail.

At the first follow-up – like the Conductor – she described her therapy as the 'turning point of her life'. Her parents think she is better than they have ever known her, and she herself feels 'a new person, almost as if I have been reborn'. She said that she doesn't need to show off any more, she can be quiet and pleasant with other people and finds that they still accept her even though she doesn't put on an act. She said that drinking, even in response to stress, is no longer a problem, and she gave an example of handling a triangular situation imposed on her by her man friend, Charles, in a very mature way, in contrast to the histrionics that she would have shown before therapy.

At 1 year 11 months she repeated that she has been much calmer and happier since her therapy, and everything is still going well. She is still with Charles and she is now pregnant by him.

Since then much has happened, as the following information from the 5½ -year follow-up will show. She said, 'I am never depressed for a long time.' However, she has twice become pregnant and has lost the baby on both occasions – the first pregnancy (mentioned above) ended in a miscarriage, and she asked for the second to be terminated because tests showed that the baby suffered from spina bifida. She responded to the severe stress of the loss of the second baby by becoming depressed, and she saw a psychiatrist for nine sessions at this time. This brings her total of sessions up to 39, near the upper limit of psychotherapy that can still be called brief.

She said, 'I don't drink any more.' However, she recounted the following story: 'When a man whom I met after breaking with Charles began treating me badly, I did not get out of control, as I would have in the past. I tried talking to him calmly, I didn't take to the bottle and I didn't get depressed. I was feeling initially very angry, hurt and bitter, but I went on working on it and I didn't drink until I had sorted out all I felt [we may note this hint of residual use of alcohol as a response to stress]. I then wrote a letter. Previously I would have written lots of letters and made lots of phone calls and got drunk [we may also note that she apparently did not go as far as getting drunk on this occasion].' She also said that she has given up taking tranquillisers.

Her creativeness seems to have improved even further. She said that her latest work is the best that she has ever done, and that her ability to be creative 'no longer depends on having a man at my side.'

As far as other responses to stress are concerned, she described with extraordinary clarity how she had converted an inappropriate reaction, on the one hand, into a highly constructive reaction on the other. This incident was described in detail in Chapter 3.

As far as relations with men are concerned, she is no longer promiscuous, and the relation with Charles lasted for 5 years. She said that there was a marked contrast from her husband, who neglected her. Charles, when he was with her, was kind, attentive, and apparently totally committed, and sex was enjoyable. However, she said that on every occasion when he moved in with her he would become 'frightened of his commitment' after a few weeks, and would have to leave. Moreover, another man whom she took up with afterwards suffered from a similar problem. She said, 'I didn't listen to the message that came from him. From the very beginning he didn't want a relationship.'

With some help from the interviewer she linked her relation with men to her father. This passage is quoted in full because it illustrates with great clarity the operation of Freud's concept of the 'compulsion to repeat' (compare the follow-up of the Victimised Telephonist, p. 201):

> My father was a little Frenchman, a god in his shop [i.e. the ladies' dress shop, before they moved to the restaurant]. I think I was competing with the ladies, doing things to get his attention. He was working so hard that he didn't give me much attention. He is still a very handsome man .... I'm afraid I chose the same thing again with a man recently. He can't give attention at all. I filtered off what I didn't want to see and hear.

Thus, even though the relation with Charles lasted as long as it did, she has not been able to escape from her pattern of endlessly forming relations with men who find it impossible to commit themselves to a woman.

Finally, she said that she gets on much better with her family, and she can understand that her father is reacting to his own childhood when he behaves badly to her, so that she is not nearly as distressed by this as she used to be. She gave up being a vegetarian, which she feels was almost a family religion, during her therapy.

Comments on outcome

It is important to note that the earlier follow-ups show clearly that most if not all of her improvements followed her original therapy rather than the nine sessions that she had after the termination of her second pregnancy. These improvements are very impressive: she is able to cope with stress and loss realistically and constructively without resorting to alcohol or over-activity; she is able to 'be herself'; her depression has disappeared except in response to the severe stress of losing a second baby; her creativity has not only been restored but has developed further; and she has given up promiscuity and has been able to maintain a long-term relation with a man.

On the other hand she still seems to express her difficulty over commitment by taking up with men who suffer from the same problem; and there are also traces of the original inappropriate reactions to stress. The score depends on the weight attached to these residual problems. One judge gave a score of 3.0 and the other the conservative score of 2.5, giving a mean of 2.75.

Discussion

These two contrasting patients illustrate with great clarity a fundamental issue in the study of brief psychotherapy, which may be approached as follows: there are patients reported sporadically in the literature – starting of course with Breuer and Freud – whose unconscious lies so close to the surface that they need little more than a single piece of insight to provide major therapeutic effects. The technique needed is usually quite simple and primitive, namely to give them the relevant non-transference interpretation and allow them to work it through on their own; and consequently the therapies of such patients are often very brief, consisting of no more than one to three sessions. Unfortunately such patients are also extremely rare, and in consequence anyone who deliberately looks for them is quite often unable to find them. This is one of the origins of the ultra-conservative view of brief psychotherapy: a more radical technique is not explored, and therefore the erroneous conclusion is reached that these are the *only* patients suitable, so that brief psychotherapy is of very little use.

The Pacifist Conductor represents an approximation to this type of patient in the present series – although his therapy of 16 sessions was not exceptionally brief. Nevertheless the features that he shares with the type of patient described above are that his repressed feelings were very close to the surface and emerged very quickly in therapy, and that this happened without the use of transference interpretation. The essential work was highly focal and consisted of showing him his various defences against aggression, and their origin in his pacifist upbringing. The result was a major emotional liberation accompanied by an entirely changed attitude to feelings of all kinds, which led to a transformation of his whole life even before his therapy ended.

The therapy of the Sculptress, on the other hand, represents an excellent example of the necessity for using a fearless radical technique and the effectiveness of doing so – the discovery of which was originally made by Alexander and French and was re-made in Balint's Workshop. This particular therapy was far more complex and considerably deeper than that of the Conductor, and cannot really be described as focal, since it involved such wide-ranging issues as highly ambivalent feelings towards both the father and the mother, the erotic attachment to the father and the consequent Oedipal rivalry, sadistic impulses, fantasied attacks on babies in the mother's womb, the 'compulsion to repeat', the depressive position, and the link between transference and past – in fact most of the issues that might have been dealt with if the patient had undergone a full scale analysis.

However, we may note a less favourable observation illustrated by both these patients: that it is much easier to deal with problems of self-assertion than with problems in relation to the opposite sex. Both patients seem to have solved the former problem, but even in the case of the Conductor there were residual doubts about the latter; and in the case of the Sculptress her major problem of taking up with men who had difficulties over commitment was apparently not solved at all. This kind of observation occurs again and again in follow-up work, and it will be discussed in detail in Chapters 27 and 28.

8

Two further patients with favourable outcome

The Nurse Mourning her Fiancé

Age 33, single, qualified nurse working as a matron in a mixed boarding school, 31 sessions, score 3.75.

A description of this therapy, on which the following account is based, was given in *Individual Psychotherapy and the Science of Psychodynamics* (Malan, 1979). We would like to acknowledge with gratitude the permission of the publishers, Butterworths, to reproduce the material here. The results of this therapy were also published in another article (Osimo, 1984).

Part of the follow-up interview with this patient has already been described in Chapter 1.

History and initial disturbances

Until 4 years ago she had never suffered from significant disturbances, despite the traumatic events represented by the sudden death of both her mother and her father. When she was 16 her mother had been killed while out shopping, by a lorry that had run out of control. Her father had died of an intracranial tumour when the patient was 28. She had mourned both parents in a seemingly normal way. However, 4 years ago her fiancé was severely injured in an explosion at a chemical factory in the North of England where he was working, and died in hospital in her presence a few days later. This time her reaction was entirely different: she neither mourned nor became depressed, but began throwing herself into hectic activity – going to wild parties, drinking too much, and working out of hours. However, 18 months ago she suffered the onset of manifest depression, which consisted mainly of the feeling that life was not worth living. This had been bad enough for her to take 5 weeks off work, but there were no endogenous features such as early waking, and she denied suicidal ideas. She was quite unaware of any precipitating factor for her depression.

About 2 years ago she had again formed a relation with a man, but had broken it off, quite consciously aware of this as a defence against the anxiety of being hurt again if she became too involved.

It also emerged that she was unable to assert herself either at work or at home.

Dynamics of initial interview

She was interviewed by an extremely skilful trainee woman psychologist. The patient showed her resistance to examining her feelings in a number of ways, which included pinning her hopes on anti-depressants and saying of her fiancé's death that 'it was all such a long time ago', and she 'couldn't go on for ever hanging on to the past.' After checking on the quality of her depression, the interviewer coaxed her into telling the details of the three traumatic bereavements, and the patient showed her insight by saying, 'When it happened once more I just couldn't go through it again.' The psychologist then offered the interpretation that the fiancé's death must have aroused feelings not only about that event, but those left over from the two previous deaths, and that instead of being aware of them she was depressed.

At this point the patient showed the beginning of her therapeutic alliance by putting her finger on the one mysterious aspect of her history: her fiancé's death had occurred 4 years ago, but she had only become depressed 18 months ago, and she now asked, 'Why so much later?' The interviewer responded by suggesting that she should examine events since she came back to London 2 years ago. It finally emerged that soon after the beginning of term, 18 months ago, one of the girls had come to her in a state of depression because her mother had just died. This had clearly threatened to reactivate the patient's own grief and had precipitated her depression, and the mystery was solved.

Reason for acceptance for brief psychotherapy

There was a clear focus of unresolved mourning, and indeed she seemed on the formal evidence to be the ideal brief psychotherapy patient – someone with an excellent basic personality suffering from unresolved feelings after being subjected to overwhelming stress. Part of the dynamic evidence was also favourable, in the sense that her unconscious therapeutic alliance collaborated with the interviewer enough to enable the recent precipitating factor to be discovered. However, her motivation to face her feelings was limited, since she still wanted to pin her hopes on anti-depressants, but she eventually decided that this would not work and asked for treatment.

Course of therapy (31 sessions)

The therapist was the woman psychiatrist who had treated the Pacifist Conductor, now with over a year's further intensive experience and training.

Work on mourning

It may be remembered from Chapter 1 that at follow-up the patient said of the first session, 'I was afraid she was going to ask me all those questions I was trying to forget about.' This remark explains the character of the session, much of which was spent in silent and passive resistance. It also puts in context the following passage, taken from the therapist's report: 'She asked, "What am I supposed to say?" I replied that she was free to mention any thought that went through her mind. She looked puzzled and was silent for a while, staring into space. She said, "I thought you would ask questions?" I: "No, as you see I don't, and you are free to say anything you are thinking of, or to be silent if you choose to do so."'

As the patient also described at follow-up, this approach enabled her to feel safe, and towards the very end of the session she was able to recognise spontaneously that she was concentrating on irrelevancies in order to stop herself thinking painful thoughts, and that this no longer worked and was why she was depressed. It was here that this patient, who had not cried for 4 years, began to become tearful. This mixture of passive resistance and therapeutic alliance characterised the whole of therapy.

In the next session (number 2) she reported that the moment she got out of the door she had been in floods of tears and had not been able to stop herself crying all that evening. Yet she said she did not know why she was crying; and in Session 3, where she reported that the process had continued, she said she was 'crying about nothing' – so that it was clear that she was suffering from 'depressive tears', which are not truly in touch with the underlying grief.

However, this state of affairs changed in Session 5. She reported a major coincidence: she had heard that the fiancé of a friend had been severely injured in an accident and was now in intensive care. This brought back memories of waiting at the hospital after her own fiancé's accident. She had been very upset by this and had lain awake for a long time. The therapist described the desolate look on the patient's face as she spoke, and her own fear of precipitating some strong reaction. As a result she probably spoke too much, rather than encouraging the patient to speak, and the session never came to life.

Between Sessions 7 and 8 the patient spent part of the Easter holiday in the North of England, where she had been living at the time of her fiancé's death. It was a measure of her continued capacity for denial that she had enjoyed herself and had felt no grief even when she visited places where they had been happy together. Nevertheless she became upset once more at the thought of coming back and facing therapy; and in Session 10 she said she was depressed again. Under some pressure from the therapist she suddenly remembered that her depression had come on after she had been told by a friend about a woman who was dying in hospital, and she offered the spontaneous insight: 'I can see that I blocked off something painful.' In the next session (number 11) she reported that she had been fighting with tears all the day before and had been unable to work, but even then she could not link this with her own mourning.

Work on anger

The question was always in our minds whether the patient's inability to face her grief was partly due to repressed angry feelings, perhaps resulting from quarrels with any of the three people who had died, and the supervisor urged the therapist to explore this area as actively as possible. In Session 2 the therapist questioned her closely about this. No trace of any such problem was ever elicited in relation to either her fiancé or her father, but she did admit that in her teens there had been quarrels with her mother, who would not let her go out in the evenings on weekdays.

A hint that this might be important was a recurrent theme, first expressed in a dream reported in Session 7, of people who are usually kind and helpful becoming *unsympathetic.* This would seem to indicate that somebody had behaved in a way to her that aroused her anger. Nevertheless the patient utterly denied that this had occurred with any of the three people who had died, and she equally denied any connection with the transference.

Very little more direct evidence on this question was elicited throughout the whole of therapy, and yet indirect evidence was considerable. On at least three occasions she reported improvement after therapeutic work directly or indirectly concerning anger. One of the climaxes of therapy occurred in Session 12. She spoke of waiting at the hospital 4 years ago and knowing that her fiancé was going to die, and of the feeling that she had had previously that her happiness with him was bound to go wrong. Once more she denied any quarrels with him. She then suddenly remembered two recent nightmares, the second with a distinctly paranoid tinge. In the first her current platonic boy-friend Derek betrayed her by taking a job that she wanted, and then *unsympathetically* told her off for crying. In the second she was looking for her cat and found instead many cats sitting and staring at her in a persecuting way; and then Derek appeared, but it wasn't Derek and he had a horrible leper face. The significance of her cat seemed to be that in her absence her parents had had it 'put to sleep', i.e. killed, but since she was not responsible for this it was difficult to make use of it. As far as Derek was concerned, she had found him somewhat unsympathetic recently, telling her to pull herself together; but this did not seem sufficient reason for the persecutory nature of these dreams, nor for the intensity of the anxiety that she had felt on waking up from the second. The explanation for this somewhat paranoid dream in such a very 'normal' person, and the link – if any – with her fiancé's death, remain a mystery to this day. Understandably the therapist was at a loss and simply said – assuming that the mechanism behind the dreams was paranoid projection of hostile feelings of some kind – that the patient must be frightened of something inside herself that was very upsetting and horrible to look at.

In spite of the fact that the nature of these feelings never became clear, the patient said in Session 15 that she had been feeling better ever since the session in which the nightmares had been reported. At the same time she had once more become extremely resistant, and in Session 16 the therapist made interpretations about anger in the transference, basing this on her feeling that the patient was deliberately trying to irritate her by being obstructive (she wrote in her account of the session, 'If counter-transference is evidence, then I am feeling more and more angry with this girl'). The patient utterly denied any anger, but in the next session (number 17) she showed her therapeutic alliance by saying that she had been trying to remember occasions on which she had been angry, and she reported three episodes of being let down by people, including a previous boy-friend who she discovered had been going out with many other girls as well as her. No such feeling could be elicited about her fianca. Nevertheless, after telling of these instances of anger, she once more reported that she had recently been feeling better. At various other times in the therapy the therapist tried to get at anger in the transference but always drew a blank.

In Session 18 the therapist returned to searching for hostility against the patient's mother, and brought out some more details of the conflict with her mother in her teens. This led in Session 19 to another of the climaxes of therapy. The patient showed her therapeutic alliance by spontaneously writing down her dreams. In one of these a woman called Anne had been murdered – Anne is the patient's second name and also that of her grandmother – and a man was following the patient and her grandmother, possibly intending to murder them. The therapist succeeded in bringing out that the patient sometimes gets so irritated with her grandmother that she wishes she would die, and then she feels terribly guilty, with the thought that she has not done enough for her. It seems that this ability to reach love and hate for the same person, the 'depressive position' (compare the Sculptress), resulted in *coming to life,* for in this same session the patient reported another dream, in which the ice of an Arctic landscape became transformed into grass.

Her ability to express anger now continued to increase. In Session 21 she reported an incident in which, shaking with rage, she had sworn at a bus conductress who hadn't waited for an old lady to get off before re-starting the bus, which had resulted in the lady being separated from her husband. In Session 26 she said that recently she had been much more aggressive, and she gave an example of a girl at school who had answered her back: 'I was so furious that I swore at her and felt I could have hit her.'

In Session 24 she told of an incident in which her friend, Derek, had failed to meet her, and she had been afraid that something terrible had happened to him. 'It's always the same thing. I'm worried that something is going to happen to people I'm fond of.' 'And,' the therapist said, 'with whom you've had a disagreement and expressed some irritation to.' This guess hit the mark, for the patient said that she had nearly quarrelled with Derek the day before.

Final phase: evidence of major improvements

In Session 27 she opened by saying that she had been trying to convince a friend who was depressed that she should see a psychiatrist, because she herself had been helped so much. She went on to tell of having burst into tears because she had been let down by another friend who had invited her out and then cancelled. This marked an important advance, because now her tears were in touch with their cause, which they had not been in the early sessions. The therapist made the link with the past, and the patient then told of two further nightmares, both about ghosts. The therapist said that often the belief that people will come back as ghosts, if they haven't been properly buried, is really concerned with the psychology of the survivors, who haven't dealt with all their memories and feelings about the people who have died.

In the last few sessions she continued to be resistant, with long periods of silence, though with occasions when her therapeutic alliance broke through. Interpretations about feelings of loss at the termination of her therapy produced no response whatsoever.

In the final session (number 31), however, she said she felt *different* – she could now tell when she was upset, whereas previously she had never been conscious of sadness or unhappiness. Recently a girl who had lost both parents in an accident came to her, and they had cried together, and she felt she was crying for herself as well as for the girl. The other members of staff could see that she had been crying, but it no longer mattered.

Follow-up (5 years 6 months since termination)

Much of the follow-up information has already been given in the patient's own words in Chapter 1, and it will only be summarised here.

Of all the features that emerged, one of the most convincing was that she spontaneously compared her state of complete non-involvement when she first came here with her quite normal reactions now. 'I just didn't feel anything then.' She described being able to cry and the resulting relief, to be happy, to laugh, and to read a book because she was involved in it and wanted to read on, instead of reading it to blot out her thoughts.

She has now been married for 2 years. She described how in a previous relation with a man she had deliberately provoked rows so that he would leave her. With her future husband she had not done this – 'I felt too strongly that the relation with him was worth risking.' Her relation with her husband seems completely normal: she is able to share her feelings with him, to feel close to him, to quarrel and make it up, to enjoy the sexual relation. She has a job in a larger school, with more responsibility. Anger and self-assertion seem no longer to present a problem to her.

She described how she now realised that if she met her first fiancé again she would not feel the same about him. She has developed interests that he would never have been able to share.

In summary, hardly any trace of her original disturbances can be detected. The scores given by the two judges were 4.0 and 3.5 – the latter based on conservative caution – mean 3.75.

It is worth noting that at follow-up she expressed a considerable degree of resentment against her therapist for refusing to advise her about whether she needed further treatment – 'she couldn't care less'. This is an example of the disadvantage to a therapist of being over-psychoanalytic: the rigid use of the passive sounding board approach, which would have been inappropriate even in an analysis, let alone in brief psychotherapy. Clearly the therapist should have said something like, 'You have made a great deal of progress, but there is no way of telling at present. I suggest we see how you get on and review the situation in, say, 6 months' time.'

Comment

It is interesting that the two patients with the highest scores, this patient and the Conductor, were both treated by the same therapist, whose great gift was the accepting atmosphere that she was able to create. It takes nothing away from her work to say that both these patients seem to have been the ideal type of brief therapy patient, whose feelings were so close to the surface that they started to break through extremely early in therapy, and with whom a relatively conservative non-transference technique was all that was needed. In both patients this resulted in an entirely changed attitude to feelings of all kinds, and ultimately a complete transformation of their lives.

As far as guilt about ambivalent feelings was concerned – which might have been expected to have complicated the present patient's grief and made it more difficult to bear – very little was unearthed except in relation to her grandmother; and yet, as described above, on at least three occasions she reported improvement after receiving interpretations about anger, even though there was hardly any response to these interpretations at the time.

In spite of all this, there was clear and steady progress towards being able to express feelings in an uncomplicated way. Thus although her tears after the first session represented a major improvement in someone who had been quite unable to mourn, she was not in touch with their cause; but in Session 5 she reported that her grief had been reactivated by hearing of an accident to a friend's fiancé; in Session 27 she reported having cried at being let down by another friend; and in Session 31 she had cried with a bereaved girl, for herself as well as for the girl.

There was a similar progress over anger. Her anger with the bus conductress who ill-treated an old lady may well have been tinged with self-hatred because of her own ambivalent feelings about her grandmother; but her anger with the girl at school who answered her back was uncomplicated and direct.

As far as relations with men were concerned, she showed similar steady progress in the follow-up period: from deliberately provoking rows in order to end a relationship, to allowing herself to become committed to her future husband.

Finally, we may note the patient's ambivalent motivation throughout. Apparently she was determined to go at her own pace and not be pushed at any time into feelings that were more than she could bear. Yet it seems that this policy paid off, since during the course of therapy and the follow-up period she changed from a kind of automaton into the utterly normal person that she had been before.

The Librarian who Sought Suffering

Age 30, married, part time assistant librarian, 30 sessions, score 3.0.

Complaint

Recurrrent depressions since puberty, worse since age 19 when she got into conflict with her parents over her intention to marry, and much worse since the birth of her second child 4 years ago. 'I want to be dead and I don't understand why.' However, she denied actual suicidal intent.

History and disturbances

She is the oldest child of a family of five, the next being a brother 3 years younger. Before her brother's birth she remembers her mother as warm and loving to her, but after his birth her mother turned her attention towards him and away from her. She describes her father as cold and aloof. She said she was very jealous of her brother, but much less so of the three later children.

She admitted that in adult life she was sexually excited by being treated badly or being forced to have intercourse. She married her husband on the rebound from a man who ill-treated her. Her husband himself had neurotic difficulties, and it became clear that their relation was on the basis of strong mutual dependence and caring of a regressive kind. She reacted badly to the restriction imposed on her by the birth of their second child and had a brief affair, about which she told her husband. He was precipitated into impotence, for which he sought psychotherapy. This helped him considerably. With remarkable insight she wrote about this situation in her application form as follows: 'He has gradually ceased to need me in my familiar role as mother-substitute. Now the persona I have built up around other people's needs is quite redundant and I have no one inside me who can tell me who I am.'

Dynamics of interview

In a highly dynamic interview the (male) trainee psychiatrist made a large number of interpretations, which included the following: the need for revenge on her husband; hostile feelings towards her parents, to which she responded by acknowledging her anger with her father for being so aloof; jealousy of her husband's relation with his therapist, which led her to speak of her jealousy of her younger brother; when she got stuck at this point, he said she was behaving as if she was helpless and wanting to be rescued, which she acknowledged as one of her patterns; she spoke of her father nearly having a heart attack, at which he interpreted death wishes. This led her to speak of a crucial incident in her childhood, in which she was in charge of her younger brother, then aged 2, and he fell into a stream – she did not know whether she pushed him or not. Most fortunately, he was rescued by a neighbour. The therapist said that 'she had pushed the wrong person in,' to which the patient, wide-eyed, said, 'You mean my mother?' She added that she had always been aware of anger with her father, but never with her mother for having a baby and then neglecting her.

Reason for acceptance for brief psychotherapy

This was based on her insight and response to interpretation, and the clear focus of her regressive and masochistic defences against anger and jealousy.

Course of therapy (30 sessions)

The therapist was a woman social worker in her 30s, Jungian in her approach, considerably experienced in psychotherapy (therapist D in Chapter 5), and active, fearless, and skilful in her interpretations.

Masochistic defence against anger and jealousy

Under the impact of much active interpretation of the two therapeutic triangles, the following emerged. In her current life the patient was actively promoting an affair between her husband and a woman called Denise. The therapist interpreted many aspects of this:

1 that it was a *defence* against anger and jealousy (the *underlying feelings* or *impulses*);
2 that her *anxiety* was that, if she expressed these feelings, she would lose both the man and the woman, and
3 that it expresssed a wish to experience vicariously a close physical relation with the woman, which had more of a maternal than a sexual quality (another *impulse*).

A second main defence against her anger and jealousy, which was repeatedly interpreted, consisted of strong masochistic tendencies – for instance, as a reaction to her jealousy and feeling of exclusion when her husband first undertook psychotherapy, she would go out into the street with the fantasy of being raped, murdered, or run over. Her sexual fantasies included being used sexually by a number of men whom she didn't know, and performing as a stripper but never allowing the men in the audience to have her. In therapy she several times spoke of being near to suicide, which was interpreted both as an aggressive act and a method of manipulating people – her husband, her GP, and the therapist – in order to get love.

In the transference, situations of jealousy were provided by her GP (about whom she had overtly erotic fantasies) and his wife, and her GP and the therapist.

The link with the past

The early situations with which all the above was linked consisted of losing her mother's love when her brother was born when the patient was 3; and the fact that her father was both seductive on the one hand, and rejecting and humiliating on the other. For instance, he confided in her about her mother's lack of interest in sex, and told her sexual jokes, but hardly ever gave her physical affection, and laughed at her and imitated her awkward gait as a teenager.

The therapist interpreted the sexual fantasies in terms of the relation with her father: that the exciting men who use her and throw her out resemble her description of the relation with her father; and the stripper who tantalises the men seems to represent a reversal of roles between her and her father.

Climax of therapy in the transference

The major breakthrough occurred in Sessions 13 and 14. These events were described in detail in Chapter 1. They are too complex to summarise briefly, and in order to avoid repetition we ask the interested reader – with apologies – to turn back (see p. 9).

After the end of the passage from Session 14 quoted in Chapter 1, the patient said that she felt that the therapist was 'trying to depersonalise' her, and she was angry about it. The therapist said that she was seeing the therapist as trying to take away her sexuality, as if it was only mothers, or therapists, who could have sex and babies. The patient responded with a frankly Oedipal communication, recounting how her father spoke of her mother's relative frigidity and was angry with the patient for having boy-friends – she was supposed to be Daddy's little girl. The therapist said that she must be angry at her mother for being the one sexually desired by her father, and that her fear that her mother and the therapist might deprive her of her sexuality must be a projection of her wish to split her mother and father. The patient spoke of an incident in which she was in the bathroom, and her father had walked in and had called her 'dirty' for having forgotten to lock the door.

Therapeutic effects

Most of the rest of the 30 sessions were devoted to consolidating this work. Therapeutic effects began to appear: instead of feeling suicidal or masochistic in response to the current triangular situation, she had dealt with it effectively; and she had been able to see Denise as pathetic in her attempts to hold on to the patient's husband.

Termination

Her feelings about termination consisted of a mixture of sadness at the loss of the therapist and exhilaration at the prospect of being able to be herself and go on alone. In the final session she read to the therapist, most movingly, the following beautiful poem which she had written (here reproduced with gratitude for permission given by both the patient and her therapist):

Moth Emerging

Tiptoe upon a tip of leaf
This shrivelled thing
Quivers with effort and expectancy.
The warmth it reaches for is waiting.
Perhaps the green life pulsing
Through its leaf-fine veins
Is painful; certainly a surprise.
It struggles, tremulous,
But cannot stop
The sudden rush of necessary joy.
Clear of the cramping chrysalis
There is no choice.
The new-born self,
Crumpled like hand-torn leaf,
Must use its wings or die.

Follow-up (5 years 10 months since termination)

She was interviewed by a member of the Individual Team. It became clear that she now has a full sense of her own identity in a way that she did not at all when she first came – in her initial application form she had written that she had 'no one inside me who can tell me who I am.' She said that she enjoys the difference from her previous life, because she now lives by her own precepts and not somebody else's. She has undertaken a training for a new kind of work which satisfies her more, has found her own creativity, has friends of both sexes, and enjoys social life. She seems to have entirely given up her masochistic tendencies. She has been able to assert herself both with her husband and in her life in general in a constructive way. As far as her husband is concerned, she finally became tired of his endless affairs and asked him to leave.

Foolishly as it turned out, she relied on a 'gentleman's agreement' between her and her husband over financial affairs and the custody of the children. This worked at first but he eventually turned against her and she is now involved in a running legal battle over custody, in which he accuses her of neglecting the house and the children. We had no means of knowing how much truth there was in these accusations, but we felt convinced that even if the house was in some kind of chaos, the children were not being neglected *emotionally*. (Evidence confirming this was obtained at very long-term follow-up – see below.)

It is in her relations with men that the main reservations lie. She said that she is frightened of intellectual men, and the result has been that she forms relations with men who are her social and intellectual inferiors, with whom she cannot share large parts of her interests, and with whom final commitment seems unrealistic. Nevertheless these relations are close and warm, and sex is enjoyable and in no way masochistic. She also quickly broke with two men who had obvious neurotic difficulties.

There seems no longer to be any tendency towards depression, and she has reacted to losses with realistic coping and appropriate sadness. She did not become depressed at the break-up with her husband. She became very close to her father before he died, reacted to his death with appropriate mourning, and was able to remain close to her mother and to discuss him with her.

She said that her writing has been much more creative than it was when she first came.

She spoke very positively about her therapy, saying that with her therapist she 'could have feelings which she regarded as wicked, but it didn't make her into a wicked person'; and also that she had been able to 'disentangle what belonged to her husband and what belonged to her father.' For her the most important moment of therapy had occurred when the therapist had relieved her of anxieties about homosexuality, by saying that 'feelings could be erotic without being sexual'.

The scores by the individual team were 3.0, 2.5, 3.0, and 3.0: mean 2.875.

Postscript

The patient has regularly kept in touch with her therapist by letter. In a letter written to one of the present authors (DM) 17 years after termination, she wrote that she was now in analysis to try and deal with the difficulties that had been left untouched. Apart from problems in relation to men, she said that she needed to integrate childhood aspects of herself into her personality, which formerly she had treated with contempt.

She wrote very warmly of her gratitude to her therapist (and the supervisor), saying that she might *literally* not have survived if she hadn't been helped to find both her anger and her potential strength at that time. Thus, even 17 years later, she remembered some of the events and crucial issues of therapy very clearly. She added that her children have 'turned out OK – much healthier than I was at their age!' This goes some way towards confirming the judgment made by the individual team at 5½-year follow-up that the children were not being neglected.

Comment

Her story gives both a striking confirmation of the effectiveness of radical brief psychotherapy, on the one hand, and an illustration of one of the main therapeutic mechanisms operating in dynamic psychotherapy of any kind, on the other. As in the case of the Sculptress, the technique that was used shirked nothing and involved most of the issues that would be encountered in a full-scale analysis. As far as therapeutic mechanisms are concerned, we may note the following sequence of events. Preliminary work consisted of repeated interpretation of the *triangle of conflict* – the masochistic defence against anger and jealousy, with the fear of losing the loved person – together with the link with the past. This assault on her defences aroused intense anger in the transference, which broke through and was directly experienced and expressed. The result was a sudden freeing of her unconscious – a major piece of de-repression ('a monster of violent anger within me') accompanied by clear insight about the link between her feelings currently and in the past.

An exactly similar phenomenon occurred in the therapy of the Borderline Graduate Clerk (see Chapters 1 and 18). In the present patient it also resulted in the beginning of therapeutic effects, consisting especially of the ability to assert herself in situations of jealousy.

This phenomenon, de-repression in response to the direct experience of anger about a challenge to defences, occurs regularly in Davanloo's initial interviews; and indeed he has recently published a book devoted largely to this subject, entitled *Unlocking the Unconscious* (1990). It is very important for the theory of psychotherapy that the breakthrough occurred in a similar way in two of the therapies reported here.

Also confirmed is one of Davanloo's crucial and repeated observations, that when violent impulses of rage are de-repressed in masochistic patients, the masochistic phenomena disappear. This gives strong evidence for one of the mechanisms lying behind this kind of disturbance, namely a turning of aggression against the self, which represents both a defence and a method of self-punishment.

It is of great interest that the therapeutic effects included an increase in creativeness, and her discovery of the ability to know her own identity and 'be herself', two of the more subtle changes – very different from purely symptomatic improvements – that were shown by the majority of the seven 'best' patients in our series.

Of course it was clear to both her and us that the therapeutic result was incomplete, and we may wish her well in her analysis.

9

Two male patients with Oedipal problems

Introduction

In this chapter we describe the therapies of two apparently very similar young men, with whom conflicts in relation to the father were taken as focus. For this reason both patients were deliberately assigned to male therapists.

The Car Battery Man

Age 26, single, driver of a minicab (a car belonging to an independent taxi service in London), 29 sessions, score 2.75.

Initial disturbances

He was referred because of severe phobic anxiety in crowded places, particularly the Underground, which had come on suddenly about 2 years before. He associated the onset with, firstly, being let down by a boss with whom he had formed a very good relation, who had promised him promotion but had then been transferred to another office, so that the issue had been forgotten; and secondly, an incident in which he had temporarily exchanged (without permission) his own defective car battery for a battery in one of the firm's cars. Although the firm treated the matter quite leniently, he said he had never felt so guilty and ashamed in his life. A few weeks later he left the job.

He also suffered from an inability to keep jobs because he could not restrain his anger with bosses – in his questionnaire he wrote in the space set aside for job history, 'I would need a whole page for this' – and an inability to commit himself in his relation with women.

Background

His parents emigrated to this country from Italy, and the family felt themselves persecuted in the area where they lived. His parents had to watch from the window to protect the patient when he was playing in the street. All this improved when they moved to an area of London where there was an Italian community. They were very poor at first, but the father worked extremely hard and enabled them to buy their own house. Both parents punished the patient physically, his mother more than his father and apparently quite severely. A sister was born when he was 4, and he remembered being very jealous of her.

Dynamic material

When in the initial interview the (woman) trainee psychiatrist pointed out that he suffered from problems with authority, he spontaneously spoke of his father, revealing strong competitiveness by saying that he was determined to become as successful in his job as his father was, or more so. He added that he was still resentful against his father for refusing to advise him on a choice of career at 16–18. This was a clear dynamic response to a minimal comment.

Later in the interview he said spontaneously that he felt unable to kiss his mother because there was sexuality involved in it.

At projective testing he told the psychologist of an incident 3 years ago (i.e. 1 year before the onset of his symptoms) in which he came home to find his mother in tears and a policeman in the home, the reason being that his father had collapsed at work and was now in hospital. He had imagined that his father might be dead and said now, 'I never knew I could shake so much.'

Projective testing confirmed that the problem was Oedipal, with the emphasis on ambivalent feelings towards the father. This was summed up in his response to Card CG in the ORT (a psychodynamically based development of the TAT – see Phillipson, 1955). Here he saw the figure at the top of the steps as a sincere and well-meaning politician who has failed to honour his promises to the crowd below. The crowd restrain their anger because they know it wasn't the politician's fault, but the atmosphere is tense and physical assault is not far away.

Here it should be added that there were also some paranoid-sounding responses in the Rorschach. One of these was the first response of all: he saw Card I – usually seen as a butterfly – as 'a person between two hooded Ku Klux Klan figures, being tortured'. He agreed with the psychologist's interpretation that this was what he felt about being tested. This is significant in view of what emerged later.

Reasons for acceptance for brief psychotherapy

These were based on the dynamic quality of his material and the obvious focus of his ambivalent feelings towards his father. His insight and motivation were high – he said in a second interview with the psychiatrist that he knew that his problems were 'deep down in there', and that they were concerned with what went on at home.

Course of therapy (29 sessions)

This was much more complex and confused than would be expected from the simple dynamics revealed at initial assessment.

The patient was treated by a male psychiatrist from abroad who at times worked well and at considerable depth, but at other times had difficulty in finding the truly accurate interpretation.

The relation with the father

One focus that developed was absolutely as predicted, namely the patient's intense competitiveness with other men, and behind this his highly ambivalent feelings about his father. Early in therapy he said that in relation to other men there was 'always a power struggle', and later he said, with reference to girl-friends, that he wanted to 'clear the field of other men'. With his father, in addition to the power struggle, there was both an intense wish for support, and anger when he did not receive it. This was manifested in the transference in the form of repeated requests for advice, which were ultimately interpreted as his need for the therapist, symbolically speaking, to give him his masculinity – or even, more literally, the therapist's penis. The interpretation that the therapist had great difficulty in giving, in spite of pressure from the supervisor, was of the patient's need to take other men's strength away from them and weaken them. This interpretation was missed especially in Session 20, and – possibly as a result – a phenomenon emerged which the Rorschach had foreshadowed but which had not been foreseen, namely strong paranoid feelings. Nevertheless this was not in any way a disaster, because the therapist was eventually able to interpret these feelings effectively and to link them with the patient's phobic symptoms.

The climax of therapy – confused, deep, and paranoid, leading to feelings about the birth of his sister

In the following account we have used italics to pick out the most significant communications in this very confused and often obscure series of sessions.

In Session 21 the patient told three dreams. The first two seemed to express his need for support. In the third there was a Chinese man with a gun who started to shoot people in the street, while every time he shot someone he shouted a line of a menu, like 'fish and chips'. The patient's main association was a recent row with his boss, in which his boss had been very angry with him for going home early. He told the boss that he had done this because he had been left alone in the office and had felt *very lonely*. He said he had begun to have feelings similar to those in the car battery incident (where he also had had an unpleasant boss). However, on this latest occasion it was the boss who went away feeling angry and frustrated, and the patient said in a very literal and concrete way that he felt better because he had succeeded in *transferring his own bad feelings to his boss*. The therapist linked this with the fact that he was about to leave the patient by going on holiday, and went on to interpret the Chinese man's aggression as really being that of the patient himself. At this the patient became emotional and quiet and spoke of themes of guilt. At the end of the session he described getting angry because he could not enjoy a meal as thoroughly as one of his colleagues. The therapist, preoccupied with primitive interpretations, interpreted this in terms of the Kleinian concept of 'envy' (leading in the direction of mother–child relations) rather than 'rivalry' (leading to Oedipal problems).

In the next session (number 22) the patient told a dream in which he was in bed and was suddenly surrounded by hundreds of insects. His boss was there and was unsympathetic, but his mother was also there and was sympathetic. The therapist said that the insects must stand for the crowds that the patient is afraid of. The patient agreed with this and went on to contradict the message of the dream by saying that his mother *is warm on the outside but cold on the inside, whereas his father is both the stronger and the warmer of the two.* Later in the session he said that in all his jobs there seems to be one man who *doesn't trust him and follows him* – for instance in one job the foreman used to drive to the patient's house from many miles away, and wait outside to check that the patient was leaving in time for work. At follow-up the patient still maintained that this was true, but it certainly sounds an extraordinarily paranoid communication.

Towards the end of the session he spoke of fearing that his boss would 'suddenly confront him with something'. The therapist linked this with the transference, and the patient spoke of *not being able to trust his therapy* because he didn't know how it functioned – another paranoid communication. He went on to speak of relieving his phobic anxiety during the week by taking a tablet, and he said that he wanted a boss who would give him things. The therapist related this to the transference, saying that the patient seems to wait for him to give him security, potency, and power – perhaps even the therapist's penis – in a very concrete way. He then – sensitively abandoning the rigid refusal to respond to the patient's communications on a reality level – spoke as follows: 'That is not the real way to growth. The aim is that you should be able to rely on your own power. After all, I can't always be there to give you advice.' He ended by saying that the patient must be angry when he doesn't receive advice, and then he is afraid that some kind of a battle will develop. The therapist wrote that this interpretation seemed to have very little effect.

Breakthrough: paranoid material successfully interpreted

Nevertheless a breakthrough occurred in the next session (number 23). The patient opened by saying that he thought the previous session was a good one. Last week he had visited several pubs and realised for the first time that it was *people* that made him afraid. He described how he had been in a pub that was empty, and that he had become *irritated when other people had begun to arrive* and had moved to another pub where there was a *more cosy and warm atmosphere.* The therapist linked this with the family's feeling of persecution by the neighbours because of their Italian background. The patient then suddenly remembered how as a little boy on two or three occasions he had been taken out by his mother and had got separated from her and lost in a *crowd.* The therapist mentioned the word 'despair', at which the patient became very moved and spoke of his feeling at the time that he would never find his mother again. The therapist asked him if that was similar to the feeling he had had in the car battery incident. He responded by saying that now he remembered that at that time, when he heard that his (good) boss was leaving, he went home holding his head in his hands and feeling a deep despair. The therapist linked this with termination, speaking of the warm and cosy atmosphere in therapy, and then – making a leap into the past – suggested that *the warm atmosphere of the patient's home had been broken when his sister was born when he was 4.*

The patient made no direct response to this interpretation, but a crucial indirect response appeared almost immediately: he said that some evenings ago, in a pub, he had felt as if *all the people coming in were aiming at him and invading him.* He felt very little and as if he was at the tip of a conical formation lying on its side, with all the crowds converging on him from the base.

This disturbed and obscure communication might have defeated many therapists, but this therapist was equal to it. He pointed out that the patient was *irritated* by the crowds who disturbed the cosy atmosphere, and suggested that he *saw his own anger in the other people*. He (the therapist) linked this with the crowds in childhood, which were associated with losing his mother, and with the hostile insects in the previous dream [we may note that insects are often thought to represent children, so that this may have linked with the patient's hostile feelings towards his sister]; and he then suggested that the patient was furiously angry with his mother [presumably about the birth of his sister, although this is not made clear]. The therapist linked this once more with termination.

There was no direct response to this, but not long afterwards the patient became quite emotional and admitted *how difficult he had found it to trust the therapist, and that he still believed the therapist was holding back a lot of information from him*. Thus he was finally enabled to admit paranoid feelings about the therapist.

The rest of therapy; therapeutic effects, the issue of termination

In Session 24 there were reiterated demands for advice from the therapist, and in Session 26 the therapist managed to bring out anger about not receiving it. By now there was evidence that the patient was beginning to be more able to acknowledge and contain his own aggression, and in Session 26 some therapeutic effects appeared: the patient had been on a training course, had felt much less anxious than he expected, and had been the only one of the trainees to get a prize. Formerly, he said, his performance would have gone 'floppy'. Much of the rest of the session was spent in expressing complicated feelings about women, involving both fear and hostility, which included:

1 unwillingness to commit himself;
2 being easily hurt;
3 leaving them the moment they did something he didn't like;
4 feeling that he could not trust them, and
5 feeling that although they put on a beautiful front there was something nasty underneath.

The therapist reiterated interpretations about the patient himself putting on a front in order to cover his fear that his own potency was false. The response to this work came at the very end of the session, when the patient said that in recent weeks his relation with his current girl-friend had greatly improved: he was able to tell her about his therapy (i.e. to trust her and admit his own weakness to her) and to discuss their future together (i.e. to contemplate commitment) in a way that had never happened before.

In subsequent sessions there was much material and increased insight about his fantasy of potential fights with other men, including the therapist, and struggles for 'potency' with them. For instance he spoke of his anxiety in the Underground at sitting opposite another man, and his fear of 'fighting his way through' to the doors of the train; and the therapist interpreted the patient's feeling that even when he merely sat opposite another man he was afraid of a terrible fight developing and had to avoid it. Soon afterwards the patient was able to recognise his own wish to overpower another man at work, and to realise without anxiety that the other man himself was weak – as illustrated by his 'floppy' handshake, a term that linked with his fears about his own potency and acknowledged the overtly genital element in many of the therapist's previous interpretations.

The last session (number 29) was extremely tense, with the patient half trying to convey the impression that therapy had done no good, and complaining with much feeling about its brevity and about the fact that the therapist had not told him how to get more out of it. The therapist reiterated interpretations about the loss of himself as the good father, and raised the question of whether the patient could preserve something good from their relation, or whether he wanted to spoil his memory of it. The therapist was left very despondent – a feeling that later events were to prove quite unfounded.

Follow-up (5½ months, 2 years 10 months, 7 years 10 months)

At 5½ months the patient was given a follow-up interview by the therapist, which turned out to be an important therapeutic session. The patient spoke of a new symptom, namely that in church he began to feel sick and disgusted and then could not imagine eating. He said that his imagination is so vivid that he *cannot tell the difference between fantasy and reality*. He then said something about 'taking things back from other people so that he can come together himself, but that this is an unbearable feeling because he would either burst into pieces or destroy everything around him.' The therapist handled this psychotic-sounding communication extremely well, saying that the patient could not cope with being powerful and was afraid of his destructiveness. In response the patient spoke of a recent incident in which another driver, an old man, forced him on to the pavement, and he became enraged and felt like killing him but managed to control himself. Shortly after this communication the atmosphere of the interview became much more positive, and the patient described how he felt much freer in his life, and how his girl-friend had said that there had been a great change in him. They both attributed this to his therapy, and he now added that he and she were able to quarrel and sort things out without breaking the relationship, and that they planned to marry in 2 months' time.

At the final, nearly 8-year, follow-up, the situation can be described under the following headings:

1 Phobic symptoms: these are still present but very much reduced in severity, e.g. he now can bear travelling by Underground but needs to stand near the door so that he knows he can get out at the next station. There was a situation somewhat similar to the battery incident, which he coped with realistically and without anxiety.
2 Self-assertion and relationships with bosses: there is some residual anxiety but he can cope with any kind of conflict situation. He can argue with bosses and get his own way. He kept his last job for 4½ years.
3 Relations with women: he married his girl-friend as planned, 7 months after the end of his therapy. This has been a very stormy relation, with physical violence on both sides (apparently initiated by her) and they have been on the verge of parting many times, but in the end he has been determined to see it through. She did not want children, though he did, but surprisingly the marriage greatly improved when she became pregnant, 'the nicest 9 months of our relationship'. They now have a son whom he clearly loves very much. Sex was good before the pregnancy – 'we had good rows and good sex' – 'now when the relation is on a steady footing the sexual side hasn't a lot of importance.' On questioning, he said that his wife didn't talk much about deeper feelings, and he was wary

of doing so because in quarrels his communications would get thrown back at him as weaknesses.

4 His relation with his parents: his relation with his father has dramatically improved and they can now go out for a drink together and collaborate happily in domestic jobs. On the other hand the relation with his mother has not changed. He still feels unable to kiss her, and indeed to relate to her properly at all.

5 Finally, his originally somewhat suspicious attitude towards his therapist – which fits in with the other paranoid features that he showed – was in no way repeated in his relation to follow-up. This is illustrated by the conspicuous openness of his remarks quoted above (some more of which are quoted on pp. 221 and 241), and the fact that he readily agreed to his material being published.

His comments on therapy were highly ambivalent. At the final follow-up he spoke of termination as losing a friend who was also an enemy. At the earlier follow-up he had been determined to convey that he received no insight from therapy, while unconsciously making clear that he had actually received a great deal.

Discussion of follow-up

There is a great improvement in symptoms (though not complete recovery) and he is now able to cope with jobs, relations with male authority, and self-assertion. Paranoid features have been replaced by openness and trust. He has committed himself to marriage. Just as in the case of the Conductor – where also there was violence – the relation with his wife is very difficult to evaluate. We were troubled both by the violence, the link between violence and sex, and the falling off in the sexual relation after the birth of his child – when the violence was mitigated. Yet, when one reads his actual words, the gestalt is of a very close and genuine bond between them, of which the storminess is somehow a natural part. If one takes this view, then the therapeutic result is very good and better than our scores would indicate. Much detailed evidence on this is given in Chapter 27 (pp. 241–2), to which the interested reader is referred.

The relations with his son and his father are both excellent, but the difficulties with his mother are unchanged.

The scores of 2.5 and 3.0 expressed our doubts, which may or may not be well founded.

Comment on therapy

It seems that the therapist brought out the main issues very clearly and enabled the patient to experience the corresponding feelings directly. Very important was the interpretation of paranoid projection, which not only met with a clear response on several occasions, but was followed by the disappearance of paranoid feelings directed both towards his therapist and the girl who later became his wife. This illustrates once more the effectiveness of a radical technique. Moreover the absence of paranoid features persisted at follow-up. It may well be that his wife greatly contributed to this by enabling him – because of her own violence – to get the violent feelings presumed to underly his paranoia out of his system.

We may also note in passing the major contribution of paranoid anxiety to what appeared to be purely phobic symptoms – a possibility of which every clinician needs to be aware.

The repressed feelings that emerged centred around anger with people of both sexes, and rivalry with men. The anger arose from two sources: the birth of his sister, which caused the loss of his mother's exclusive attention (and hence the anger was directed against both his sister and his mother); and his father's lack of support.

Therapy revealed that the Oedipal rivalry took the form of fantasied struggles for power with other men, which resulted in intense hostility against bosses and a consequent inability to hold down jobs.

In our view the therapist used transference interpretation to just the right degree, neither over-emphasising it nor avoiding it when it was required. It was clearly crucial to have brought out the patient's suspiciousness in the transference in Session 23.

However, we may note one feature missing from this therapy, namely bringing out the erotic element in the patient's relation to his mother – which the patient had mentioned spontaneously in the initial interview – and hence the source of rivalry in his jealousy of his father's relation with her. This omission may possibly account for the fact that the patient's difficulties with his mother remain unchanged.

The Betrayed Son

Age 25, married, manager of a small chain of delicatessen stores, 30 sessions, score 2.25.

Reasons for referral

His GP referred him because of physical symptoms for which no cause could be found. These had apparently been precipitated by a virus infection 2 years previously and consisted of loss of energy, headaches, shortness of breath, and chest pain. Other symptoms, of a depressive kind, were that he felt unable to get on with things and was moody, irritable, and listless. In addition he suffered from hypochondriacal and phobic anxiety: whenever he felt physical pain he was afraid he had some serious illness, and he suffered from feelings of panic that he would collapse when alone or in the middle of a crowded room.

Background

He was the second of five children, the next sibling being a brother 7 years younger. His father formerly owned a garage business, but now works as manager for a garage owned by somebody else. There was little information about the relation with his mother. He did not do well at technical college but his work history has been progressive. He is now working as manager for a chain of delicatessen shops.

He has been married 4 years, has a son aged 3, and his wife is now pregnant again. Originally the sexual relation was highly satisfactory, but recently his wife has become indifferent to the preliminaries of sex and this has caused tension between them.

Dynamics of initial assessment

He was given two highly dynamic interviews by a woman trainee social worker (later the therapist who treated the Psychiatric Nurse with Attacks of Rage). When she drew his attention to his move from a subordinate to a managerial position he immediately free-associated to his father. Here he gave evidence of very complex feelings, which included great warmth, identification with him, guilt, and hidden ambivalence. His first association was to a memory, as a boy, of helping his father make a model aeroplane. He later conceived the ambition of setting up his own business, financed by his father, doing something with his hands. He went on to make clear that his father suffered from considerable problems over achievement. The garage business had gone into liquidation not once but twice, and his father had said, 'Why does everything I touch fail?' During this time, in his late teens, he had become much closer to his father and had worked with him, helping him to build up a new business. Previously he had been closer to his mother. His father had been under great strain and one day collapsed. He himself linked this with his own fear of collapsing.

However, in the second interview he gave evidence of a powerful source of unconscious negative feelings: his father had originally bought the family house for a small sum. He had the idea of selling it to the patient for the same figure, but eventually sold it to someone else for a large profit. The patient was quite out of touch with any resentment about this betrayal.

Another important communication, giving evidence of a strong unconscious therapeutic alliance, also emerged in the second interview. He had originally said that his symptoms were precipitated by a virus infection, but he now suddenly remembered the following: at that time he and his wife were living with his parents, and there was friction between his wife and his mother. One day, without previous warning, his wife phoned him at work to say that she had walked out and had moved their belongings into her family home, i.e from his family home into hers. Not long after this, he got an attack of panic in the Underground, on his way to work.

Reason for acceptance for brief psychotherapy

This was based on his highly dynamic response to interview, and the fact that there seemed to be a clear focus in his mixed feelings for his father.

Therapeutic plan

A detailed therapeutic plan was drawn up. He was assigned to a male therapist (a psychologist), with the aim of bringing out the following unconscious feelings about his father:

1 hidden competitiveness;
2 anger that his father had let him down and not helped him to be a man, and
3 guilt and sorrow about having in fantasy caused his father's downfall.

Course of therapy (30 sessions)

The therapist had been on the Tavistock Four-Year Course in Psychotherapy for 2 years full time, but had had no psychotherapeutic experience before that. He worked skilfully and missed little, and there was a steady progression along the chosen focus. Naturally much material also emerged that had not been foreseen, and therapy was very complex.

The theme of death wishes emerges at once

In Session 1 the patient spontaneously spoke of thoughts that 'certain people' might die, and the therapist fearlessly interpreted that he might feel violent, even murderous, towards people close to him. The patient spoke of feeling let down by his father, and by implication admitted conscious thoughts about his father's death.

The themes of sibling rivalry and 'being himself'

In Session 3 two entirely new themes emerged: rivalry with his younger brother, and the conflict between putting on a façade and 'being himself'. These themes developed from his announcing that his new baby had been born, but entirely avoiding any mention of feelings about this, or even saying whether it was a boy or a girl. He then spoke of intense competition over material things with a colleague whose wife had just lost a baby due at about the same time, and the therapist suggested that rivalry might go deeper than this and that maybe he 'wanted to have a better baby than the other chap'. The patient responded with a highly positive unconscious transference communication to this acknowledgment of his anxiety-laden feelings of rivalry. He spoke of a fantasy of a house with two rooms, in one of which he could be himself and do creative things with his hands, while the other was just for show. *He would only allow people into the first room when he knew them very well.* The therapist brought out the transference implications of this response. Associating to the theme of rooms, the patient went on to speak of a time when he came back from holiday and *found his brother installed in his room.* The therapist emphasised powerful competitive feelings directed against both the brother and the father.

It must have been this mention of rivalry with his brother that had an extremely disturbing effect. The patient came back for Session 4 saying that he felt 'terrible', 'completely confused', and 'unable to concentrate'. The therapist made interpretations linking the new baby's birth with the fact that the patient had been displaced by his brother's birth, and suggesting that he felt resentful against both his wife and the baby for being the centre of attention. In response the patient at last revealed that the baby was a girl, and went on to speak about a number of things that his brother could do which he himself couldn't. He ended with another highly appreciative unconscious transference communication: that he had recently found a new friend with whom he could be himself.

Negative transference, hostility towards female members of the family

In Session 5 other transference issues began to emerge. The patient began to ask questions of the therapist and said that he wanted some kind of response from him. The therapist did not respond and interpreted that the patient was afraid of getting into a fight with him. In Session 7 the patient spoke of being verbally aggressive in a 'putting down' way to his mother, which happened mainly in the presence of his brother. In this session on more than one occasion the patient said, in response to an interpretation, that he 'had just thought of that himself', and the therapist interpreted that the patient was in competition with him, as with his brother. In Session 8 the therapist interpreted that the patient was afraid that therapy would become a 'mutual putting down', and that they would end up lashing out violently at each other. The patient said that when he was younger he used to get uncontrollably angry, and that recently he had experienced recurrent fantasies of his baby dying or his wife bleeding to death. In Session 9 he revealed one cause for his anger with the female members of his family, namely that the incident in which the tension between his wife and mother had caused his wife to move house – which probably contributed to the precipitation of his panics – had made him angry with both of them. Here the supervisor commented that it really seemed as if the patient was angry with everyone close to him: his wife and the new baby, behind this his mother and his brother, and of course also his father for betraying him.

In Session 10 he made a slip of the tongue, describing his wife's and mother-in-law's idea of going into business together as a 'plot' when he meant to say 'plan'. The therapist interpreted that he seemed to expect everyone to conspire to prevent him from getting ahead. In response the patient said that whenever he heard about these plans he felt 'very strange', tense and angry, and wanted to lash out at everyone. He then said he had the same feeling about his father, who was always making promises that he never kept.

The relation with the father

This began a period of work on the relation between the patient and his father, together with a number of PT and PC links, which lasted till the end of therapy. The patient spoke of one pair of contrasting aspects of his father, namely weakness (when his business went into liquidation, and when he collapsed), and strength (he once held the patient in a 'bear hug' and the patient said he had no idea his father was so strong). The therapist chose to emphasise the weakness, and the patient said that 'if we told this conversation to my father it would break him'.

Another theme which the therapist brought out was the patient's need to be given something by a man, which linked with the patient's repeated questions, and his disappointment and anger when he did not receive it. This led to another pair of contrasting aspects both of the father and the therapist: on the one hand helpful, and on the other hand only concerned with their own interests. The therapist pointed out how difficult it was to integrate the two.

All this work led to what seemed the central issue in his relation with father-figures: the way in which they all seemed to be trying to keep him down and prevent him from being a success; and the mirror image of this, namely his own wish to deprive them of their power. In Session 17 the patient spoke of resentment about the off-hand way in which his father had offered him money, and said he preferred the relation when his father was broke. The therapist interpreted that the patient couldn't stand his father being in a position of having something to give, and wanted to 'strip him of his present powerful position'. Similarly, when the patient was resistant in therapy he was resenting the therapist having anything to give and attacking his power to give it.

The climax of therapy

It was probably this work that led to the climax of therapy in Session 18. The patient said that in Session 17 he had felt the therapist was trying to 'break him down', and he had gone away feeling 'crucified, dead, empty, like a broken man'. All week he had felt shaky, panicky, sleepless, nauseated, and now he was beginning to feel this in the session itself. Moreover this was exactly how he had felt when his panics started for the very first time.

This led to an entirely new picture of the first precipitation of his symptoms, together with crucial work on the TCP link. The patient described how at that time he was working for an immediate boss who was 'using him as a messenger boy', which he felt was trying to 'break him down'. Moreover, he wanted the boss's job. Thus the highly Oedipal theme of wanting to supplant a man in a superior position, with the latter trying to keep him in his place, was very clear. He had had his first panic attack while travelling to work in this job, and he said that he had had a very similar struggle with previous bosses. He added spontaneously that he was beginning to feel exactly the same about the therapist – thus himself making the current–past or CP link. He then said that it was strange that he could remember everything about that time so vividly – he was re-living it as if it had happened yesterday, and moreover talking about it gave him immense relief.

The therapist now suggested that he must have the same kind of feeling about his father, thus completing the triangle of person (current, transference, past). This led to an account of events that happened when the patient was in his teens. He left school at 15 and was encouraged by his father to go to art college. It was soon after this that his father's business collapsed. The patient wasn't doing well at college and repeatedly asked his father to let him leave and help set up the business again. His father refused and the patient felt put down and rejected. He eventually did leave and help his father, but he now complained that his father never taught him anything about the managerial side of the business, and once more he felt put down and rejected. [Here we may note the deep emotional significance of the social worker's comment about the move to a managerial position, which she had made in the initial consultation, and which had led him to begin to talk of his complex feelings for his father.]

The theme that now emerged consisted of the frankly genital aspects of his conflicts. He spoke of taking various qualities from men that he felt he lacked himself, and making up his own identity with them. He said that his worst panics occurred when he felt he did not have the power that he was trying to imitate. The therapist brought in the idea of masculinity, in work, social life, and sexual life, and suggested that the patient was afraid of getting into a confrontation with him over who was the most potent. The patient said that from early adolescence he had thought of other men as 'infertile', and began to muse about why he had always wanted to have six children – which was of course one more than his father had had.

Many themes come together; the issue of termination; therapeutic effects

In Session 19 he said that the previous session had been an 'attack on his masculinity'. Another important theme now emerged, namely the conflict between rebelling and trying to find his own identity, on the one hand, and needing to be accepted and supported, on the other. In Session 21 he spontaneously brought this into the transference, saying that he had had the feeling that all the therapist wanted for him was that he should become a satisfied businessman; but now he realised that if he found out what he really wanted to be, then the people who would be most upset would not be the therapist, but his wife and parents.

In Session 24 he spoke of resentment against his mother, who seemed to keep his father in a passive position; and in Session 25 he said he got put down by his wife in the same way as by his mother. The therapist used the word 'castration', and the patient said that his wife spoilt his confidence sexually as well as in other ways.

The major theme of Session 27 consisted of repeated interpretations about conflicting feelings for other men, linking the therapist with the patient's boss and his father (a TCP link). On the one hand there was the man who gave him something, worked closely with him, and made him feel warmly inside; and on the other hand there was the man who exploited him and withdrew support at the critical time (the issue of termination). The patient agreed, but said that nowadays he was more able to work things out for himself – in the old days he would have panicked. The one thing that he was now determined to do was to make a decision on what *he* wanted, and not on his mother's ideas, his wife's, his boss's, his father's, or the therapist's.

The sequence between Sessions 28 and 29 illustrates a crucial phenomenon, namely the resurgence of symptoms, resolved by constructive action on the patient's part. In Session 28 he had an actual attack of panic, which seemed to be related to a situation at work about which he had failed to confront his boss. In Session 29 he reported that he had carried out the confrontation, had found the response unsatisfactory, and though seething with anger had quietly but firmly given in his notice, and he felt much better for it (an example of constructive self-assertion). He had then confronted his father and asked him to lend him money to set up a business of his own, to which his father had agreed. He told the therapist that he was going to change his whole way of life. He added that when he thought of the end of therapy he got a knot in his stomach, but when he thought of his plans the knot went away.

In the final session he said that his recent decisions would have been impossible a year before.

Follow-up (with his therapist at 3 years, with Dr Rodin at 4 years)

At the latest follow-up the situation was as follows:

1 *Symptoms:* The physical symptoms of which he originally complained have disappeared, and he no longer suffers from depressive symptoms, but he still gets some attacks of anxiety, which are not as frequent or as severe as before. He is able to do some self-analysis and 'talk himself out of them'.
2 *Work and achievement:* After trying various business ventures he finally decided to give this up, and eventually got a job as a craftsman instructor in a rehabilitation centre, also doing some group therapy. Thus he is both doing something of his own, fulfilling his wish to use his hands, and making use of the experience gained in therapy. He is able to function effectively and to work closely with the staff. However, he has not been able to fulfil his ambition to be a teacher, since he has failed the exams for getting into training college. Thus he may well have a residual problem over achievement.
3 *Self-assertion outside the home:* He is able to express his opinions at work constructively and not to 'let things stew'.
4 *The relation with his wife:* This is very difficult to assess. He said that 'there is much greater communication about how we feel', but he also added that this

did not necessarily make them any closer. He had a number of complaints about her, and a situation has developed in which both are expressing hostility in indirect and destructive ways. Their flat needs re-decorating before they can sell it and get a larger one, and he is putting this off. In order to put pressure on him she has started withholding sex and told him if he didn't like it he could find sex elsewhere, which he did.

5 *The relation with his children:* This seems good and well balanced. He wants to allow them freedom, but is firm with them when they go too far. He now feels that his parents did not consider their children sufficiently and he is determined not to repeat this with his own children.

6 *The relation with his parents:* He has freed himself emotionally from his parents, saying that his own family is more important, but keeps in touch with them by phone. He spoke of his mother's double standards in his childhood, namely that she allowed the children freedom in public, wanting to show them off, but often 'gave them a good thrashing' when they got home, because she felt they had over-stepped the mark. This throws some light on his need to do something of his own.

An important statement that he made to the therapist at 3-year follow-up was that in therapy he valued the opportunity to see his therapist in any way that he wanted – to feel resentment, to feel helped, to feel indifferent. He thus showed clear insight about the function of the transference relationship.

Summary

Symptomatically he is considerably improved; he has been able to find a job that represents what *he* wants and to do well at it; he is much better able to relate to people and to assert himself outside the home; there is a good relation with his children.

But his relation with his wife is highly unsatisfactory, with indirect and immature ways of expressing hostility on both sides. This problem, together with the residual symptoms, represents the deficiencies in the therapeutic result. The scores given by the two judges were 2.5 and 2.0, mean 2.25.

Here it should be added that his wife was subsequently interviewed and behaved in a hostile, destructive, and self-destructive way towards the Clinic (details are given in Chapter 27). It is very difficult to assess a therapeutic result in a patient who has made an unsatisfactory marriage before coming to therapy, and has not yet been able to resolve the situation.

Discussion

An observation of great interest is the marked similarity between these two patients, which can be seen in the following features:

1 *In their history:* both patients suffered from the acute onset of phobic anxiety precipitated by an incident involving their boss.

2 *After initial assessment:* the focus chosen in both was the highly ambivalent relation to the father.

3 *In therapy:*
   a. both felt the lack of support from their father, and this was expressed in the transference as repeated requests for advice from the male therapist;
   b. both were in intense competition with their father, which was also expressed in the transference;
   c. in both an additional and crucial constellation of feelings concerned the birth of a younger sibling, the de-repression of which caused great disturbance in the patient;
   d. both were revealed as angry not only with their father but also with their mother.
4 *At follow-up:*
   a. both showed a massive improvement in their relation with men and
   b. in their ability to assert themselves; but
   c. in both there were still residual phobic symptoms; and
   d. in both there were difficult relations with the marital partner, still not fully resolved.

The one major difference between the two patients was the much more disturbed, paranoid material in the Car Battery Man.

The main feature that needs discussion is the pattern of therapeutic results, with marked improvements in all areas except for the presence of major residual difficulties in the marital relation. It could perhaps be argued that if one assigns a male patient to a male therapist and takes as main focus the relation to the father, dealing much less with the the relation with the mother or the triangular relation with the two parents, then it will not be surprising if there is more improvement in the relation with men than with women. This might also be confirmed – with the sexes reversed – by such patients as the Sculptress and the Librarian, both of whom were *women* patients treated by *women,* and in both of whom there were major improvements in other areas but serious residual disturbances in the relation with *men.* Yet in both of these latter two patients the relation with the father, and the triangular relation, were dealt with in great depth, so that this argument does not really hold.

The alternative explanation arises simply from the observation, already mentioned, that the relation with the opposite sex is by far the most difficult of all disturbances to correct. There will certainly be plenty of evidence to confirm this view, and it will be discussed in further detail in Chapters 27 and 28.

10

A woman patient with Oedipal problems

The Girl and the Mountain Tarn

Age 25, separated, civil servant working in the Ministry of Health, 33 sessions, score 2.0.

Disturbances

Her complaint consisted of episodes of tension resulting in hysterical attacks ('shouting, laughing, crying, and general collapse'). In addition, she had a conflict over 'being herself', she had not been able to establish a lasting relation with a man, and she suffered from a repetitive pattern of getting involved in triangular relationships – six such relationships were counted since her mid-teens.

Background and history

1 She is the younger by 4 years of two sisters. Her father is director of an art gallery, her mother a solicitor.
2 She was born and brought up in the country and described her childhood up to the age of 13 as idyllic.
3 She was her father's favourite, her sister was her mother's. There was always extreme competition between the two sisters.
4 There was much tension between her parents, who 'often did not speak to each other for weeks at a time'.
5 When she was 12 or 13 the family moved to the town and her mother went back to work. At about this time the relation with her father deteriorated, and there were 'fierce rows' between them.
6 She said that her father was disappointed that she was not a boy. In her early life she was a tomboy.
7 The circumstances of her first hysterical attack, at age 18, were concerned with her being forced to take a decision between pursuing her artistic interests (which her father encouraged and her mother discouraged), or entering a business course (which her mother was pressing her to do). She eventually chose the latter.
8 She married at age 20. It is not entirely clear what went wrong between her and her husband. It seems he was made to feel inferior by her intelligence and she

had to act a 'charade of a 6-year-old girl'. He was inexperienced sexually and suffered from premature ejaculation. The marriage broke up after a year-long enforced separation owing to the location of her husband's job.

Dynamics of interview

When the (male) trainee psychiatrist – who later became her therapist – pointed out at the very beginning of the interview that there were tears in her eyes, she responded by telling of a recent incident on holiday in which she had asked her father to come up a small mountain with her to see a tarn, and he had refused – 'which typifies something for me about hopes'. She compared it to Sisyphus, who was condemned for ever to push a stone up a mountain, but it always rolled down before he could get to the top.

Much later in the interview the therapist made use of this communication, saying, 'You were very close to your father but were always unable somehow to quite make it with him' (deliberately ambiguous wording). She responded by picking up the sexual connotations of the therapist's remark, saying that he 'wasn't good at kissing and hugging'; and at another point she said that he used money as a substitute for understanding and affection. The therapist made an explicitly Oedipal interpretation, saying that there was a sexual closeness with her father which was always denied her, and it was symbolised by his not wanting to climb the mountain to see the tarn. Also there was a struggle with her mother, which was perhaps made more dangerous because her father and mother were estranged. He went on to say that when at 18 the battle inside her occurred about whether to follow her mother's or her father's way of life, she had to let her mother win. She responded, 'And I thought my father-problem was over. I used to have older boy-friends and I once nearly got involved with a 45-year old man.'

Reason for acceptance for brief psychotherapy

She was accepted because of the high degree of communication that she showed and the clear Oedipal focus, with special reference to the disappointing relation with her father.

Course of therapy (33 sessions)

This was a case of a gifted therapist – perhaps not at his best – treating a difficult patient, which resulted in a rather confused therapy. There were a number of different themes, but all hang together in terms of her desperate attempts to please both her mother and her father, in spite of her intensely ambivalent feelings about both of them, and the consequent loss of her own identity. Therapy is best described by means of a series of important moments.

'Being herself'; many losses at age 13

In Session 3 the patient introduced the main focus by speaking of the inability to 'be herself' in relation to her husband, saying with great intensity that her husband 'totally swamped her', and that she had to leave him or lose her identity. Thus this choice of partner seems to be an example of the 'compulsion to repeat' the relation with her parents – something that was not seen at the time.

In Session 4 the therapist spoke of the disappointing relation with her mother as well as with her father, at which she burst out, 'What does Mother have to do with home and security?' This led to her realisation of the confluence of losses at age 13, in which the family moved (without consulting her about the decision, which they had promised to do), her mother abandoned her by going back to work, and she both lost her friends by moving to a new school, and her idyllic childhood in the country by moving to the town. She had written in her diary that this was the most terrible year of her life. It was also about this time that she had her first menstrual period, and the therapist pointed out that she must have felt that she lost her father as well, at the very time that she was becoming a woman.

Two hysterical attacks

In Session 5 the therapist raised the question, 'What had you done to lose both your father and your mother?' and added that sexuality seemed to have something to do with it. In a very distressed voice she said, 'Why in me and my sister can sex and security never go together?' As she got up to go at the end of the session she had a hysterical attack, sliding down the wall and collapsing on the floor, which was accompanied by the feeling that she 'couldn't go back and she couldn't go forward'. The therapist was unable to make clear sense of this incident, though in subsequent sessions he did draw the parallel with her first attack at age 18, where she had to take a decision between identifying with her father or her mother.

She arrived for what would have been Session 8 to find that the therapist was away with flu, and his secretary had been unable to contact her to let her know. In the next session the therapist tried to deal with her feelings about this, and though he apparently said all the right things concerning her anger and her defences against it, she did not really respond. However, the delayed response seems to have come immediately after the session, since she had another hysterical attack in the car as she was about to be driven away by her boy-friend, screaming and bashing her head on the dashboard. She was brought back to the treatment room. The therapist handled the situation calmly, and eventually made the following interpretation: that this was the only way in which she could express her anger at failing to find in him, or anyone else, what she was looking for (an implied reference to her father); and moreover she was manipulating him and others into caring for her in a way that made them feel impotent, which possibly linked with what she had done to her husband, who felt inferior to her and suffered from sexual difficulties. This seemed to calm her and she was able to leave.

At 5½-year follow-up she said that in the session she had been 'resisting everything' (which explains the lack of response described above) and it was very important that the therapist had taken her back and that his other patients had had to wait – 'nothing shocked him, he accepted me, he wasn't cross, threatening, or rejecting.'

Trying to please both her father and her mother

In Session 12 the theme appeared of not being able to bring sex and love together. The therapist said, referring to age 13, that he wondered if there was the 'feeling of being in the wrong, never knowing where you were'. She burst out with, 'I know, it was that I should have been a boy.' She said that she tried to please her father by being a tomboy, but her mother would tell her off and put her in skirts.

The therapist said that she could never relax into being either a boy or a girl, with her mother and father pulling in opposite directions. She responded, 'So true', and later said that she had told her father 'I'm going to have to be a girl', but that that meant being miserable and alone. In the next session (number 13) she confirmed the accuracy of the therapist's interpretations by saying that 'to please Dad was to go against Mum, and vice versa. I always felt wrong in one way or another and it wasn't only the boy/girl thing but art versus financial security' (which of course further elucidates the original hysterical attack at age 18).

The transference linked to the mother

An important moment in the transference, linked to the past, occurred in Session 17, after a 3-week break. She had had an angry outburst with a shopkeeper, which the therapist related to having felt abandoned by himself. She said that if she expressed what she really felt she wouldn't be able to stop. He said that she must be angry because he 'stopped her emoting', to which she said with venom, 'You *make* me control myself. One has to control oneself all the time.' It eventually emerged that the person in the past who required her to control herself was her mother, and she gave a number of imitations of her mother's voice and sayings.

Sexual feelings in the transference, leading to the relation with the father

In Session 27 the therapist made interpretations about defences against sexual feelings in the transference, linking it with her father, to which there was no clear response. However, in the next session (number 28), she spoke for the first time of four positive incidents with her father, in one of which he had 'overwhelmed her with cuddles', and she wished he wouldn't because it made her sister jealous. As the session went on she then provoked the therapist into a quarrel, causing him to address her unguardedly by her married name, 'Mrs ——'. She burst out in fury, 'I could never pour out anything to someone who called me Mrs ——. People address memos to that name. It's not *me*. I might answer to "Pat".'

In the next session (number 29) he spoke of her difficulties in 'being herself' with him or her father, and she responded by saying that her father would still treat her the same if she weren't his daughter, and that 'he was keen on any girl between the ages of 17 and 25, which included her; and this would mean that her mother might have thought she was the "other woman".' The therapist remembered that at her initial interview she had said that she 'had had to behave like a 6-year-old' with her husband; and he suggested that she had always wanted to remain a child, as a defence against her underlying wish to become her 'father's woman'. He linked this wish both with her behaviour in the transference and with her previous tendency to have affairs with married men.

In the final session (number 33) she said that many things had been uncovered, but that 'inside her it feels like a tangled ball of wool with many ends.'

Follow-up (5 years 7 months)

The most important issue is her relation with men. She had one relation which ended up in another triangle – the man left her for a woman friend of hers – but since then no further triangles have occurred. For the past 5 years she has been deeply involved with a man, Howard, to whom she feels totally committed, and thus on the face of it her problem over commitment has been solved. They 'fell madly in love', and they have a great deal in common, share artistic and intellectual interests, and have a fulfilling sex life. The only problem is that now it is Howard who gives considerable evidence of suffering from a difficulty over commitment – e.g. whereas she wants children, he does not, saying that he 'cannot commit himself for the next 18 years'. Their homes are hundreds of miles apart and they can only live together for 6 months of the year; and he is proposing to go on a solitary exploration of the jungles of South America, which will take him away for a year. It is impossible to know the degree to which he is thus expressing for her any residual difficulty over commitment from which she may suffer. (A patient from the Individual Series who described an exactly similar kind of relationship in the most graphic terms, and who also was entirely happy with it and was well aware of the issues involved, is described in Chapter 28.)

She has found highly satisfying artistic hobbies. She left her former job and took up work that makes use of her creativity, though she is now beginning to get bored with this.

She showed evidence of being able to deal constructively with situations that formerly would have ended in a histrionic outburst – a type of response which has entirely disappeared. (For details please see Chapter 30.)

She is still deeply involved in her relation with her father, though she doesn't see him very often. Every time she visits her parents she 'has a knotted gut for days afterwards', and Howard has said that it's not worth going there if it makes her so ill. She said that two things in the future might 'freak her out', one being an inability to have children, and the other her father's death.

As far as 'being herself' is concerned, she said that she no longer *needs* to put on a show for people, but can put it on and take it off as necesssary, 'like clothes'. At follow-up, however, she did give the impression of having to entertain the interviewer, 'talking at a tremendous rate, and using a whole range of catchy phrases and amusing anecdotes.' Two of the four judges of the Individual Team felt that her whole lifestyle was still very adolescent in quality – to which anyone might answer, why shouldn't it be, if that is how she feels?

Reading between the lines, it is probable that these two judges were also sensing that she is still a 'hysterical character', full of feelings that are in some way always being *acted,* even though they may be genuine underneath.

In summary, there have been clear-cut gains, but there is also considerable evidence for residual problems. This applies particularly to her relation with her father. Moreover, in her choice of Howard as a partner she seems to have laid up trouble for herself, since the relation seems likely to be threatened by the question of having children whichever way it is decided. She is now over 30 and this issue will become increasingly urgent as the years go by. (Here she shows a potential resemblance to the Sculptress, whose marriage broke up at her age of 34 over the issue of having children.) However, it is debatable whether this is relevant to a judgment of her current therapeutic outcome.

In consequence of all the above problems and unanswered questions, the scores given by the Individual Team covered a most unusually wide range (1.0, 1.5, 2.5, and 3.0: mean 2.0). This reflected the different emphasis of each judge on the genuine improvements, on the one hand, and the clear or suspected limitations on the other.

We have always held the view that where a legitimate case can be made out for either kind of emphasis, it is right and proper for this to be reflected in the scores, and a wide spread in scores does not constitute a criticism of the method of assessment.

11

The seven 'best' cases, discussion

'Total resolution'

This is a concept which rouses considerable passions at symposia on short-term psychotherapy, with participants speaking contemptuously of 'impossible goals' and 'trying to make patients into perfect people'. This view is misconceived. The concept is an empirical one: it simply means that none of the original disturbances can any longer be detected, and that as far as can be seen all former 'inappropriate' or 'maladaptive' reactions in terms of behaviour or feeling have not merely *disappeared* but have been *replaced by the corresponding appropriate or adaptive reactions*.

At the risk of repetition, because this is such an important subject, we can describe the original disturbances in the Nurse Mourning her Fiancé, and their resolution, as follows:

1 Depression.
2 An inability to experience feelings of any kind, particularly grief or anger.
3 A corresponding general inability to involve herself in anything.
4 A quite conscious and deliberate avoidance of relations with men.

During therapy she achieved the ability to experience grief and to recognise its source, and to experience and express anger – there is little that could be more convincing than her description of the relief of crying after the first session, of her sharing the grief of the bereaved child and 'crying for herself' as well as for the child, and of her 'shaking with anger' in an incident in which she swore at a bus conductress who had treated an old lady with callous unconcern.

At follow-up she made absolutely clear that she was aware of the pathological nature of her former position and the major change that had taken place. In addition, her depression had not recurred and her ability to experience grief had been maintained; and she had now quite consciously taken the decision to allow herself to become involved emotionally with a man. She had married, and the relation seemed to be satisfactory in an entirely 'ordinary' way, with closeness, common interests, the ability to share deep feelings, to quarrel and make it up, and a satisfactory sexual relation.

After this evidence, it is difficult to see the relevance of 'impossible goals' and 'making patients into perfect people'. No one is suggesting that she is a perfect person, but she does seem to be an 'ordinarily normal' person within any definition of that phrase that can be formulated.

Total resolution and the rest of the sample

It must now be said that no other patient in the sample of 24 gave a result that could be judged with certainty as total resolution. A possible exception to this statement is the Conductor. Our score of 3.0 was conservative, and the truth is that there is really insufficient information to lay to rest our doubts about the quality of the relation with his wife. All the other disturbances seem to have been resolved.

A case could also be made out for regarding the Car Battery Man as a 'near miss' to total resolution, since if we regard his relation with his wife as essentially 'normal', his only residual disturbance was the presence of mild phobic symptoms which inconvenienced him very little. (The gestalt of his relation with his wife is described in detail in Chapter 27.)

'Character changes'

This is another subject that raises strong passions. The usual implication is that changes in character disorders are the province of long-term therapy or psycho-analysis, and it is presumptuous and unrealistic to claim that they can be altered by anything shorter. Once more, this is mistaken. The most striking example is the Librarian, who could hardly be described as suffering from anything other than a masochistic character disorder, and in whom the masochistic tendencies disap-peared and were replaced by the ability to feel jealousy and rage freely and to assert herself constructively.

One of the difficulties is that the term 'character disorder' is very difficult to define, and it is much better to abandon it and to refer instead to 'repetitive and inappropriate (or maladaptive) patterns of behaviour', an empirical definition which *includes* the manifestations of character disorders but takes in various other – sometimes more short-lived – disturbances as well. The empirical definition of 'resolution' is then simply that these should be replaced by the corresponding appropriate patterns.

Resolution of this kind occurred in at least six of the seven patients, the possi-ble exception being the Betrayed Son, in whom the criterion appears to be irrel-evant because no such pattern was identified. The details of these maladaptive patterns are as below:

1 *The Nurse Mourning her Fiancé:* Deliberately breaking off relations with men.
2 *The Pacifist Conductor:* Withdrawal from creative work; getting other people to express anger while he remained calm.
3 *Librarian who Sought Suffering:* Masochistic handling of anger and jealousy.
4 *Car Battery Man:* Inability to hold down jobs because of quarrels with bosses.
5 *Sculptress with Nightmares:* Promiscuity; drinking and histrionic behaviour in response to conflict with other people.
6 *Mountain Tarn Girl:* Hysterical attacks in response to stress.

All these disturbances disappeared and were replaced by the corresponding appropriate patterns.

Similarities within the sample

One of the most interesting features of this sub-sample of seven patients is the uniformity of the types of therapeutic effect that *were* observed, on the one hand,

and *were not* observed on the other. This whole subject will be considered much more fully, with detailed clinical evidence, in Part Four. Here it will only be summarised.

All seven patients showed major *emotional freeing,* and in five this was also expressed in *increased creativity;* six of the seven (as described above) showed improvements in *maladaptive behaviour patterns*; in six, *self-destructive ways of expressing anger* – or failing to express it – were converted into constructive self-assertion; and six discovered the ability to '*be themselves*'. Finally, five also showed *symptomatic* recovery, and the other two showed major symptomatic improvement.

However, although six also showed significant *improvement in relations with the opposite sex,* in only one was this relation free from reservations, and in the seventh (the Betrayed Son) there was possibly deterioration.

In other words the overwhelming pattern is for major improvements to be found in all areas, including relations with the opposite sex, but for this latter area to show substantial residual difficulties.

Relations with the opposite sex

Throughout the many years of follow-up work in which these carefully thought out dynamic criteria have been used, a 'satisfactory relation with the opposite sex' has always figured prominently. During discussions among the Individual Team we tried to specify exactly what were the crucial elements in this, and through repeated interaction with the clinical material we concluded that two of these – but obviously not the only ones – could be formulated as *commitment* and *emotional closeness.*

From this point of view we may summarise the data on these seven patients as follows:

1 The Nurse Mourning her Fiancé changed her position from withdrawal from men to commitment and marriage. She apparently achieved a fully satisfactory relation with her husband.
2 The Conductor changed his position from 2- or 3-year relations (in which 'sexual boredom' set in) to commitment and marriage. He achieved emotional closeness; but there are reservations in terms of the residual violence between him and his wife.
3 The Librarian gave up her masochistic pattern and achieved emotional closeness with a man; but this latter was only possible with men who were her intellectual inferiors, with whom final commitment seemed unrealistic.
4 The Car Battery Man changed his position from short-lived relations, which he deliberately broke up, to commitment and marriage. He achieved emotional closeness; but there are reservations in terms of the residual violence and the falling off in the sexual relation after the birth of his child.
5 The Sculptress changed from ever-repeated relations with men, each lasting no more than a fortnight, to a 5-year relation. She achieved emotional closeness, but did not change her pattern of taking up with men who had a fear of final commitment.
6 The Betrayed Son, who was already married, showed a deterioration in his relation with his wife and started expressing resentment in indirect and destructive ways.

7 The Mountain Tarn Girl gave up her pattern of getting involved in triangular relations. She committed herself to a man with whom she achieved great emotional closeness – and indeed her description is of an extremely fulfilling relation – but the reservation is that he himself seems to suffer from a fear of final commitment.

All the previous follow-up studies carried out at the Tavistock Clinic during the past two decades indicate that the over-all criterion of a satisfactory relation to the opposite sex is the most difficult of all therapeutic effects to achieve. The present series turns out to be no exception.

Nevertheless, whatever the reservations, it must be said that six of the seven patients formed far closer and warmer relations, and five formed more lasting relations, than had been possible before they came to therapy. When in addition we take into account the changes in other areas, it becomes clear that all seven of these patients experienced therapeutic effects of incalculable value, which have resulted in a complete transformation of their lives.

12

False solutions

I General
II Two patients with relatively adaptive false solutions

Introduction

In all the follow-up work in which this outcome scale has been used an empirical observation has emerged, namely that once the judges give a mean score below 2.0, even though certain important changes may have occurred, the result can no longer be described as satisfactory. The changes in patients whose scores lie between 1.0 and just under 2.0 can be put into two main categories: improvements in subsidiary areas with little change in the most important areas; and 'false solutions', i.e. apparent improvements which on close examination turn out to result from either an avoidance of, or a hidden expression of, the patient's basic problem, leading to a judgment that this problem remains largely unresolved. Among our 24 cases there are 5 who come into the latter category. They are of the greatest interest and will form the subject of this chapter and the next.

False solutions: general

An archetypal false solution was described by Bandler (in Oberndorf, Greenacre and Kubie, 1948) and quoted in *A study of Brief Psychotherapy* (Malan, 1963):

A girl when first seen suffered from agoraphobia, dressed very attractively, and complained about men's attentions. At follow-up she reported that there had been no recurrence of her agoraphobia, but now she dressed unbecomingly and complained that men weren't interested in her.

Any experienced psychotherapist can read between the lines of this story as follows. Very likely the patient's agoraphobia expresses sexual anxieties, and her recovery from the agoraphobia is the result of her changing her appearance in such a way that her sexual anxieties are no longer aroused. In other words there is no evidence for any internal change, but she has recovered from her symptoms by *avoidance* of what for her is the *specific stress*.

This whole question of false solutions was discussed at length in a study of untreated patients (Malan *et al.*, 1968), where 13 examples were found among 45 patients followed up. Of these the most striking was a woman who had twice developed symptoms on exposure to a particular kind of situation, which for her represented the specific stress: namely the arrival of a new baby who became an intruder in a formerly exclusive relation, and against whom she probably felt a considerable amount of guilt-laden hostility. The first occasion was the birth of her sister, who disrupted the exclusive relation with her parents when she was 13; while the second was the birth of her son, who disrupted the exclusive relation with her husband when she was 31. At 3½-year follow-up she was symptomatically much improved, but she said spontaneously that her improvement had begun at the point when her son first went to school – 'I had him in smaller doses and I felt more relaxed'. Thus the evidence strongly suggests that the improvement occurred, not because of any internal change in the patient, but in response to the *relief of stress brought about by an event outside the patient's control.*

The patients from Balint's Workshop also provided examples. One of the most interesting was the Unsuccessful Accountant. This married man of 31 was trying to give up his job as an accountant in private practice, where he had been unable to make a living, and had been seeking personnel work, for which he had been turned down at about 20 interviews. He was seeking advice about what sort of job to take. It seemed clear that he had been turned down because he was unsuitable for personnel work, and the psychodynamic evidence suggested that he suffered from severe problems over competitiveness and his relations with men in general, which for him represented the specific stress. After a brief therapy in which he experienced some of his problems in the transference, he decided to settle for a job in a commercial firm. This job held few prospects of advancement but it made use of his qualifications in accountancy, and it seemed clear that it served the purpose of avoiding the competition with which he would have been faced if he had continued in private practice – i.e. in his case, like that of Bandler, the improvement was the result of *relief of stress by avoidance.* Moreover, at follow-up there was clear evidence that competitiveness still caused him severe problems, i.e. that what may be called his *specific internal predisposition* to react maladaptively to the specific stress was still present. For instance, he had twice failed an exam on a subject in which he had specialised knowledge – the second time because he became so anxious that he walked out. Nevertheless he was contented in his job and had made fair progress in it.

The scoring of these false solutions on our scale is extraordinarily difficult. If the judgment of outcome were to be based solely on the clear lack of resolution in these patients' basic problems, then the score should be 0 regardless of any other consideration. But this fails to take into account the degree of adaptiveness in the patient's solution, or the quality of life that results from it. Here, for instance, there is an important difference between Bandler's patient and the Unsuccessful Accountant. There is little adaptiveness in the position of a young girl who suffers from so much anxiety about her desire for men that she has to dress unattractively in order to keep them away. On the other hand, a patient who settles for a relatively pedestrian job because of his anxieties about competition, but makes a go of it, may not be doing as well as he might if his problems were resolved, but at least he has found a realistic solution and is not acting self-destructively. It was for this reason that the score given was not 0 but 1; whereas Bandler's patient would certainly be given a score of 0.

These considerations arise particularly in two of the patients to be described below, the Script Writer and the Concert-goer, both of whom decided to stay in relationships which were satisfying to them, on the one hand, but which enabled them to avoid the specific situations which caused them anxiety, on the other. This whole question will be discussed more fully in Chapter 13 after the five case histories have been presented.

The Rebellious Script Writer

Age 32, single but living with a man, freelance writer, 29 sessions, score 1.75.
   For reasons of discretion the following account is highly abbreviated.

Presenting problem

The patient sought treatment because of the acute onset 6 months previously of a distressing preoccupation with the word 'lesbianism'. This symptom seemed to be associated with the break-up of her relation with a man named Colin, which had occurred 1 year previously. She showed no evidence of homosexual tendencies. The two men in her life possessed very contrasting personalities: one was Dick, who was steady and reliable, with whom she got on very well, but whose life principle seemed to be the avoidance of any kind of difficult feeling; and the second was Colin, who was passionate and impulsive, by whom she felt liberated, and yet at the same time whom she did not really like and with whom she could not imagine settling down. After much conflict she had finally broken with him, as a result of which he had had a depressive breakdown and when she was first seen was still in hospital. She did not seem to have faced her true feelings about this.

Reason for acceptance for brief psychotherapy

She was taken on with the aim of dealing with her feelings about the break-up with Colin, and trying to find out the connection – which was by no means obvious – between this and her obsessional symptom. The therapist was a woman psychiatrist, inexperienced but mature, sensitive, and very willing to learn (Therapist A in Chapter 5).

Course of therapy (29 sessions)

For reasons that are not clear, the patient's feelings about the break-up with Colin never arose in her therapy.
   The theme that developed was the link between the relation with these two men and that with her parents in her upbringing, particularly her mother (the patient is an only child). This was typified by her saying that she had never been *troublesome* in any relationship, that the only time that feelings had been evoked in her family had been when she decided to leave home, and that she had wanted to *make trouble* between her and Dick by the relation with Colin. Correspondingly, the climax of therapy came in Session 13 with *making trouble* in the transference – she became almost belligerent, demanding to know why the therapist was always linking herself with the patient's mother – what was the point of it? In the next session she described herself as having almost burst with anger, imagining herself standing on the table and waving her fist. The therapist made a TCP interpretation, linking herself with the patient's parents and with Colin, which brought out that, although the relation with Colin had started as a bid for freedom, it had

ended up like the relation with her parents – in the sense that Colin needed to control everyone and she had felt that she had to get out or be swallowed up. In the next session (number 15) the themes of *guilt* and *loneliness* as consequences of getting out of these relationships were dealt with, and in Session 16 she said that since Session 15 she had felt better.

In Session 19 she spoke of the closeness with her mother as representing a 'stranglehold'; and in Session 22 she said that she felt she had been born into a 'whirlpool' of feeling which lay under her mother's façade, and that in all her relationships she was hanging on to the edge of the whirlpool and in danger of being drawn into it. It is worth noting here another aspect of the way in which the relation with Colin, beginning as an attempt to break free, ended by resembling the relation with her mother.

In Session 23 the therapist spoke of the patient as meeting a surge of needs in other people which threatened to overwhelm her, in contrast to the 'safe, unadventurous' relation with Dick. The patient spoke of being able to tell the truth to the therapist in a way that she could never do with her mother – 'to face her mother with her true feelings would be like destruction.'

Finally, in the last session (number 29) the patient herself made the link between Colin's over-protectiveness and that of her *father* – one of the few times that her father was mentioned in the whole therapy.

Follow-up (6 years)

She recovered completely from her obsessional symptom during therapy and has suffered no recurrence, though a phobic symptom, fear of flying, still remains. She has settled for the relation with Dick, with which she is very contented. This relation is essentially unchanged from the position when she first came. There is some inner freeing and she feels more confident in herself.

Discussion

Therapy was highly focal and some of the dilemmas in her relationships became extremely clear. The meaning of her obsessional symptom was never properly clarified, but perhaps it can be said that a preoccupation with lesbianism is concerned with relations with *women*; therapy brought to light the immensely loaded and ambivalent relation between the patient and her *mother*, and therefore there may well have been enough resolution in this area to cause the symptom to disappear.

It is worth noting that during therapy there were no overt feelings expressed about Colin's breakdown or the loss of him, and her father was very rarely mentioned, and consequently any Oedipal problems which may have been present were not dealt with at all.

As far as relations with men are concerned, the evidence suggests strongly that she has settled for safety. Nevertheless, her relation with Dick is highly rewarding to her. The judges took this into account in giving scores of 1.5 and 2.0, mean 1.75.

The Concert-goer in an Acute Panic

Age 24, single, lecturer at a technical college, 26 sessions, score 1.625.

Precipitating event

The patient had gone to a concert with his woman friend, Ruth, and a male acquaintance of hers, a Norwegian, whom he described as good-looking and a very forceful personality. He immediately took a dislike to this man, sensing that Ruth was attracted by him, and feeling intensely competitive. As the evening progressed he became more and more irritable, angry, and anxious, and he finally reached such a state of agitation that they all had to leave and return home. He was in a daze and it took him 3 days to recover.

Long-standing disturbances

The patient was well aware that the above was only an acute manifestation of lifelong problems. He suffers from considerable anxiety in relation to other males, especially in three-person or group situations. He also has difficulty with men in authority, tending to react aggressively in a way that threatens to damage his career.

Current situation

Ruth is a married woman of 40, living with her husband and three children, the eldest of whom is a son nearly as old as the patient. The patient spends most nights in the same house. Her husband, who is 59 and is crippled with multiple sclerosis, turns a blind eye to her sexual relation with the patient, which is highly satisfactory to both partners. However, the patient does not envisage this relationship lasting more than about another year.

Background

He is the younger of two boys, with a brother 5 years older. There were problems of rivalry with his brother from an early age. The patient became very close indeed to his father, and the two of them engaged in many activities together such as fishing. The mother probably tried to compensate for this by forming a close relation with his brother, and he feels his relation with her suffered in consequence.

The trauma of his life occurred at the age of 11 when his father died suddenly of a stroke. The patient was so upset and disturbed by this that he had to remain in bed for 3 weeks under heavy sedation.

In view of material that emerged in therapy it is important to note that his mother is still alive.

Reason for acceptance for brief psychotherapy

The theme of competition with another male for a woman runs through his story. It seems that currently he suffers no anxiety when he is the successful rival, but that he becomes overwhelmed with anxiety when this success is threatened. There was therefore an obvious focus in terms of competition for his mother with his much loved father and his elder brother. A possible additional focus was incomplete mourning for his father. The patient showed high motivation for treatment and clear insight, saying that he had understood much more about himself since the incident in the concert, and had been able to modify his behaviour so as to be 'more rational' in competitive situations.

Course of therapy (26 sessions)

He was given a termination date which would allow for 26 sessions. The therapist was a psychiatrist from abroad who was not very experienced and highly oriented towards analysis. At times he made psychoanalytical interpretations 'out of the book', or out of his imagination, some of which were of questionable relevance, while at other times he was excellently on target.

From this confused therapy we will pick out one crucial theme.

Fourteen sessions of resistance

The therapist did his best to maintain the focus, but the patient – as, with hindsight, might have been predicted from his extreme anxiety in the precipitating situation – remained highly resistant, employing much rumination about non-emotional topics such as the relative merits of different kinds of building material. Throughout this part of his therapy – and indeed later as well – his pattern was to shy away from strong feelings as soon as they began to be aroused. The therapist did his best in this very difficult situation, often being forced into making rather far-fetched interpretations, particularly about the transference, which the patient treated with well deserved scepticism. The most important work consisted of reiterated interpretations about the patient's need to avoid his feelings and keep control.

The patient partially reveals a secret

Finally in Session 15 the patient acknowledged that because of this need for control the therapy had so far been superficial. He said he had decided to go deeper, and he then told a dream: he was with his woman friend, Ruth, in the town where the family had settled after his father's death, and his father came in and tried to persuade him to give the relationship up. He said that the last time he had dreamt of his father was when he was 14 and had dreamt that his father had made his mother pregnant.

It would seem that one of the main interpretations to the dream should have been concerned with the transference – the therapist trying to make him give Ruth up – but this seems to have been missed. Instead, the therapist interpreted, correctly enough, that the patient must feel guilty at wanting the woman for himself, and perhaps he had felt the same about his mother. The patient said, 'That is the obvious thing,' but in a disappointed voice, as if he felt that the therapist had missed something. The therapist then, clearly thinking about the warm relation between the patient and his father, said that perhaps the person whom the patient really longed for was the therapist, at the same time making a hint about homosexuality. Although there is no evidence that this was in any way correct, it touched on something unexpected which turned out to be crucial. The patient said, 'Everyone has fantasies, and I do too,' but he would not reveal what these fantasies were.

During the rest of therapy, between bouts of extreme resistance, he revealed further details of these fantasies bit by bit, with great anxiety and distress. In Session 16 he said that if he went any deeper he was afraid he would not be able to function sexually and would have to break off treatment. In Session 17 he got as far as saying that his fantasies were 'perverse,' and 'a bit masochistic but more masochistic on the part of the woman'. He emphasised that they only occurred when he was on his own and that they in no way interfered with his relation with Ruth. In Session 18 he was highly resistant, with much obsessional rumination; but he eventually said that the previous two sessions, in which he had spoken of his fantasies, were of an intensity that he does not remember ever experiencing before. In Session 20 he said openly that he was withholding further information because he believed that at the last moment the therapist would grant him an extension of his therapy. In Session 21 he said that he had been thinking that he hates his mother; and the therapist, making an informed guess, asked whether his fantasies involved 'inflicting pain and punishment on the woman'. This did not appear to be so, but the patient eventually revealed that the fantasies involved a dead woman. He said that it was all too difficult to talk about and he begged the therapist not to press him. He then returned to the subject of his mother, speaking of a possible cause for being angry with her, namely that to compensate for the close relation between him and his father she had paid more attention to his brother.

At some point in this period he also allowed his idealisation of his father to slip, describing him as 'exacting, critical, and severe'.

The last session

In the final session, number 26, he started by chatting about superficialities for 15 minutes and then spoke about someone who talked and talked and didn't get to the point. The therapist made the obvious interpretation, at which the patient got quite angry, asking why the therapist kept calling him a 'bad student' – perhaps it was the therapist who talked and talked and wouldn't give his own opinion. Anyhow, he didn't agree, and he listed a number of ways in which he had improved. These consisted of his being more able to assert himself and demand his rights, and being both less afraid and more tolerant of men in authority – formerly he wouldn't listen to them. The therapist interpreted this refusal to listen as an expression of anger, suggesting that it had occurred in the transference and might well be displaced from the patient's father. The patient responded by saying he recognised that the therapist had said the right thing on many occasions.

There was then a long passage in which the theme was concerned with *winning* and *losing*. The therapist said that perhaps he saw the relation with his father in similar terms, implying that he had regarded his father's death as a victory. This brought out that the patient had never seen his father's death as real. The therapist then said that the patient had blocked off his feelings about his father's death in the same way as he was blocking off his feelings about this being the last session. This brought out the following revelation: 'I can't explain why I didn't mention it before, but you bear a close physical resemblance to my father.' He went on to compare his own physical symptoms with those suffered by his father just before his death.

Here the therapist made an excellent interpretation: that the patient needed to identify with a sick father to avoid both the guilt of having wanted to win against him, and the pain of losing someone so dear to him. He reminded the patient that his father and Ruth's husband had the same Christian name, and he said that the patient had taken Ruth away from her husband, comparing this with the fact that after his father's death he had gone to another town to live with his mother. The patient now spoke again of the dream in which his father had made his mother pregnant, revealing a new detail, that his father was both alive and dead at the same time. The therapist tentatively linked the dead father with the patient's sexual fantasies, which now brought out the final and most obscure revelation of all: that the fantasy consisted of having sex with a woman who was dying. (Here it is important to note that the patient's mother was still alive and well.) 'I know this is a crucial part of therapy, but now it is too late, and it is my fault that I wasn't able to speak of it earlier.' This was almost at the very end of the session. He was in a highly emotional state as he said good-bye.

First follow-up, with the therapist (1 year 5 months)

He had moved in permanently with Ruth in the later part of therapy and he was still there. He said his relation with her was 'better than ever'. He gave evidence of having been able to assert himself with his brother in a way that would have been impossible before.

When the therapist touched on his way of dealing with feelings by rationalisation, he said he had thought about this a lot, and added, 'Perhaps it has to do with my father'. He then tried to shy away, and the therapist brought him back. He spoke of his father's death with tears running down his cheeks, which had not happened in therapy.

However, when the therapist tried to investigate his sexual fantasies he became resistant again, saying that he did not want to talk about this any further. 'It is like going to a dentist who wants to look at *all* your teeth, and there comes a point at which you don't want any more.'

The therapist asked to see him again. The following is the therapist's description of this truncated interview – typical of the patient's severe anxiety about facing his feelings: 'He came on time, sat down, and said at once that he had not wanted to come and had thought of writing and telling me so. He said he felt angry with me, but this didn't mean that I hadn't helped him – he had wanted to come and tell me this personally. He then stood up, and since I didn't feel I had any right to keep him, I said good-bye and wished him luck.'

Final follow-up, with a member of the Individual Team (5 years ll months)

His acute anxiety, as experienced at the concert, has never recurred. There has been a major improvement in his ability to compete, and in his relation to rivals and men in authority. Some of his leisure activities involve competition, and this is no longer anxiety-laden. He is much more able to relax and be himself in group situations, including those in which other males are present. He is more at ease with male authority-figures. He has recently pressed for promotion and been given it, but the interviewer felt that if he had been more assertive earlier he could probably have been promoted before. Whereas, during therapy, he was constantly complaining about the way he was treated by his superiors at work, he now feels creative in his work and enjoys it.

Contrary to his expectations and ours, his relation with Ruth has continued throughout the whole of the follow-up period; and it is only now that, on her gentle insistence, he is contemplating leaving her and moving away. There seems little doubt that his relation with her has been an exceedingly rewarding one, intellectually, emotionally, and sexually, so that in this area his 'false solution' would seem to be in many ways highly adaptive.

It was research policy that the Individual Team should not have access to the events of therapy, so that the follow-up interviewer knew nothing about the patient's sexual fantasies and could not ask about them.

The patient was genuinely grateful for his contact with the Clinic. He emphasised that he had been enabled to look at problems, relationships, and himself, in a new way, and that this had helped him throughout the follow-up period.

Comment

This was an exceedingly difficult therapy for a relatively inexperienced trainee. The patient was so resistant that the therapist is to be congratulated for having produced any therapeutic effects at all. Apparently the original precipitating event served the purpose of acquainting the patient with his problem over competition, and he was able to allow some work to be done on this during therapy. This seems to have mitigated both his anxiety in competitive situations and his hostile relation with male authority. On the other hand he was so anxious not to have his feelings mobilised at any depth that – although these subjects were touched on – he succeeded in blocking most of the attempted work both on his grief about his father's death, and on the presumed, deeply repressed, intense hostile rivalry with his father. The description of his father as 'exacting, critical, and severe', in contrast to the previous idealisation, provided a clue here, but it was impossible to work with it. The first follow-up, with the patient almost in tears about his father, certainly indicated that there was much unresolved feeling in this area. No light was shed on the meaning of his sexual fantasies, which remain entirely obscure to this day.

A critic could possibly say that a more active, even confronting, pursuit of the patient's feelings about his father might have paid dividends; and yet the constant severe anxiety about having his feelings touched at all, and the almost unbearable anxiety about his sexual fantasies, indicates that this would have been very difficult, and that unless it was very carefully graded it might well have driven the patient away.

The final outcome is almost impossible to assess, and we really need a further follow-up to see how the patient fares if he leaves Ruth and tries to find another partner, and particularly if he has to face competition for her and is in danger of losing – which for this particular patient constitutes the *specific* stress. Yet there seems little doubt that there has been some genuine resolution in what may be called the patient's 'specific internal predisposition', namely to react to the stress of competition in general with intense anxiety.

There are many questions without clear answers, of which the following two are the most important:

1 How does one judge a relation with a woman which on the one hand was so rewarding, and on the other hand was never likely to lead to a final commitment and was so clearly based on the expression of unresolved Oedipal problems?

2 Was the successful competition with a crippled and colluding rival still being used as a defence against anxieties about competition with more effective rivals?

As is quite appropriate, the spread of scores reflected this dilemma: 1.0, 2.0, 2.5, 1.0, mean 1.625.

13

False solutions

III Three patients with less adaptive false solutions
IV General discussion

The Hypomanic Advertising Executive

Age 28, married, 26 sessions, score 1.375. The description 'hypomanic' is derived from the final follow-up.

History and disturbances

He met his wife 6 years ago. He said that she was a consummate actress and he spent 2 years getting through this to her real self. Eventually her acting dropped away from her 'like a curtain'. Their early sexual relation was described as 'hectic'. He encouraged her to let herself go to the maximum degree, which she apparently did. However, 6 months ago she confessed that she had been acting a part the whole time and had never in fact had an orgasm. This precipitated him into impotence, which is his complaint.

In addition he seems to have had a problem over competition, and fulfilling the potential indicated by his high intelligence, from an early age. At 9 he was sent to an analyst because of vomiting attacks at school and general tension. In this previous therapy there emerged a great deal of rivalry with his brother, 2 years younger, who was always top of the class and made him feel very inferior. In his mid-teens he was advised to leave school early because the teachers thought he would never get to university, but in fact he then went to a crammer, passed into university, and got an Upper Second in Economics, 'just missing a first'. He entered the world of advertising. Again he was regarded as not very bright, but he enjoys his work and has done reasonably well at it.

Background

His family background is Polish. He is the elder by 2 years of two brothers. He described his mother as considerably more intelligent than his father, very warm, and possessing a magnetic personality which drew many people to her. He said he 'did not really know what to think of his father', but described him as generous.

Projective testing

It was here that the most important material emerged. In the ORT (as mentioned before, a psychoanalytically based test similar to the TAT), he described a card which is usually seen as a heterosexual scene as 'two men urinating against a tree'. He expressed the fear that homosexual and sadistic fantasies might be exposed in him. The psychologist later asked him if he felt 'his marriage was a field in which he had succeeded and his brother hadn't, and when his wife confessed about her lack of sexual enjoyment, did he feel he had failed?' He replied that this was an important piece of insight, and indeed he was afraid his wife might be attracted by his brother.

He also told the psychologist that he 'wants to be aggressive but doesn't know how'.

Reason for acceptance for brief psychotherapy

His motivation was at first ambivalent, since there had been a recent improvement in his potency and he felt he might not need to come at all. However, he relapsed after a few weeks and asked for treatment.

In view of the fact that his wife's problems were so clearly bound up in the situation, we regarded the treatment of choice as conjoint marital therapy, but his wife refused to come. He was therefore taken on for brief individual therapy because of the obvious focus of rivalry with men and his clear response to interpretation on this theme.

Course of therapy (26 sessions)

The therapist was the woman social worker who treated the Librarian (see Chapter 8), relatively experienced, fearless, and accurate in her interpretations.

Family relationships; hostility towards women; a mixture of hostility and incestuous wishes towards the mother

The kind of work that the therapist did with this patient, the correct and repeated use of the two therapeutic triangles, the high degree of communication between patient and therapist, and the picture of family relationships that emerged, may be illustrated very clearly by Session 10.

The patient spoke of having defied his wife by refusing to change his clothes before going out with her, to which she had retaliated by saying that she had almost agreed to go to bed with a man whom she had met on the Underground. The therapist said that this mutual humiliation reminded her of the patient's previously mentioned fantasies of humiliating women (impulse, current). He said that he had a lot of anger locked up in him because he feels weak, and the therapist led him towards the relation with his mother (current–past link). He spoke of a very unhappy childhood, saying that now for the first time he was beginning to feel that his mother was to blame. He had been sent away to Warsaw to school, where he stayed with a woman who 'engulfed' him, but he could not ask to leave because it would have hurt her. The therapist linked this with similar feelings about his mother – saying that he both wished for and resented being engulfed by his mother (conflicting impulses in the past). He spoke of coming home from school every week-end because he had to 'report back' to his family and 'see things through their eyes'. His mother thought that anyone who disagreed with her was unintelligent (the theme of the importance of intelligence emerges here). The therapist said that 'it sounded like a straitjacket in which he also voluntarily stayed', to which he said that he had to agree with his mother for fear of losing her or making her angry (defence and anxiety in the past). He added that his father always agreed with his mother, which didn't help, and that even nowadays his brother is often depressed and deliberately tries to upset his mother.

The therapist now made the link with herself, saying that he needed to agree with her in order to get her to respond warmly to him (defence, past linked with transference). To this he said that he gets both anxious and angry (anxiety and impulse in the transference) when she doesn't respond, and he tries to use his power to cause her to show weakness. She said that he both wanted to keep her down and wanted her to reassure him that she cares for him (mixed impulse and anxiety in the transference). He then spoke of his fear (the anxiety) that his mother would 'flip over' into being more interested in his brother, who was very clever and took all the prizes (here the patient himself implies the link from trans- ference to past). The therapist now made the link from the past back to the trans- ference by saying that perhaps he had a similar kind of anxiety about her, i.e. that she (the therapist) would be more interested in someone more intelligent than he was, perhaps someone like his brother or his father. This was completely confirmed when he said that he gets anxious when she asks about members of his family, wondering if she'd be more interested in them than in him, 'and when will the subject get back to me?'

As foreshadowed in this session, the central theme of therapy now became the patient's hostility towards women, which was repeatedly linked with his feelings about his mother, often via the transference.

The following sexual fantasies and impulses emerged:

1 Physical violence against women.
2 Exposing women to humiliating situations such as having sex with animals.
3 Voyeuristic impulses (watching women undress).
4 Looking at other women in the street in the presence of his wife.
5 Looking at women 'with venom,' and also
6 Violent and humiliating attacks on men.

Side by side with these violent and hostile elements in his fantasy life, the thera- pist brought out his passive defences in real life, which he described as consisting of 'behaving like an amiable clot', and avoiding all forms of aggression. The hostile elements in his fantasies gradually mitigated. In Session 12, for instance, he said that he now looked at women 'with *half-hearted* venom'. He added that the thera- pist had 'taken the steam out of him', had 'got at the cracks in him'. The thera- pist said that he must see her as making a castrating attack on him. He agreed, saying that it made him think of doing sadistic things to her. This was linked with his mother, whose contemptuous and competitive attitude to male sexuality now emerged: e.g. she speaks of her other son's sexual promiscuity as 'going to the lavatory', denigrates male sexuality on principle, and says that women 'have the flame' and experience more intense and more spiritual pleasure than men.

In Session 13 he spoke of being made anxious by his wife's wet kisses, being afraid of being 'sucked in and engulfed'. The therapist commented on his seeing himself as so small and said that it's as if he was back in an incestuous relation with his mother. He said that his mother's weapon is keeping him as a little boy, and the therapist interpreted that he colludes with this 'in order to avoid the combat with other males'.

In Session 17 he spoke of self-hatred because of his wish to follow girls in the street, with the impulse not only to undress them and hug them, but also to murder them. The therapist linked this both with herself and with his mother. In response the patient said with much feeling that he did indeed feel this about his mother, and he added that she is seductive and promises warmth but does not give it.

In Session 18 he thumped the chair and said that he 'had had no adolescence – they were so bloody understanding I couldn't rebel'. Later he shut his eyes and described with strong feeling a fantasy of sadistic attacks on the therapist's breast, anus, and vagina, saying what a relief it was to be able to tell her this.

Rivalry with men

In Session 19 he said that the Managing Director at work thought him a fool. The therapist interpreted that his protestations of impotence were a defence against his rivalry, and perhaps he thought the Managing Director was a fool. The patient said with surprise that this was true, and he later spoke of having for the first time openly criticised his mother for putting his father down.

The theme of independence; therapeutic effects

In Session 21 he said that he 'felt in charge' when visiting his parents. He has thought of taking up training for another job, and if he does it will be *his* decision and he wants to 'throw off the fetters'. He feels he has learnt a lot from people at work, but he no longer wants to be a disciple. He has started to do metalwork as a hobby, using designs of his own which people like, and selling the things he makes. The therapist said, 'No longer the impractical clot'. He said, he doesn't know how, but he's changed. He had a feeling of not wanting to come to the session, 'perhaps because I can do without you. I've got mixed feelings – I want Mummy's approval, but I also don't care whether you approve or not. I seem to be going through an accelerated adolescence.'

Climax of therapy: return to hostility against the mother

Perhaps the climax of therapy occurred in Session 22. The patient said that his mother subtly tells him how thankful he should be for the way she brought him up, 'but now I estimate it differently'. The therapist pointed out how mild his comments were and linked this with his defence of submission both to her and to his mother. He shut his eyes and said, with intensity, 'I avoid getting to the core of my feeling about her, which is tremendous locked-up anger – a lack of respect, that's what it is – it's terrible to say that. I feel as though a thunderclap has happened.'

Further therapeutic effects

During the course of his 26 sessions the patient reported a considerable number of therapeutic effects. In addition to those mentioned in Session 21, these were as follows:

1 He became more sexually active and more forceful in other ways with his wife, which they both enjoyed.
2 He lost his fear of women's genitals and enjoyed exploring those of his wife, discovering the clitoris for the first time.
3 He constrasted his new-found confidence with his feelings of helplessness when he first came.
4 His sexual fantasies occurred less often and were 'more gentle'.
5 His relation with his wife became closer and they became able to discuss their problems with each other.

Comment

In our view this was an extremely skilful and highly focal therapy, with extensive and correct use of the two triangles, leading to the emergence of intense feeling botfi in the transference and about the past.

First follow-up (with DM, at 1 year 3 months)

It may be remembered that one of the issues in the patient's history was the degree to which his wife was 'real' or was – consciously or unconsciously – acting a part. In the whole follow-up period the same issue emerges about the patient himself, with the inference that it was a shared problem in the marital relation. The assessment of outcome depends very largely on the view taken about this.

At this first follow-up he said that there had been a 'quantum jump' in the sexual relation with his wife, and that now there was 'congruence' between the two of them. They can admit their feelings completely to each other, whereas previously there had been two different relations going on at the same time, one superficial and the other containing their real feelings underneath.

The interviewer tried to pin him down over this issue. Eventually he said that at times he was 'able to hate her completely', but he was unable to give a concrete example of expressing anger to her.

He no longer suffers from trouble with his potency. His wife enjoys sex very much, but she has never had an orgasm. The previous sadistic fantasies against women no longer come even if he tries to revive them – 'except rarely'. However, sexual fantasies are still very important to him, and it seems that some of them are homosexual in a highly ambivalent way, involving both affection and some kind of castrating attack.

Second follow-up, with a member of the Individual Team (5 years)

Again the important issue is the relation with his wife. He said that he and she had got to a serious pitch of resentment with each other, and eventually (about 9 months ago) he had said something to her that he had never dared to say before, namely that he was afraid that if he didn't give her an orgasm she would leave him. She said, 'Is that what it's all about?' and from then on their relation, though not their sexual relation, had improved – there was more open discussion between them. Moreover, there are times when he can be 'gloriously angry' with her.

Finally, about 2 months ago, he had met a woman who had shown him how to give her an orgasm by stimulating her clitoris, and he has managed to give his wife an orgasm by this technique on three successive nights. He feels that this has 'cut the Gordian knot' and – though it is not clear why – has 'cut the links with his mother'. It has increased his confidence immensely and the sexual situation is much better.

His relation with men seems much improved and he can hold his own with them and get on well with them at work. Here he has done extremely well, being head of a team training executives, and – as he said – using some of his psychotherapeutic experience and thus repaying a debt to the Tavistock.

As far as his relation with his mother is concerned, he spoke as follows: 'I was virtually bound by a steel hoop to my mama. Now the links have been cut and have dropped into the mud without trace. My mother didn't let me rebel, but now I'm jolly well doing so. She used to be my mate and colleague in arms, and my wife was very jealous of the links between us. Going home was really going back to her, but now the link is broken and things are just pleasant between us.'

He is closer to his father, who currently is worried over business problems and is able to share his feelings with his son.

He also feels closer to his brother and less jealous of him.

Comment on follow-up

On the face of it the patient has shown remarkable improvements in all areas: his relation with his wife, his potency, his self-confidence, his achievement in work, his emancipation from his mother, and his improved relation with his father and brother. This would mean that he should score in the region of 3.5.

However there is much evidence to cast doubt on the overall picture, particularly that of the relation with his wife:

1 The patient's sexual improvement is very recent and he has described similar improvements in glowing terms on two previous occasions, on both of which he subsequently relapsed. For instance, when he first came to us he said that there had recently been a 'tremendous' improvement in his potency, but the interviewing psychiatrist wrote: 'He seems to lay great emphasis on what I think is a rather tenuous and very recent improvement', and in fact he did relapse and came back asking for treatment. Equally, at the earlier of the two follow-ups he mentioned a 'quantum jump' in his relation with his wife, which in view of later information obviously did not go very deep.
2 His attitude to sexuality still seems unrealistically all-or-nothing. He claimed that his wife had always thoroughly enjoyed their sexual relation, and yet he also said: 'When I left the Tavistock, I was no longer impotent, but so what? As my wife hadn't had an orgasm, it was still an unconsummated marriage.'
3 Probably the most important reservation is that there was considerable evidence at the final follow-up that he was actually in a hypomanic state. Thus he took his shoes off and sat cross-legged on the chair; his flow of words was described by the interviewer as 'torrential'; he said of his work that he was 'indispensable' and the 'mainspring of his group' (which of course may be true), and that he 'had more power than his boss'; of his relation with his second son he said he had a 'magic touch with babies', and so on.
4 Returning to the relation with his wife: an overall view of this is that it has consisted of long periods of *falseness,* punctuated by moments of honesty which have produced improvements that turned out to be transitory; and there is little

reason to suppose that this pattern has been finally broken. Hypomanic and manic states might be described as the epitome of falseness, and they surely cannot be regarded as an adaptive form of false solution.

All these considerations make it very difficult to believe that his improvements are as genuine as he makes out, and at best they must be regarded as 'not proven'. Many of his claims to have improved may really be hypomanic phenomena, which would include the relation with his wife and his apparent liberation from the tie to his mother. One major improvement consists of his changing from the role of an 'amiable clot' to becoming leader of a team at work, which is presumably an objective fact; and yet his account of his effectiveness in this area may well be highly exaggerated.

At the same time, on the other side, there were touching moments of genuineness in the final follow-up interview. Two of these concerned his changed view of events and situations in the past. The first was his original initiation into sex by an older woman in his teens. When he first came he had described this woman as having 'initiated him rather gently and pleasantly'; now he said, 'the degradation of the experience overshadowed everything else'. The second was his changed view of his childhood, which at his initial interview he had described as essentially happy, but which now he described as having contained 'a lot of pain, a lot of seriousness, and not much laughter'.

Once more the judges were faced with an almost impossible task. Three members of the Individual Team were highly sceptical and scored 1.0, while the fourth gave a score of 2.5 – which is entirely justifiable if the patient's improvements at work, in self-confidence, and in relation to his family, are taken at their face value, and if he is given credit for some improvement in his relation with his wife. The resulting mean value was 1.375.

This fascinating story, more than any other in our series, illustrates the extraordinary difficulty of assessing psychodynamic change, and the complex issues that have to be taken into account.

The Secretary in a State of Nirvana

Age 34, single, secretary and personal assistant to an architect, 29 sessions, score 1.0.

Like the description 'hypomanic' in the title of the previous patient, the description 'in a state of nirvana' is derived from the follow-up.

Referral

She was referred by her Tavistock-trained GP to whom she had gone, first, with a series of physical complaints, then with depression (lethargy, lack of concentration, insomnia), and finally with a request to be allowed to talk about her problems.

Presenting problems

One of her main problems emerged with great clarity as a preoccupation with everybody else's needs and difficulties, and a powerful inhibition against considering those of her own or asking anything for herself, which was now breaking down into intense resentment.

At the initial interview, with the woman psychologist who treated the Sculptress, she opened by saying that she had too much to cope with at work, and she went on to describe other people's problems in great detail. It seemed that almost everybody, including her immediate boss, had either recently had a breakdown or was about to have one.

The interviewer pointed out that she was not speaking about her own problems, which led to her describing her relation with a very difficult boy-friend who imposed on her with total lack of sympathy or consideration, and apparently did not lift a finger to help her. Nevertheless the sexual relation was highly satisfactory.

She had had a previous 4-year relation with a married man, whose wife colluded with their affair. She described him as very gifted but rather mad, suffering from terrible tempers, and causing her to become quite hysterical at times. He threatened suicide when she left him.

It is important to note that she described her boss also as a very difficult man and she made no mention of wanting to look for another job, so that there is evidence that she tends to gravitate towards men who ill-treat her or cause her trouble.

Background

The background to this was as follows: her mother clearly suffered from 'helping profession syndrome', which in her case meant that she was always involved in good works which she put before the children's interests (there was one brother, younger by 3 years). The mother's background was extremely deprived – her own mother ill-treated her, both of her parents were alcoholics, and she was eventually sent away into the care of guardians. In describing her own background the patient typically emphasised her mother's deprivation rather than her own.

Unlike her mother, her father made considerable sacrifices for the children's sake, staying in a job that he hated in order to pay for their schooling. She said, however, that she felt little warmth between him and her – there was some sort of barrier.

In addition to the above problems, the patient suffers from attacks of fairly severe depression – she said she can't remember when last she felt it was good to be alive.

Reasons for acceptance for brief psychotherapy

There was an obvious focus in terms of the altruistic position that she adopted as a defence both against expressing her own needs, and against her anger about not having them met. At interview she showed a clear response to interpretations along these lines, expressing considerable resentment and seeing the parallel between her own behaviour and that of her mother.

Course of therapy (29 sessions)

Focal work

The therapist, a woman psychologist, was moderately experienced and worked hard and well.

Session 1 showed a clear sequence, from the patient's state of suffering, through her defence, to some of the underlying feelings. She said that she had had an operation on an infected tooth, but the thought of going and staying with her boy-friend would have been impossible because he would have expected her to carry on as normal, cooking and cleaning for him. She had become very ill with a reinfection and had asked him to buy something for her from the chemist in his lunch hour, to which he had said that he didn't have the time. In addition her father had started telling her to pull herself together.

After some tentative comments by the therapist, the patient went on to speak of her unsuccessful attempts at keeping up her defence of compliance, saying that she couldn't live up to her parents' expectations. The therapist pointed out her life pattern, that she is like her mother, always attending to other people and finding it difficult to make her own needs known. This very simple interpretation produced a clear response in terms of *anger:* the patient said that she cannot go on like this, and told of an incident in which a man had pushed in front of her in a pub, at which she had just 'snapped', shouted at him in fury and rushed out in tears.

This highly focal and encouraging session was followed by a warning. She arrived for Session 2 in a state of psychomotor retardation, saying that over the week-end she had been severely depressed, hardly able to do anything but sit in her room with the curtains drawn.

In this session she reported what seemed to be abominable behaviour on the part of her boy-friend, and the therapist pointed out that she got herself involved with such men, that she felt she had no right to expect anything for herself, and in spite of her underlying resentment could not extricate herself. This was linked with the family situation, in which both her mother and her father sacrificed their own needs in favour of those of others – the mother by her good works, and the father by providing the best education for the two children. The patient nodded, but made no other response.

Therapeutic effects appear and focal work continues

However, in Session 3 she reported having had a terrific row with her boy-friend, who had criticised her for complaining to a superior at work about her immediate boss. Her boy-friend walked out, saying he never wanted to see her again and had never liked her anyhow.

In Session 4 she said she was feeling much better and had been taking a lot of pleasure in doing exactly what *she* wanted. She went on to speak of the previous married man with whom she had had a relation. It appeared that she had ended up practically supporting him. Once more the therapist pointed out that although she appeared to be a passive victim, in reality she actively got herself into this kind of situation. In response the patient described how in her childhood the family was very poor and her mother didn't have time to have her meals ready or her school clothes ironed. Once the patient had had to go to a school dance with tacks and pins keeping her dress together, because her mother had not had time to have it ready, though she had promised to do so. The therapist interpreted that she was almost making excuses for her mother, but that underneath she must be angry and resentful, when her mother spent so much time caring for others. This was linked with the patient's own altruistic pattern.

Work of this kind led to a major breakthrough in the patient's relation with her parents, which she reported in Session 8. She had been depressed, and her father had said 'he hoped she'd be more cheerful and less moody on her next visit'. At last she had become aware of anger with both of them, and she had later phoned her mother and said she wasn't going to come home any more, since it was obvious they couldn't accept her as she really was. In fact she did go home and had a long talk with her parents, confiding in them about her relation with her boy-friend and her consequent depression. She said to the therapist that this was the first time she had ever talked to them in a meaningful way, and that it had been made possible by her therapy.

Transference

In Session 10 the therapist made a determined attempt to get at anger in the transference, without success. She said that the patient had got some good things from therapy and therefore found it difficult to complain about such things as breaks in treatment or not having her questions answered. The patient denied any anger or irritation and said how much she valued the sessions. The therapist pointed out the difficulty of allowing resentment when she also felt warm feelings, linking this with the patient's mother. The patient eventually admitted resentment towards her mother, and the therapist said that to be angry with someone she cared about made her feel guilty and bad, to which the patient said 'and it's also like that with my boss'.

Further therapeutic effects

The patient's continuing progress may be illustrated by Session 11, in which she said, 'What really gets me is that my father is so sanctimonious'; and later that she was 'sick to death' of the way her mother gave up all Saturday morning to helping at the Church. A highly symbolic incident which had happened at home was that her mother had complained that some house plants were not doing well, and the patient had said the trouble was that they *needed more light,* and had put them on the windowsill. In this session she said that she always used to think that people were doing her a favour by employing her, but she now realises that she puts a great deal into her work and it ought to be acknowledged – and she has asked for overtime pay.

A protracted state of resistance; the issue of termination

In the second half of therapy the patient became increasingly resistant to further work. She repeatedly said that she didn't know where her therapy was going. There was much attempted work on her feelings about termination, but little response. At one point she suggested stopping a month early, at which the therapist suggested that she was dissatisfied with the number of sessions and was trying to get out before the situation got any worse. She eventually agreed to stay. Although she acknowledged the important gains that she had made she remained basically in resistance.

Towards the end of the final session (number 29) the patient asked if people were ever seen again after the end of therapy, and the therapist responded by making a further appointment for 6 weeks' time. The patient said how much she had got from the therapy, and the therapist said that she herself also had got a lot from their work together, to which the patient made the depressive, self-deprecatory comment, 'I can't imagine what'. The therapist said that the patient couldn't acknowledge what she (the patient) had put into the sessions. The patient gave the therapist a present, by which the latter was very touched, and they parted on a note of warmth.

Comment on therapy

Although, as will be seen, the final result was disappointing, this seems to have been a well conducted therapy. The early sessions were highly focal, exactly as planned, and the patient made unexpectedly rapid progress in being able to relinquish her altruistic pattern and both acknowledge and make use of her anger. It seems, however, that she then felt that she had gone far enough, and she resisted further work. Very probably this was concerned with her resistance against facing her transference feelings, which the therapist in spite of considerable effort was unable to penetrate. Consequently the patient did not experience her basic problem in the transference, and – as follow-up showed – she was left with considerable unresolved resentment. This probably accounts for the unsatisfactory nature of the therapeutic result.

Follow-up (4 years 4 months)

The patient showed clear insight into her original problem: 'I tried to please everybody except myself. I have become more selfish. I am infinitely better at standing up for myself at work and also with my parents. Now I go home when I want to, not out of a sense of duty.'

Apart from this, however, she was unable to give any concrete examples of her changed behaviour.

She is in fact still in the same job, working for the same difficult man. She said that the situation didn't bother her at all, and she could cope much better. She no longer suffers from depression or psychosomatic symptoms.

All this seemed decidedly hopeful, but when she was questioned more closely it began to become clear that she was coping by means of some kind of emotional withdrawal. She spoke of 'distancing herself', 'adopting a philosophical approach', becoming 'more objective', and finally of getting into 'a sort of nirvana state'. The true meaning of nirvana is the *absence of desire*, and although of course it is possible that she did not know this, the term seems highly appropriate for describing her position.

When she was asked about her relation to men the above impression was thoroughly confirmed. She referred to her relationship with the apparently unpleasant man who left her at the beginning of therapy as possessing 'depth and intensity', and contrasted it with the present one which started soon afterwards and has continued since then. The man is married, but, as she said, 'Nobody has been harmed by this'. She spoke warmly of his support of her and his ability to communicate with her on an intellectual level. However, she also spoke as follows: 'The relation is very stable, possibly because there is no question of its progressing to anything different. It's limited and therefore it's easy to live with. It makes no demands on me at all.' They do not see each other very often because he is frequently away on business. She said that sexually it is not very satisfactory because of the difficult circumstances under which they have to meet. She went on to say that with her previous boy-friend there were no sexual problems, but since then 'it has been like a switch turned off'.

Socially, she has a number of good friends.   Her reply to a question about anger in personal relationships was: 'Apart from work, I don't find any anger. In other relationships I don't feel there is any sort of connection with anger.'

In contrast to the apparent warmth of her relation with the therapist as reported in the final session, and also in contrast to the clear insight that she showed about the nature of her problem, her remarks about her therapy were full of denial and ambivalence. Although she regarded the therapy as responsible for her improvements, she said that in therapy she 'didn't discuss things in detail' and that she 'began to think that she could do much better by distancing herself'. She mentioned that during therapy she had suffered from severe toothache, somehow implying that this was her only problem, and adding that 'all the rest was a waste of time'. The main thing that she remembered apart from this was that at one point she had wanted to stop coming, and her therapist had persuaded her to stay. She said that this was important because she felt lonely and isolated – in her chaotic and confused life, the very fact of going somewhere on a regular basis was itself of value.

Discussion

There seems little doubt that she has given up her altruistic position. Moreover, if we set aside her inability to give examples of 'being more selfish' and we thus give her the benefit of the doubt, we can say that she appears to be able to assert herself constructively at work, to cope with her difficult boss, and to please herself instead of adopting a compliant position in relation to her parents. All these are major gains.

On the other hand, the evidence for a false solution by emotional withdrawal in her life in general is overwhelming. This includes her relations with men, where she has settled for a relation that is *undemanding*; and since one of her main problems was coping with demands, it is clear that in this area her specific stress is being avoided. Moreover, there are strong indications that she was sexually aroused by a man who ill-treated her and not by a man who was kind to her, thus suggesting that her original altruism contained an element of masochism, and that this extended to the sexual sphere where it has not been resolved.

Thus her solution cannot be regarded as adaptive. Both judges gave a score of 1.0.

The Self-driving Physicist

Age 21, single, research physicist working for an electronics firm, 29 sessions, score 1.0

Disturbances

His complaint is nervousness for 2 years, precipitated when a girl-friend left him. This is present all the time – 'I wake up tense and don't seem to relax day or night.' There is an element of claustrophobia, since his tension is worse when he is in an enclosed space.

His material is permeated by a sense of inadequacy. He met the girl-friend mentioned above at 16 and described how this relation helped his confidence and his ability to achieve; but he then said that she had left him because she wanted a proper man. The result has been a profound loss of confidence which has resulted in impotence. His nervousness is made worse in the presence of people whom he feels to be superior to him. At work he said that he tries very hard but is never praised, and instead his supervisors always criticise, control, and diminish him. He would like to attack back but feels like 'somebody with a gun containing one bullet against somebody with an automatic with a full magazine.' He described a recurrent nightmare in which he is being attacked by big, tall men, and has to run to his mother or his girl-friend for help. He said that he feels at ease with an ugly girl but 'If I try to talk to a pretty girl I just want to dig a hole and bury myself.'

Background

He is the middle of three children, with an older and a younger sister. His father is also a research physicist. The features that stand out from his background are his highly ambivalent feelings about his father, and the sterility of his parents' marriage, with his profound sympathy for both his parents, especially his mother.

He mentioned one good aspect of his relation with his father, namely being taken fishing when he was small – fishing is still one of the patient's main relaxations – but apart from this most of what he said was negative. He felt that his father was always criticising him, diminishing him, and pointing out his inadequacies (exactly what he had said about his superiors at work). His father seems to suffer from a high degree of competitiveness, having been extremely disturbed on more than one occasion when his son saved up and bought possessions, such as a car, that were better than his.

The patient's despairing, depressive, feelings about his home life and his parents are best illustrated by his responses to the ORT, which were frankly autobiographical: 'I see my mother and father. They're moaning at each other. Very familiar. The person standing up is thinking, "Oh God, what an existence". He must want to stay with them to protect them... The ending will be some unhappiness in that house. It will just become empty.' 'If my mother died I'd be terribly upset. When my grandad died, my uncle was crying and wishing he could have done more for his Dad. I'd hate that to happen to me. I think I'd go mad.' To the Blank card he said, 'Go off to work, come home, have tea, moan and groan. Miseries can't be expressed and drawn out of you with a kiss and a cuddle. My mother is just drying up, worn out.'

Reasons for acceptance for brief psychotherapy

There was an obvious focus in Oedipal rivalry, and the patient responded with unconscious material to interpretations relevant to this focus: e.g. when the interviewing psychiatrist spoke of the pain of being left by his girl-friend, he responded with what seemed to be a reference to castration – 'It was like losing an arm or a leg'.

Course of therapy (29 sessions)

He was taken on by the initial interviewer, a male psychiatrist from abroad, soon to be in psychoanalytic training, a good therapist though perhaps rather over-psychoanalytic in his interpretations.

The central triangle of conflict

The patient made clear that he was profoundly disappointed in the relation with his father, who never gave approval, always criticised him, and did not respond with understanding when the patient confided in him. As with so many male patients suffering from this kind of problem (see the Car Battery Man and Betrayed Son), he began to reiterate his wish for the therapist to give him advice or prescribe drugs for him. The therapist gave transference interpretations, linked with the father, of defences against anger at not receiving the love he craved. In response to one interpretation about his father, the patient confirmed the anger by saying, 'I was never violent, I preferred to smash *things*.' From this kind of work the triangle of conflict emerged very clearly: the patient tried to be nice to everyone and to deny all his negative feelings (defence), which included anger with both sexes and rivalry with men (impulse), in order to get love and to avoid being deserted and left alone and desolate (anxiety); but – as so often happens – this did not seem to have the desired effect of making him acceptable.

The patient began to respond in his outside life, and in Session 12 he reported that he was feeling great because he had had an argument with his current girl-friend and for the first time had been able to express himself.

Emergence of manifest Oedipal rivalry

Towards the middle of therapy the theme crystallised of guilt-laden Oedipal rivalry of a very literal kind, which can be illustrated by Session 18.

Early in the session the therapist gave an interpretation of defence and impulse in the transference: that the patient expressed only love in his therapy, but he expressed his anger and disappointment about not getting advice and encouragement from the therapist by missing sessions. The patient made a clear response to this, speaking of his fear of losing his girl-friend and his parents (anxiety in current situations), and going on to describe his anger with his father when his parents quarrelled (impulse in relation to a parent). This led to two openly Oedipal communications: first, how uneasy he felt when he was being cuddled by his mother in his father's presence; and second, 'I felt embarrassed because my mother used to be a mother to me and not a wife to my father, and came to kiss me good-night in my bedroom, and I felt I should push her away and send her back to my father. I felt my father was really angry with me.' The therapist tried to bring in sexual rivalry with the father, but the patient said he never felt like that, and it was his father who was competitive, who told him he was stupid, and is still jealous of him, e.g. of his new car – 'I don't know why I feel so guilty'.

In later sessions the theme of highly guilt-laden Oedipal rivalry now emerged in the transference. The psychologist whom the patient had seen was a very attractive young woman, working as Mrs —— under her married name; and in Session 22 the patient confessed to the idea that she was really the therapist's wife – in spite of the objective evidence against this idea arising from the difference in their names. He said that he felt extremely guilty and embarrassed at 'some of' his thoughts, and that seeing her was 'like going to a friend's house without his knowing that I was interested in his wife.' The therapist linked this with the parents, and the patient said that he can see now that he always had to avoid competition, as if saying to his father, 'I am not in the kitchen to cuddle and take my mother – you take her.' He now made the triangular situation in the transference even more explicit by saying that he was quite sure that the psychologist was the therapist's wife and it was terrible being attracted by her – how could the therapist be prepared to help him in that case? The therapist said, 'like your father, deserting you and leaving you alone.' The patient described how throughout his current life he constantly found himself in triangular situations, coming between two other people and feeling very uneasy about it.

Termination

The patient became strongly attached to the therapist, who clearly represented the father that he once had known but had lost, and the last session (number 29) was very painful, with the patient openly distressed, feeling bereft and deserted. He wanted the therapist to give him a piece of paper on which were written some of the things that had emerged in therapy, so that he could take it away with him. He told a story about a man who had confessed to the murder of a woman that he didn't commit, so as to get put in prison where he would be surrounded by people and would not feel lonely. Five years later the real murderer confessed, the man was discharged from prison, and he threw himself into the river. Later he said, 'I can accept that therapy has finished, but what I find difficult is that somebody else will take my place.' The therapist linked this with the patient's father expressing admiration for the boy next door, or his mother paying more attention to his sister.

The therapist reassured the patient that if he got into further difficulties he could get in touch. They shook hands, and the patient left in an extremely distressed state.

Comment

The reconstruction of the family situation in the patient's childhood that emerged very clearly from this therapy was as follows:

1 When he was small he had a good relation with his father.
2 This was spoilt by the development of intense Oedipal rivalry.
3 The mother, because of her bad relation with the father, directed much of her affection towards the patient and made the father jealous.
4 The father, now very insecure, became in his turn hostile and competitive towards his son, and more hostile towards the mother, thus perpetuating a vicious circle involving all three of them.
5 The patient tried to cover his anger and intensely guilt-laden competitiveness towards his father by being nice; but
6 This did not work and in no way improved the relation; and finally,
7 The patient was left with intense incompatible feelings for his father, consisting on the surface of anger and competitiveness, but underneath this a deep longing for the close relation with his father that he had once had and had lost.

Most of these feelings emerged with the utmost clarity in the transference relation.

The patient's experience of his feelings during the therapy was extremely intense, and it is both surprising and disappointing that the therapeutic result was no better than it was.

Follow-up (5 years 1 month)

The patient has made major progress at work. He has moved over to the management side and is now in charge of about 80 men, which is extremely good for his age of 28. His boss is extremely pleased with him because of his ability to work hard and get hard work out of the men under him. It is clear that the patient handles the men well.

The trouble with this is that it is shot through with a compulsive need to prove himself. In his own words, he must work hard 'in order to prove something'. He gets into a state of tension if output is dropping. There is a great sense of urgency even if the situation is not urgent. 'I need to run at 100 mph even if it is only necessary to run at 50 mph.' It is very important to him that he should feel admired.

In his relation with other men he is greatly preoccupied with strength and weakness. Although he described being able to disagree with his boss and bring him round to his point of view, he also said that he feels insecure with strong people. With men in a weaker position he sometimes tends to over-react and may become rude.

It may be remembered that in his original history one of the important features of his relation with his first girl-friend was that it gave him confidence, and the loss of her precipitated the anxiety state that brought him to therapy. At follow-up he described a friendship with a younger man who became very attached to him, which he said did an immense amount to bolster his self-esteem.

He said something similar about his relation with his current girl-friend. 'In some ways she is tough and capable, in others she's a big baby, and this feeds my egoistic needs.' The relation seems to be very limited. She likes physical contact but is not interested in sex. He is no longer impotent and would like more sex but is not willing to leave her. He said that he cannot allow her to put restrictions on his life and that she will leave him eventually, like all his previous girl-friends. 'I won't listen to them, won't marry them, won't build homes for them. I see marriage as a death.'

Symptomatically, he still feels tense all the time, but less so than before. He clarified the claustrophobic feelings mentioned at initial assessment by saying that he no longer feels 'enclosed, as if he could explode'. Considering the mass of pent-up feelings that were brought out in his therapy, the meaning of this claustrophobic symptom emerges clearly. He has not had any periods of overt depression.

Discussion of outcome

There are some improvements: in his depression and claustrophobia, his potency, and his ability to be successful at work and to hold his own with other men in certain situations.

However, whatever area we examine we find it shot through with neurotic problems. Thus, though there may be a reduction in manifest anxiety, there is a thread of compulsive anxiety running through his whole life, which is clearly based on a need to compensate for a profound underlying feeling of inferiority. He is still greatly preoccupied with strength and weakness; he uses relations both with men and women to boost his ego. He is quite unable to commit himself to a woman and his life is still overshadowed by his view of his parents' marriage.

He himself said, 'I have not got an aim in anything. I am like a bird without a perch.'

In response to this tragic and distressing story, there was total consensus in the scores of the members of the Individual Team: 1.0, 1.0, 1.0, and 1.0, mean 1.0.

General discussion of false solutions

False solutions are at once the most difficult and the most interesting category of result to assess. On the one hand they require the maximum use of psychodynamic insight, and on the other hand – as discussed in Chapter 12 (see pp. 96–8) – they require the integration of this insight with entirely non-psychodynamic judgments about the adaptiveness of the patient's position and the quality of life resulting from it.

Mechanisms of false solution

If the large volume of psychodynamic follow-up material available to us is reviewed, it becomes clear that false solutions are reached by a large variety of different mechanisms. In the present material there seem to be three broad types.

The Script Writer and Concert-goer – avoidance

Although the details are very different, these two patients show a fundamental similarity. In both, the solution consisted of staying in a relationship in which the basic conflict, or anxiety-provoking situation, did not occur and could thus be permanently avoided.

The Script Writer had tried to break away from a steady relationship in order to express her turbulent, rebellious, and passionate feelings, a move which had ended in catastrophe. At follow-up she had settled for the steady relationship, and the evidence suggests that the conflict with the more instinctual side of her nature had been solved only by avoidance.

The Concert-goer had suffered a paralysing anxiety attack in response to the threat of becoming the loser in a triangular situation. He solved his problem by staying in a relation in which he was the victor over a crippled rival – a situation of 'no contest'. His ability to cope with true competition was therefore never put to the test.

Yet in both these cases the relationship in which the patient stayed was a rewarding one, which is what makes the final assessment – though very difficult – relatively favourable.

The Nirvana Secretary – withdrawal and repression

This patient improved symptomatically and became better at asserting herself, but settled for a superficial relationship with a man, which she knew could not lead to any commitment or true fulfilment. The evidence was overwhelming that she had bought a life of relative tranquillity at the price of massive emotional withdrawal and repression of feeling.

The Advertising Executive and Physicist – over-compensation

The feature that these two patients have in common is *over-compensation for feelings of inadequacy*. In the Advertising Executive this took the form of a hypomanic state, in which he made such claims as 'being indispensable' and 'the mainspring of his group' at work, and 'having a magic touch' with babies; in the Physicist it took the form of compulsive achievement, in which he felt he needed 'to run at 100 mph even if it is only necessary to run at 50 mph'. In both patients this over-compensation clearly indicates that the underlying feeling of inadequacy remains unresolved.

Genuine improvements

Although the *over-all* psychodynamic judgment in these five patients was of a false solution, all five also showed some improvements that were important and apparently genuine. Thus the Rebellious Script Writer attained some degree of increased confidence and emotional freedom, and in addition lost her very distressing obsessional symptom; the Concert-goer became more able to compete, to assert himself, to get on with male authority, and to face group situations; the Hypomanic Advertising Executive gave up his defence of being an 'amiable clot' and became a leader at his work; and similarly the Self-Driving Physicist escaped from his 'impotent' position and became effective at work and in his relation with other males, and in addition became literally more potent sexually; and the Nirvana Secretary apparently gave up her compulsive altruism and became able to seek her own interests.

Thus the evidence suggests that some degree of true resolution did occur in all these patients. This is reassuring in view of the intensity and psychodynamic clarity of the work that was done with all of them.

The scoring

It is clear that the judges took a considerably more favourable view of the Script Writer and Concert-goer, both of whom scored 1.75, than they did of the Advertising Executive, Physicist, and Nirvana Secretary, who scored 1.375, 1.0, and 1.0 respectively. The reason for this difference is concerned mainly with the view taken about the degree of adaptiveness of each patient's final position – a view which of course is highly subjective and about which there is much scope for differences of opinion.

Both the Script Writer and the Concert-goer settled for relationships which enabled them to avoid their basic problem, but which nevertheless were rewarding to them, and their position could therefore be called adaptive. The other three patients show a contrast from this. The Advertising Executive had struggled throughout the whole of his marriage for genuineness and true feeling in his relation with his wife, but he seemed never to have attained it for any length of time, and at final follow-up he was judged to be in a hypomanic state – a highly maladaptive position which (as mentioned above) represents the epitome of emotional falseness. The Physicist's major area of improvement, namely his extreme success at work, was made less valuable because it was so obviously compulsive and anxiety-laden; and his emotional life appeared to be a desert. And finally, although the Nirvana Secretary had made some important gains, no one can judge an overall position to be satisfactory that is so clearly based on serious emotional withdrawal.

This leads to a consideration of these patients from two related points of view: the degree of emotional closeness of which they were capable, and the elements that were *missing* from this same area. The Script Writer attained emotional closeness but at the price of losing some aspects of instinctuality; the Concert-goer attained a high degree of emotional closeness, but in a situation where competition was carefully excluded; the Advertising Executive attained some degree of emotional closeness, which probably lacked full genuineness; and finally the Physicist and Nirvana Secretary settled for relations that contained a certain amount of closeness but were basically superficial and uncommitted. Thus the final rank order given by the mean scores makes some additional sense.

Conclusion

These patients illustrate many important features of the assessment of outcome. They illustrate how necessary it is to interview the patient directly, in a free manner, and how deceptive the supposedly 'objective' answers either to questionnaires or to structured interviews may be. For instance, neither questionnaires nor structured interviews would be likely to include the fact that the Advertising Executive sat cross-legged in the chair and delivered a torrent of words, which formed essential factors in the diagnosis of a hypomanic state. Nor would they be likely to give sufficient emphasis to the Nirvana Secretary's repeated use of terms like 'distancing herself', or adopting a 'philosophical' or 'objective' approach, and finally the use of the word 'nirvana' itself.

Similarly, these patients illustrate the importance of psychodynamic thinking in any assessment of outcome. This is shown most clearly by the Concert-goer and Physicist. In the first, only the psychodynamic diagnosis, namely a problem over rivalry in triangular situations, calls in question the patient's solution of staying with his original partner. In the second, only the psychodynamic diagnosis of an underlying feeling of inadequacy calls in question the patient's apparent high achievement at work.

Thus these five patients have added to the stockpile of well documented false solutions, a type of outcome of which researchers must be fully aware if they are to reach a valid conclusion about the effectiveness of psychotherapy.

Finally, perhaps we can note the following: although this kind of work may appear to be so subjective, in fact all five of these patients illustrate the possibility of accumulating powerful evidence, which points almost inevitably both to a particular psychodynamic diagnosis and a particular conclusion about outcome: the Script Writer's conflict between instinctuality and safety, and her solution of settling for safety; the Concert-goer's severe anxiety about competition so clearly illustrated by the incident at the concert, and his solution of settling for a situation of no contest; the underlying feeling of inadequacy present in both the Advertising Executive and Physicist, solved by a hypomanic state in the first and compulsive over-compensation in the second; and the solution of emotional withdrawal adopted by the Nirvana Secretary. It is on evidence of this kind that psychodynamics can make the claim of being a branch of science.

14

Two women patients who showed limited improvements

In Chapters 12 and 13 we described patients who, side by side with their false solutions, showed some genuine though limited improvements. The two patients in this chapter showed limited improvements without clear evidence of false solution, and in their cases the assessment of outcome presents far less of a problem.

The Allergic Receptionist

Age 22, single, medical receptionist, 30 sessions, score 1.75.

The description 'allergic' is derived from the follow-up, in which the problem of allergy emerged for the first time.

Referral and history

The patient was referred to a hospital for a check-up, complaining of attacks of dizziness and fainting, palpitations, breathlessness, headaches, and dysmenorrhoea. She was told that these were psychosomatic and there was nothing to be done. She refused to accept this and demanded referral to a psychiatrist.

She is the youngest of four children. She attended a special boarding school for slow-learning children between the ages of 11 and 17. At this latter age she was about to return home, hoping to get to know her father who was described as having shown very little interest in his family; but he left to live with his mistress, and she has had hardly any contact with him since.

Apart from the symptoms mentioned above she described lifelong feelings of depression and mood swings, worse in the past 5 years. She has difficulty in communicating with both sexes. She described violent feelings which she cannot express, with consequent difficulty in asserting herself. She has not been able to form a satisfactory relation with a man, and said that 'as soon as she wrote a man's address in her diary she lost interest in him'.

Dynamics of initial interview

She responded with strong feeling to a number of interpretative comments, e.g. the (male) interviewer pointed out that she looked aggressive when talking about her father, to which she said, 'I mean, blow it, he walked out on us just when I might have got to know him, that's why I'm aggressive.' At the end of the interview she showed both high motivation and clear insight. Without mentioning her symptoms, she said that she knows therapy will be painful, but that it is necessary *if she is to solve her problems in relationships.*

Reason for acceptance for brief psychotherapy

She was accepted because of her high motivation; her insight; the strong feeling shown at interview, and the clear focus of her disappointment with her father leading to her defence of avoiding involvement with men.

Course of therapy (30 sessions)

The therapist was a male psychiatrist from abroad, with moderate experience, who threw himself into his therapeutic work. Unfortunately he was often over-enthusiastic in his interpretations and at times seriously lacking in psychotherapeutic tact.

The focus developed exactly as foreseen, with the patient sometimes admitting emotional involvement in the transference relationship but alternating this with slapping the therapist down and saying she was indifferent. The therapist confronted the patient with the issue of termination much too early – already in Session 9, before the transference had become clear.

The extraordinary alternation of involvement and denial, warmth and aggressiveness, insight and the lack of it, on the patient's part, and the alternation of sensitive work and tactless work on the therapist's part, may be illustrated by Sessions 12 to 14.

In Session 12 the patient spoke of her father's strict and demanding attitude to the children. The therapist said that since she had been so badly hurt by her father she was not prepared to give her most precious part, her feelings, to any man. At this point 'she became soft and sad and emotionally very close' to him.

In the next session (number 13) she came up 'with a radiant smile' saying that she had been happy this last week and for the first time had been longing to come – there was quite a change in her but she didn't know why. The therapist said, of course she knew, she had allowed herself to experience her feelings of being in love with him (!). 'At this she blushed and said that maybe that was going a bit far'. She then said that her sister had said that she was quite a new person. However, she also said that she had had a severe headache for 3 days soon after the last session. When the therapist later said that 'she had found new ways of expressing her feelings, and was able to show how much he meant to her,' she 'reacted by laughing in a very aggressive and triumphant way, explaining that she had no feelings at all for me.' The therapist pointed out how dangerous it was for her to let anyone approach this very intimate and loving part of her. To this she agreed, saying that she had been able to let her defences down and that she did like to come to these sessions. When he finally said it was time, she said that she 'felt like throwing all the clocks away'.

In Session 14 she arrived with a happy smile and said that she had been longing to come and meet the therapist again. She again said that her sister had spoken of her improvement, namely that she had matured a lot, and that this was right – she had been a child until recently but was now aware that she was becoming a woman. Also, she said, she was becoming capable of thinking properly, of being more constructively active, of being independent, and of setting goals and reaching them. She now felt more like going out, and she had met a very charming and handsome man, and had experienced one of the most beautiful times with him that she had ever had in her life. When she mentioned missing this man the therapist linked this with himself, at which she 'all of a sudden became very aggressive, saying that she was not going to miss these sessions at all, and on the contrary she had already thought of stopping early. From the beginning she had avoided getting emotionally involved, and the therapist didn't mean a thing to her.' The therapist said that this was a reaction to his hurting her feelings, at which she instantly calmed down and said that she knew she just had to go through all this. As she left, she said the sessions were very helpful.

The climax of therapy

This occurred in Sessions 20 and 21 when, in response to the TP link between termination and the loss of her father, she re-lived the events at that time with great feeling, both grief and anger. Her father had arrived home with a van in order to collect his furniture, everybody was shouting at everybody else, and she felt she was losing all her good memories and all her hopes. She alternated between saying she wanted to forget all this and saying that, through talking about it, she felt very much happier deep down inside.

Oedipal feelings

Towards the end of therapy the issue of erotic feelings for her father was touched on. In Session 24 she said that she had gone out for a drink with a man from the office and had felt uncomfortable because he resembled her father. She had asked herself whether she really wanted to go to bed with a man who resembled her father to that degree. The therapist said that she had never had the opportunity to relate to her father as a grown-up woman. She said that she was now experiencing all the feelings that she should have had as a teenager. The therapist said that maybe she was discovering that there were erotic feelings for her father, which she at once strongly denied. In Session 26 she said that she was going to share a flat with this new man. She then spoke of a wish to be dominated, and said that her father was extremely powerful and perhaps she was looking for a man who resembled him.

Termination; therapeutic effects

In this same session she said that her therapy had been 'the most important experience of her whole life', and in Session 27 she said that 'it had been the best investment she had ever made'. The therapist said that it must be difficult to give up such a precious possession, to which she said yes, it had indeed been precious, but it had enabled her to become independent and live a life on her own.

During this later part of therapy she described a number of therapeutic effects: new feelings of ambition, the ability to relax, loss of headaches, better coordination of her body leading to the ability to take driving lessons, clearer thinking and increased ability to express herself verbally.

Comment

Although there was much to criticise in the therapist's handling of the patient, he never lost touch with her, and there is no doubt that the result of his interventions was an intense and meaningful interaction. On the other hand the therapy was very typical of that of a hysteric, and the question was to what degree these therapeutic effects were real or simply the manifestation of a hysterical 'mirage' (a term coined by Davanloo), and thus merely temporary or illusory.

Follow-up (5 years 1 month)

The most important positive change is in the ability to assert herself constructively. Her original living conditions, in her grandmother's house, had been highly unsatisfactory, and immediately after the end of therapy she told the local council that if they didn't help her they would have to pay for more psychiatric treatment, with the result that they arranged a flat for her, with which she is very contented. She also won a court case against some noisy neighbours. (These highly entertaining incidents are described in detail in Chapter 29.) She said, 'Now I can tell anybody what I think. I am me, I am answerable to nobody.'

She had been allergic to various foods since an early age, e.g. she had to avoid dairy products, and her face would swell up if she ate pork; and 4 months ago she finally forced the doctors to investigate her more thoroughly for this. In consequence she has been put on a diet which has resulted in her feeling as if she was a new person – she has lost all her symptoms, together with the constant feeling permeating her whole life that there is something wrong with her. When the interviewer mentioned her previous inner feelings of violence, she also attributed their disappearance to her diet.

In trying to disentangle psychological and physiological factors in her improvements, we may note that she reported a number of therapeutic effects, including loss of headaches, before the end of therapy. On the other hand, chronic food sensitivity, together with the seemingly miraculous effects of treating it specifically, are phenomena that are becoming increasingly recognised, and we have no reason to disagree with her judgment that her diet is responsible for her recent improvements.

Although she said she wants to get married, she has not yet met any man with whom we would want to settle down. She is currently involved with a married man who has a grand-daughter with the same name as hers. This sounds like the expression of unresolved Oedipal problems. Commitment with him is obviously impossible – her attitude is, 'when the end comes, it comes'.

Of her father she said, 'He can go to hell', and she has had nothing further to do with him.

She is going to evening classes learning pottery, which she enjoys very much.

She spoke most warmly of her therapy, saying that it had helped her a great deal. 'Many people say the sessions have altered me completely. I have become far more decisive.' She did not know how this had happened, and it was also clear that she was entirely denying anything negative. She particularly remembered the 'in love' session, which she spoke of with amusement and without bitterness.

Throughout the follow-up interview she chattered in a way that seemed to the interviewer tiresome and potentially endless, conveying the impression of very considerable superficiality. The only time he felt he made any true contact with her was when she spoke about severe dysmenorrhoea, saying that she often cried herself to sleep and wanted to be cuddled.

Summary and discussion

Apart from her dysmenorrhoea she has made a symptomatic recovery, some of which is almost certainly due to her diet rather than to therapy. On the other hand, apparent dynamic changes are that she has made remarkable progress in 'being herself', becoming more decisive and self-assertive, and making something of her life. As far as these aspects are concerned, her position can be described as highly adaptive. Against this, however, it is clear that her problem with men remains entirely unchanged. Moreover it is very noticeable that she seems to have less insight, and to be far less in touch with her deep feelings, than when she first came, which represents a deterioration. The judges gave scores of 1.5 and 2.0, mean 1.75.

Mother, or Teenage Daughter?

Age 26, divorced, telephonist, 30 sessions, score 1.5.

Referral

She was referred by a Tavistock-trained GP because she was a frequent attender at his surgery, and on several occasions had burst into tears without knowing what she was crying about.

She wrote an incoherent, demanding, and in places somewhat uneducated questionnaire, ending: 'Yes please send me an appointment but no more bureaucratic forms like this, I need some-one too talk to not forms to fill in. Why waste your and my time. . .?'

Initial assessment

She is the younger of two sisters, both parents being unskilled workers. At the age of 17 she took up with a violent man who, she said, more or less raped her and got her pregnant. They married, he left her after a year, and they were later divorced. She returned home, where her mother took over the role of mother to her baby son, who is now 8. Not only this, but the father behaves as if he were her son's father. The household is thus full of confusion of roles. The patient is dissatisfied with her upbringing and feels that she never had her mother to herself, and moreover that her son now gets more attention than she ever did.

The patient's sister had a depressive breakdown, which the patient said was caused by the father, but she was never able to say what the cause might be. However, when she spoke of her father, a beatific smile came over her face.

The patient was aware that although she wants a man to relate to, her choice of men tends to be inappropriate. She is tense in her sexual relations and is not satisfied when she has an orgasm.

The interviewer made a sustained attempt at reaching the source of tension in her. She spoke of 'something in her wanting to come out', and of her crying attacks with her GP as 'like a boil coming to a head'. What seemed to crystallise was the conflict between staying at home and being looked after, on the one hand, and trying to find her own independence, on the other. After an unpromising start to the interview she eventually said with considerable feeling, 'Perhaps I want to tell the lot of them to go to hell', and the interviewer felt he had made true contact with her.

Projective testing

She used the ORT to express some of her hidden feelings. She said she had never been able to give anybody the full blast of what she felt about her experiences. She expressed jealousy of her sister, the feeling that she had not got enough from her mother, and anger with her father for causing distress in the family. She said she wanted attention, but not the kind of attention got by having screaming attacks – she wanted someone both to stand up to her and not to give her advice. She said she wanted to explode about all her boy-friends who had upset her by not seeing beneath the surface.

Reason for acceptance for brief psychotherapy

The focus seemed to be the conflict between dependence and independence. By staying at home she is hoping to make up for something missing in her childhood, but on the other hand she very much wants to get away from her family and make her own life.

Her feelings were clearly close beneath the surface, and her motivation seemed both high and realistic.

Course of therapy (30 sessions)

The therapist was the woman psychologist who gave the projection tests. She was very analytically oriented and in the first few sessions tended to relate everything, inappropriately, to the transference. When the supervisor pointed this out she worked well and sensitively and dealt with many important issues.

In early sessions the main themes were as follows:

1 Fear of violence getting out of control, especially towards her son.
2 The feeling, expressed very strongly, that her mother had neither given her enough attention and care nor allowed her independence.
3 She 'has not had a good argument for years', and her mother always insists on keeping the peace.
4 Confusion of roles – she doesn't know whether she's a mother, a teenager, or a divorced woman.
5 She has never had a proper adolescence nor the opportunity to express all her adolescent rage and rebellion.

The patient sorts out her relation with people close to her

Probably the most important session was number 10, the first after a break for Christmas, in which she reported a number of events which seemed to represent real progress. During the break she had felt abandoned by her therapist, but though she had started by acting out, she had ended by using the opportunity to sort out her relationship both with her boy-friend, Stephen, and with her family.

When she received a phone call from Stephen saying he would be late for her, she had thrown a tantrum, kicking the doors and screaming. She felt she wanted to 'rip him apart', but when they actually met she and he had discussed their relation in a constructive way; and when on a later occasion they had been about to go to bed together, she had said, 'You don't have to do this to oblige me, you know, and I'm not going to do it just to be obliging to you.' They had talked about it and had decided that in fact it was something they both really wanted, and it had been a very fulfilling experience. In a later discussion with him she had said that in her therapy it was seen to be all right to be selfish, and that she had never really been selfish about her own needs before. 'I want a few *nows*, I'm fed up with waiting for *laters*.' (This beautifully expressed epigram goes a long way towards contradicting the initial impression of lack of education.)

Then, over the New Year, when she had been unable to see Stephen, she had found herself for the first time seeking cuddles from her father. The result had been an open discussion of the family situation, in which she spoke of feeling that they had never given her the right sort of care and that her mother always prevented anger from being expressed in the home. This prompted her mother to say that the reason for the latter was her experience of terrible rows in her own family. The patient's parents now said openly that they had always felt she had been pushed out by her sister's depressive illness, as she was now pushed out by the presence of her son. After this, it became a sort of family joke – but in a pleasant way – that whenever she showed signs of being upset they would come and cuddle her. Here she said that she had felt very abandoned during the break, but she added the very healthy comment that on the other hand it had been good because she had felt pushed to sort things out at home. Moreover, after the open discussion with Stephen, he had been quite charming to her, and had even thrown her up in the air, like a father with a young daughter. Thus she had given considerable evidence of finding her own self and the capacity for asserting herself in a way that made other people meet her needs. The therapist, at the end of her account of the session, wrote: 'I am constantly amazed by the strength of this girl.'

However, 3 weeks later she asked for, and was given, an emergency session caused by the fact that Stephen had been paying attention to another girl, and she had broken with him. The fact of asking for this session in many ways represented a therapeutic effect, because it meant that she was now able to express her needs in the transference relationship as well as at home. The session contained a great deal of entirely normal feeling, consisting of a mixture of anger and misery, a furious sense of hurt and betrayal, and the wish just to go to sleep and shut it all away. In this session she also said that it had suddenly got through to her how little of a mother she was to her son, which she had never really dared to look at before. She ended by saying to her therapist, 'Thank you. Something broke. I feel I can scream at you as well now.'

The rest of therapy

This was spent in working over these themes, although unfortunately the impression now is more of going round in circles than of genuine progress. There was further evidence of her being able to complain about situations that caused her distress, but at the same time there seemed to be some degree of relapse into inability to express her real feelings at home. Perhaps the most important material that emerged consisted of her feeling of being in competition with her son for her mother's attention; and, later, a 'day nightmare' in which she was forced to watch someone torturing him, which was interpreted as her fear of angry impulses against him going over into open cruelty.

In the final session she said that she felt she was at 'square one and a half' rather than back to square one, which was perhaps a remarkably accurate assessment.

Follow-up (6 months, 3 years 10 months)

At the 6-month follow-up, she was now living in a flat of her own just round the corner from home. She attributed her being ready to leave home at least in part to her therapy. Her son remains with her parents. She is no longer depressed and no longer suffers from outbursts of temper. Her life in general seems to be going well and she is enjoying her independence.

The later follow-up was pre-empted by a letter from her GP asking for her to be assessed for further treatment: 'She has been having serious difficulties in her relations with men. She is again concerned about her inability to mother her son and wonders what has become of her maternal feelings. Unfortunately also, her son has been exhibiting severe behavioural difficulties at school.'

At interview it appeared that in fact she is less moody and her various psychosomatic symptoms are much better. She is still living away from home and has found her own life and her independence.

She said that she seeks out men who boss her around because they take responsibility and decisions for her, but on the other hand she is afraid of commitment because it threatens her independence. Thus her original conflict between dependence and independence has now been transferred to her relations with men. This means that her act of leaving home was in some sense a false solution, since it has not solved her inner problem.

She is trying to sort out her relation with her son, who is now 13 and is still not living with her. She has him round at week-ends and is enjoying his company more than she used to, sharing activities with him. But there seem to be many occasions when she makes excuses not to see him, about which she feels very guilty. Sometimes when he comes round she may retire to bed to sleep, no doubt as a way of coping with her conflicting feelings about him.

She said she is able to express herself better, but she was able to give little evidence for this, and she still seems to express anger in an immature and histrionic way.

The positive features are the ability to leave home, the attempts to make better contact with her son, and the symptomatic improvement; but in other areas the progress represented by Session 10 seems to have been lost, and her conflict between dependence and independence is still in operation. Both judges gave her a score of 1.5, which is perhaps something of an over-estimate.

Eventually both the patient and her son were taken on for individual treatment in the Department for Children and Parents at the Tavistock Clinic.

Comment

We may note the residual difficulty in her relation with men, which may well be connected with the fact that Oedipal problems were largely absent from the themes dealt with in her therapy.

15

Patients who showed minimal improvements

The Acting-out Accounts Clerk

Age 22, single, 13 sessions, score 0.5.

Disturbances

Her main symptom is claustrophobia in situations such as social gatherings, pubs, and restaurants, since the age of 16. She is unable to travel by Underground.

Her relations with men have been superficial and unsatisfactory. She has had two boy-friends, both of whom seem to have used her. The most recent left for Canada after making her pregnant. She had her pregnancy terminated.

She is unable to express anger except against herself, e.g. by banging her head against the wall.

Background

She was the middle of three children, with an older sister and a younger brother. Her father is a successful business man, but suffered from polio when younger and has a much weakened left arm. He is shy and nervous and blushes in company. Her childhood was disrupted by constant rows between her parents.

Initial assessment

She was seen twice by the (male) psychologist who eventually took her on for treatment. In the first interview she was distant and evasive, but in between the two interviews she made a major response – she experienced a flood of memories of the time when she was 15–16, about which she brought up written notes. These were mainly concerned with events involving her mother, who continually picked on her two daughters and criticised them if they showed any signs of nervousness resembling that of their father, such as blushing. The patient said that it was this that had caused her current nervousness in social situations. Interpretations suggesting that she was angry both with her parents, and with the boy-friend who had left for Canada, produced some confirmation, while there was no response to attempts to link her social symptoms such as blushing with sexual anxieties.

A prominent theme in her ORT was guilt about aggressive feelings, e.g she told stories about murderers being put to death.

Reason for acceptance for brief psychotherapy

She was taken on because of two favourable criteria: her marked increase in motivation in response to the first interview, and the clear focus of her inability to express her anger.

As will be seen, the focus was correct, but her apparently high motivation was a hysterical mirage.

Course of therapy (13 sessions)

Her therapist was the male psychologist who treated the Betrayed Son. He had been at the Tavistock under intensive training on the four-year Course for 2 years, but had had no psychotherapeutic experience before that. He was careful and competent, but whereas he did well with the Betrayed Son, he found this acting-out hysteric to be more than a match for him – as indeed she would have been for most therapists.

The first session encapsulates both one of her main problems and the difficulty of dealing with her. She arrived 10 minutes late and opened with three communications about avoiding or terminating relationships. The therapist interpreted that in these situations she was in conflict between wanting to become involved and wanting to escape, and linked this with her feelings about therapy. She admitted that she nearly didn't come today and went on to say that perhaps she needed something stronger than he was offering, such as hypnosis or ECT.

She failed to turn up for the next session, and in fact she missed four out of the first eight appointments. The main theme that developed in the rest of therapy, and the only theme on which any useful work could be done, was her fear of expressing aggressive feelings (Oedipal interpretations were tried but failed to lead anywhere).

In Session 3 she spoke of having to keep control in the therapy, and when she was asked what would happen if she lost control, she spoke of losing her temper – sometimes she says horrible things. With her mother she 'wishes it would all come out into the open', she would like to swear and shout. In fact the only therapeutic effect that appeared during therapy was that she was able for the first time to begin to speak her mind to her mother. She told her mother over the phone that she made her (the patient) feel worse, which reduced her mother to tears. In later sessions she spoke of 'blaming' her mother, and under pressure she spoke of a time at the age of 12–13, when her parents had a period of severe quarrels with screaming and physical violence and her father sweeping the crockery off the table and smashing it. She used to think he was some kind of maniac and that he wanted to kill her mother.

This led to a TP interpretation, that she blamed the therapist for being a bad parent who made her feel worse rather than better (a link with the phone conversation with her mother mentioned above), to which she said, 'Where is it all leading?' Then, in perhaps the most important moment in therapy, she answered her own question with a piece of spontaneous insight: perhaps the reason why she is afraid in public places is that she wants to come out with something aggressive – she has the impulse to say something really hurtful if someone gets in her way or pushes in front of her in a queue.

Typically, after this moment of apparent progress, she failed to turn up for the next session.

Under supervision, the therapist made a supreme effort to deal with her provocativeness in the transference, pointing out to her with his own graphic words the pattern that she showed of 'Come on. Go away. Now you see me, now you don't.' In response she admitted that she had a fantasy of coming in and shouting that the therapy was no good and going out slamming the door. In a later session she said that sometimes the therapy makes her think deeply, sometimes she thinks, 'What's the point?' If she thinks deeply she gets murderous thoughts, e.g. working out ways of killing her woman boss. Later she admitted to murderous thoughts against her parents.

This apparent progress was illusory. She wrote a letter to the therapist saying that therapy was no good, but was eventually persuaded to come back to discuss the situation.

In this session (number 13) she mentioned in passing that a few days ago she had taken an overdose after having a tremendous row with her woman boss. She then said that she felt she could not go home at Christmas, and she admitted under pressure that this was because of her intense mixed feelings about her parents. The therapist said that she felt him to be as useless as her parents, and she would rather kill herself than kill them. He pointed out that she could only express her anger with him indirectly, by provocativeness, messing him about, teasing him, wanting (by her suicidal gesture) to bring a medical consultant down on his back. She said she didn't realise she was doing these things, they just happened. She went on to maintain her position that what she really needed was hypnosis. The therapist pointed out that in fact she had previously gone to three different hypnotists and had broken off with all three, but this didn't alter her position in the least.

This session was to be the last before the Christmas break. The therapist tried to link her suicidal gesture with her feeling that she was being abandoned, which she totally denied.

She did not return.

Follow-up (7 years 10 months)

There was limited improvement in her claustrophobia. She was able to travel to the follow-up interview by Underground, which would have been impossible before. However, she still gets extremely tense and anxious in social situations and lost one boy-friend because of this. She also mentioned getting depressed.

She appears to be slightly better at speaking her mind to her mother, but apart from this she has almost as much difficulty over expressing anger as before. She had gone over to Canada to see the boy-friend mentioned above. Things had gone all right for the first week, but then something went wrong and he started longing for another woman with whom he was currently involved, and ignoring her. She admitted that she felt angry. In answer to the question of what she did with her anger, she said, 'I smoked and smoked and smoked, and got a headache.'

She had come back to England and taken up with another former boy-friend. She knew from the beginning that he did not want a deep relationship, and he eventually broke with her because of her phobic symptoms which occurred when he took her out. When she later met him by chance and found that he was involved with someone else, she went home and 'smashed the door and screamed and yelled'.

She was very disparaging about her experience of therapy. She said that she began to dread going to the sessions, that she really needed help and advice, and instead of this her chief memory was of her therapist just sitting and glaring at her, and of her feeling desperate after every session. 'I didn't like him. He didn't do me any good at all, and I don't suppose he did any good to anyone else either.' She was as ambivalent about committing herself to further therapy as ever.

Comment

The therapist handled this patient well, but such patients are exceedingly difficult and they probably need a much tougher approach than he – or his supervisor – were able to provide. The minimal improvements found at follow-up, for which both judges gave a score of 0.5, are in keeping with the limited progress during therapy. It is worth noting that this is yet another patient who suffers from a total inability to establish a committed relation with the opposite sex.

The Actress with Elocution Problems

Age 33, engaged (married during therapy), 30 sessions, score 0.25.

She was seen twice, with an interval of 3 years between the two consultations, by two different male psychiatrists. The second interviewer became her therapist.

First consultation

Referral and precipitating factor

Her first referral was for an attack of depression which had lifted by the time she was seen. It became clear that she had suffered from recurrent depressions for as long as she could remember. The precipitating factor for recent exacerbations was her mother's personality change following a stroke 14 months ago.

The patient has been living alone with her mother since her parents separated 10 years ago. Her mother, after her stroke, 'has been asking the same question a thousand times, going round and round in circles', and has become extremely dominating. The patient feels that this tendency has always been present beneath the surface in her mother and has now manifested itself overtly.

Main problems

The patient showed considerable resistance, trying to find out things about the therapist rather than talking about herself. When her resistance was pointed out she said that her real problem is her *relationship with people*. This concerns both intimate relations with men and more superficial relations with people in general. She has never been able to establish a satisfactory relation with a man. She wrote in her application form: 'I seem to attract emotional parasites. Those I am not interested in flock to me. Those I am interested in sometimes begin to like me, but then I seem to handle it quite wrongly and it doesn't work. I become terribly afraid and quite unable to act naturally.' She also wrote: 'I find it difficult to work closely with people who do not see things my way. I have alienated many people.' Under the question of 'things that have given you most trouble' she wrote: 'A very bad relationship with my father, which has carried on in the form of clashes with authority or anyone I felt was destructive.' All this has prevented her from making progress in her career as an actress.

In response to the interpretation about her resistance, mentioned above, she also mentioned another complaint, namely that when she is acting, she loses the power in her voice in dramatic passages, making it difficult to project the part effectively. This seems to be an aspect of a general inhibition affecting her ability to express herself physically. She has been to very many drama and elocution teachers about her voice problem, and one of these remarked that she was the most physically inhibited person she had ever met.

In view of the final follow-up, it is worth noting that she also wrote in her application form, 'I am over-analytical about everything'.

Background

She was an only child. She said that her mother and father never got on with each other. She described her mother as kind and gentle at this time and her father as violent and cruel. She took her mother's part against her father and was frequently at loggerheads with him, as a result of which he used to beat her. She has not seen her father since her parents separated when she was 20.

Events between the two consultations

She was put on the waiting list for either group or individual treatment. However, when she was offered an individual vacancy some months later she refused it, saying that it was no longer necessary.

Subsequently three important events occurred, namely that both her father and her mother died, and she became engaged.

Second consultation (3 years after the first)

A change in emphasis in her complaints

She applied for treatment once more because a new drama teacher had told her that there was nothing basically wrong with her voice, that there was no point in her trying to cure it with technical lessons, and that her problem was emotional.

Dynamics of second interview

The second interviewer went deeply into the apparent connection between her voice problems and her relation with her parents, which was extremely complicated. He wrote that although on the surface she presented the early relation with her mother as all white and that with her father as all black, there was an opposite side to both. There was a father whom she wept for, and who appreciated her acting when she was a little girl and rather admired her later successes, though he could never bring himself to say so and didn't really appreciate the artistic side of things. Her mother came from a family much connected with the theatre and herself had considerable acting ability, but the patient felt that her mother had never had the courage to make use of it. It was she who had introduced the patient to acting, and she had tried to live through her daughter's successes, which had resulted in a subtle kind of domination even before her stroke. The father had liked the idea of the patient becoming an actress, when she was about 8, but had become opposed to it when she was 14.

As far as her relation with her fiancé was concerned, it seemed that there was very considerable sexual inhibition. She regards him as a friend and they spend much time together, but for the most part they avoid sexual relations. She said she is 'not really responsive' sexually.

- In accordance with all the above information the interviewer gave her three main interpretations, the first two of which were basically Oedipal:

1 He tentatively linked her voice problem to an inhibition against competing with her mother – 'if she is to become a successful actress she can only do this over her mother's dead body'.
2 He also linked her inhibition over acting to her very mixed feelings about her father – her guilt-laden wish to please him and her wish to rebel against him.
3 He drew the parallels between her general physical inhibition, her lack of sexual responsiveness, and her inability to let herself go in her acting.

He wrote that her response to these interpretations was mixed. 'Ostensibly she was prepared to look at them and consider that they had some possible significance, but beneath this I felt there was considerable resistance and a wish to flee from all kinds of unpleasant aggressive and sexual feelings into a world where everything was as beautiful as she wanted it to be.'

Reason for acceptance for brief psychotherapy

It was felt that her mixed feelings for both her mother and her father, and the connection between these and her problems with her voice, could be made into a focus. However, it was by no means certain that she could work with such a focus, and she was therefore offered six exploratory sessions to obtain evidence on this question.

Course of therapy (30 sessions)

The six exploratory sessions

The male psychiatrist who treated her was the second most experienced of all our therapists, already half-way through psychoanalytic training. He was a mature and excellent therapist – in view of the nature of the therapy, he needed to be.

The scene was set for subsequent events when the patient arrived 20 minutes late for the first session, said that she 'hates having to wait for things she doesn't like', and promptly denied that therapy came into that category. She then remained silent and eventually asked what the therapist wanted her to talk about. He said that she must want to find out how to please him, to which she said, on the contrary, her silence was a kind of rebellion. She said that she could not tolerate uncertainty, and the therapist said that she fears not being in control. She said, 'That was how I felt as a child, with everything being uncertain and violent.' The therapist linked her fear of losing control with her voice difficulty, and she spoke of being unable to 'let herself go' in a play in which she took the part of a prostitute. He tried to link this with her difficulty in letting herself go physically. This caused her to go into resistance, and she started to talk of her difficulty with her voice as a purely technical problem.

Already by Session 3 the therapist was writing of his mounting rage in the therapeutic situation. The patient seemed to invite obvious interpretations, but whatever he said she managed to nullify, while remaining (as he wrote) 'nice, polite, and prissy – "I see what you mean but somehow I don't really feel it."'

This came to a head in Session 6, the last of the exploratory sessions. She started with intellectualisations about the previous session and he got the feeling of being systematically opposed. Ten minutes before the scheduled end of the session he therefore made a long interpretation, pointing out this systematic opposition and suggesting that it occurred in her life outside as well. He proposed to her that they put the problem of her voice aside and take this as her central problem for a further 24 sessions.

She responded remarkably favourably. She agreed that this happens in her life outside and mentioned being told that she could never get any help with her voice because she was always at loggerheads with her teachers. She said that if she was not in total opposition to the other person she was afraid she would have to agree with everything. He linked this to her 'difficulty in differentiating herself from her mother' (an interpretation linking the areas of T, C, and P). He wrote: 'She did not take this up directly but there was a tremendous relief of tension all round. She seemed very positive about the proposed project, and said that I had absolutely put my finger on what the problem was.'

The rest of therapy

Apparent progress alternating with resistance

The pattern of therapy was a continuation of massive resistance punctuated by moments of apparent breakthrough which only served to intensify subsequent resistance. The therapist repeatedly pointed out her resistance in the transference and repeatedly made TP interpretations, at different times making the link to both her mother and her father, without any sustained progress. The following are some of the more important sequences.

In Session 10 she spoke of people 'moulding children into some alien image'. The therapist tried to confront her with her resistance in the session and linked it with her behaviour outside and her feeling of being forced into a mould by her father (a TCP interpretation). Her response was to say that she didn't think she fought the therapist, nor did she fight everyone outside. She thus totally denied the relevance of the focus on which she had agreed so enthusiastically in Session 6. At the end of the session she asked whether there was any point in her coming again – she had the impression she was wasting the therapist's time.

In Sessions 11 and 12 the therapist made an attempt to reach erotic feelings about the father. Surprisingly, she did not deny these and talked about various incidents of a sexual nature involving her father, in one of which she had refused to go to bed and he had ended up by undressing and washing in front of her. Nevertheless the exploration of this theme did not result in any apparent progress, nor did the link with the transference, which the therapist tried to make.

Apparent breakthrough

In Session 16 she started plying the therapist with questions, wanting to know how she compared with other patients. In a previous session she had devoted a great deal of energy in trying to get him to be more human with her, and he therefore said that she must feel he possessed what she wanted but deliberately withheld it. He then asked whether she had felt like this with one or other of her parents. Close to tears, she said, 'I think it was my mother'. For the rest of the session she was crying on and off in an apparently genuine way. She said that her mother seemed quite unsympathetic to what she needed, though knowing perfectly well what it was. She would feel furious with her mother and attack her verbally and hurt her, about which she felt extremely guilty because she also loved her. As she got older she tried to control this, and she felt it was then that she became 'emotionally dead'. (Here we may note the similarity with two patients to be described in later chapters, namely the Psychiatric Nurse with Attacks of Rage and the Robot Man, both of whom suffered from severe emotional inhibition as a result of feeling forced to control outbursts of temper.) She went on to repeat what she had said in the consultation period, that her mother had behaved since her stroke in a way that seemed to reveal nakedly what she had really felt underneath. This was that instead of loving her daughter she had been utterly ruthless and self-centred and only wanted her to be an extension of herself. The patient also said how guilty her mother had made her feel whenever she did anything on her own like going out and enjoying herself. Her mother did this by conveying how abjectly miserable she had been in her daughter's absence. The therapist said she must have felt that her mother's stroke was the result of her (the patient's) attack on her; and when her mother died, freeing her from the prison in which she had been held, she must have felt too guilty to go ahead and make a success of her freedom. He linked this with her voice difficulty. The patient sat sobbing through most of this, but her manifest reaction was resistant – 'This may well be true, but what can I do about it? My mother is dead.'

Intensification of resistance

Her basically resistant position was only too completely confirmed in the next session (number 17). She arrived a quarter of an hour late (with foolproof excuses), minimising the importance of the last session and saying that nothing had emerged that she didn't already know – 'it isn't as if any deep secrets are being uncovered.'

In Session 18 she went on to deny even what seemed to have been established, which occurred as follows. She said that her fiancé's parents only find people acceptable who don't step out of line. The therapist made the obvious comment that this sounded like her mother, to which she said that on the contrary her mother 'had always accepted that her daughter had a viewpoint different from her own'!

In Session 19, in spite of the therapist's best efforts, she spent the time chatting in a jolly way; and in Session 20 she said that the whole problem concerned her father, not her mother. Thus in the end the apparently deeply felt work of Session 16 was completely nullified.

Break in therapy, marriage

There was then a 6-week gap in therapy due to the summer break, during which she and her fiancé got married.

Massive resistance

She cancelled the first session after the break and arrived half an hour late for the next (number 21), saying: 'Actually I was coming today to tell you I had decided not to come any more.' The therapist made the clearly indicated interpretations about her wanting to avoid painful feelings, without any obvious effect. At the end of the session she said she would let the therapist know whether or not she was coming to the next session. In fact she turned up 5 minutes late without letting him know.

Transference manifestations

In Sessions 21 to 25 there were a number of dreams and associations with transparent transference implications, which the therapist interpreted without making any apparent progress. In Session 21, for instance, she told of a dream in which she was being chased by a black man who wanted to do unspeakable things to her, and she tried to devise schemes and decoys in order to slip away without his noticing. In Session 24 she told of a dream in which she got into a discussion of acting technique with a male drama teacher who was much warmer and friendlier than she remembers in reality, and she thought of having private lessons with him. The therapist tried to make the link with her feelings about losing him at the coming termination, but she denied that she was at all concerned with this issue. In Session 25 she spoke of a boy-friend who chased her but was never there when he was wanted, and another who was more interested in his piano than in her. She said that after this latter experience she changed in her attitude to men and 'conducted her affairs through her head'. The therapist related this to the transference, pointing out that she had tried to break off treatment just as she was afraid she was going to be made to feel something, to which she said, 'It would be rather a problem if I found I could feel after all.'

Climax of therapy

This led to a climactic period of therapy in Sessions 26 to 28. In Session 26 she spoke of two incidents involving rows with women in authority. The first was with a woman director many years ago who had constantly picked on her. The patient had eventually had an outburst in which she had called the director all the names she could think of. The director spoke of not knowing why she picked on the patient, but 'there was just something about her' (which, in view of the events of therapy, is not difficult to understand). Surprisingly, the director also said that until then she thought the patient had no spirit, and in fact this outburst didn't result in the patient's expulsion from the cast. The second incident, which occurred just before she came to therapy, involved a drama teacher who kept giving her interpretations based on tenuous evidence. She had become very angry, but when she protested she was told to leave, which she did rather than cause a scene.

The therapist said that perhaps she felt resentful about many of the things he had said, and was wondering whether to have a showdown with him before she left. After initially meeting this with bland denial, she said that he had said 'so many obvious things' about her sexual life and her anger and the end of therapy, which were all completely untrue, and she did feel resentful but felt she had to be polite. However, she just couldn't see how he could have such a distorted picture of her, and – with increasing anger – he must need his eyes examined if he couldn't see the emotions which she constantly felt. He had said she was 'dead' when in fact she was an impulsive, passionate person. He pointed out that it was she who had said she was dead (see Session 16), and suggested that she was attributing this to him because she didn't want to look at it.

When it was almost time for the end of the session she spoke about her love of beauty, and she then threw in the remark that she and her husband weren't very compatible because he couldn't see beauty even when it was staring him in the face. The therapist felt that this was a pretty serious thing to be saying at the very end of the session, but simply said, 'I'm afraid we'll have to stop there.' At this she became extremely angry, and with tears of hate in her eyes shouted: 'How can you cut me short like that? I've just told you something important. You're all the same, you just go by the rules.'

She looked daggers as she came into the room for the next session (number 27), opening with, 'Will you answer me one question? Why do you sit in silence?' She went on with a series of criticisms: how unhelpful, unsympathetic, and cold he's been, how she has to do all the work herself, how it's been a waste of time coming here, and has he been trying to provoke her? He said, once more, perhaps he reminded her of someone in the past, to which she said he was always saying this and sometimes she thought he was 'trying to impersonate her mother'. It then became clear that in the battle between her and her therapist she felt he was trying to make her angry, and in order to win she had to remain calm. Did he think it was good for her to show her feelings? She thought it wasn't. And so on.

This led to a further apparent breakthrough in Session 28. She said that she used to be direct and emotional with people and tell them what she thought of them, but it drove them away; and she also used to fall in love at the drop of a hat and had then been hurt and disappointed; it was better to control one's emotions and live by common sense – but this wasn't really her, though she didn't see how one could live any other way. She went on to say that in her childhood she was like a little savage, attacking people, throwing things about, leaping on people. The therapist asked her who she meant by 'people', to which she said 'my father of course'. She described his violence, his completely uncontrolled temper, how furious and wild she would get with him and how she wanted to kill him – she would have done if only she had been strong enough. He beat her, he took her belongings away from her, and what was worst he destroyed beautiful things, which made her want to destroy him. She said all this with intensity and in a state of great distress.

However, she later spoke of a director 'whom she couldn't stand and who had seen it as his job to break the actors down and then build them up again into what he wanted them to be.' The therapist made the obvious TCP interpretation, linking this with her father and the transference, speaking of the murderous feelings that she must have been sitting on during her therapy, to which her response was a very sweet, 'I don't feel angry with you'.

The therapist wrote that she maintained her attitude of 'bland denial and sweet bloody-mindedness' to the end – typified by her final remark as she was putting on her coat after the last session (number 30): 'I feel perhaps I ought to have brought you a present.'

First follow-up, with the therapist (1 year 3 months)

There were a considerable number of slight improvements. She appeared more real and more likeable, more able to admit difficulties rather than idealising everything. She is now less depressed. She said her voice is improved, though she still has difficulty in dramatic passages. She has now found a new elocution teacher who thinks the whole problem is related to muscular control.

She still has difficulty with women in authority, particularly her current woman boss. However, she finds herself much better able to get on with her husband's family than she could during therapy (when she spent a good deal of time in complaints against them). She has a lot in common with her mother-in-law – 'we are both emotional people' – and although her father-in-law is difficult and moody she is able to give him as good as she gets. She said in fact that therapy had put her more in touch with her anger and had made her less afraid of it, so that she is somewhat freer with people and less anxious about having to please them.

In her marriage, however, there are major difficulties. She and her husband are quite good companions, but there seems to be very considerable lack of communication between them. He doesn't understand her and makes no attempt to do so, with the result that she rejects his physical overtures, which she feels are without sufficient preliminaries in terms of relating to her mind. Sexual relations are therefore infrequent.

This result was not formally scored but would probably be given a score of 1.0 to 1.5 – say 1.25.

Second follow-up, by a male psychiatrist from the Individual Team (4 years 8 months)

There are five areas in which she appears to be improved:

1 Her depression appears to have lifted. She could not remember having said that she had been depressed all her life.
2 She and her husband can carry on social relations with other couples without strain.
3 She feels much more self-confident.
4 Her feelings of tension are much improved, especially since she took up yoga.
5 She is able to make herself look more attractive.

Against this the following needs to be noted:

1 Her voice problem remains unchanged. She still goes from one teacher to another, idealising each new one before finding her a failure and passing on.
2 Although she now has a stable relation with her husband, he appears to be highly obsessional and withdrawn. He spends most of his time working and pays her little attention. Their sexual relation has changed from his occasionally having some interest while she has none, to her very occasionally having some interest while he has hardly any. The interviewer's impression was of two highly neurotic people trying to help each other with a great deal of obsessional rumination couched in psychoanalytic jargon. (It is worth comparing this situation with her description of her relation with men in her original application form.)
3 We need to take into account the over-all nature of the follow-up interview. The interviewer said he started by liking her and being impressed by her apparent friendliness, pleasantness, warmth, and insight. As the interview went on he began to realise that she was really regurgitating theories written in the notes

of the original consultations, and as she went on further, that she must have suffered for many years from ruminations of an analytical kind (see in fact her statement about being 'over-analytical' in her original application form). He wrote, 'I remember noticing just for one moment that, behind this smiling expert constantly talking to me of hope and change and interpretations and relations, there was some complicated mixture of sadness and anger which I felt frightened to say anything about.' He said in the end that the interview left him feeling muddled and chaotic, swamped with useless interpretations, tense, and utterly exhausted.

The members of the Individual Team agreed that this kind of obsessional rumination must be a massive defence against attaining any true insight about herself, or getting in touch with her real feelings. It even calls in question the improvements that she does show, which may be the result of extensive denial. The score must depend on the view taken about this.

It emerged that she has been having counselling from a woman therapist for the past 2 years. The main feature that has come out of this consists of positive feelings for her father, which her mother tried to discourage. She described memories at the age of 3 or 4 of being told by her mother not to love her father, and said that this occurred at about the time that her mother started to refuse to sleep with her father. She also remembered playing with her father, and her mother interfering and forcing her to reject him. She is still seeing this therapist, but she has now become interested in Transactional Analysis, and she and her husband are occupied trying to analyse themselves and each other and interpreting everything in their relation in transactional terms. She has great faith that this will resolve everything. Thus it looks as if her pattern of moving from one helper or helping system to another, idealising each new one before finding it inadequate, is being repeated with her psychotherapy as with her elocution and drama teachers.

She was extremely critical of her Tavistock therapy and her therapist. 'We did not get anywhere at all, though I think he felt we had touched on a number of important things.' She said that among these things touched on was a particularly sore spot, namely her relation with her father, but 'we did not find out why it upset me – it should have been thoroughly investigated.' 'The worst thing was that Dr —— never explained what his aims and methods were. I was very upset by his complete non-involvement, shutting the door and staying silent. I think it was extremely unfriendly and upsetting.' The interviewer said she must be very angry with him, to which she said, 'Yes, I identify him with my father, don't I? He was projecting his ideas on to me the whole time.'

Scores: 0.5, 0, 0.5, 0. Mean 0.25.

Comments

Four main points are worth making:

1 Her subsequent therapy revealed clearly that there had been a period in her early childhood when she was very close to her father, and moreover that at this time there was more or less open rivalry between her and her mother for him. Therefore perhaps the important interpretation that was never reached, and for which there was abundant evidence in the transference, was that her anger with her father was partly being used as a defence against realising her intense

disappointed love. With a patient as resistant as she was, however, it seems very doubtful that this interpretation would have made much difference, and indeed the realisation of her love in her subequent therapy obviously made no difference to her neurotic state. This having been said, her therapist handled her extremely provocative behaviour with great skill and maturity; and if the above interpretation would indeed have helped, the failure lay in the supervisor as much as in the therapist.

2 This patient illustrates one of the effects of an initial trial period, namely that under the pressure of threatened rejection the patient makes a major response in the final trial session, which does not necessarily mean that she is suitable for continued therapy. A similar phenomenon was observed in the Girl with Eye Problems, to be described in Chapter 18.

3 Although the patient was so resistant, therapy was of a highly dynamic, interactive kind. It is worth saying that a patient like this is crying out for the use of Davanloo's technique, and that a purely interpretative technique, however skilfully applied, is unlikely to be effective over a brief period.

4 This is a patient who was regarded as worse at a later follow-up, after subsequent therapy, than she was at the first follow-up. Obviously the second follow-up must be accepted as more valid than the first.

The Miner's Daughter

A young woman aged 25, single, working as a lathe operator for a small firm making specialised components, 22 sessions, score 0.25.

Disturbances

She was interviewed by a woman psychiatrist from abroad, who later became her therapist.

Before she had an abortion 3 years ago the patient was unaware of any difficulties. Since then she has suffered from the following severe disturbances:

1 *Social anxiety, claustrophobia:* If she is in a room with people, she suddenly starts blushing and is overcome by claustrophobic anxiety severe enough to make her have to leave. As a result she refuses invitations.

2 *Disturbed relation with her boy-friend, hysterical outbursts:* The young man who had made her pregnant behaved in a highly ambivalent way towards her, at one time offering to give her money for her abortion and then failing to send it, and at another time phoning from abroad to suggest that they get married, and then not following this up. She had the feeling that he simply did not care. However, she then went on an extended holiday with him. During this time she became overwhelmed with feelings of hatred for him, so severe that she described 'coming near to doing him physical harm'. She began to have fears of killing people, or being killed, in an accident involving their car. About 15 months ago this culminated in a major hysterical attack which took place in the car. At the time she was suffering from severe toothache. She 'seemed to go berserk', became terrified of objects in the car, and started screaming uncontrollably, with the feeling that she was going mad. Since then she has suffered from other violent attacks, in which she may tear at the wallpaper or bang her head on the wall.

Background

She was an only child, brought up in Wales, her father being a miner. Her parents were devout Methodists. She described her childhood as exceptionally happy. Her father doted on her, though she said she was closest to her mother who was extremely self-sacrificing. She said her parents were very sensitive to her needs.

However, indications of underlying disturbance in the family emerged when the patient said that her mother and father never slept in the same room, and that when she was small she shared her mother's bed for a number of years. It also became clear that in this home neither aggression nor sexuality could be openly expressed.

Dynamics of interview

The interviewer made a number of linking interpretations, two of which arose as follows:

1 The patient told of an unsympathetic consultant who had said, 'Why don't you just go and have an abortion?' – as if it were no more difficult than having a tooth out. The interviewer linked this with the toothache which had contributed to the patient's major hysterical attack. The patient said, 'You mean the tooth represented the baby?' and went on to say that on a card given to patients in the abortion clinic there was a reference to an abortion being like having a tooth out.
2 The interviewer linked the patient's current social anxiety and blushing to guilt about the abortion, and particularly to the time when the patient was desperately trying to conceal her pregnancy from her parents. The patient said that she felt no guilt at the time, but when the interviewer asked her if it would have 'destroyed' her parents to learn of her pregnancy, she fervently agreed, describing how good they had been to her – how could she hurt them in this way? She said that these feelings applied especially to her mother.

At the end of the interview the patient showed herself as very keen for treatment and brought out her work timetable in order to indicate the times when she would be available.

Reason for acceptance for brief psychotherapy

We felt that it would be possible for the patient to work with the following three linked foci:

1 Grief and guilt about the abortion.
2 The upsurge of hitherto repressed anger against her boy-friend.
3 The link with the avoidance of sexuality and aggression in her childhood.

The patient responded well to interpretative comments and showed good motivation at the end of the interview.

Course of therapy (22 sessions)

As mentioned above, the therapist was a woman psychiatrist from abroad. Her work was highly sensitive and usually accurate. The number of sessions was limited to a maximum of 27 by the therapist's planned return home – though in fact there were only 22, largely owing to the patient's acting out over appointments.

Therapy was characterised by pursuit of the chosen focus, resulting in a clear identification of the problem, without any apparent progress towards resolving it; and by the development of very strong regressive dependence in the transference.

An important factor in therapy concerned the relation between the patient and her boy-friend, Louis, who had been responsible for the pregnancy which had ended in her abortion. He was living with her, but she announced in the first session that she had asked him to leave – though not immediately. As emerged later, this eventually resulted in her being faced with the expiry of a second time limit which roughly coincided with the end of her therapy.

The therapist had to cancel the first scheduled session; and the patient (ominously, as later became clear) failed to phone to say she could manage the next time offered, though she had been asked to do so. The main theme in Sessions 1 and 2 was the need to keep people at arm's length, including the therapist, which the therapist interpreted as fear of getting involved in relations like that between her parents, which were both dependent and hostile.

In Session 3 the theme emerged once more of how her abortion seemed to mark a turning point in her recent life. The therapist said that the abortion must have made her feel 'bad', and suggested this might be due to things that had happened before the abortion. The patient replied, 'And I always thought I had such a nice childhood.' She went on to describe the shock of learning at the age of 11 that her friends' parents shared the same bed. She had never been able to talk about sex, and it was this inability to discuss sex with Louis that had caused her to take inadequate contraceptive precautions.

In Session 4 there emerged a further aspect of the abortion, namely her buried grief about the baby who had thus been killed. This theme arose as follows. The therapist interpreted the patient's fear of others' disapproval as a disapproval within the patient herself. The patient described sobbing after leaving the hospital where she had had the abortion, feeling that she had left part of herself behind. She then went on to rationalise about how impossible it would have been to have had the baby, which the therapist interpreted as a defence against her true feelings. This interpretation penetrated the defence, and the patient said with deep feeling that if only she could have *that* child she would get pregnant again, but she could have a hundred children and none of them would be that child. She went on to say once more that it was as if she were two people, one before the abortion, whom she liked, and one after. The therapist asked her what the cause of this could be, to which the patient made a highly indirect but crucial communication about her regressive wish to return to her childhood: could it be anything to do, she asked, with a feeling she had had after a row with Louis, which was *sadness,* the wish that she could be a small child again, whose Mummy could pat her head and make everything all right? But after the abortion she realised that she could no longer take care of herself, and her Mummy couldn't either.

With hindsight we can see that this communication also was ominous, because her regressive wish was extremely intense, and the attempt to work it through in the transference was ultimately doomed to failure.

In Session 5 the theme emerged of not wishing to destroy her parents' denial of their own problems. She said she could have told each parent separately about the abortion, but not both together. The therapist said it would mean confronting them with their lack of sexuality, to which the patient said that she didn't want them to know she knew about this – they had stayed together for her sake. To tell them of her pregnancy would have destroyed their idealisation of her and undone the sacrifice of their lives. She then added that their goodness and altruism were 'too good for her good' and had not prepared her for the realities of life. It would have been better if they had fought openly – their goodness hid the emptiness of their existence.

This theme was continued in the next session (number 6), in which the therapist said that the patient must have felt profound guilt at hurting her parents if she did not live up to their extraordinarily high expectations. The patient said that perhaps her wish to be a child again was concerned with returning to an idyllic world in which no one got angry, or shouted, or threw things.

In Session 7 the patient spoke of being let down on three different occasions by women friends. The therapist said that she must wonder about the therapist's reliability, and interpreted the wish not to get involved as a fear of being hurt. In response the patient described how, if a man became interested in her, she 'overnight' lost interest in him. She went on to extend her need for an idyllic relation to her relations with men, saying that she dreamed of a man who would be all things to her at all times, be a friend and teacher, be exciting and interesting for ever. The therapist interpreted this as a defence against any true and deep involvement with a man. The patient said that her mother had often told her, 'Don't get married, have fun while you can'. The patient felt that to become deeply involved would result in being deprived or taken for granted, like her mother.

The theme of Session 8 was her guilt about hurting people, especially Louis, who is shortly due to leave. The therapist spoke of fear of destructiveness – the anxiety must be that harm would come to someone whom she both cared about and was angry with. The patient was silent for a long time, her face flushed.

The therapist now had to cancel a session once more, but did not have time to let the patient know. The patient's reaction was a period of considerable acting out over appointments. She failed to turn up for the next session. When she did come (Session 9), she told of a dream in which she was talking to the therapist but not about what really mattered, and was crying. The therapist suggested that the dream must speak the truth, and that she must have strong feelings about having been let down. In response the patient blurted out that the missed session had been 'just awful'. She was already upset because she was late for the session, and then had been told at the desk that the therapist couldn't come. She had walked to the Underground in a daze, crying. She had left it too late to phone that she couldn't make the next appointment, so had just not turned up. She was utterly hurt and disappointed, as if unknowingly she had become too attached to the therapist. The therapist suggested that her failure to keep this appointment was a way of getting her own back, and the patient said that she must have felt some anger – how could the therapist have missed that particular session, just as Louis was due to leave? It then emerged that in fact she could have come to the next session, which completely confirmed the therapist's interpretation. At the end of the session the therapist mentioned that there would be a gap of 2 weeks around Easter, and that therapy would end in June.

Perhaps in response to this mention of termination, the next session (number 10) did not produce any worthwhile communication. The therapist failed to make an effective link with the previous session.

In Session 11 the patient spoke of her 'blood running cold' at the thought of Louis leaving in 3 months' time – in spite of the fact that it was she who had asked him to leave. The therapist seems not to have made any connection with the issue of termination – not that it probably would have made any difference.

Session 12 was the last before the Easter break, during which in fact only one session would be missed. The patient spoke once more of how her childhood had not prepared her for the realities of life, to which the therapist said that perhaps the end of therapy represented the harshness of the real world. The patient had previously questioned whether she had got any benefit from treatment at all, but she now said that even if the therapist were to disappear tomorrow, she felt she had been helped. She went on to say that she had always felt very deeply about loss; and later she spoke of her dependence on Louis and how she had not really been able to accept this in herself.

Little progress seems to have been made in the first session after the break (number 13) and the patient then failed to turn up for the next session, having forgotten to phone that she couldn't come because she had to have a tooth out. In the next session (number 14) she reported a panic attack the previous night. There seemed to be three – apparently minor – precipitating causes for this: first, that she had not received a birthday card from her parents; second, that she had asked a woman friend to cut her hair and she had agreed, but had put it off for half an hour to a time that was more convenient for her; and third, that the patient had then suddenly remembered that she had forgotten to do something for her father, as promised. She had felt abandoned and panicky and had begun to cry uncontrollably. The therapist said that though she talked about how independent she wanted to be, it only served to hide how dependent she really was, and linked this once more with termination. The patient confirmed this, saying that during her attack she had felt, 'Why isn't she [i.e. her therapist] here? I need her now.'

The patient now gave clear evidence of her regressive need for total and unconditional maternal care, which emerged as follows. The therapist mentioned that she was leaving 1 month later than originally planned, and offered to continue until then. At this the patient's face lit up, but it fell again when the therapist said she would like to insist on a more regular appointment time. The therapist linked the patient's dismay at this with the fact that she had been so completely gratified by her mother in childhood, to which the patient said that since she was 100% prepared to care for others, why weren't they prepared to care for her in the same way? However, she now mentioned a possible therapeutic effect, namely that she was beginning to be able to modify her behaviour so that things could be more on her terms, e.g. by deliberately withholding certain actions on behalf of others -for fear of being taken for granted.

In Sessions 15 and 16 there was further evidence of the breakdown of the patient's idealisation of her childhood. She said that her parents never really got on together and that there was hidden hostility between them; and in her description of her father it now seemed clear that he was miserly and obsessionally rigid.

In Session 17 she mentioned that Louis and her therapist would be leaving at about the same time, and she spoke of how desolate she would feel. She went on to list Louis' deficiencies, e.g. his obsessionality, which seemed to be exactly those of her father. The therapist said that the fantasy of marrying Louis seemed to consist of repeating her parents' marriage.

In the next session (number 18) the therapist raised two important questions: first, was there anger about termination in addition to grief, and second, how was it that the patient never spoke of longing for her father? The patient said that there was growing anger against both parents, and went on to speak of a time when her mother was in hospital and her father insensitively had not allowed her to do the housework for him. She went on to tell of a half-waking dream in which her father was dying and her mother did not seem to care. In the dream the patient rushed to the phone to tell the therapist, but her mother tried to prevent her. She wrapped the cord round her mother's neck but stopped, suddenly realising what she was doing. She then woke up fully, crying. The therapist underlined the anger with both parents, but raised the question of whether in the present circumstances this was being deflected from her, the therapist. The patient did not respond, and – significantly, after this potentially important material – rang up to cancel the next session.

In the next session (number 19) she described a volte-face in relation to Louis, for she was now thinking of marrying him. In this session and the next (number 20), she was given the interpretation that she was trying to console herself for the loss of the therapist. The patient said that when things go badly for her, she wants to be consoled by a mother who will make everything all right. The therapist said that the patient wanted to hold on to her, but failing this to replace her with her mother, which the patient readily accepted.

Once more there was acting out over appointments, with the patient missing two offered times before coming to the next session (number 21). The patient started by avoiding eye contact with the therapist, which was unusual. The therapist again raised the question of anger over termination, and the patient spoke of a renewal of irrational quarrelling with Louis. The therapist said that this could be better understood if she, the therapist, were recognised as the proper object of the anger. The patient must feel that termination is a rejection because she isn't good enough. Put like that, the patient said, she could understand it, and from then on eye contact was restored. The therapist then asked who it was the patient felt she was losing, to which the patient said, someone all understanding, all able, all caring. The therapist said that there was a distinction between losing someone idealised and losing someone real. The supervisor noted that the therapist had not pointed out the need for idealisation as a defence against anger.

In the last session, number 22, the patient brought up a large bunch of flowers, saying that on the way to the session she had had the feeling that she would like never to have to leave. Throughout this session the therapist made a determined attempt to bring home to the patient some of the realities of the situation – e.g. that the patient wasn't worthless and was much valued at her work, that there were aspects of Louis that were very understanding even if he wasn't the perfect carer, and that the all-caring mother whom she was seeking was neither possible nor necessary. The patient said that she had been told at work that at the beginning of therapy she had walked about as in a dream, but that now she was much more alert, more engaged.

It was still not clear whether or not she would marry Louis. At the end of the session she said that of course she would miss her therapist, and she went on to say how unequal the relation had been, how little she knew about her. Was she going back to her home country? The therapist said 'yes' and wished her luck. The patient left with a smile.

Follow-up (8 years 2 months)

The important life events that had occurred since her therapy were as follows. Shortly after termination she left Louis. He went abroad, and she has never had contact with him since. She said, 'We would have gone on to destroy each other. He used not to show any interest in what was going on for me. I really felt very alone with him.'

· She then met a man who made no secret of the fact that he was married and loved his wife, but apparently they couldn't have children. The patient and he had regular and enjoyable sex together. One day she said, almost in passing, 'Sometimes I think I'd like to have a child,' to which he said, 'Well, if you really think you want it, please let me be the father.' She stopped taking the Pill and got pregnant straight away. Ironically, his wife got pregnant almost at the same time, and at this point the patient decided to stop their sexual relation, feeling that she didn't want to be 'the other woman' when there was a child involved. The patient now has a daughter, Ellen, aged 4. She has kept up the relation with Ellen's father, feeling that 'a father every 2 months is better than no father at all'.

She said of her decision to get pregnant, 'I could accept that I might not get married, but not to be without a child.'

The only other important relation was with a man whom she met 2 years ago through an agency. In the end she felt that he and she had little in common, and when they were alone together she was bored. She finally broke with him. 'Ellen will have to get used to the idea of growing up without a father.' She added, 'I can't help thinking that I was never able to make a reasonable relationship with a man.'

Of her relationship with Ellen she said: 'It is a very loving one, my whole life. I have really felt fulfilled in what I wanted in having her.' She said that Ellen goes to school in the mornings and that the two of them go out together 'every single day', meeting friends who have children, and going to various kinds of entertainment such as fairs or circuses. In a few months' time Ellen will go to school in the afternoons as well, and she knows she will miss her. 'I will probably have to get a job. I am not going to worry about that now, but I don't like the idea.' She is currently living on Social Security.

She has very little social life apart from what she shares with Ellen. Sometimes her friends try to do some match-making, but she said she found this kind of thing so much of a strain that she'd rather not go. 'I have got used to not going out, it doesn't bother me.' She said it was very difficult being sociable when one is on one's own, an unmarried mother. It is made even more difficult by the fact that she still suffers from fairly severe claustrophobic anxiety, accompanied by blushing, in social situations, especially when she is with men. The fear is that other people will find something out about her, in particular that she had an abortion, about which she still feels very guilty. She said that her anxiety was better in the sense that she can control it now, which she couldn't before: 'I fight it down, I tell myself that the other person can't know what I am thinking, or I change the subject. If I really can't bear it I find a suitable excuse to leave.' Of the abortion itself she said she felt less guilty and could probably talk about it now if the subject came up in conversation, but that if people made critical remarks about abortion she would find it very difficult to bear.

She has never had a panic attack and lost control in the way that she did before therapy, but she has come near it on more than one occasion. One of these was after both smoking marijuana and drinking alcohol, when she felt she was 'drifting away' and had the same feeling as before that she was losing her mind or going mad. However, she managed to control it.

Concerning self-confidence and self-assertion the position is as follows. She said that her self-confidence had increased since she had a child – 'When I first came here I had a very low opinion of myself. I think having a child has helped me. Now I am somebody's mother.' She has been able to be self-assertive for her child's sake, and told a story of Ellen being mismanaged by a doctor, and how she insisted on seeing someone else and getting the right treatment for her. She then said that she couldn't have done this if it had been for herself, and this was confirmed when she failed to lodge an appeal with the Local Council – which she was entitled to do – for a grant which had been refused. She said, 'I am not very aggressive really. I have always found it works better to be nice.'

Similarly, of her relation with her parents she said, 'It has always been on a sort of nice level.' She had had tremendous difficulty telling them about her second pregnancy, and went home five times trying to do so but failing. When she finally managed it, they were very kind and helpful after the initial shock, and her father said he was glad she 'hadn't done anything silly', by which he meant having an abortion. Thus she has never been able to tell them about the previous pregnancy and the abortion that she did have. They help her with money when she is in need.

When she was first asked about her view of her therapy, she said that previously she had never been able to blame anything on anyone else, but now she could be quite critical. 'When my therapist left, it was really quite terrible. It was wrong to be abandoned when I wasn't ready. I felt very rejected. I was attached to her and it was really bad that she was going. Now, I could have told her, but I couldn't at the time. I had a friend who had the same experience with a psychiatrist – they sit and stare at you, it was absolutely awful. I remember racking my brains for something to say to start the conversation.' Later in the interview, however, she said that therapy had helped her to see her parents as they really were. 'I had seen them as the perfect parents. Maybe I did feel angry inside and that they were not so wonderful. I think it helped me just that somebody was listening and trying to help, even if she didn't succeed.'

Assessment of follow-up

Of course we must respect the life style as a single parent that she has chosen, which is very fulfilling for her, and in this sense she has made an excellent adaptation. It has clearly been an effective way of partly overcoming her grief about the loss of the baby who was aborted. It has also resulted in some increase in her self-confidence, but we may note that she only seems able to assert herself for her child's sake and not her own. Symptomatically she is marginally improved in the sense that she can now usually control her anxiety, which she couldn't before, but it remains fairly severe.

However, the evidence suggests strongly that her life style is also being used as a defence against her social anxieties and her fear of commitment to a man, both of which are essentially unchanged. She also made clear that her pattern of being 'nice' remains the same, though she was certainly able to be critical of her therapy.

We may note her ability to have an enjoyable sex life in the follow-up period, but this enjoyment was present before she came to us, so that it does not represent a change.

Perhaps the fairest score, which acknowledges the small improvements, is 0.5, given by one judge, and the score of 0 given by the other judge is unduly pessimistic. Mean score 0.25.

Discussion

In spite of occasional missed interpretations, this seems to have been a good therapy, carried out by a sensitive therapist. Moreover the work concentrated on the problem areas formulated at the beginning, namely her feelings about the abortion, the idealisation of her parents and her childhood, her guilt about sexuality, and her inhibited aggression. Nevertheless, although each of these problems was brought to the surface, there is no evidence that any effective working through took place at all. Thus, her feelings about her abortion were discussed extensively, but her guilt and grief about it, though certainly quite understandable, were little changed and – particularly since these feelings are still expressed in severe phobic symptoms – are far beyond what would be considered 'normal'. Equally, much work was done on her idealisation of her parents, but though her *view* of them changed, her *relation* with them remained much the same as before. Work was done on her inability to be aggressive, but she remains unable to be self-assertive on her own behalf. Finally, her feelings about termination were brought up repeatedly, but she remains as distressed about this now as she was at the time. It seems, therefore, that the anxiety and pain at the heart of the patient's problems were too great for her to work through in a short period.

An issue that never came up in therapy was her feeling of hatred for Louis, the boy-friend who had made her pregnant, the extreme intensity of which was never explored.

We may note the patient's marked drop in motivation early in therapy, the acting out over appointments, the clear problem over commitment in relationships – including her commitment to therapy – and the longing for regression, all of which were ominous signs.

16

Patients who showed no improvement

It is particularly unfortunate that these two patients who failed to improve were in fact treated by the same therapist, a most gifted woman Social Worker, well experienced in psychotherapy. This result does no justice to her work. which was characterised by great sensitivity, creativeness, and flexibility. With the first patient the therapist's creativeness matched that of the patient's dreams; while with the second patient the therapist's flexibility was shown in her sudden decision to switch over to a 'Gestalt' session, which resulted in a major change for the better in the transference situation.

The therapist's approach resulted in extremely interesting and dramatic therapies. However, one of the problems of great creativeness is that a therapist may get carried away by her (or his) own ideas and pay insufficient attention to gathering further evidence from the patient. With these two therapies, as a result, we find ourselves writing that certain aspects of the patient's material were missed, which is only partly due to hindsight and many years of further experience.

With the first patient these omissions almost certainly made no difference to the therapeutic result at all, since the patient was clearly unsuitable for brief therapy because of her underlying profound disturbance. This was the therapist's misfortune. With the second, on the other hand, it may have been a factor contributing to the unsatisfactory final outcome.

Yet another unfortunate feature of these two therapies was that the therapist was going through a period of poor health, which resulted in a traumatic incident in the first therapy, and premature termination in the second.

The Anorexic Museum Assistant

Age 25, single, 34 sessions, score 0.

It is difficult to do justice to this extemely interesting and complex case history within a limited space, and our account must of necessity be somewhat selective. The material of her therapy is remarkable for the literal quality of the Oedipal feelings that emerged.

Initial disturbances

She wrote in her application form as follows:

Acute depression, anxiety. General sense of insecurity, lack of self-confidence and self-esteem. Fatigue, impaired concentration.

Physical symptoms: itchy skin, minor digestive disorders, weak bladder; stiffness of body, aching legs. Spasmodic attacks with increased itchiness, swollen eyelids, troubled complexion. General sense of physical discomfort, headaches.

The condition has gradually developed and worsened over the past 2 years, since completing university studies and starting work.

No menstrual periods for 2½ years. Insomnia, disturbed dreams from childhood on. Excessive nervous perspiration from early adolescence.

Psychiatric history

This revealed considerable disturbance. Her sleep pattern included fairly severe early waking, and she said that she had longed for death, though she had not actually contemplated suicide. When she was asked about eating patterns it emerged that the onset of her amenorrhoea had coincided with an attempt to diet, in which her weight dropped from about 8½ stone (120 lb, 54 Kg) to 6½ stone (90 lb, 41 Kg), without clothes.

Background

She is the eldest of three children of a working-class Scottish family, with a sister and brother younger by 5 and 8 years respectively. Her father is a carpenter. There was also another sister who died soon after birth when the patient was 10, an event which plays a crucial part in the story. The patient was brought up in a small isolated village in North-East Scotland. Her academic history was progressive, and she managed to get into Dundee University, where she got an Upper Second in German and then an MA.

Her family

Her description was of a united and close family, though with considerable under-lying tensions about which no one could speak. She was close to her mother but could not talk to her about emotional subjects. When she was small she was very close to her father, but there seems to have been a loss of intimacy with him at about the age of 11 (we may note that her periods did not start at that time, but at 13).

Important life events

The theme that emerged very clearly was of *something repeatedly going wrong with the process of growing into a woman*. This involved the following four incidents:

1 She said that she had no recollection of her mother's pregnancies with her two living siblings, which were never talked about. However, her mother shared the final pregnancy openly with the patient, aged 10, who looked forward with great pleasure to having a new brother or sister. The sharing of this aspect of her mother's femininity was of course a departure from the family's inability to talk about intimate subjects, and it meant a great deal to

her. Here everything went wrong: her mother became ill and was admitted to hospital, the baby was born, and the patient received a postcard saying that it was a girl. Some time later her father told her that there was 'something wrong with the baby's mouth and it wouldn't be coming home just yet'. Her mother arrived home without any baby, and the family reticence was now re-established, for the whole thing was never talked about. The patient never dared ask her mother what happened, and only recently did she get a clue when she overheard a conversation between her mother and a relative, from which she made the deduction (on slender evidence) that the baby had been born spastic and her mother had chosen to allow it to die. This whole episode affected her very deeply – so much so that she kept the postcard and read and re-read it many times.

2 The second incident emerged at interview as follows. The interviewer pointed out to her that she had denied the existence of sex to an extraordinary degree. The patient said that she hadn't realised this at all, and she then became extremely upset and embarrassed and recounted the following: ever since the age of 11 she had suffered from severe excessive perspiration, especially in her armpits. Her mother never discussed anything about puberty with her, and she only had the haziest notion, picked up from a friend, that one bled from somewhere. One day in class at school, at the age of 13, she was teased by another girl because she was showing interest in a boy, and suddenly her armpits began sweating profusely. She came to the conclusion that it was blood, and was tremendously relieved when she was able to rush to the toilet after class and find that it was only sweat.

When she was 21 and at University, incidents 3 and 4 occurred within 24 hours. In both one can see the theme of parental disapproval of her need to break free and live her own life.

3 She was invited to Germany to stay with a friend with the aim of helping the friend to prepare for her wedding. Here something went very badly wrong, because the friend's parents arrived home, asked what on earth she was doing there, and said they didn't want her. She was put in the position of having no alternative but to leave.

4 She arrived home in the midst of a family crisis in which her father was extremely angry with her sister, whose boy-friend he disapproved of. She realised her father was jealous, and she was greatly shocked at the violence of his anger. She said it changed her whole attitude to him from then on.

Dynamics of two initial interviews with one of the present authors (DM)

The following were the main interactions that occurred:

1 The interviewer put together in his mind two observations, that the patient's facial expression seemed to express an underlying bitterness, and that whenever the subject of angry feelings was touched on she became tearful. He therefore suggested that the patient felt some kind of deep anger about deficiencies in her childhood, but was profoundly guilty about it. The patient responded by saying that whereas her sister tended to flare up and get her anger off her chest, she herself used to retire to her room and sulk. The main thing that set this off seemed to be that her parents failed to understand her need to grow up.

2 The interviewer put to her that the four life events described above could all be seen in terms of her anxieties about sex and growing into a woman, her wish to share these with her parents, and her encountering silence or disapproval wherever she went. She took this interpretation seriously but did not make any clear response. The interviewer then brought in the loss of closeness with her father at around the age of 11, and tried to suggest that it was because she was beginning to grow into a woman. This was possibly confirmed because, although her periods started at 13, she said that the loss of closeness occurred over 2–3 years, and it also seemed to emerge that it was she who had withrawn from him rather than the other way round.

Projective testing

She told the psychologist that she had given much thought to her interviews and that since then *she had had her first menstrual period for 2½ years.*

The main features that emerged from her ORT stories were: that she has difficulty in accepting her physical self, and tries to make it spiritual; she cannot tolerate three-person situations and denies their existence; and there are primitive and violent feelings underneath, which she tries to avoid. It was also significant that in her stories there were five *sinister* percepts, which seemed to indicate the possibility of deeper disturbance than appeared on the surface.

Reason for acceptance for brief psychotherapy

There was much discussion among the members of the case conference, who saw on the one hand a highly responsive and well motivated patient with whom very clear dynamics had crystallised; and on the other hand someone with evidence for considerable underlying disturbance (the severity of her depression, the anorexic episode, and the sinister percepts in her ORT).

The final view was that she could be worked with in brief psychotherapy, and that the deeper disturbance could be handled by a reasonably skilled therapist. Two foci were formulated: strongly guilt-laden anger with her parents, and severe anxieties about growing into a woman, based on Oedipal problems. The two foci were connected, in the sense that her main anger seemed to be about her parents' failure to understand her need to grow up and become independent.

Course of therapy (34 sessions)

Initial transference resistance resolved by interpretation

Although the patient talked quite freely in Sessions 1 and 2, there was clearly an underlying resistance, since the therapist gained the impression that therapy was not really getting off the ground. The reason for this became clear in Session 3, when the patient began to speak of her need to be sensitive to her mother's feelings, and the therapist interpreted this as a communication about the need to be sensitive to the therapist's feelings. The result was a clear response, the patient saying that she had found it easier to talk to the male interviewer (DM), and that she was very aware of the therapist as a woman and the need 'not to cause any offence'. She said she had resented this and was afraid that it might result in her wasting the whole therapy.

A significant Oedipal memory

A further response to this piece of work on her resistance came in the next session (number 4). The patient first said how much easier she now felt with the therapist, and she went on to tell of a highly Oedipal incident in her childhood. When she was 8 her mother had gone into hospital to have her brother, and her father – entirely innocently – had invited her to spend the night in the big double bed with him, 'just for company'. Although her father clearly thought nothing of it, she had been extremely uneasy, spending much of the night awake at the far edge of the bed, feeling that it was wrong and her mother ought to be there.

An Oedipal nightmare

In the next session (number 5) the therapist wrote that there seemed to be 'an alarming floating quality' conveyed by the patient, as she spoke about her mixed feelings for her mother – affection on the one hand, and intense resentment on the other. She added that something of the same kind seemed to be happening with her feelings about the therapist (i.e. the patient gave her own PT interpretation). Later in the session she described a disturbed dream from which she had woken up in a terrible panic. She was with a man belonging to another woman, and they were being chased by the woman and hid in a grave. In the grave were the dismembered bodies of Jews, and their assailant came to the grave and was trying to get at them. The therapist linked this with the patient's having spent the night in her father's bed and being afraid of what her mother might think; and linked this in turn with a triangular situation involving the transference, suggesting that the patient had become attached to Dr Malan during the initial assessment, but that she felt he belonged to the therapist. The patient responded with warmth and said that she would have liked to see Dr Malan again to tell him about re-starting her periods.

In the next session (number 6) she opened by saying that she had become very aware of warm feelings for the therapist. It was as if, together, they had lifted up the corner of a veil and looked underneath, and it wasn't so frightening after all, so that she felt as if a burden had been lifted from her shoulders. There was then a striking confirmation of the therapist's interpretation about Dr Malan, because it turned out that the man in the dream was the hero of a film whose name was David!

Further Oedipal material

In Session 7 she spoke of two women friends, one of whom had become pregnant, much to her parents' disapproval; and the other who had become attached to a married man, who had then been unfaithful to her with one of her friends. The therapist made interpretations about guilt-laden sexual feelings spoiling potentially good experience, including that with Dr Malan. The patient again went into her 'floating' state, and said that somehow she couldn't believe in holding on to something good for herself. She went on to say that she had been quite unaware of her parents' sexual relation until after the birth of her brother when she was 8. Her living sister was born when she was 5, and although she remembered nothing about the pregnancy, her parents had been very careful to make her feel included by letting her hold and look after the baby. She had been proud rather than jealous when people made complimentary remarks about her sister's appearance. She went on to speak of doing well at school, and how the main person who was pleased about this was father. The therapist summed up by saying that she could feel included as long as she wasn't aware of her parents' sexual relationship, but that once this happened she was faced with a competitive situation that she couldn't cope with, just like her women friends mentioned at the beginning of the session.

In Session 8 some negative things emerged about her father, in particular that – for reasons unspecified – he used to boycott the family meals and go and eat in another room. In the next session (number 9) she spoke of resentment against the therapist for bringing this out, and the therapist said that she must feel it to be unsafe to have mixed feelings. In response the patient spoke of the severity of her symptoms and how they lead to her isolation. Her sweating in particular is so bad that she cannot go into shops, and she now has difficulty in going out anywhere, e.g. to art galleries, which she used to enjoy. The therapist interpreted the symptoms, not in terms of guilt (which might have been more correct), but of intense feelings struggling to get out and activated by the therapy.

A further dramatic dream

In response the patient spoke of recurrent dreams, in which the main theme consisted of having to cross a bridge. She mentioned one in particular which went back to her childhood, as follows.

There was a fire in a village, from which she had to escape by crossing a bridge made of fabric. The adults crossed safely but she was afraid; and when she did try to cross, the fabric began to fray. She could see the river open out into two channels, very wide and open, and though there was something cool and calm about the openness she was also afraid because she did not know where the river would lead.

The therapist interpreted the fire as the burning feelings of sexuality and anger aroused by her family, which she was afraid would cause damage. The river was the path to growing up, and she found this difficult because her feelings were still involved with her mother and father, and particularly with her need to protect them from her criticisms and her wish to break free.

The patient responded by speaking of her experience of her home as claustrophobic because her parents demanded total allegiance, and of her father's possessiveness towards both of his daughters in relation to boy-friends. The therapist said, 'Should you take the risk of losing your father's love by finding a man of your own, and what would your mother think?'

In Session 10, after a break of 2 weeks, the patient reported what seemed to be a therapeutic effect, which was that she had been able to take the decision to pay a visit to her home because she wanted to go and not because she felt she ought to. Moreover, she had been able to relate to her parents much more freely than before. However, she had also become depressed because her father was again in conflict with her sister over a boy-friend.

A transparent Oedipal dream

Session 11 began with further emphasis on the severity of her physical symptoms, and how she felt at war with her body. With some skilful work the therapist now brought out something that the patient had concealed, namely that she had had the following dream. She and her father were having supper together, and there was another woman there who was both glamorous and blonde (an obvious reference to the therapist). The woman asked whether it was time for the patient to go to bed with her father. Her heart sank at this because, although – owing to her mother's recent death (in the dream) – she had just married her father, she had not expected a sexual component to the relationship, and her intention had been only to look after her father and be his companion.

The first thing the therapist said was, 'And you never told me!' which made them both laugh. She then made the following interventions: she linked the dream with the incident in which the patient spent the night with her father while her mother was in hospital giving birth to her brother; and she said that the patient wanted to retreat from sex because it involved forbidden feelings towards men, representing her father, and rivalry with women, representing her mother. It is worth noting that two other themes that were not mentioned were transparent death wishes towards the mother, and the guilt and self-punishment that must follow; and the obvious reference to the patient's view of the therapist as a rival who was also driving her towards acknowledging her sexual feelings for her father. Nevertheless the patient agreed with what the therapist said and left the session looking active and very alive.

She opened the next session (number 12) by saying that she had been feeling better. She had been out helping with the local election and had enjoyed it, but her sweating had been very troublesome and she had been afraid people would notice it. She spoke of a man there who had been telling interesting stories, and the therapist interpreted that she had been afraid other people would notice how excited she had been inside, like the little girl listening to her father's stories – admiring him and even being excited in a sexual way. The patient's response was, 'Never, the man was at least 50', to which the therapist said, 'Exactly'. This led on to the family's implicit taboo on sexuality, the result of which was that it became easier for the patient to remain at home – as now she stayed in her own bed-sitting room – and comply with the taboo rather than allow her own sexuality to become alive. The patient said that it was especially her father who condemned sexuality, and the therapist said that it was the patient who was particularly close to her father, so that sexuality became more than ever dangerous for her.

A further dramatic and significant dream

The patient responded by telling two dreams, in the first of which she visited a foreign family and left her bag behind, and they forgot to give it back to her. It crossed her mind that they intended to rob her. (It would seem now that this must have been a reference to her traumatic visit to the German family mentioned in the initial assessment.) The second dream was as follows: she was walking downstream in the shallow part of a river, which gradually narrowed and got deeper between mountains. There was something blocking the river and when she saw the water getting deeper and rougher she was worried because she was not a good swimmer. She could see beyond the block to the beauty of the valley beyond, in which there were flowers and fields. Suddenly everything went wrong and the block was broken down by the force of the water, and she watched the water rushing through the break, and it was reddish like the red sandstone soil around her Scottish home. But there was also some black in it, like coal dust. She became sad and swam resignedly back upstream.

The patient asked the therapist what she thought, denying that she had any thoughts herself. As a result the therapist did not press for associations, but made a long interpretation based on her own associations and intuition. She spoke of something being 'carried' in both dreams, the bag being carried by the patient in the first, and the patient being carried by the river in the second. Both dreams had ended in disaster. She wrote in her account of the session: 'I said I thought both dreams were about her mother's "carrying" the baby and the excitement and then the pain that she had felt as she participated in her mother's pregnancy, at times almost robbing it as if it were her own, and then finally feeling robbed herself by the disaster of her baby sister's death; the "waters breaking" over the land [a reference to the "breaking of the waters" at the beginning of labour], red and black – just as she was in sight of that beautiful view ahead, her own fertility and sexuality, so she had to swim back resignedly upstream, as she had been doing ever since.'

Although there may have been some details of this highly creative interpretation that were inaccurate, the essential message must surely have been correct. Moreover, the interpretation was couched in anxiety-relieving rather than anxiety-provoking terms. This leaves us mystified at the patient's extremely ambiguous response, raising doubts as to whether she was saying that the interpretation was wrong, or that it was right and she was becoming resistant because claiming her own femininity was too disturbing for her. This ambiguity is illustrated by the fact that on the one hand she made no helpful immediate response; but, on the other hand, at the end of the session she gave an important piece of fresh information, namely that she had saved the postcard from her mother about the birth of the baby to this day.

There was similar ambiguity in the next session (number 13). She arrived very prettily dressed, in a new outfit, which seemed to indicate a major response to the work of the previous session. On the other hand, she now said she had suffered an exacerbation of her physical symptoms, and she went on to attribute this to her feeling that in the previous session 'there has been no communication'. Moreover, later in the session she talked about a woman boss who was 'lunatic' and 'only interested in power', which looks like a disguised reference to the therapist, and she also mentioned a book on the subject of suicide.

The rest of the session was extremely confused, and the therapist had no idea what was going on. Towards the end she decided to comment on the patient's appearance, saying that she was dressed very differently today and looked very pretty. At this the patient blushed, and said that it made it all the more difficult at work, where the fact of being dressed differently made her symptoms worse.

The patient's ambiguous response in Session 11 to 13 can be made more understandable if we make use of two themes from her later analysis. The first is her total inability to allow herself pleasure, which indicates the extreme anxiety with which the whole area of emotional fulfilment was surrounded. This leads in turn to the second theme, namely her repeated 'negative therapeutic reaction', which meant that in addition to pleasure she could not allow herself *progress*, so that she responded to each apparent step forward by becoming more disturbed rather than less. Nevertheless, in her response to these present sessions there was an extremely positive component, and it is all the more tragic that the negative component was so strongly reinforced by the events about to be described.

A traumatic transference experience created by chance events

This session was followed by a very unfortunate train of events. The patient had felt much better after the previous session, apparently because she was surprised and pleased that the therapist had noticed her appearance, and as a token of gratitude she had bought some flowers to bring to the session. She had then received a message saying that the therapist was ill and couldn't see her, but offering another appointment in the same week. She had gone out and bought some more flowers, only to receive another message cancelling the second appointment. During this time also she had been referred by us to a physician about her excessive sweating. She said he had been very abrupt with her; and she had been extremely embarrassed at his asking about her periods, getting off the subject as soon as possible by telling him that they were now normal when in fact in her last period she had bled severely. When she finally did come for Session 14 she gave a very moving account of her double disappointment over the flowers, at which the therapist herself openly cried in the session.

Interpretation of the meaning of these events leads to major communications and fresh memories

The patient said that she had felt like a little girl who knows her mother is ill but at the same time wants to say, 'Why can't you pay attention to *me*?' Here the therapist gave a TP interpretation, saying that there was much in these events that was reminiscent of what was happening between the patient and her mother around the time of adolescence – 'in the present events it was as if something exciting to do with femininity was happening between us, and then it had all gone wrong.' It resembled her mother both not coming home without the baby when she was 10, and failing to help her over the start of her periods when she was 13.

These were two of the traumatic experiences described in her initial interviews; and we may note that the present chance event seemed to repeat for the patient the pattern of the other two traumatic experiences as well (the incident with the German family and the quarrel between her father and her sister over the latter's boy-friend), since the common theme of all four was something going seriously wrong each time she made a step towards growing into a woman.

It is noticeable that the above TP interpretation did not mention the loss of attention caused by the mother's illness and the birth of the new baby, which was so clearly hinted at in the patient's remark about loss of attention in the present situation. However, it led to the following major communications in the rest of the session:

1 The patient said that around the time of her adolescence she had been very confused about the lower part of her body and had thought that there was only one opening there; and when she had begun menstruating she had thought that the blood was coming from her anus, and she was very frightened. The therapist, creatively using material from a previous session, linked this with the dream in Session 12 – the red sandstone soil (blood) mixed with black coal dust (faeces).

2 The therapist said that at the time of the pregnancy the patient must have wondered what was going on in her mother's body. The patient said that she had been alarmed at the size of her mother's belly, had thought it was all baby,

and had wondered how it could possibly get out. The therapist linked this also with the dream – the waters breaking, what could it be that was inside, and how did it get to the fertile valley beyond?

3 Although it was almost the end of the session, the patient asked if she could tell two further dreams. In the second of these she had had a baby but had abandoned and neglected it, and it was given to a friend to look after. There was also a theme of trying to keep men away from the situation. In fact the friend's name was very similar to the therapist's, but the therapist did not mention this in her interpretation. She said that the patient must have been so identified with her mother that she thought there was a baby somewhere whom she had neglected, and that she had failed in her role as mother. The patient said, 'It's funny you should say that, because when my mother was pregnant I used to go around with a cushion under my skirt, wondering what it felt like for my mother, and treating it very carefully because I knew how vulnerable it was.' The therapist said that when her mother didn't bring the baby back it was as if she herself had failed in the mother role, and had been somehow responsible by not being good enough. In the situation in therapy she had wanted to put the experience right by bringing flowers. 'The flowers and the creativity of the work we did together were something about wanting to have a baby here with me, just as she wanted to have a baby with her mother.' The patient smiled and seemed much happier at the end of the session, and the therapist felt that deep emotional contact had been made.

Here it is worth noting that although there is no doubt about the emotional contact, the feelings dealt with consisted almost entirely of *disappointment* and *distress,* and the supervisor pointed out that hints of over-compensation for negative feelings, towards the mother, the baby, and the therapist, were not taken up. This was probably because of the therapist's own distress and guilt about the pain caused by her cancellation of the two sessions.

Failure of an attempt to deal with negative feelings

However, when in the next session (number 15) the therapist tried to bring in negative transference feelings, the result was only that the patient became very upset and felt that the good part of the relationship had been spoiled by misunderstanding. This was followed by a breakdown of communication in the next few sessions (numbers 16 to 21) up to the summer break, in which much of the material was obscure. An important moment was the following dream: the patient was travelling in the Underground and there was a baby in someone's arms which was then given to her. The baby had been ill with vomiting. She now handed the baby to someone else who was able to treat it medically, and her own (i.e. the patient's) work changed from boring to pleasurable. This was an obvious reference to the baby sister who died, but otherwise the therapist was unable to find any useful interpretation. With hindsight one can see the most likely meaning: that if only the baby could have been cured and have lived, the patient would have been relieved of her guilt-laden depression and her life would have become pleasurable again.

In association to another dream during this period the patient remembered an incident from her childhood in which she was entrusted with carrying her baby brother across a stream and had nearly dropped him (cf. the Librarian), and her mother had been very understanding. The therapist seems not to have taken up the evidence for ambivalence towards the younger siblings.

The rest of therapy (Sessions 22 to 34) gives the over-all impression of obscurity and lack of further progress, though with moments of important communica-tion. In Session 26 the patient brought up the postcard announcing the birth of her baby sister, which – as mentioned above – she had kept to this day. In Session 27 the therapist introduced the subject of masturbation, and it now emerged that at 13 the patient became aware that masturbation was accompanied by thoughts of having a baby. The therapist first reminded her of putting the cushion under her skirt, indicating an intense wish to be in her mother's shoes, and then reminded her of the earlier baby (her brother) who had been born while she was sleeping in her father's bed. The therapist interpreted that there must have been thoughts of marrying her father and having sex with him (as shown by the dream reported in Session 11), about which she must feel very guilty. The patient seemed much relieved by this and mentioned that recently her mother had come across another postcard, this one referring to her *brother's* birth, and had said quite openly, 'I bet you slept with your father that night, didn't you?' The therapist said that in spite of this the patient must feel very guilty, and she must have had thoughts of killing off her mother and taking her place (an oblique reference to the dream in which her mother was dead and she married her father). The patient said: 'It makes a lot of sense but I can't take it inside me.'

The issue of death wishes towards the baby sister

In Session 30, under pressure from the supervisor, the therapist made a determined attempt to reach negative feelings about the birth of the baby sister. A way into this was provided by the patient's remark that she had a 'furious' rash on her body. The therapist spoke of the patient being angry and envious of her mother for having a baby, for having sex with her father, for being his wife and sharing his bed – and then the terrible thing was that in reality the baby didn't return and she must have felt that she had killed it. The patient tried to make an intellectu-alised response to this, which the therapist pointed out, reminding her of her dream of marrying her father, the horror in the same dream about sharing her father's bed, and the moment when she nearly dropped her baby brother in the stream. The patient responded by saying: 'it's strange that you should mention these things, but I had a dream recently.' In the dream she is at a railway station and looking after a little girl, and she takes her eyes off the girl and hears an awful thud, and the girl has fallen on to the railway lines with the train just coming in. In the session she followed this by saying that she felt she should have looked after her mother better, and then her mother wouldn't have had to go into hospital so soon. She went on to remember a recent incident in which she was in the museum and a little boy was run over in the street. She was completely unable to mobilise her concern and it was a colleague who had rung for an ambulance. She then told of a third incident in which a lame pigeon had alighted on her windowsill, and she felt she should have brought it in for the night, but she has a phobia of touching such creatures and couldn't do so, and in the morning it was dead.

These associations would seem to have completely confirmed the therapist's interpretation, but in the next session the patient seemed to be in despair and spoke of the 'alien ideas' that the therapist was putting forward, in particular that she might have wanted to kill her baby sister. She spoke of the pigeon that died as having a deep significance for her, and she felt very guilty about it, but this was as far as the therapist could get.

The therapist wrote that facing the patient with her ambivalent feelings about the members of the family seemed to be an impossibility.

Termination

Later in this session the patient said that flowers have a very deep significance for her – flowers are better than people because they don't cause the same kind of pain and disappointment. The therapist spoke of the patient's feeling that termination was like 'just being dropped', and thus taking no account of the depth of her experience in the therapy.

In the next session (number 33), in the context of a discussion of her feelings about termination, the patient said that she had used the previous session negatively in order to get nothing out of it, and she felt she went away with nothing. The session then got into deep waters, seemingly concerned with her inability to take anything in from the therapist because of her fear of her uncontrollable instincts – reminding us that at one time she had apparently suffered from anorexia nervosa. She said that her 'head', i.e. her intellect, had a superior and condescending attitude to the rest of her. She contrasted this with a friend who enjoys 'eating, and window-shopping, and speculation, and intrigue'. The therapist interpreted that instinctual life, and all aspects of bodily functioning, were felt to be inferior and needed to be kept under control, and perhaps she was afraid that 'if she gave them an inch they would take a mile' and she would be overwhelmed. This seemed to be confirmed when the patient said that 'if she really allowed herself to take in the ideas that she had read or thought about, then she might well be overwhelmed by them and have no energy left over for anything else.' She then spoke about eating, and how she regarded it not as something to be enjoyed but as a boring task that had to be got through. We can see now that this communication might have been connected with the patient's inability to 'take things in' from her therapy and thus make full use of it.

In the final session (number 34) the patient brought a most beautiful orchid, which the therapist accepted, deeply moved. The patient said that she was less depressed and her symptoms were somewhat better. The session appeared fragmented and very little further communication seems to have taken place. They made an appointment to meet again in 2 months' time.

Follow-up

Subsequent events

She was seen by her therapist for a number of follow-up interviews, and then, since she was so little improved, was taken on 1 year 2 months after termination for analysis on the couch at three times a week, under supervision, as part of the four-year training in Adult Psychotherapy at the Tavistock Clinic. Her new therapist was a woman social worker, well experienced in psychotherapy, and under psychoanalytic training.

During this period much of the material of her analysis was negative, in the sense that she spent a great deal of time in complaints about her physical symptoms and her isolated, empty life. The therapist concentrated on trying to show her that she herself was spoiling the potential for good experience, including that with her therapist. The therapist wrote: 'She experienced me as either repeatedly interrupting her obsessional ruminations, or alternately leaving her alone and neglecting her. I was in danger of losing sight of minute, more positive shades of feeling in her responses to events.' 'Any brief improvement in mood was immediately followed by a negative therapeutic reaction, often extending for weeks.' Nevertheless, in the final year there were definite signs of improvement: 'She acknowledged that she was more appreciated at work, she was regularly going to concerts, operas, films, and art galleries – although usually on her own – and she had more friendly relations with her landlord and the other lodgers. She had a few acquaintances and two tenuous friendships. Also she began to wear all her new and tasteful outfits of winter and summer clothes, and I realised with surprise that I had not heard a word about her perspiration for the past 18 months.' (Unfortunately this did not mean that the problem was any better, though her reaction to it may have been.)

Finally, 9½ years since the termination of her brief psychotherapy, and nearly 5 years since the termination of her analysis, she applied for treatment again at the age of 38.

The information given below is based on the 1-year follow-up by the original therapist, supplemented by information from subsequent events. As will be seen, at 1 year there was hardly any change; but at 9½ years, even though she felt she had nearly had a breakdown, there were very great improvements in her personal life.

One-year follow-up, supplemented by information at 9½ years

Symptoms. Though some of the details may have changed, her physical symptoms remained severe throughout the whole 9½-year follow-up period. She has never had any interest in food, and although at 1 year she was eating regularly, at 9½ years she still suffered from attacks of loss of appetite. She continued to menstruate but at 1 year her periods were highly irregular, the cycle varying between 14 and 98 days, and the degree of bleeding sometimes being very light and sometimes severe. As far as her sweating was concerned, it was unimproved at 1 year, and at 5½ years she had an operation for removal of sweat glands. The symptom improved temporarily but at 9½ years it is still severe – 'it makes buying and wearing clothes complicated and can be a nightmare on social occasions.'

At 9½ years she wrote that her physical symptoms occasionally make her feel extremely ill, but that she has twice been on holiday abroad and then 'the physical symptoms vanish and I feel happy'.

Depression. Immediately after her brief therapy she was probably less manifestly depressed, but at 1 year and throughout a large part of her analysis her whole life style was both depressive and obsessional in quality. She lived an isolated life in a bed-sitting room, hardly ever going out except to work; and one of her most striking characteristics was her continuous and desperate struggle to get through the everyday chores and her almost complete inability to allow herself pleasure. Indeed during this time the whole of her life continued to involve an immense effort even to keep going. In the later stages of her analysis this improved considerably. However, at 9½ years she wrote of her constant worry about work, and a 'feeling of not being able to cope, even with small everyday matters', and she also wrote that she very nearly had a breakdown in which she felt unable to go to work, and only the knowledge that the work would pile up in her absence kept her going.

Her feelings about the baby sister who died.   At 9½ years she wrote: 'During my first course of therapy I lost my preoccupation with the death of my baby sister – it doesn't bother me very often now and I feel quite distant from it.'

Summary of the position at 1 year after termination of brief therapy

At this time the only apparent improvements were the loss of preoccupation with the baby sister and possibly some improvement in manifest depression. Her obsessional life style had presumably always been present; but it is clear from the account of her analysis that she was now much less in touch with her feelings than she had been in her brief therapy. Her other symptoms remained severe.

A most interesting observation, however, is that after the intensive working through of her Oedipal problems in her brief therapy, such problems were hardly mentioned in her analysis. It really seems that the excellent work done by her therapist brought about substantial resolution in this area. Moreover, at 9½-year follow-up the patient herself attributed an improvement in her relation with men to her brief therapy, which both confirms that this resolution had taken place and represents a major reward for the therapist's work; but unfortunately the patient remained entirely withdrawn from men for many years, so that there was no tangible evidence for any improvement at the point at which the therapeutic result was scored. Thus the over-all result of her brief therapy seems to have consisted largely of the exposure of an underlying severe disturbance, which had not been evident when she was first seen. Moreover, in some ways she appeared to be worse, as is shown by the contrast between the lively and intense young woman who first came to us, and the chronically inhibited, isolated, and obsessional person that she had become by the time she entered analysis.

Both judges regarded her as unimproved and gave a score of 0.

Major improvements at 9½-year follow-up

In spite of the severity of these problems involving her everyday life, at 9½ years there were two immensely important areas of improvement. First, she now wrote of many things that gave her pleasure: 'Going out to operas, art galleries, cinemas, theatres, restaurants etc. Evening classes and holidays abroad. My relationship with my boy-friend.' This last is of course the second area of improvement. Whereas during the whole of the period up to the end of her analysis she had kept entirely away from men, she now has had a steady boy-friend for 3 years, and an enjoyable sexual relation with him for a year. There is the possibility of their living together or getting married.

Experience of therapy

Of her brief therapy she wrote: 'I remember this mainly as my first opportunity to discuss my difficulties with someone and to build up a relationship at the same time. It was important that my therapist was a woman. I remember her as intelligent and active but [sic!] also quite feminine, and I think this has had an effect on my relationships with men since then.'

Of her analysis she wrote: 'This felt quite different and was very important to me. I had more space and time to develop. I started to do things I hadn't done for years – went out more, made new relationships – and felt my therapist valued any progress I was making. The experience seemed enriching in itself, and I also left feeling optimistic about my life and held on to those feelings for years.'

Comment

This was a most interesting and dramatic brief therapy, packed full of significant communication, and with transparent dreams and fresh memories revealing major Oedipal problems. Yet it is clear that after her brief therapy the residual problems were severe and all-pervading. We can probably see the reason for this in the material of her anaylsis, in the sense that there was a very powerful thread of self-destructiveness running through her whole life. The origin of this in the past never became clear, but it must have been based on severe superego pathology, which in turn implies profound guilt. Quite possibly it had its origin in her feelings about the death of her baby sister, but there also seems evidence of disturbance in her early relationship with her mother. From the patient's description it appeared that in the early years her mother had been depressed and withdrawn.

Could the immense difficulty of treating her, and her unsuitability for brief therapy, have been foreseen at the beginning? The answer is that the evidence was indeed seen, and consisted of such features as her anorexic episode, the severity of her depression (with early waking), and the disturbed and sinister responses in her projective testing. However, we took the decision – which even with hindsight seems justified – to work with the major positive feature that she showed, namely her responsiveness to interpretative work, of which perhaps the most striking illustration was the restoration of her periods – after a gap of 2½ years – in response to two initial assessment interviews. It is tragic that, even after a 3½-year analysis, we were not able to do more for this exceedingly responsive but deeply troubled young woman.

The Psychiatric Nurse

Age 25, single, Staff Nurse at a Mental Hospital, 20 sessions, score 0.

Reason for referral

Her original complaint was depression. The precipitating factor consisted of the death within 2 weeks, 10 months ago, of three people: first her father, and then two more distant relatives who had been close to her. Premonitory symptoms in her father, which had been present for some years, had been dismissed as psychosomatic by his GP.

In her application form she wrote: 'At present I am feeling quite well but I feel there are lot of underlying problems that need bringing to the surface – feelings of guilt, an inability to channel anger, and my feeling that I damage people, which inhibits my actions at work.'

Background

She was the third of a family of four girls. Her father, a professional man, appears to have been obsessional and chronically depressed – 'it was an event if he smiled'. He had a violent temper and punished the children physically. Her mother was scatterbrained and untidy. Both parents were very Victorian and she did not feel close to either of them.

In her childhood she felt excluded by her two older sisters, which caused her to have violent outbursts of temper. Her fear of damaging people goes back to this time. At the age of 11 she made a conscious effort to put a stop to her outbursts, and the result seems to have been a state of general inhibition accompanied by withdrawal from the family circle. When she was 14 her younger sister, Beth, developed multiple sclerosis, became progressively paralysed, and has required a great deal of attention.

Dynamics of interview

The interview was carried out by an experienced (male) psychiatrist. The patient was highly insightful and, in dynamic collaborative work, there was little difficulty in identifying the issues in her life. Those in her upbringing have already been described above. More recently – for reasons that are not entirely clear – the death of her father seems to have set in motion a process of emotional liberation, involving both sexuality and anger. She began to have fantasies of being a prostitute and, as she described it, 'going through every kind of degradation – I just wanted to get right down into the earth'. Her work was in a ward for disturbed adolescents, and the liberation of her anger culminated in a violent and uncontrollable – and also extremely effective – outburst of rage against some of the children, who had provoked her beyond endurance. She described an inner feeling of immense power as a result, and since then she has felt better. It was clear that her aim in asking for treatment was to get help in completing the process of liberation in every way possible.

Gynaecological history

Her periods had always been infrequent and highly irregular, and she had some degree of hirsutism; and it became clear that she suffered from mild adrenogenital syndrome (an excess of masculinising hormones). She had seen a specialist about this and was told that there was nothing to be done until she wants to have children.

Reason for acceptance for brief psychotherapy

The present period of her life seemed to provide an important opportunity for trying to help her complete the process of emotional liberation begun by recent events. She was well motivated and highly responsive to dynamic work.

Course of therapy (20 sessions)

As mentioned above, the therapist was the woman social worker who treated the previous patient.

The focus of competition between women and its dangers

In Session 1 the patient gave evidence of a marked drop in motivation. She had been feeling better since her interview with the psychiatrist and almost didn't come. The scene was then set for the issue of competition between women when she made some disparaging remarks about social workers. The therapist suggested that after her good interview with the psychiatrist she felt palmed off on a social worker. The patient laughed and admitted this, and she then agreed to come.

The therapist had to cancel the next appointment because of illness, and in Session 2 the theme developed of the patient's fear of her own anger. The therapist made the link between fear of expressing anger in the transference (because of the cancelled session) and the fear of expressing anger to the damaged sister, Beth. The patient said that she did resent the way Beth had to be protected all the time. She later described having a furious row with her boy-friend, James, who had been late for her, which seemed to confirm the above transference interpretation.

In Session 3 the patient reported another furious row with James, who hadn't come to meet her after the last session. This was followed by an 'anti-men' theme. The therapist linked this with the patient's father, who saw his daughter as a kind of son and wanted her to succeed, in contrast to her mother, who seemed to want her not to be intelligent and to be tied to the kitchen sink. As a consequence, whatever the patient did she would displease one or other of her parents, with the result that she found it difficult to enjoy a relation with a man or to become intellectual, on the one hand, or to enjoy domesticity, on the other. (This theme is similar to the main focus in the therapy of the Mountain Tarn Girl.)

In the early part of Session 4 the therapist had to deal with a complicated piece of reality which had intervened. The patient had attended a meeting at the Tavistock involving two highly loaded situations: actual professional competition with the therapist, which the therapist brought into the open; and the impossibility of expressing anger against a male colleague of the therapist's because he suffered from a physical disability, which the therapist linked both with the damaged sister and the ill father. The patient spoke of her attempts to get close to her father in her teens, and also of the fact that she was the only one of the family who realised that he was more ill than appeared, but when she tried to speak of this he had brushed her aside. From these themes there developed the interpretation that competitive feelings contained anger, and therefore the patient felt it impossible to succeed because she was afraid someone would get damaged. The patient spoke both of her competition with her sisters and of her extreme success at school. She said that each time she had climbed on to the stage to receive a prize she had 'died inside' with embarrassment. The therapist interpreted that it was better to *die inside* than to have someone *die outside* as a result of her success.

A hypomanic episode

These themes were continued in the next few sessions, and in Session 8 they appeared to be bearing fruit. The patient spoke of an 'incredible week,' in which she had done all sorts of new things. This included leaving the flat where she had been living with her boy-friend, James, and finding a flat of her own (though she has continued to see him). She also had been on a 'high-powered' course, which she paid for herself. However, she had taken time off work for this and then had felt so guilty that today she had had to stay late and consequently had come late for the session. In talking about this she made a strange slip of the tongue, saying 'dishes' when she meant 'decisions'. The therapist interpreted that she felt guilty about getting something for herself and had to go back 'tied to the kitchen sink' as her mother wanted. 'Competing intellectually had meant becoming Daddy's girl, but now she had to go back and become Mummy's girl.' In response the patient spoke of open competitiveness with the therapist – she has entered a competition to win an Alfa Romeo, whereas the therapist probably has only a 'crappy little sports car' – a communication which conveyed a distinct flavour of masculine strivings.

This was followed by a session (number 9) which made clear that the patient was in a hypomanic state. She found it difficult to stop talking and said, 'I have so much energy I don't know what to do with it. Incredible things have been happening.' These included having 'completely taken over' in a family therapy session, refusing to work overtime, and chairing a meeting with great success. She linked all this with a new-found ability to express her aggression. The therapist also linked it with sexuality, saying that the patient had found a 'potency' without feeling it was destructive, and added that she had always been confused about her sexuality. This brought out first that – in contrast to the whole of her previous menstrual history – she has had regular periods ever since the initial consultation (it is worth noting the comparison with the previous patient); and second, that because of her excessive bodily hair she had felt there was something wrong with her femininity and that she was really a man. Later in the session the therapist spoke of the patient's need to protect her (the therapist) from her new-found success, both in professional areas and in the kind of car she owned.

The hypomanic state is followed by depression

This in turn was followed by a session (number 10) in which the hypomanic bubble had burst. The patient was depressed and retarded and had had the impulse to throw herself under a train. The therapist eventually managed to get from her that she had been home over the week-end, and she now described with deep feeling how much her crippled sister, Beth, had recently deteriorated. 'On the way back to the train she had felt she just wanted to find a husband and stay at home and have children, and not fight any more.' The therapist must have been having an off day, because she apparently did not make any interpretations linking success-ful competition with damage to Beth, nor pointing out the abandonment of mascu-line strivings, which the patient must have felt in some way to be dangerous.

In Session 14 the patient announced that her boy-friend, James, who was a highly successful young man, had been offered a job at Bristol University and would soon leave. Towards the end of the session she spoke of wanting to 'smash' him, presumably for leaving her (this word is significant, in view of the events reported at follow-up).

In Sessions 15 and 16 she returned to the theme of being successful: she had been transferred to another ward, which represented promotion, though she seemed to need to play this down. She also revealed that she now had a new boy-friend, which she had kept secret until now; and she started being provocative to the therapist, talking about the therapist's 'counter-transference', and then laugh-ing at her when she didn't know what to answer.

The climax of therapy; therapeutic effects; premature termination

The climax came in Session 17. There seemed to have been a major therapeutic effect: the patient had gone for interview for a course at London University, and had argued extremely effectively with her interviewers, refuting their suggestion that she was aiming too high. The therapist took up the competitiveness in this, and (being well trained in gestalt work) suddenly suggested that she and the patient should exchange places in the treatment room. This completely altered the patient's perception of the therapist – she now saw the therapist as smaller, and noticed wrinkles round her eyes and various nervous habits. She also said that she was afraid that she might hit the therapist, who partly resembled one of her older sisters. She mentioned that a senior colleague, with whom she had been assertive, had recently died; and the therapist reiterated interpretations about fear of damaging people with her competitiveness, linking this with the father and sister.

In Session 18 there was more evidence of therapeutic effects. London University had commended her for the way she had handled the interviews and had said that they would accept her next year if she applied. However, she has now been accepted for a course at Bristol (which is where James is going).

In Session 19 there was even further evidence of her effectiveness: she has attended a conference at the Tavistock because the psychiatrists at her work could not come, and she presented a case without preparation and with great success. People there related to her 'on the same level'. The therapist linked this with the gestalt session, in which the patient had felt that she and the therapist were on the same level.

After Session 20 the therapist fell ill. Shortly afterwards the patient had to take up her place at Bristol, and therapy – intended to be 30 sessions – was terminated prematurely.

Follow-up (4 years 1 month)

At Bristol she had returned to living with James. He finally broke with her, not surprisingly, after she had had a violent outburst of rage in which she smashed up one of his treasured possessions – 'that's for keeping me awake till 3 in the morning, that's for always leaving me to do the washing up, that's for. . .' and so on. It was clear that this outburst had resulted from accumulated resentment about bending over backwards to please him and never complaining about his lack of consideration. She is now as depressed as ever. She is clearly functioning below her potential at work, where she has refused promotion, and she is now abandoning this career without knowing what alternative to take up.

Improvements are: that she has been able to prevent herself from being exploited at work (though obviously not in her relation with James), and that she feels more like a woman, which is reflected in the way she dresses. Nevertheless, there is still considerable residual anger against men, as is shown by her remark, 'I would never cook for a man'.

Thus her improvements are balanced by deterioration, and both judges saw little justification in giving her a score other than 0.

Two years later she accepted further therapy with a male trainee psychiatrist, in which she was considerably helped, but this is not considered in the present work. Some details of this follow-up are given on p. 265.

Comment

The focus of her original brief therapy consisted of guilt and anxiety about competition with women, including death wishes, arising from the relation with her elder sisters, who excluded her, and her crippled younger sister Beth, who perforce got so much attention. There seems litle doubt that this focus was highly relevant, as is indicated by the following sequence, which started in Session 8:

1 She becomes extremely successful in various areas.
2 She gets into a hypomanic state.
3 The bubble bursts and she becomes severely depressed after witnessing the deterioration in Beth, which the therapist succeeds in bringing into the open. This is then followed by
4 Apparently more genuine ability to be highly effective in a number of areas involving her work.

Nevertheless, follow-up showed that most of this improvement was built on sand.

The main focus of her subsequent therapy was her pattern of bending over backwards in order to be accepted, with immense underlying resentment about not being cared for herself – a pattern which in her upbringing had taken the form of allowing herself to be exploited and endlessly doing the chores. Presumably she had had to adopt such a stance as a way of coping with the exceedingly difficult situation caused by the presence in the home of her crippled sister, who not merely occupied much of her parents' attention but had an absolute need and right to do so. *This aspect of the patient's problem was not touched on in her original therapy.* It is worth noting that a clear hint of this theme did arise in Session 8, when she made the slip of the tongue 'dishes' for 'decisions;' but it was interpreted in terms of her conflict between tying herself to the kitchen sink, as her mother wanted, and competing intellectually as her father wanted. Subsequent events indicated that this problem was quite unresolved, as is shown by the continued pattern of bending over backwards in order to be accepted by James, the theme of her final outburst against him; and her statement, 'I would never cook for a man'.

Of course it is quite possible that, if this most gifted therapist had not been forced to terminate prematurely (because of her illness), she might have found this second focus and been able to work it through, with profound effects on the ultimate outcome.

From the point of view of psychodynamics, it is important to note the following sequence spanning her whole life, which shows that not only the above pattern of bending over backwards was unresolved, but equally unresolved was the problem of what to do with her anger when it emerged:

1 A feature of the patient's early childhood consisted of outbursts of rage, which she finally decided she had to control.
2 One of her original complaints was 'inability to channel anger'.
3 The outburst of rage at work which she described at initial assessment – though not to be encouraged in a psychiatric nurse! – had been extremely effective without being destructive, and had resulted in a feeling of liberation, so that in a way it could be described as constructive and valuable and might have marked a major step forward.
4 On the other hand, her final outburst of rage against James had not only been exceedingly destructive but had resulted both in his leaving her and in her becoming depressed, so that in the end it achieved nothing – not even a feeling of liberation.

17

Discussion of the five patients who showed minimal or no improvement

The main question to consider is what factors led to the poor outcome in these five therapies. The patients are very heterogeneous and few generalisations can be made, but the following observations can be made.

We may divide the patients into two categories: those who appear, with hindsight, to have been basically suitable for brief therapy (one patient only); and those who do not (four patients).

The first category is represented by the Psychiatric Nurse. She was taken on for treatment at a turning point in her life, in which she was experiencing an upsurge of hitherto buried feelings, and it seems even now that brief therapy should have been able to capitalise on this situation. However, most unfortunately, therapy had to be terminated prematurely because the therapist was taken ill. Moreover, one of the patient's major problems, namely her pattern of leaning over backwards to please, was entirely left out and therefore remained quite unresolved. This pattern led to steadily accumulating resentment in her relation with her boy-friend, and a final explosion in which she smashed up one of his possessions and lost him for good.

In the second category, three patients (the Accounts Clerk, Miner's Daughter, and Actress) illustrate the phenomenon of *false motivation*. Of these, the first brought up highly relevant written notes at her second assessment interview, and this apparent increase in motivation was one of the reasons why she was taken on. Nevertheless she arrived 10 minutes late for her first therapeutic session and opened with three communications about avoiding relationships. The transference that developed was graphically described by her therapist as 'Come on. Go away. Now you see me, now you don't,' which was accompanied by denial of involvement and repeated missed apppointments. It thus became clear that she was an acting-out hysteric, and that her apparently high motivation was really a hysterical mirage.

The Miner's Daughter responded well to interpretation and showed high motivation at the end of the initial interview, but in her case also this was followed by much acting out over appointments. However, these phenomena occurred in the setting of an entirely different personality from that of the patient described above. For her it seemed that feelings were too intense, and involvement was too great, with the result that she missed appointments to avoid pain. Moreover, because of the intensity of the pain, she was unable to work through her grief about traumatic experiences – not only her abortion, but also the termination of her therapy. Therapy gave the impression of working *over* important themes without working them *through*. Corresponding to this, there was an extremely intense wish to regress, which also could not be worked through and which provided a serious obstacle in her therapy. These observations raise the suspicion that really she was unsuitable for brief therapy, but this would have been very difficult to foresee at the beginning.

The Actress presented a very different problem again. Because of our doubts about her suitability she was offered six exploratory sessions, in the first five of which she was in a constant state of malignant resistance. In the sixth, the therapist brought this into the open and suggested that it should be made into the focus of therapy, to which the patient agreed enthusiastically, apparently showing a marked increase in motivation. However, in her subsequent therapy the resistance returned in full force, with the patient deliberately trying to confuse the issue, alternating between attributing her problems to her mother and to her father, and nullifying each element of apparent progress almost as soon as it was made. The result was that in spite of intense interaction, there was – once more – no working through, and at follow-up she was judged to be hardly better than when she started. Here we should add that the (male) therapist handled this very difficult and provocative patient with extreme skill and maturity, and the final judgment must be that she was unsuitable for brief therapy; but we do not believe this could have been foreseen, and it does seem that it was appropriate to make the attempt.

These patients confirm two linked research findings described in *Toward the Validation of Dynamic Psychotherapy* (Malan, 1976b), that motivation at initial assessment is not what matters, but motivation after therapy has got under way; and that acting out over appointments, which is an indication of poor motivation, is an ominous sign. Unfortunately this observation is not of much use clinically, since the drop in motivation often appears after the commitment has been made to accept the patient for treatment.

The final patient to consider is the Museum Assistant. Here the possible contra-indications were seen clearly at initial assessment – the severity of her depression, the anorexic episode, and the disturbed and sinister percepts in her ORT. Yet the calculated risk of taking her on for brief therapy seemed justified at the time, and perhaps still seems justified to this day. In any case no harm was done, since it was possible to take her on later for analysis. What was not seen was the severity of her superego pathology, which was the chief obstacle to her improving in therapy of any kind. Nevertheless it is worth pointing out that in her brief therapy there was extremely intense interaction on Oedipal themes, and that it really did seem that these problems had been largely worked through, since they played only a very minor part in her subsequent analysis.

Thus for these five patients we do not feel that the choice of brief therapy, on the evidence available, was necessarily a clinical misjudgment. This, we are afraid, is not the case with some of the patients to be presented in the next three chapters.

18

Patients who were worse

I Three patients who were wrongly diagnosed at initial assessment

The Girl with Eye Problems

Age 26, married, housewife, 20 sessions, score –0.5.

A case history emphasising the need for a proper psychiatric diagnosis at initial assessment.

Complaints: depression and eye symptoms

She has suffered from recurrent attacks of depression all her life. Two years ago she was treated with anti-depressants by her GP with apparent benefit. She wrote: 'My current tiredness, sickness, lack of appetite, and dizziness have been increasing now for 1 year. Over-reaction to any stimulus results in complete exhaustion.' She has attacks lasting a fortnight in which she doesn't want to do anything and just sits on the floor at home crying, for no reason that she knows.

One year ago she went to the hospital because of inability to focus her eyes. She was given atropine drops. She wrote that the eye drops gave her 'strange, remote, surrealistic views that I find quite unnerving.' The specialist wrote, 'Of course ciliary muscle spasm in otherwise normal eyes is the expression of emotional disturbance.' Ten weeks ago she visited her eye specialist, who wrote: 'She was in quite a critical emotional state. She had difficulty in controlling a great outburst of weeping. I was unable to understand her problem.'

History

As foreshadowed by some of the material described above, an important theme which runs through her story consists of outbursts of emotion which she is quite unable to link to any cause.

She was an only child, her father working on the management side in industry. At the age of 8 she remembers going out of the house to cry by herself on her father's vegetable patch, but she has no idea why this might be. She described frequent quarrels with her parents in which she would shout at them and hit them, but she was quite unable to say why. Her parents would respond by sending her to her room. At 10, almost certainly because her parents wanted a rest from her behaviour, she was sent abroad on a holiday for 6 weeks. The night before her departure she cut the curtains of her bedroom to pieces with a pair of scissors. Again she could not account for this, though now the reason seems obvious in terms of her fury at being rejected. Her parents were angry, but when she came back new curtains had been bought and no more was said.

Four months ago a fact about her parents' relation was revealed which may have a bearing on her history. Her mother told her that she had just discovered that her father was having an affair, and then added with some glee that the other woman couldn't have got much out of it as he had been impotent since the patient was 8. The patient's comment about this was that it made her parents seem 'less perfect and more human'. We may note that she described her attacks of crying as having occurred at the age of 8, so that one of the contributory causes for these may have been some kind of tension within the home.

The patient married 6 years ago. She wrote, 'I have a full, happy marriage although most decisions are made by myself.' (Her husband was later interviewed by a social worker at the Clinic, who cast considerable doubt on this – see below.)

There is a clear resemblance between the relation with her parents and that with her husband in that she described violent quarrels with him in which she shouts and hurls abuse at him – she has no idea why. In a recent incident he arrived home saying that the windscreen of *his* car had become shattered while he was driving it. She flew into a rage and hurled a chair at him, breaking its leg. The reason for her reaction was no clearer on this occasion than on any of the others. In the interview with the social worker her husband said of this incident: 'I assumed she knew what she was doing', and he denied having any idea that she might have been feeling angry.

She told the following story concerning the decision about whether or not to have a child: she decided to stop taking the Pill and leave it to God to determine whether she was fit to become a mother. She became pregnant but the pregnancy was ectopic and had to be terminated. She now feels that this has solved her problem, because she has proved that she and her husband are fertile but she is not fit to become a mother, and therefore she does not have to face the responsibility of having a child.

The interviewer (a male trainee psychiatrist) wrote that he was unable to give her any effective interpretations.

Comment

We found it very difficult to make sense of this story. A possible theme was disturbance in relation to men, the early evidence of which was crying on her father's vegetable patch (though this might simply have been a place where she could be alone), the later evidence being her attacks of rage against her husband.

It was decided to see her husband with a view to exploring the possibility of conjoint marital therapy.

Her husband

Her husband, a pharmacist working for a drug company, was interviewed by a (woman) social worker.

She wrote: 'The interview consisted of non-talk. He thinks you should not talk about feelings and there certainly should not be any clashes. Both he and his wife are sure that the cause of her problems lies outside the marriage. He said their sexual relation is wonderful.' She summed up: 'He appears to be an utterly defended young man, scared of any emotional experience, sceptical about psychiatry, and determined that his wife's problems are physical. He seems exactly the sort of man to have a non-marriage with.'

Therapeutic plan

We considered going ahead with our plan of conjoint marital therapy, but in view of her husband's obvious difficulty in discussing anything to do with feelings we eventually abandoned this idea.

The final decision was to offer her six exploratory sessions (as with the Actress with Elocution Problems) to see if something clear would crystallise, and then to review the situation.

The aim in these sessions was at least to get her to start thinking about some of her current behaviour patterns and their possible roots in her early history.

This was clearly an experimental case, since she hardly fulfilled any of our criteria. In particular, the psychodynamics were extremely obscure and there had been no response to interpretation.

A later hypothesis about the cause of her disturbance

Because her story as told so far makes so little sense, it is worthwhile mentioning here the hypothesis made many years later by the Individual Team, and *reached solely on the basis of the above material without access to any information derived from her therapy.* They made the inference that the problem in her childhood was that her parents were quite incapable of true emotional contact, that her outbursts were an attempt to get a genuine response from them, and that the 'compulsion to repeat' had driven her to marry a man with whom she continued exactly the same pattern. This idea makes a great deal of sense of some of the material of her therapy (particularly the patient's letter written after Session 5); and indeed the therapist did see it and work on it, with some response from the patient (see Sessions 1, 11, and 12). Moreover, it makes sense of the patient's refusal, at times, to react to her children, which she described at follow-up. It is a vindication of the Individual Team's method of working, which consisted of highly experienced clinicians putting their heads together over every scrap of available material, that this hypothesis could be reached on such slender evidence.

The first five of the exploratory sessions

The therapist was a male psychiatrist from abroad, not very experienced, but remarkably sensitive and competent with this extremely difficult case.

He did not tell her immediately of the plan, but since she started very silent he said that perhaps her silence had to do with not knowing what to expect from him. She said that this was true, and he therefore said that he would see her for six sessions and then reconsider. She now started talking quite freely, saying that when she gets depressed she sits alone in her room for hours, and the main thing that relieves her depression is 'doing something noisy, like having a row with my husband'. She tries to provoke him but instead of hitting back he just becomes worried. The therapist said that it must be frustrating to get no reaction from him, to which she said that his main fault is that he is perfect. The therapist compared this with her feelings about her parents, and added that probably she was suspicious of their perfection as well as that of her husband. To this she said, 'Yes, I just noticed it while you were saying it. I must admit it sounds true.' He therefore linked her current behaviour with her husband to that with her parents, saying that perhaps her outbursts had the aim of getting them to look after her. She said: 'It was exactly like that', and added that she was an angry child and is now an angry woman. (All this represented work on the Individual Team's hypothesis described above.) As always, the therapist was unable to get her to say any more about the cause of her anger. However, she did describe another dramatic incident in her childhood, in which she had drawn 'a splendid tree' on the wall of her bedroom. It wouldn't wash off and her parents had made her re-paint the wall.

This session contained a considerable amount of communication and was distinctly hopeful, but in Session 2 she went into resistance. The therapist tried again to explore her need to get reactions from other people and mentioned her underlying anger with her parents and her husband. She now completely nullified her previous communication by saying that she was happy most of the time, and why did he insist that she was angry?

For brevity we will give few details of Sessions 3 to 5. An important remark that she made in Session 3 was that 'she used to cry, curl up, and be alone, and it was cosy, but now. . .' and she started weeping. The therapist tried to get from her what had caused the change, but she wouldn't answer.

In Session 5 she said that her eyes were now as bad as ever, 'and she can make things disappear by voluntarily blurring her vision.' The therapist mentioned the therapeutic plan and said that next week they would take a decision about the future.

Thus the first five sessions had contained moments of communication; but these had alternated with resistance, and it was not at all clear where they were leading. We were not prepared for the following bombshell, in the form of a letter written to the therapist after the fifth session.

A letter to the therapist

I feel obliged to write things down and clarify them. Firstly when young I found that saying my eyes hurt brought a different response than, say, stomach ache. I even discovered that dwelling on imaginary symptoms gave me a strange lurching sensation in my stomach (looking back, an orgasm?). When I first married I found I could only reach a climax in intercourse if my husband was aware of my rather dim sight. To this end I called upon an old habit of unfocusing my eyes. I acquired a pair of glasses and became 'short-sighted'. My husband is not a confirmed Christian and I managed easily to forget my lie. Then I told myself that it would be too dramatic to change back and that it would be just as sinful in reverse. Knowing that I mustn't use 'eyes' as a comforter I became more remote, depressed. The sin came home to me when I realised that the damage was for real. I am still not sure that I am not using the 'cure', yourself, eye drops, poor sight etc. etc. to the same ends although I am giving my visits to you as a sign of my good intentions.

At first reading this letter appeared utterly bizarre, but with more careful thought it does in fact make complete sense in terms of the extreme lengths to which she had to go in order to get attention from her parents – as clearly formulated in the Individual Team's hypothesis. Moreover, intensive study of the material during the writing of this book does suggest an explanation for the connection between her eyesight and sex: namely that dim sight is connected in her mind with becoming the centre of attention and being cared for; that when her husband is *aware of* her dim sight she can feel that he is caring for her; and it is only then that she can become sexually aroused.

However, because the supervisor was blinded by the strange quality of her writing, none of this was seen at the time. We felt that we needed more information to confirm or contradict our impression that she was psychotic, and – in spite of our knowing that this might seriously disturb her – the therapist was instructed to suggest in the next session that she should come for a Rorschach. This he did, saying that it was to help us decide what our next step should be. In this session she said, 'I don't think at all about what I have written. I have carefully forgotten it.' She went on to say that if she does not think about it it doesn't exist. 'Thinking about it is *it*'. With great tact the therapist did not press her to elaborate on her letter.

A very disturbed Rorschach

The Rorschach was given by a woman psychologist. The patient's behaviour in the interview was extremely bizarre. She made curious repetitive movements while sitting curled up in her chair, and her statements were accompanied by florid expressions of inappropriate affect. 'Her performance on the test reveals severe disturbance of her thought processes, and on several occasions she appeared to go off into a fantasy world of associations, seemingly impervious to any intervention from me... The quality of intense anger which came through in her voice was carried over into her percepts, nearly all of which were of violent, destructive forces or damaged objects. Her fear seems to be of engulfment by primitive forces. No relationships are seen in the record, either human or animal. If two figures are seen they are seen as one, with no sense of their being in any way separate.'

Revised therapeutic plan

We were now faced with a serious dilemma: we had no vacancy for long-term treatment and it was difficult to see what could be achieved in a few sessions. To reject her at this point, after she had given us such a revealing glimpse of her inner world, would be utterly traumatic. The crucial thing was not to make her worse. After much heart-searching we decided to offer her 14 more sessions, making a total of 20, in which the therapist was to follow the principles for treating psychotic patients laid down in *Individual Psychotherapy and the Science of Psychodynamics* (Malan, 1979, p. 178): to go along with her thoughts, share them with her and try to understand them where possible, not to make any attempt to weaken defences, but to feel free to make major interpretations if the defences broke down.

The last 14 sessions

Session 7 – communication

She came up for Session 7 wearing new glasses which had been prescribed for her and said that now 'all was splendid'. She went on to say that this made her letter *seem* ridiculous, but it was *not* ridiculous and it was true that she herself had caused her eyes to become short-sighted. She said that she enjoyed being ill, but now because of the glasses she wouldn't be attracting people's attention any more. The therapist offered her the 14 more sessions, saying that he knew that her eyes were not the real problem – otherwise she could now say that she was cured and go away – but that he made his offer because he knew she believed in what she had written. She accepted gratefully.

Depression and resistance

The above session, full of communication, was followed by three sessions in which she was depressed and resistant, with long silences. The therapist could not understand what was going on and felt unable to make any useful interventions. He wrote of feeling tired, bored, bewildered, and confused, and being left with a headache.

Apparent improvement

In Session 11, however, she reported a sudden change of mood, which possibly represented a hypomanic state. She had been shopping in the West End of London, something she had not done for years. She had been extremely demanding sexually on her husband, and they had been having sex sometimes twice a day and more at week-ends. The therapist asked her if there was any change in her eyes, to which she said no, they seemed to be worse, and her glasses weren't helping any more. The therapist said he wondered whether this state of happiness served the same purpose as previous ways of trying to get a reaction from people, such as drawing the tree, or getting angry; and thus whether it was also designed to get a reaction from him, as a means of getting attention and care. She said, 'Yes, I haven't stopped talking all session and you too talked more than ever.' (All this represented further work on the focus formulated by the Individual Team, now in the transference.)

However, in between sessions she phoned to say that her eyes were much worse. In the next session (number 12) she showed the therapist a vase that she had made. The therapist made a creative interpretation: that she was shaped like the vase and needed someone to find out how to fill her, and that perhaps her phone call was an attempt to get him to do so. She said she does feel like that, and added that she could communicate better with things if she touched them. She went on to say how important it was to see well when one did pottery, and the danger was that the base of this particular vase might be too weak and the whole might collapse. He interpreted that she must feel this about herself, and that maybe the weak base could be taken as her childhood, which was insufficient to hold what came afterwards. Perhaps she was talking about a feeling of isolation, of being 'out of touch', and that eyes were not a sufficient means of communication. She said that this sounded true; and she added that she did feel isolated at home, and that she thought she could get affection and attention from her parents by complaining about her eyes, but it wasn't very successful. This again represented work on the Individual Team's focus.

Total resistance

Once more, this session of communication was followed by resistance. In the next two sessions (numbers 13 and 14) she talked almost incessantly about her eyes in a confused and sometimes bizarre way; and at the end of Session 14 – as in Session 2 – she nullified her communications of Session 12 by saying that she had been given all she wanted by her parents, and why did the therapist keep insisting that she wants attention and love?

In Session 15, which was in November, she said that her parents were always unhappy and had to pretend to enjoy Christmas, and she herself always gets depressed at this time. The therapist said that perhaps she felt neglected and was angry about it, but could not allow herself to admit it. This mention of anger now produced an immediate denial: she said she was more amused than anything else.

Perhaps because the therapist had mentioned anger – though she herself had spoken of being angry in Session 1 – she rang up and cancelled the next session (this cancelled session is counted as number 16).

Transference and termination

Sessions 17–19 were characterised by the therapist's giving well thought out transference interpretations, which included the issue of termination. In Session 17 the patient said that she did not come for the previous session because she had to buy some clay for her pottery; and that coming this time had resulted in her being rushed and spoiling the pottery that she was making. The therapist suggested that she was angry with him for interfering with her enjoyment, and added that maybe she finds it difficult to enjoy good experiences because she spoils them. She said that her husband has bought her a big machine for her pottery, which she doesn't understand, and now that she has all the materials for her pottery she is afraid of spoiling it. Her husband leaves her with all the responsibility. The therapist linked this with the transference, though without specifically mentioning the issue of termination, saying that she feels she has to be grateful and she is angry about this and expresses it by spoiling things, e.g. by staying away last session. She said yes, she wondered if the same thing happened when she stayed late in bed.

In the next session (number 18) she came very well made up, and said that she had had the best pottery class since the summer holiday. She added that she didn't understand what the therapist had said about spoiling. He said that she had to make good things into bad ones so that she could part with them without pain, and this included her treatment here. She said that this made sense. However, she then asked, 'What has all this to do with my eyes? All I get is my depression cured.' The therapist interpreted that she needed to keep the depressed part of her as a shield to avoid her feelings of being neglected by him, just as she did with her parents in her childhood. She said she misses the emotion that she feels in her depression – now that she is not depressed she feels indifferent. He tried to link this with her eyes, to which she said that she was perceiving things now as dull, and he pointed out that this was like her current feeling of indifference. She said that she quite likes her eyes as they are but she wants to stop herself from feeling like this.

In Session 19 she said that she did not consider the therapist or anything to do with the Clinic as real. He interpreted this as a defence against her feelings about termination – it is easier for her to separate if she does not consider him as a real person about whom she might have real feelings. She said this might be true, but her subsequent material showed no obvious other response.

However, before the next session the therapist received another letter, now confirming how strongly she felt about the issue of termination. A condensed version of this is as follows:

Please don't think too badly of me for sending this to you. It is 3 o'clock in the morning and I am about to panic at the thought of your abandonment. It seems like that to me now. I hate the way I see, it is the inhibition of my eyes that makes me depressed because I cannot use my eyes as an emotional release, but I am continuously reminded by their inefficiency of my 'secret'. Can I really go back to just not thinking about them? I don't think I can. I could say that you have spoiled that for me. But not true, or I wouldn't have sought you out in the first place, would I?

All I seem to have got from these visits is a mass of questions. Last night a woman made a pass at me and said that it was my eyes that attracted her. So now she knows the password.

She enjoyed them large and drugged.

I enjoy them small and myopic.

But I am constantly aware of them.

I must post this, as I say so many things during the week that you don't hear.

The therapist opened the last session (number 20) by saying that he had received her letter. She said that she was expecting people for Christmas and hadn't started preparing. She had thought of committing suicide, but had changed her mind because she thought it would be a nuisance and she knew she could cope. She went on to speak of the woman mentioned in her letter. The therapist asked what she had meant by 'password', to which she said she meant 'eyes' because talking about them made her feel erotic. The therapist translated this into a transference interpretation, including the issue of termination, saying that perhaps she was depressed now because talking about her eyes in the sessions gave her sexual pleasure and she was now going to be deprived of this. She said that she felt precisely that, talking with him. Last night she had become extremely excited sexually just by thinking about her eyes. She asked what she should do about this. He said it was very difficult to get rid of a source of pleasure like that, but that he did not think he could help her further for the time being, and that he would be available in the future if she needed to get in touch with him. She left very sadly.

Comment on therapy

It is interesting that for most of the time there was little, if anything, that was overtly psychotic in her communications, but at the time the connection between her eyes and sexual excitement remained as strange and mysterious as ever. The therapist handled her with considerable tact and skill, and since the aim of therapy was simply to hold her, to let her communicate, and not to make her worse, then he succeeded. Moreover, the Individual Team's hypothesis reveals the therapy to have been more focal than it originally appeared. Looking back over the sequence of events, we can now see that on three occasions when this focus was touched on, the patient went into intense resistance. This occurred between Sessions 1 and 2, 12 and 13, and 15 and 16 (the session that she cancelled). This pattern was not seen at the time, but it suggests now that the focus was both correct and extremely disturbing to her.

Follow-up (6 years 10 months)

Children, depression

She now has two boys, Trevor aged 6, and Christopher aged 3. She breast-fed them both up to 9 months and enjoyed it very much. However, she now appears to be so depressed and exhausted that she can hardly look after them. She described a clear pattern: when she wakes up she feels as if it is too much effort to do anything at all, but she gradually gets better during the course of the day. She manages to force herself to take the children to infant school and play school respectively. Then she hurries home and goes to bed. 'I lie in bed head first.' What this meant was that she puts her head under the bedclothes and leaves her feet hanging over the edge, feeling too lazy to take her shoes off. She lies there until 11.30, when she has to fetch Christopher back. She made the somewhat bizarre statement: 'I have *hardly ever* forgotten to fetch him.'

During a recent relatively severe attack of depression – for which no precipitating cause could be found – she fed the children on breakfast cereal three times a day. She said that she cries a lot and lets the children see her cry. At one time she used to lie on the floor and Trevor would tear at her to try and get a response from her, but the more he did so the more passive she would get. It seems possible that this behaviour unconsciously aims at repeating for the children her experience with her own parents.

The older boy, Trevor, appears to be quite normal. On the other hand, Christopher suffers from temper tantrums if she says no to him, in which he may slap her on the face. Her response is just to let him do it. He demands to have his drink in his own way, sometimes hot, sometimes cold, and out of a certain cup etc. She gives in to him, because she hasn't the strength not to.

Attacks of anger

She said that since she had the children her attacks have largely disappeared. The last time that she remembers was an occasion when Trevor, at the age of 1, had fallen downstairs, and she had screamed and shouted.

Is she in touch with the cause of her emotions?

The answer is, emphatically not. She could account for neither her attacks of crying nor her attacks of anger. She spoke as follows: 'They are surface emotions, easy emotions. They're *bodily* emotions, they're not really *my* emotions. My body cries and my body throws things.'

The relation with her husband

Her immediate answer to a question about this was, 'It's fine. We enjoy each other very much. He is rather untouched by what goes on.' This seems to imply that the situation of non-communication continues as before. Recently she went to the Headmaster to find out how Trevor was getting on, and her husband was surprised that she should have done so. However, they do seem to have a fair amount of companionship, including social relations.

Sex, and her eye symptoms

As far as sex is concerned, there has been a recent falling off. 'We both feel old and tired. I mentioned this to him but he denied it.' She can only get orgasm either if she is on top of him, or if she thinks about her eyes. She could no more account for the connection between eyes and sexual feelings than she could before, though she said she knew it went back to when she was very small.

Because of her difficulty in focusing she cannot drive a car. She continues to use eye drops every day.

Creativeness

She continues with her pottery, which makes her some money, but she regards it as a chore, tends to skimp it, and gets little pleasure from it. We therefore cannot describe this as an expression of her creativeness.

Borderline phenomena

Obviously some of her remarks and her reported behaviour, as described above, are very strange. In addition she said, 'When I was pregnant with Trevor I felt he wasn't my husband's child. It was just me and my eyes. He wasn't even a proper baby.' She said that sometimes Trevor looks 'flat, like cardboard', and added that this only began to happen when he was out of the baby stage, and it hadn't yet happened with Christopher.

Her comments on her therapy

Her main feelings about her therapy were of resentment. 'I am no better. He didn't do anything for me.' He had written a final letter to her GP, which she had pressured the GP into allowing her to read, and she was particularly annoyed that he had written that he didn't understand a communication about her eyes till the very last session – she thought she had made it absolutely clear. She had felt very let down when her therapy finished. The only positive thing that she said was that her therapist had made her realise that her 'laziness' was an illness, and therefore she had felt less guilty about it.

Discussion of follow-up

If her present state is carefully compared with her state when she first came, all the evidence suggests that in herself she is little changed, though the birth of the children has introduced a disturbing factor into the situation. She is still severely depressed, her eye symptoms are unchanged, she remains as unable to account for her emotions as before, there is no obvious change in the relation with her husband, and the borderline phenomena remain.

She was assessed by the four members of the Individual Team. Two judges gave a score of 0, while two regarded her as worse because of the disturbed relation with her children. Thus the scores were 0.0, –1.0, 0.0 and –1.0: mean –0.5.

Postscript

The follow-up interviewer was extremely worried about the children, feeling that they were considerably at risk. He therefore phoned the (woman) psychiatrist by whom the patient was currently being supported. The psychiatrist was fully aware of the situation and was in touch with the Social Services, who had sent a social worker to visit the home. It seemed that nothing more could be done.

The Borderline Graduate Clerk

Age 28, single, score –1.0.

This patient was given a total of about 50 sessions. To anticipate what emerged early in his therapy, he turned out to be far more disturbed than was originally detected. He had originally been offered 30 weekly sessions; but because of the nature of his condition he was then given further sessions – of a largely supportive kind – at 2-monthly intervals over a period of 2½ years. This would seem to be a much more realistic way of handling such a patient than the more strictly time-limited therapy offered routinely to our other patients.

Complaints and precipitating factor for seeking treatment

His complaints, of long standing, consisted of a typical constellation of apparently Oedipal problems: severe difficulty with male authority; extreme shyness with women, to whom he can only relate to in fantasy; and generalised tension.

He sought treatment after a woman at work, with whom he was in love at a distance, announced her engagement.

History

He was the elder of two children, his father being a solicitor. The two disturbing factors in his childhood were the birth of his younger brother, of whom he was extremely jealous, when he was 2; and the relation with his father. He was very close to his father up to the age of 11, when he feels that his father turned against him, becoming a 'tyrant' and repeatedly and arbitrarily punishing him. His father himself was going through some kind of emotional crisis at this time, precipitated by difficulties in finding a job.

In his adolescence there were many quarrels between his mother and father, in which he took his mother's side. He said that at this time he felt much closer to his mother than to his father.

The patient was very intelligent and clearly had considerable potential. His academic career started well at school, but from University onwards it showed a marked deterioration. He studied engineering and got a poor degree. He then tried to enter the teaching profession but failed the Certificate of Education. He left a job that made use of his qualification in engineering and from then on took a series of jobs well below his capacity, frequently leaving because of difficulties with bosses. He gets extremely angry with bosses but swallows it and never disagrees with them. He is currently doing a humdrum job as a clerk.

He has never had an adequate relation with a woman except in fantasy. He often feels himself in love with a girl at work and may succeed in asking her out, but he then completely freezes up and finds himself quite unable to make conversation with her over dinner.

Dynamics of interview

He was seen by a male trainee psychiatrist who gave him a highly dynamic interview, but did not give enough detail in his report to make clear exactly what happened.

In the early stages of the interview the patient was extremely apprehensive, and the psychiatrist made a number of interpretations about the patient's rage at being in the interview situation. At this the patient experienced what the psychiatrist described as 'tremendous' anxiety, but when he was able to speak of his anxiety openly he calmed down considerably.

Further quotations from the psychiatrist's report indicate the kind of work that was done in the interview: 'Interpretations as to his resentment of authority, and his rage at being in a subordinate position, were easily accepted and facilitated his associative work in this area.' Later in the interview the psychiatrist linked together the patient's difficulties at work, his difficulties in the interview situation, and rage against his father. 'On several occasions he extended the interpretation even further, making links between his current situation and the situation in his childhood.'

Towards the end of the interview the psychiatrist wrote: 'He was also able to link up tremendous feelings of rejection and dependency in his relation with his mother, stirred up by the birth of his brother, with his current reaction to women: that with them too, as with male authority figures, he experiences very intense rage and thus becomes frightened of his own aggression.'

Projective testing

He was given the ORT and Rorschach by a male psychologist. In view of the severity of the patient's problems, the tests showed remarkably little disturbance, and the psychologist wrote of the Rorschach that 'it appears to have many features of a normal healthy record'. There were no psychotic features.

Reason for acceptance for brief psychotherapy and therapeutic plan

The psychodynamics seemed unusually clear. We formulated the focus as intense anger against both of the other two people in a triangular situation, originating in two triangles in his childhood, namely those involving first, his mother and brother, and second, his mother and father. He had obviously responded very favourably to interpretations along these lines.

Course of brief therapy (33 sessions)

The therapist

The therapist was probably the most experienced of all our trainees (see Therapist E in Chapter 5). As will be seen, he was extremely sensitive and mature. His one fault – presumably a consequence of his being in psychoanalytic training – was a somewhat compulsive use of transference interpretations. This was entirely appropriate in the first three sessions, but not always appropriate thereafter.

Therapy with this patient was exceptionally rich and long, and it is necessary to be selective in describing it.

The first three sessions: transference resistance followed by near-psychotic communication

The initial assessment, including the Rorschach, had given no inkling of the patient's true disturbance; and indeed the supervisor was so blinded by the clarity of the patient's Oedipal material that he even failed to note some transparent clues, consisting of communications with a paranoid tinge, in Sessions 1 and 2. This was therefore an example of the saying that 'there is no greater enemy of a psychiatric diagnosis than a psychodynamic diagnosis' – which applies even more strongly to the next patient to be described, the Robot Man.

The first three sessions were almost entirely taken up with his anxieties about therapy and his relation with the therapist; and the therapist's long experience in the use of transference interpretations stood him in good stead.

Early in Session 1 the patient said that his initial interview had been very helpful, but he went on to use the material of the interview in what seems a highly intellectual way: 'I used to think I lacked mothering, but now I feel perhaps it was fathering. My father punished me for ridiculous reasons. He locked me in a room for not eating certain beans.' He went on to say, 'My mother went away to have my brother when I was 2 and I then turned against her'.

The therapist correctly perceived this material as defensive and concentrated on the transference. When the patient spoke of a fear that people would not listen to him, the therapist related this to himself, to which the patient said, 'Yes, I fear I'll disappoint people and their expectations of me.' The therapist asked whether he feared disapproval and being pushed away in his therapy. The patient said he did fear being abandoned, and that at the end of the 30 sessions there would be no more treatment and he would feel very cut off.

This work on the transference now gave the patient the confidence to bring out his negative feelings towards the Clinic: 'The psychiatrist who interviewed me said it was hard for me to talk about the rage that I felt at the coming of my brother. I resented that theory being forced on me. It was just like the psychologist. He gave me theories that I resented very much.' The therapist linked this with the patient's father; and at the end of the session the patient admitted that he felt resentful when the therapist tried to push similar theories on to him.

There was some misunderstanding about the date of the next appointment, and the patient failed to come. In the next session (number 2) he again started highly intellectual, saying he thought he was a 'schizoid personality', and speculating about paternal and maternal deprivation in his childhood. He added a new detail, that when his mother returned home with his baby brother, he had 'thrown muck' at her. The therapist eventually suggested he was ambivalent about coming for treatment and this had shown in the mix-up over the appointment. Very soon the patient spoke of two men, a chaplain and a psychiatrist, to whom he had gone for help but who had ended by saying they could not help him, which the therapist linked to fears about his therapy here. The patient associated to the hostile relation with his father in his childhood. At the age of 13 this had progressed to his singing insulting songs about his father's peculiarities in his presence. He said he regarded his father as a 'vampire-lover' who wanted literally to take the blood of life from him. Eventually he said that he wanted strength from his father but couldn't get it, and that his father had said that he washed his hands of him – thus clearly making the link with the chaplain and psychiatrist mentioned above. The therapist asked if he was afraid that he would do something that would make him (the therapist) wash his hands of him, to which there was an extraordinary response: 'When I pulled my cigarette pack out and stumbled with the cigarette, I felt you were disapproving, but if I told you this you'd ridicule me.'

The remark about the 'vampire-lover' and this last communication represented the first clear-cut indications that the patient was borderline, but if we had had any doubt it was soon swept away by the disturbed and often paranoid quality of his communications in the next session (number 3). Early in the session there was a silence, and the therapist urged him to say what he was thinking. He said that he was having confused and vicious fantasies, many of which were about arguments with his father, and the feeling was that if he didn't win the argument he would be 'annihilated'. He went on to speak of conflict with authorities at work over their rigid approach. He then said that someone had come into the office and had threatened to smash all the windows. The therapist asked whether he also would like to smash things and do away with people who restricted him. The patient said yes, and went on to speak of various thoughts and fantasies, which included both descriptions of his failure with women and further details of his hostility towards authority, now with a clear paranoid flavour. He spoke of patients rebelling against their doctors and nurses, and 'using tablets as missiles to undo the evil medical team with'. He spoke of people who were planted with drugs and then arrested; and of a patient who had drawn a 'doodle' which had been shown to a psychiatrist, who had said that he was undoubtedly mad. The therapist linked all these communications with the transference, with which the patient partially agreed. He ended by speaking of being able to 'tune in on people's wavelengths', a manner of speaking which, taken literally, appears as a delusion in schizophrenia.

Revised therapeutic plan

When this session was reported to the Workshop we were put in the same kind of dilemma as with the Girl with Eye Problems – but the outcome was a different decision. It appeared that the patient was much too disturbed for brief psychotherapy as we knew it, but as always we had no vacancy for long-term treatment; and on the other hand it would be unthinkable to reject him. We therefore decided on a therapeutic experiment designed to answer the following question: is it possible to help a patient like this substantially in a short time, as originally planned? Because the degree of communication that he showed was so deep and strong, we also decided to pull no punches in the work, and to give him interpretations as deep as his material seemed to indicate.

From now on it is only possible to give the highlights of his therapy in order to convey the flavour of the work that was done with him, including some of this excellent therapist's mistakes.

A summary of the patient's pathology

It may help to make sense of the material if we give our interpretation of the main pathology that emerged. This consisted of violent and primitive impulses aroused in him when he was rejected by a woman in favour of another male. These impulses, originally directed against both his mother and his brother, seem to have been perceived as coming back at him from the outside world (the mechanism of 'paranoid projection') and thus to have given rise to paranoid feelings. The whole constellation of feelings was then incorporated into his Oedipus complex and his relation with his father, which resulted in a similar mixture of hostility and paranoid anxiety in his relation with male authority.

It is worth noting that on the face of it this hypothesis is identical with the initial focus as formulated above; but of course that focus took no account of the much more primitive psychic mechanisms that were revealed.

Sessions 5 to 8: missed focal interpretations lead to increased disturbance

In Session 5 the patient described a feeling of emptiness which went back to early childhood. 'It happened when I felt rejected or shunned.' This led to a flood of anger, expressed in the session, which he had experienced at school from age 9. 'I was an aggressive child. I hit people. I hit a friend with a rock and my parents kept me confined in the garden.' Shortly after this he said, 'Cain didn't get a fair hearing over his aggression towards Abel. The emphasis should have been on Cain's rehabilitation.' Very surprisingly, the therapist seems to have missed relating this to the obvious interpretation of murderous feelings towards the patient's brother.

In Session 6 the patient reported that he had felt 'numb', 'bored', 'like being half dead', over the week-end after going out with friends on Friday night. It eventually emerged that there had been a girl in the party with whom it had not gone well; and he also mentioned a 'very sensual' girl at University with whom he had spoiled the relation and who had eventually left him. This was a clue to exploring the intense and disturbing feelings aroused in him by rejection, and interpreting the corresponding defence of 'numbness' and 'boredom'. However, the therapist missed this, and since the patient also said that the relation with the girl was an emotional thing and not just a 'professional meeting of minds', the therapist got diverted on to the patient's feelings about the professional relationship in the transference; and at the end of the session the patient said, 'this numbness isn't reduced'.

In the next session (number 7) the patient's early remarks were tinged with paranoid feelings. He spoke of resenting being laughed at by people who were superior. 'I view those who are older as somehow more gifted and *cunning*.' 'Authority has an inner security. It's what I want, but I don't want it tinged with off-handedness and charity.' The therapist linked all this with the transference, which was obviously correct, but it seems now that he was not specific enough and that the real problem was the missed interpretation of the previous session. This was confirmed when the patient's unconscious clearly asked again, and more literally, for an interpretation of the disturbing degree of violence evoked in him in response to rejection by a woman. He spoke of having been 'given the push' by a girl at University (it is not clear whether this was the same girl as the one mentioned above). A little later he said, 'One night I got a knife out and slashed at my books. I had feared I was going to do this.' Once more, the therapist missed the connection and got involved in the transference (as mentioned above, this over-use of transference is one of the disadvantages of being in psychoanalytic training when one embarks on brief psychotherapy). His account continues: 'I interpreted that although he wanted what was in the books, the wish to slash at the books, the container, the authority, was very strong. Further, these feelings of slashing out could well be present towards me, as being a person whom he would like something from, yet feels constricted by. The response was, "It hasn't happened yet. It did happen with a missionary-like categorising friend, who was over-bookish and tried to be too clever".' We hope this excellent therapist treating a very difficult patient will not mind if we relate this communication to himself.

This was followed by a session (number 8) in which some very clear material about relations within his family alternated with two utterly obscure dreams. The material about his family was as follows: he had experienced protective as well as hostile feelings towards his brother, and the first dream made a reference to this; but he also had many fights with him up to the age of 16, and at one time 'refused to speak to him for 2 years'. As far as his parents were concerned, the important information was that he was quite close and intimate with his mother in adolescence, and she confided in him that she never enjoyed sex and 'would rather have a good cup of tea'. His father had tried to talk personally to him after the age of 16, but he didn't respond. The therapist said that in a way he was closer to each of his parents than they were to each other; to which the patient said that he seemed to have some 'mystical power' (another borderline communication) that was needed to draw them together. He told of an incident at the age of 14 in which he had a cold and was taken into bed between his parents. 'My father said "now it is complete", as though I fulfilled their love. I felt very embarrassed, sensing great frustration in him.' (It is worth noting that this incident seems to contradict the almost wholly black picture that he painted about his relation with his father in adolescence.) He went on to say that he caused division between his parents as well as bringing them together. At the age of 16 he bought a present for his mother and his father flew into a tantrum, accusing him of bribing her. His mother said that his father was jealous of the attention that the patient took away from him.

Amongst this very clear Oedipal material there were the two dreams mentioned above. The first, which he dreamed the night before the session, contained such details as the following: he was trying to help his brother get through a hole in a fence. Through the hole there was a road, and there were two dogs guarding 'coal or something'. 'There was another substance in the road which was reddish-orange-brownish' – in his associations he said it was 'rather like afterbirth'. The second was a recurrent dream, told late in the session: 'It's a sensation of being closed in, yet expanding, like in a womb. There is a bright and sharp needle being enclosed in a blanket. This closes in and it's a "feeling" kind of experience'. The therapist did his best with these two dreams, but their relevance to the rest of the material, and the relevance of his interpretations, is not at all obvious. Because of the dreams, the impression that this session created was of confusion and disturbance of a near-psychotic quality.

Session 9: resolution of the situation with the help of supervision

One of the advantages of being in possession of written accounts of the therapy is that supervisors can re-acquaint themselves with the material of previous sessions, and thus are better able to put a current session in context. In this particular case, the supervisor formed the hypothesis that the disturbance shown in this session was the result of the missed interpretations of Sessions 6 and 7 about violence and paranoid projection in response to being rejected. He urged the therapist to create as many opportunities as possible to give this interpretation in the next session.

In the next session (number 9) this supervision bore fruit. The patient opened by speaking of being 'used' by his parents but holding his anger inside. Later he described feeling rejected by some women at a disco. 'I never have ideas of women in chains or using whips on them. If I feel an erection – I mean rejection – I just end up turning my back and feeling regret.'

The therapist interpreted that his anger at being rejected by women 'seemed to be projected on to people about him, such as parents'. The patient spoke of feeling rejected by authority-figures, and also of his feeling that his parents had worked their hang-ups out on him; and he went on to say that as soon as he sensed any kind of rejection it set up a vicious circle and intensified these feelings. He then spoke of being unable to kiss a girl at a party when he was at High School, and feeling that the 'wise guys' at the party were sneering at him. This paranoid feeling about rival men was to play an important part in subsequent sessions. The therapist gave a summing-up interpretation: that the patient had started by speaking of his parents as 'using' him, and had then gone on to talk of rejection by women; and was he perhaps really talking about his mother as the rejecting woman and his father as a kind of wise guy? The patient agreed enthusiastically and said that these were very powerful feelings. He ended by saying that he felt cheated and resentful because he had been 'programmed' by his parents all his life.

Sessions 11 and 12: anger in the transference leads to sudden freeing of the patient's unconscious

Session 11, which was described in Chapter 1, represents the climax of therapy. Please turn back to that chapter for the account of this.

Between sessions there was now a further freeing. In the next session (number 12) the patient reported a mass of dreams revealing very literal and primitive Oedipal feelings, but without much of the previous flavour of paranoia. One dream involved a woman who seemed to be a sort of sister. He wanted to fondle her breasts, and she seemed like 'someone close to him with whom he had shared his life for a long time' – a fairly obvious reference to his mother. This was followed by dreams containing male enemies, his father and a priest and (slightly paranoid) 'two fighting, vicious guys'. Then, an obscure, primitive dream in which a brother-figure turned into a mother-figure and her nipples grew long and protruding. The therapist took this as a highly disguised reference to sexual feelings for the mother, and hinted at this by saying that the nipples seemed to grow into an erect penis; to which the patient spoke of discovering masturbation at the age of 14. The therapist then spoke more openly of the Oedipal constellation, suggesting that the patient had been sexually stimulated by his mother and felt hostility from his father. This led first to literal fears of castration: a priest who had denounced masturbation, and his mother saying that if he didn't wash his penis a dog would come and bite it off; and then to a literal reference to sexual feelings for the mother, when the patient asked if babies became sexually stimulated while feeding.

Therapeutic effects

The apparent consequence of this deep and effective work was that in Session 14 the patient reported a number of improvements: he had successfully got through a probation period at work, which he had not expected; he was enjoying expressing himself by playing the piano; and there was evidence that authority-figures seemed less threatening, for his father had been friendly to him and he had managed to get on well with an uncle whom he disliked.

The rest of therapy: work on termination

An important moment occurred in Session 19, when the patient reported a dream in which his mother was pregnant again, and in his associations he expressed considerable anger against her. The therapist, mindful that termination was approaching, suggested that the end of therapy might seem to the patient like the therapist 'getting pregnant with another patient'. The patient eventually said, 'I guess brother-figures are all around me.'

In later sessions the therapist concentrated further on interpretations about termination, the main theme of which was the issue of whether the patient could preserve good feelings about his therapy inside himself in face of his anger about being abandoned. The patient continued to work very hard and responded well to this kind of interpretation.

Continued supportive therapy (17 sessions)

There was a preliminary termination after 33 sessions, but with a definite appointment made for a follow-up interview in 2 months' time. This developed into his being seen at 2-monthly intervals for the next 2½ years, a total of about 50 sessions. The therapist wrote that therapy was largely supportive during this period. There was one exception: a session towards the end where the patient reported a series of vivid dreams, in one of which he felt great envy of his brother who was having sexual relations with his mother in the next room.

The position at final termination

At the end of the 50 sessions the patient had got a job as proof-reader for an engineering journal, which made use both of his degree and his interest in writing. He remained very isolated from people of both sexes, but he visited his family from time to time. There seemed to be considerably better contact with his father. Moreover there was a general lessening of persecutory feelings, both with his family and at work.

Long-term follow-up (5 years 5 months since session 33)

Four years after Session 33 the patient applied for treatment to the London Clinic of Psychoanalysis, but he was turned down and referred to another psychotherapy centre. Here he was taken on by a woman therapist. His follow-up interview was given while he was still in this later treatment.

The follow-up was carried out by a member of the Individual Team without the knowledge of the very disturbed material that had emerged during therapy. Nevertheless the interviewer said that there were a number of occasions during the interview when he thought of the possibility that the patient was borderline.

The essence of the follow-up is that the patient seems to have given up almost entirely on human relations, and indeed on emotions.

He is still living alone in the same bed-sitting room, and sees few friends of either sex. He had one relation with a very disturbed girl which ended in disaster, with the result that he has withdrawn from women and has even found his fantasy life considerably stunted.

As far as work is concerned, after a series of extremely menial jobs he got the proof-reading job mentioned above, and he has now given this up to become a student again. The extraordinary aspect of this is that he denied having given any thought whatsoever to what he would do when his studies finished.

His problems over employment seemed clearly to be related to his difficulties with authority, but he at first denied this. When pressed, he admitted that his relation with authority produced in him 'on the one hand a paralysis, and on the other a deep blackness'. This was one of the strange remarks that gave an impression of his being borderline.

He seems to have entirely accepted his present state of withdrawal, which represents a major contrast from his original state, in which his written material was shot through with descriptions of the pain of loneliness.

In the interview he showed a quite amazing degree of denial. On a number of occasions he not only denied that he had feelings now but denied that he had ever had them. This applied particularly to anger. He said that his rage was 'just irritability'. He also denied his original statement that his relation with his father had changed for the worse when he was 11, saying that it had always been inadequate.

For his paranoidally tinged and extraordinarily distorted recollections of his therapy please see Chapter 1.

Final comment

This was a very disappointing end to an extremely intense and apparently effective therapy. Particularly disapppointing was the amount of paranoid-tinged resentment left in the patient about both his therapy and his therapist, and his contemptuous dismissal of anything of value in his experience. This was hardly the anticipated reward for the therapist's excellent and sensitive work, which involved a great deal of attention to the transference, including much work on termination, and which would have been expected at least to have taken the edge off the patient's negative feelings. Moreover, the format of therapy, with long-term supportive treatment following the original 33 sessions, would seem to have been a realistic experiment.

The whole story only serves to show how difficult it is to treat patients of this kind, and indeed how unrealistic it is to attempt to treat them with brief psychotherapy.

All four members of the Individual Team gave scores of –1.0.

The Robot Man

Age 26, single, Patents Officer, 30 sessions, score –1.0.

For reasons of discretion we can only give a skeleton account of this patient and his therapy.

Initial assessment

The patient's complaint was a form of 'derealisation', as if everything was happening outside him and he was watching a play on the stage.

He was an only child. Up to the age of 12 he was totally compliant, but at this age he became extremely rebellious. The result was a series of major rows with his parents, some involving physical violence, which continued for several years. He dated the onset of his symptom also from the age of 12. At first he could switch it on and off voluntarily, but eventually it became permanent and he was unable to get rid of it.

He was interviewed by an extremely experienced Consultant psychiatrist, well aware of the need for a psychiatric diagnosis. Although the patient's written material had indicated considerable disturbance, this impression was mitigated at interview, and eventually good contact was made. Interestingly, the patient was quite unaware of the coincidence in time between the onset of his rebelliousness and his symptom, and when this was pointed out it was something of a revelation to him. He then agreed wholeheartedly with the interpretation that he had developed his symptom with the aim of preventing the situation from getting completely out of control, but that in the end it had become automatic. His response was: 'I just had to. I didn't know what might happen.'

Thus this history shows a pattern that is frequently encountered in psychiatric work: the patient quite consciously employs a device in order to distance himself from his feelings and prevent them from getting out of control, but this then becomes automatic and involuntary. Another example in the present series is the Psychiatric Nurse with Attacks of Rage, who at the age of 11 made a conscious effort to blank off her anger in order to stop her outbursts of temper, with the result that she lost most of her capacity for feelings of all kinds. However, there was a difference between the two patients, in that the Psychiatric Nurse succeeded in stopping her outbursts, while the present patient did not – and indeed his symptom was still present even during the rows themselves – but the end result, with the symptom becoming automatic, was the same.

Towards the end of a second initial assessment interview the patient spoke of being split into two parts: there was his 'Self' and the 'Robot', and it was the Robot who reacted to things and people outside. As a result his Self was 'unshakable'. More recently, however, this seemed to have broken down, and he had felt 'raw', for no reason that he could discover. Interpretation of the obvious defensive nature of this split as a way of protecting himelf from being hurt brought a moment of important insight: he suddenly realised that the recent precipitating event for this feeling of rawness had been the break-up of a relation with a girl.

Reason for acceptance for brief psychotherapy

The psychopathology seemed absolutely clear and good contact had been made on the focal problem. The patient was highly motivated for treatment but also highly resistant, not really being sure that he wanted to give up the protection of his symptom.

Therapy (30 sessions)

The therapist was a mature, highly competent, and sensitive (male) psychiatrist, later to become qualified as an analyst, who handled the patient's material extremely well.

Therapy went exactly according to plan. The focus consisted of the various devices that the patient used in order to avoid true involvement, which included both his main symptom and the split between his Self and the Robot. This focus was dealt with in the transference as well as in his life outside.

Follow-up (5 years)

His main symptom was still present but somewhat better. He said he was 'more positive' with people and described a moment of constructive self-assertion at work.

His relation with girls seems disturbed and he hasn't had a girl-friend for 2 years. He said that if he stayed in a relation for any length of time some internal process was set in motion which caused his mind to become 'jammed up'.

So far, it might seem that there were some minimal improvements, indicating a possible score of about 0.5. However, in talking about work he gradually made it clear that he was developing ideas about being spied upon by his boss. Both judges gave a score of –1.0.

Comment

With hindsight we can see that the symptom of derealisation, together with the split into his Self and the Robot – however intelligible these might be in psychodynamic terms – should have been regarded as possible pointers to deeper pathology than was considered at the time. Yet he showed no trace of disturbed communication either at initial assessment or during his entire therapy; and a final judgment is that the attempt at brief psychotherapy was justified on the evidence, and that no one could have foreseen the ultimate outcome. Nevertheless, this patient illustrates once again that there is no greater enemy of a psychiatric diagnosis than a psychodynamic diagnosis.

19

Patients who were worse

II A patient who ought to have given a favourable outcome

The Victimised Telephonist

Age 33, single, 12 sessions, score –1.0.

Referral

This was the result of sensitive work on the part of an osteopath, whom she consulted for trouble with her back. He detected the extreme degree of emotional tension in her and suggested she should ask her GP to refer her to the Tavistock.

History

She was the middle of three children, and the only girl, in a working-class family in the far West of England. The family appears to have been largely empty of affection: there was hardly any physical affection from her mother, and none whatsoever from her father. Nowadays, if she tries to kiss her father goodbye he just stands rigid and doesn't respond at all.

In spite of this she clearly has considerable resources. She went to work as a salesgirl in a department store at 15, but by her early 20s had been made a manageress. It was here that she met the only important man in her life, the immediate cause of the present trouble. He is a Greek businessman, married, and 20 years older than she is. She fell in love with him and they started a sexual relation. She finally came down to London in order to be near him. He installed her in a flat and used to visit her several times a week. They could never have long together except when she accompanied him on business trips abroad. Her relation with him continued for 7 years.

However, one day about a year ago he reminded her that their original agreement had been that he would be open with her if he wanted to terminate the relationship. He said that now was the time, but she could not get out of him any reason for this. (In fact it became clear later that this was the point at which she had begun for the first time to express her own needs to him.) The result was the precipitation of her current state of depression.

Dynamics of interview

The (male) psychiatrist pointed out how calm she was in recounting these events. She said, 'I am basically like this. I don't want to cry any more.' He confronted her repeatedly with her avoidance of her anger, which brought out that after their parting the man friend had said he was tempted to come back, and he was still physically attracted by her. 'He never said he missed *me* as a person, he just missed sex. I felt so *insulted.* When we were together I had to protect him from exposure wherever we went.' The interviewer said, 'You protected *him,* he didn't protect *you,*' to which she said, 'I can see it better now. He never really looked after me.'

At this point the interviewer made the link with the lack of care in her child-hood, and brought home to her a lifelong pattern of leaning over backwards to please in an unsuccessful attempt to get some love. She described how her mother wanted to go out at week-ends and therefore left her to look after her younger brother, with the result that she had to refuse invitations from potential boy-friends.

She said she sometimes used to wish she was ill so that her parents would be forced to look after her. The psychiatrist pointed out her recent physical symptoms, 'Then your body has been saying. . .'. She interrupted, 'Please help me.'

At the end of the interview she said, 'I feel there are a lot of things deep down which I have never talked about and need to get off my chest, like being angry. I could have phoned his home and pestered him, but I couldn't do it. That night I did throw a glass at the wall. Perhaps I should have smashed everything in the house.'

Side by side with this evidence for high motivation, however, she ended by saying that she wanted therapy to be as short as possible.

Reason for acceptance for brief psychotherapy

The whole story hangs together in terms of her pattern of compliance, starting as a way of getting love and ending as a defence against her anger about not receiv-ing it. She repeated her childhood pattern in her recent relationship. There was thus an obvious focus.

She responded very clearly to interpretations on this focus – although the inter-viewer wrote that he never quite succeeded in getting in touch with the true inten-sity of her feeling. Her motivation was clearly ambivalent but contained a strong positive component.

Course of therapy (12 sessions)

The therapist was a (male) psychiatrist from Canada, competent and responsive to supervision. The length of therapy was limited by the date of his departure for home, which was explained to the patient at the beginning.

The impression created by this therapy is that, just as in the initial interview, the patient expressed a certain amount of feeling and responded well to interpre-tation, but always held something in reserve – which was symbolised by her keeping her coat on throughout the sessions, mostly buttoned up, though sometimes unbuttoned and sometimes draped over her shoulders. This meant that, hard as the therapist tried, he never achieved a true breakthrough.

Sessions 1–5: Non-transference work brings some therapeutic effects

She opened Session 1 by saying that after the initial interview she had felt happy for the first time for many years. She went on to talk about her relation with her man-friend, half denying anger, but ending by saying that it was a pity the Turks didn't exterminate the Greeks in the recent troubles in Cyprus.

In Session 2 the therapist made the link once more between her man-friend's indifference and that of her parents. She told of specific incidents involving her man-friend's lack of care, and the therapist gave her a number of interpretations about her defence of being 'good' and 'almost servile', which brought her to admit that she had felt some anger at her man-friend's lack of support during a difficult time.

Session 3 showed the first of a number of therapeutic effects. Her mother had been admitted to hospital with an exacerbation of a chronic lung infection. She felt that the expectation was that she should go home and give up going to the tennis at Eastbourne, for which she had got tickets. However, it came to her that this was just being 'pleasing' again and was probably not necessary. She then showed some of the practical qualities that had made her a manageress: she arranged for flowers to be sent to her mother and called a neighbour of her parents, giving a phone number where she could be contacted in an emergency. In fact her mother's admission was a false alarm, since she was discharged after 2 days. Thus the patient's refusal to be panicked was completely vindicated.

In Session 5 the patient reported that she had decided to go out with a man for the first time since the break-up with her man-friend. The new boy-friend is called Peter, is single, owns his own business, and is attractive. He has asked if she would like to become involved in his business.

Her younger brother is getting divorced and phoned up to share his unhappiness with her, and she had to support him. She felt that this responsibility should have been shouldered by her parents, and said 'Will this burden my family puts on me never leave me?'

Sessions 6–9: Work on resistance against expressing her needs, both in the transference and outside, brings some response

Throughout all these sessions the patient had kept her coat buttoned up, and the supervisor pointed out that in spite of the therapeutic effects she must be in some way withholding herself.

The therapist responded by saying in the next session that there was a part of her that was 'closed off' from him, and suggested that this might be concerned with the fact that therapy would be coming to an end in a few weeks' time. She said that recently she has become more aware of this, and after further associations said that she needs someone to love her. He related this to himself.

This work on the transference seems to have produced a response in terms of greater trust. She first began talking about similarities between her man-friend and her new friend Peter, who had cancelled an apppointment with her. She then suddenly became exasperated at refusing to mention her man-friend by name (which she had done throughout in order to protect him) and said that his name was Andreas. Further pressure on her feelings about her therapist brought out, with embarrassment, that she had been afraid of doctors making passes at her, which has happened in reality before. She also said that it was important to her that her therapist should know that she was doing better, and he pointed out her need to please him.

In Session 7 she reported an incident in which her new boy-friend, Peter, had suddenly said that he had to leave in order to meet some friends. She had been concerned that she was being 'used' by him and had expressed this, making clear that she wasn't to be walked over. He apologised profusely, in a way that had never happened with Andreas throughout their whole 7 years together. This had left her with a feeling of exhilaration.

Later in the session she said that during her years with Andreas she had felt 'as if she was in a cage'. The therapist drew the parallel with her childhood, saying that the feeling consisted of not being able to express her own needs and desires, having to bend over backwards to please, and getting nothing in return.

The response to this last interpretation came in the next session (number 8). She said that she has been considering what her needs really are, something that she has never done before. She needs to be with people, to have someone to love her, someone to lean on. The therapist now concentrated on the transference once more, speaking as follows: the expression of her needs and feelings in the sessions seems to be a problem. In the previous session she had again mentioned her wish for therapy to be short, and perhaps she wanted to limit her involvement and the degree of closeness with him. This might be because of the rejections she had suffered in the past, and because of the fact that he would shortly be leaving. Nevertheless he and she should try and work out these problems in the remaining sessions.

In response she came much nearer to her feelings, speaking with open sadness about many situations both in the present and in the past. She said that since her parents were unable to give to *each other* in any way, how could *she* expect anything from them? She never expected anything from Andreas either. Her needs were never mentioned because she knew they would never be met. It was when she first began to communicate her needs that Andreas left her. She went on to express some open anger with her mother who always expected support from her, when it ought to have been the other way round.

Later she said that though she has been feeling depressed recently she hasn't been able to cry. The therapist said that she is 'walling herself up', and – in a veiled reference to her coat – that she is 'buttoned up' in the sessions. She said, 'I have a fear of talking to people'.

This work produced some effect, for in the next session (number 9) she said that after the last session she had been very upset and had cried a great deal, thinking how 'stifling' the relation with Andreas had been.

Sessions 9–12: Work on resistance against expressing anger in the transference produces only limited response

Again in response to supervision, the therapist now made a determined attempt to reach anger in the transference. The main reason, he suggested, was that he had not solved her concrete problems by giving her advice. She responded by listing, with increasing anxiety, the failures of a number of doctors who had not helped her with physical problems. He suggested she was becoming anxious as she got closer to expressing angry feelings against him, and that the anxiety – as with Andreas and her parents – was that he would respond by rejecting her (a TCP interpretation). She then spoke of a woman at work who, when she wanted the patient to do something, set about it in a very devious way. The therapist interrupted, saying he thought she was talking about him, and that when he asked her to reveal more of her feelings she felt he had something in mind that he was not telling her, which made her angry. She agreed with this, as she did with a number of other interpretations about her anger with him, but without expressing it in any way. Though he pointed this out, he was unable to make further progress.

In the next session (number 10) she said that she felt better after the last session, but had been feeling 'flat' all week. She had forgotten what they had been talking about. When he reminded her, she admitted that she had been angry with him for not taking decisions for her, particularly about what she should do over her relation with Peter. However, she went on to say that she eventually realised that this was a good thing, and she now felt better about taking decisions herself.

Again the therapist was unable to make further progress. She agreed with interpretations about her anger with him but without giving the impression that she was experiencing it. He attempted to get at the possibility of sexual transference; but she simply said, quite straightforwardly, that she had 'never fancied him in that way'.

In Session 11 she reported that her new boy-friend, Peter, seemed to be backing away from both the business and the social relation with her, and she thinks this is because she has stated exactly what she wants from him. She went on to say that she had asked a woman whom she had met at an evening class to come out and have a drink with her – something entirely new in her recent life. She added that the class was ending, and the therapist linked this with the fact that the next session would be the last. She said she was very sad about this and knew that she would spend the next session crying. However, she went on to say that the reason why she had been able to invite the woman out was because she had been thinking a lot about being unable to trust people – something that the therapist had pointed out to her. She also said that now she is able to think more clearly, whereas during the past 2 years her thoughts have been slowed down and muddled.

In the last session (number 12) she unbuttoned her coat but kept it on. She was sad and tearful, but she said that she had been more involved with people during the past week than in the whole of the previous 7 years. The therapist made some supportive comments, saying that it was natural and entirely acceptable for her to have sad feelings at this time. She again became tearful as she left.

First follow-up (5 months)

The 5-month and 2-year follow-up interviews were carried out by the original interviewer.

The first follow-up was hopeful on the one hand, and – with hindsight – ominous on the other. She looked entirely different and much more attractive, and she had clearly recovered from her depression. She had been making many efforts to contact people, but they didn't seem to invite her back. She had been able to express her anger to Peter, and she described an incident almost identical to that in Session 7: he had suddenly said he must leave, and she had very angrily said that just because she had been 'used' before it didn't mean that she could be used now. This didn't prevent him from leaving, but he did phone her up the next day. However, he had then let her down over a further promised meeting. The position over her joining him in his business venture remains uncertain.

The most unsatisfactory aspect was that she was still doing a series of temporary jobs well below her potential.

Second follow-up (2 years)

The position was very unsatisfactory. The relation with Peter has ended. She has applied for a number of permanent jobs but has been turned down for all of them because she has either too much experience or too little. She showed evidence of starting once more to become involved with people who ill-treated her. There was a married man by whom she felt sexually 'used'; and a woman friend who treated her callously when she tripped and fell and was quite badly hurt. In the interview she spoke briskly and cheerfully about distressing subjects, but this defence was penetrated by pointing it out, which resulted in her speaking over and over again about her loneliness.

Final follow-up (3 years 9 months)

This interview was carried out by one of the present authors (FO).

She described an utterly disastrous situation. First, she felt ill-treated in a recent job, gave in her notice, but left before the notice expired. As a result the firm refused to pay her, saying that she was incompetent in every way. She has not yet found another job.

The second situation was even more disastrous: she went on a visit to Warsaw where she met a man called Stefan and fell in love with him. It emerged that he reminded her of Andreas. He asked her to marry him and she consented. At first he was very attentive, but when she visited him on a later occasion his feelings seem to have entirely changed. He didn't kiss her at the airport, he lost interest in her sexually, and – whereas she had been expecting a trip in the country – he remained at work for the entire period, leaving her to cope with his family alone. She no longer wanted to marry him but felt she had to go through with it. 'I got terribly depressed. I was trapped. I didn't have enough courage to leave. It was like a blank all over my head. I didn't want to hurt him or create a big scene. I wanted to help him. His family would think I was a terrible, terrible creature.' When pressed about the irrationality of this decision, she said: 'I think it belongs to my childhood'. The interviewer pointed out that Stefan resembled her mother in needing help, and her father in being unable to communicate with her. She said, 'Now that you say that, it's funny, but Stefan reminded me of my father.' She went on to make the most extraordinary statement about someone whom she proposed to marry: 'He couldn't talk to me. He would raise his voice and shout, like my father, so I felt I couldn't live with him.' Nevertheless, she did in fact marry him. He is still in Poland and can only get to Britain if he has a work permit, but she is putting off applying for one for him. She made clear that she does not propose to live with him and expects eventually to get a divorce. She ended by saying, 'It's funny that I always like horrible people'. She seemed almost disoriented, and incredulous about her situation.

We should add that she is on anti-depressants and that her back trouble is still present.

She forestalled the interviewer's offer to explore the possibility of further treatment by saying that she was 'terrified of being asked to come here again'.

Both judges gave scores of –1.0.

Final comment

This tragic story illustrates with great clarity the extraordinary power of the masochistic 'compulsion to repeat', a phenomenon that would be almost unbelievable if it were not encountered in clinical work over and over again. Davanloo has demonstrated almost conclusively that this is often caused by self-punishment for feelings of extreme violence, and that it can be eradicated if the violent impulses can be brought to the surface and *experienced* in their full intensity. It is therefore highly significant that although she agreed with many interpretations about her anger, she never fully experienced it.

Further evidence on this issue is provided by the contrast with the Librarian. This later patient experienced intense anger with her therapist, saying that she now realised that she had a 'monster of violent anger within her', and she then apparently recovered completely from the manifestations of her masochistic pathology.

20

A calculated risk ending in catastrophe

The Acutely Suicidal Receptionist

Age 28, single, 9 sessions, no score.

Referral

She was referred by a psychiatrist from an Outpatient Department, whose letter included the following: 'She was referred to me by her GP because her sister felt that she may be suicidal. However, I found no real evidence for this.'

Complaints

She wrote on her application form: 'Depression, headaches, suicidal'.

Family history

She is the youngest of a Catholic family of four. Her father owned a small business in Liverpool. The family history showed very severe disturbance: her father became bankrupt when she was 6, after which he became progressively more depressed or possibly demented; her mother then became alcoholic; one brother was in a mental hospital, probably schizophrenic; and another brother was withdrawn and schizoid.

Precipitating factor

Two years ago she became engaged to a man whom she knew to be a heavy drinker. Trouble developed between them because of her tie to her family. Eighteen months ago she went to a dance with him, where he got so drunk that she asked the husband of a friend to take her home. Her fiancé got to her home before her and beat her up. She said that he 'nearly killed her'. She broke off her engagement and it was at this time that she became depressed. Shortly afterwards she left Liverpool and came to London. One year ago she received a letter from the sister of her ex-fiancé telling her that, since she left, he had gone into an alcoholic decline and had died suddenly of a coronary thrombosis. The letter implied that the patient was to blame. Not surprisingly, there was an increase in her depression. This now consists of wanting to cry much of the time and not to meet people, but she has only taken a few days off work in the past year. She said that because of her Catholic faith she felt she wouldn't actually commit suicide.

Dynamics of interview

She was interviewed by a (male) trainee psychiatrist,

She opened by saying that although she had become depressed after the break-up of her engagement, she felt that the real cause of her trouble was her unhappy family life. She mentioned that she would often come home to find her mother in an alcoholic stupor on the floor. She had wanted to leave home but had felt that she had to stay to look after both her mother and her father. At one time she had actually left home but had been forced to give this up when her mother wrote that she must come home and work to help pay off her father's debts. Asked whether she ever got angry, she did not openly admit this; but she said that her father was very demanding and used to take her for granted, that this meant that she never had a mind of her own, and that the result was that she became confused between her wishes and her duty. Later in the interview, however, when she became more relaxed, she spoke with considerable feeling about her guilt over her fiancé's death and her extreme anger with both her parents.

Projective testing

She was seen four times by a (female) psychologist and given the ORT and Rorschach. The psychologist did a considerable amount of interpretative work and wrote: 'She was responsive to interpretation and was able to bring into awareness her anger against her parents, particularly her mother, and to face the fact that this was of an intense and overwhelming quality. She was not able to deal with her guilt at the fantasied damage that her anger has caused to both her fiancé and her parents.' When her sexuality was discussed, she gave indications of feeling she had to control it in case it got out of hand and she became pregnant, with the result that she might be rejected by her parents.

Thus she appeared to be afraid of the intensity of both her aggressive and her sexual impulses. However, the psychologist wrote that she had considerable strength and there was no evidence of severe disturbance.

In view of later events, it is worth noting that the patient expressed her need for support by asking both the psychiatrist and the psychologist for advice about whether to give up her current job.

Reason for acceptance for brief psychotherapy; therapeutic plan

We were well aware of the possibly grave significance of her background and family history, but realised that she needed immediate help. Obviously, we were lulled into a false sense of security by her denial of suicidal intent both to us and to the referring psychiatrist, and by the reassuring psychological report.

Her material offered a clear therapeutic plan, which was formulated as follows: to start by interpreting her guilt about her fiancé's death, and to link it with the fantasy that her aggressive feelings inevitably harm people who get close to her. To link this in turn with the way she sacrificed herself to her family, and all the anger there must be about this.

This plan seemed feasible since she had responded to interpretations along these lines.

We recognised the severity of the problem and decided to offer her 40 sessions rather than 30.

Course of therapy (9 sessions)

The patient was assigned to a male psychiatrist from abroad who was, unfortunately, not very experienced. This was the only current vacancy available.

The therapist started well, concentrating on the chosen focus; but he also adopted a rather psychoanalytical stance, with the result that he got involved in the patient's regressive need for support and her feelings about his refusal to give it, with consequences that in the end were catastrophic.

Focal work, early therapeutic effects

Early in Session 1 she said that she had recently had to go and help an aunt whose husband had died, and that her parents had opposed her engagement, adding 'perhaps if I had ignored my parents' objections things would be different now.' The therapist gave a highly focal PT interpretation, pointing out that she had always done what her parents wanted and deprived herself of her own needs; and he then linked this with the transference, suggesting that she might feel similarly trapped after being transferred to him for yet another assessment interview (the letter to her had mentioned 'further assessment', since we wanted the therapist to be sure that he felt he could work with her). The patient said that this was true and went on to speak with more confidence, mentioning that she had never liked her aunt, and that everybody in her own home had had to cover up the fact that her mother drank. The therapist now made another highly focal interpretation of the defence, anxiety, and impulse: that perhaps the patient herself had to maintain the image of the nice obedient daughter, and that this might cover up intense resentment, which she couldn't express for fear of being rejected. This seems to have had the effect of freeing her even further, for she now spoke with anger about how her mother had commanded her to go and help her aunt, whom she disliked; and she went on to speak of her mother's drunkenness, hitting the arm of the chair to emphasise her feelings.

This seems to have been an excellent session, but in view of later events it is worth noting that at the end of the interview she again asked for advice about whether she should give up her job, to which the therapist did not respond.

Apparently the therapist was half an hour late for Session 2, but there is no mention of how he handled this in his account. However, most surprisingly and most hopefully, the patient already reported some therapeutic effects, and it was clear that she fully understood their significance. For the first time, when at her sister's, she had been able to ask for things for herself instead of always being the giver – 'not bossy or demanding, just able to ask'. In a later part of the session, however, she reverted to saying that she felt she did not do enough for other people. The therapist said that she did not want to see her own deprivation and the anger that it caused, and as a result she had to be the giver rather than the receiver to counteract her feeling of guilt. She again showed her insight by saying that her habit has been to feel compelled to give to other people without considering whether she wanted to or not.

The patient leaves her job and moves in with her sister

She opened Session 3 by saying that she had left her job, adding with apparent resentment that she had not received any advice from the therapist about this. She is intending to go and stay at her sister's. In her job she had been given extra work and had been criticised for taking too much time off. The Manager had said she 'should leave her problems behind'. Typically, the patient said he was a good person and she quite understood his position. The therapist pointed out her inability to stand up for herself, linking it with her background and also with the fact that he had been half an hour late for her in the previous session and she had not mentioned it (a TCP interpretation). She had tears in her eyes when she said, 'You are right in what you say'. Towards the end of the session she spoke about being unable to show how miserable she was in front of her sister's children, and the therapist linked this with her inability to show her real feelings in her childhood.

In Session 4 she reported that she had moved into her sister's home. She had many doubts about this, particularly as she had been told that there was some tension in her sister's marriage. She said she would like to take a job without any responsibility, like that of a chambermaid, where she was just told what to do. The therapist suggested that she was annoyed with him for not taking these decisions for her, with which she agreed.

– Later in the session she mentioned that she was very depressed when she was alone and had suicidal thoughts. Correctly, the therapist questioned her closely about this but came to the conclusion that suicide was not a serious risk.

The problem of management versus interpretation

In the next session (number 5) she appeared to be depressed and retarded. She now presented us with a kind of situation which it is always extremely difficult to deal with: she said that her sister – who was clearly very worried about her – had asked to be allowed to come and talk to the therapist. As if it was an analysis, the therapist did not reply, and the patient repeated her question. He now asked why her sister wanted to see him, to which she said that she (the patient) couldn't watch TV for more than an hour without crying. The therapist asked what she felt about her sister seeing him, to which she said that she didn't mind; and she went on to say that she always wanted to be told what to do and to have no responsibility. He said that she wanted him and her sister to get together and take responsibility for her so that she could be like a child. She nodded. At the end of the session she asked about the possibiity of her sister coming, to which he suggested that they should talk about it in the next session.

It is always very difficult to know when psychotherapy should pass over into management; and now, looking back, it seems certain that her sister should have been seen. The information from her about the patient's state might have caused us to take more active steps to protect her from her suicidal impulses.

The next session (number 6) seems to have been largely uneventful, but there was one hopeful moment when she reported that her sister and brother-in-law had asked her to come out with them, and she had said she didn't feel like it – something she would never have dared to do in the past.

The patient tries to break off treatment; an ominous remark

Before the next session the therapist received a letter from the patient saying that she felt better and had decided to discontinue. Correctly, he wrote back inviting her to come and discuss this with him, which she did,

It was an example of the therapist's passivity that when she came for this session (number 7) and did not mention her wish to stop, he did not raise this with her either. Early in the session she spoke of not wanting to get close to people, which the therapist linked with the transference.

She went on to speak very favourably about her sister, and the therapist pointed out how difficult it was for her to criticise people close to her. The patient continued to speak of her sister, but blaming herself for anything that went wrong. As she spoke, it was noticeable that she was becoming more and more depressed.

This led to the really significant moment in the session. She spoke of the tremendous effort it had been to keep up a front at a dance to which her sister had invited her, saying that in her mind she was 'miles away'. The therapist asked her where she was, miles away, to which she replied: '*I am sorry if I am rude, but I imagined myself deep in a grave.*' The therapist did not ask at once about suicide, but interpreted that in that kind of situation she would cut off her feelings of anger towards other people – rather than be critical she preferred to blame herself. She said she recognised these critical feelings in herself, but felt she shouldn't have them. However, she did later mention an incident when she had got very annoyed with her sister for ordering her about at the age of 9.

It was only at the very end of the session that the therapist raised the question of her wish to discontinue. She looked startled, as if she had forgotten the subject altogether. She gave the depressive answer that she 'did not seem able to appreciate the treatment' and then, after a long and tense pause, that she wanted to stop. The therapist suggested that they might explore the possibilities next time.

The supervisor wrote in the margin of the therapist's account, against the patient's remark about imagining herself deep in a grave, 'ask about suicide?'; but it has to be confessed that he did not take this remark seriously enough, and did not emphasise it in his supervision of the session.

A new job

She opened the next session (number 8) by saying that she was going to start a new job in 3 days' time. This was as a maid in a private home, living in, which was what she wanted. She also said she has decided not to stop coming after all. Much of the rest of the session was concerned with talk about the job, where she had been told that she would be 'like one of the family'.

Later she mentioned that her fiancé used to get annoyed at her need to help at home because he wanted her to be with him. This was probably a disguised communication about the therapist's attempts to keep her in treatment, but he did not interpret this.

She gives up the job

She opened Session 9 by saying that she had given up her job. Whenever she did anything in the house it seemed to be wrong, and the woman of the house had criticised her for coming down 2 minutes late. She said that she is very fond of people in general, but only when they are at a distance from her. As soon as she gets close to them she has to become real, and she doesn't like them any more. The therapist said that perhaps there exists in her mind an idealised psychotherapist and an idealised family, who will look after her; but that reality is different, and it stirs up feelings in her that she has to avoid. She spoke of the situation in her family, where she tried to give them advice about what to do after her father went bankrupt, for instance to sell the house, but they were too proud to do so – 'how difficult it is to grow up and become an adult'. The therapist said that there seems to be a conflict between a part of her that feels it has to take responsibility for her family and another part that feels deprived and needs to be looked after. She said that this is exactly how she feels. She ended the session by saying, with anger, that she doesn't think the therapist could possibly imagine what it was like at home – there was such a strict and rigid environment, in which you had to eat and drink religion every day, every minute, every second. You had to learn to love all the time. The therapist said that perhaps she finds it difficult to admit how resentful she feels about all this. She was silent and he brought the session to a close.

The therapy ends in catastrophe

She failed to come for the next session, and soon afterwards we received a phone call from the Coroner's court to say that the day after the last session she had taken an overdose, and had died 2 days later. Post-mortem showed the overdose to be of anti-depressants.

Comment

It is perhaps significant that the patient's suicide followed a moment when she had expressed more anger than ever before about the situation in her family. Her suicide suggests that we failed to understand the depth of her intolerance of her own anger.

Looking back at the evidence we had at initial assessment, it seems even now that the original focus was not unreasonable. We realised the possible ominous significance of her family history, but decided to take a calculated risk.

Much of the therapist's work was on the chosen focus, but he was too psycho-analytical and not supportive enough. It is clear now that her sister ought to have been seen, and the hint of approaching suicide in Session 7 was not sufficiently emphasised.

The patient's life situation was very unfavourable. She was originally living alone in a bed-sitting room, which is obviously dangerous for a potentially suicidal person. On the other hand, living either in her sister's family, or in that of her new employer, meant that she had to keep up a front and cover her feelings the whole time, which was equally unsuitable and repeated the situation in her family of origin. We know now that she ought to have been in hospital, the only environment where she could be as depressed as she felt yet receive appropriate support. Many hospitals are glad to allow a patient out for weekly sessions of skilled psychotherapy, which they may be unable to provide themselves.

Would a more experienced therapist have been able to be sufficiently supportive, and then to pick up the danger signals and convey them to the supervisor, so that she could have been admitted to hospital and the final catastrophe could have been avoided? It is impossible to say.

21

The five patients who were worse: discussion

What can be learnt from these five patients? Three of the patients, the Girl with Eye Problems, the Graduate Clerk, and the Robot Man, were all thought at initial assessment to be 'ordinary neurotics', but turned out in therapy or at follow-up to be borderline or psychotic. This emphasises the paramount importance of a psychiatric diagnosis before therapy is undertaken, and it also suggests that there are dangers in having initial assessment interviews carried out by relatively inexperienced trainees. It is possible that a more experienced interviewer would have detected the borderline quality in both the Graduate Clerk and the Girl with Eye Problems, and in fact both the interviewers in these two cases were rather overconfident young men. However, perhaps it can now be revealed that the interviewer in the case of the Robot Man was one of the present authors (DM), who himself coined the phrase about a psychodynamic diagnosis being the enemy of a psychiatric diagnosis, and fell into his own trap. Nevertheless, it can be said in his defence that it is very difficult indeed to detect a slowly developing paranoid illness in an otherwise intact personality, before the pathological manifestations actually appear – though the symptom of derealisation and the split into the 'Self' and the 'Robot' were certainly pointers that should not have been overlooked.

This is a small sample, but the three final follow-ups do suggest that to try to give brief psychotherapy to such patients, at any rate when the therapists are trainees, is a mistake. In each patient the underlying deep disturbance manifested itself more overtly after the end of therapy and caused a deterioration in the situation. In the Robot Man the disturbance led to the development of a paranoid illness; in the Graduate Clerk it led to a state of general and severe withdrawal (often a risk in borderline conditions); and in the Girl with Eye problems the birth of the children led to a situation for which the patient was simply not emotionally equipped.

In the case of the Suicidal Receptionist the danger of suicide was considered both by the referring psychiatrist (who was highly experienced) and by the initial interviewer, but the patient's answers were reassuring. Very thorough psychological testing also failed to give us any warning. The ominous feature, of course, was her family history; and one of the mistakes that we made was to give her to a relatively inexperienced trainee who was much too psychoanalytical in his approach. The supervisor did not see the danger signals in time, and should have urged the therapist to give up his psychoanalytical approach and adopt the standard technique used with disturbed patients: that is, to give a good deal of support, and then to join forces with the patient's therapeutic alliance so that therapist and patient can look at the patient's illness together. In addition, the patient should have been admitted to hospital. For these failures the supervisor is entirely to blame.

Finally, the Victimised Telephonist was a patient who in our view ought to have provided a successful therapeutic result, but palpably failed to do so. In her case, as in the three borderline patients described above, the underlying severe disturbance reasserted itself after the end of her therapy, leading to a disastrous deterioration in her life. Surprisingly, during her therapy she had shown as many therapeutic effects as any other patient in the series – possibly even more. Here it needs to be said that her therapy of 12 sessions was much too brief, cut short by the therapist's return home; and that in spite of her apparent responsiveness, she showed a subtle underlying resistance throughout, and never really experienced the depth and intensity of her true feelings. Here was another patient who cried out for the Davanloo technique, which unfortunately we were in no position to provide.

Part Three

Types of Change found at Follow-up

22

Types of change: general

Introduction

In Part Three we have two main aims: to present some of the raw data on which the assessment of outcome was based; and to illustrate the kinds of change that were found in these patients at follow-up, and their remarkable uniformity.

The validity of psychotherapy depends entirely on *changes in the patient's life outside the clinical situation,* and since it is impossible to observe these directly, we have no better means of assessing them than by asking the patient about them and critically evaluating the replies that we receive. With this in mind, the follow-up interviewer should never accept a patient's statement – e.g. 'I am far better at asserting myself' – at its face value, but must always ask for specific examples. It is these examples which make up much of the raw data of our follow-up material, and which we present in the following pages. By this means we hope to share the evidence on which our judgments of outcome are based, and thus to enable the reader to make judgments that are independent of those made by us.

As described in Chapter 3, our method for judging outcome consisted of laying down before follow-up a list of criteria for an ideal therapeutic result, and matching these criteria with the changes actually found. Beside the obvious criterion of symptomatic recovery, there were some criteria which recurred repeatedly, such as 'constructive self-assertion' and 'a satisfactory relation with the opposite sex'. However, we could not be expected to foresee every possible issue in the patient's life, and we often found changes at follow-up that were not included in our original criteria. For instance, a recovery of creativity was laid down for the Conductor and the Sculptress, where this was known to be a problem; but it was not laid down for the Betrayed Son, who at follow-up showed an increase in creativity by changing his vocation. Equally, whereas 'being herself' was included in the criteria for both the Librarian and the Mountain Tarn Girl, it was not included for the Allergic Receptionist, and the discovery of an improvement in this area was, so to speak, a therapeutic bonus. Thus the criteria on which the therapeutic results were based included some judged retrospectively as well as those laid down in advance.

In Chapter 11 we noted the striking uniformity in the kinds of change that occurred in the seven 'best' cases – a surprising observation in a system of such complexity as the human psyche. These changes can be described under the following headings:

1 Emotional freeing (including the freeing of creativeness).
2 Being oneself.
3 Resolution of maladaptive patterns.
4 Symptomatic improvement.
5 Relations with the opposite sex: commitment.
6 Relations with the opposite sex: emotional closeness.
7 Relations with the opposite sex: relation free from serious reservations.
8 Constructive self-assertion.

Overview

The changes in these eight criteria are summarised in Table 22.1. The criteria are scored simply as 'fulfilled' (+) or 'not fulfilled' (0), which helps to keep the data clear so that it can be easily grasped. Improvements are mostly given the benefit of the doubt, and possible reservations are discussed under each individual patient. An entry is left blank if either there was never a problem in this area, or information is lacking. Inevitably some of the criteria overlap with one another – e.g. a patient such as the Conductor who had changed from reacting passively in situations that made him angry, to being able to use aggression effectively, scores '+' for both 'resolution of maladaptive patterns' and 'constructive self-assertion'. Equally, the Sculptress changed from promiscuous relations with men to a close relation lasting 5 years, and therefore scores '+' for three criteria: 'resolution of maladaptive patterns', 'emotional freeing', and 'emotional closeness'.

Discussion of Table 22.1

For reasons that will become clear below, a line is drawn in the Table between the 'best' therapeutic results, with scores of 2.0 or more for outcome, and the 'intermediate and poor' results, with scores less than 2.0.

The Table contains information of the greatest interest. First of all we may consider the three criteria referring to *relations with the opposite sex*. It will be seen first that 8 patients were judged to have achieved *emotional closeness* and 6 to have achieved *emotional commitment,* while 5 achieved both together*. However, when other aspects beside closeness and commitment are considered in addition – such as the residual violence in the case of the Conductor and Car Battery Man, and the suppressed resentment in the case of the Psychiatric Nurse – then only 1 patient in the whole series achieved a *relation free from serious reservations.* As we have mentioned many times in Part Two, this observation both illustrates how difficult it is for patients to achieve a truly satisfactory relation with the opposite sex, and reveals a serious deficiency in the therapeutic results in the present series. In particular, these patients exemplify with extraordinary clarity the various devices used by people for avoiding true commitment – a condition that seems to arouse the greatest resistance in many people. This will be considered in detail in Chapter 28.

---

*In the case of the Concert-goer, Miner's Daughter, Psychiatric Nurse, and Girl with Eye Problems, one or both of these two areas was never a problem, and the entries are left blank. The entry under 'closeness' for the Hypomanic Advertising Executive is also left blank because of uncertainty about the true quality of the relation with his wife.

Table 22.1. Types of change found at follow-up

						Relations with the opposite sex			
Patient	Constructive self-assertion	Being oneself	Symptomatic improvement	Resolution of maladaptive patterns	Emotional freeing	Emotional closeness	Commitment	Relation free from serious reservations	Score for outcome
Nurse Mourning her Fiancé	+	+	+	+	+	+	+	+	3.75
Pacifist Conductor	+	+	+	+	+	+	+	0	3.0
Librarian who Sought Suffering	+	+	+	+	+	+	0	0	2.875
Car Battery Man	+		0	+	+	+	+	0	2.75
Sculptress with Nightmares	+	+	+	+	+	+	0	0	2.75
Betrayed Son	+	+	0		+	0	0	0	2.25
Girl and the Mountain Tarn	+	+	+	+	+	+	+	0	2.0
Rebellious Script Writer	0	0	0	0	0	+	+	0	1.75
Allergic Receptionist	+	+	+	0	+	+	0	0	1.75
Concert-goer in an Acute Panic	+		+	+	0	0	0	0	1.625
Mother or Teenage Daughter	0	+	+	0	0		0	0	1.5
Hypomanic Advertising Executive	+	+	+	+	0	0	0	0	1.375
Secretary in a State of Nirvana	+	+	+	0	0	0	0	0	1.0
Self-driving Physicist	+	0	0	0	0	0	0	0	1.0
Acting-out Accounts Clerk	0	0	0	0	0	0	0	0	0.5
Actress with Elocution Problems	+	0	0	0	0	0	+	0	0.25
Miner's Daughter	0	0	0	0	0	0	0	0	0.25
Anorexic Museum Assistant	0	0	0	0	0	0	0	0	0.0
Psychiatric Nurse	0	0	0	0	0	0	0	0	0.0
Girl with Eye Problems	0	0	0	0	0	0		0	−0.5
Borderline Graduate Clerk	0	0	0	0	0	0	0	0	−1.0
Robot Man	+	0	0	0	0	0		0	−1.0
Victimised Telephonist	0	0	0	0	0	0	0	0	−1.0
Acutely Suicidal Receptionist	−	−	−	−	−	−	−	−	−
Total +	14	10	10	8	8	8	6	1	

There is one criterion which most clearly distinguishes the best results (above the line) from the intermediate and poor results (below the line), namely 'emotional freeing'. The Table shows 7 out of 7 '+' entries for patients who score 2.0 or more, compared with 1 out of 17 for the rest (the freeing shown by the Rebellious Script Writer was minimal and was not considered sufficient for a score of '+').

Second in line for distinguishing the best results is the criterion that is probably most closely related to 'emotional freeing', namely 'emotional closeness', for which the corresponding figures are 6 above the line and 2 below – the 2 in fact being the patients who scored next highest for outcome. This is therefore a a slightly better distinguishing criterion than 'maladaptive patterns', for which the over-all figures are the same; but the two patients below the line who are given '+' scores lie further down the table.

As far as *symptoms* are concerned, it is noticeable that 2 of the 7 patients above the line still suffered from residual symptoms, whereas 5 of the 8 below the line were symptom-free – but of course the latter included several 'false solutions'.

Finally, and perhaps surprisingly, it seems that the easiest improvement to achieve is *constructive self-assertion,* which extends right down the table and is found even in one patient who was judged as 'worse'. One of the most striking observations in the present series is the way in which improvements in this area occurred during the process of therapy, which helps to provide evidence for the validity of dynamic psychotherapy in general and this form of psychotherapy in particular. This subject will be considered in detail in Chapter 33.

In Chapters 23 to 31 we will consider each of these types of change in turn over the whole sample. This will inevitably involve some repetition; but we will include considerably more detail than was given in Part Two; and where possible we will give verbatim quotations from statements made by the patient or material written by the follow-up interviewer. The section on each individual patient often consists of a living vignette concerned with the realities of human relationships, and we hope that this will heighten the interest of a subject which has such a clear relevance to the twin problems of judging outcome, on the one hand, and assessing the validity of dynamic psychotherapy, on the other.

For scientific reasons we have wanted, as far as possible, to include evidence on every patient for whom each criterion is relevant. We suggest that the reader may wish to browse through this extensive material rather than read these chapters from beginning to end.

23

Emotional freeing

Since this is the criterion that most clearly characterises the best results, it will be considered first. The details are as follows.

The Nurse Mourning her Fiancé

This patient had blocked off all her feelings after the third major bereavement in her life. She had not cried immediately after her fiancé's death, nor at any time in the 4 years that had elapsed since then. She had coped with her feelings by a form of manic defence – throwing herself into hectic over-activity. At follow-up she was fully aware of this total emotional block: 'Then, I just didn't feel anything.'

The steady progress during therapy towards being able to feel both grief and anger is described in Chapter 8, and the fact that this ability was maintained at follow-up – together with the ability to be happy and to laugh – was made clear by the extracts from the follow-up interview presented in Chapter 1.

Thus the evidence for permanent emotional freeing, a process which started at the very beginning of her therapy, is conclusive.

The Pacifist Conductor

This patient resembles the Nurse Mourning her Fiancé in the sense that he also had blocked off all feeling since his recent bereavements, and like her he had adopted a manic defence against his grief, getting a job as a gravedigger and empathising with his colleagues who made fun of the whole process. However, his situation was also more complicated than hers: whereas she had apparently had what one can call a normal upbringing and before her recent trauma had been a normal person, he had been brought up in a home which severely restricted emotional expression, and he had been quite unable to express aggressive feelings for many years. During therapy he got in touch with both his grief and his anger. In Session 4 he was able to speak of his feeling of despair at not being able to get close to either of his parents when they were dying. In Session 11 he reported having had an intense outburst of rage, the results of which were entirely beneficial – a clear example of constructive aggression.

These changes were accompanied by the rediscovery of his creativeness after a gap of 5 years, which was expressed from the time of Session 10 onwards in a highly successful conducting career continuing throughout the whole of the follow-up period. However, his new-found ability to be aggressive also expressed itself in violence against his Indian girl-friend – a situation which to some degree continued after his marriage to her, right up to the final 6½-year follow-up.

During therapy his whole attitude to feelings underwent a swift and revolutionary change, the evidence for which is scattered liberally throughout the account of his sessions, as follows.

When he first came to us he was, so to speak, in a state of alliance with his defences, but this began to break down very quickly. In Session 3 he began to realise that his façade of independence prevented him from forming a lasting relation with a woman. In Session 5 he said that he had originally taken a job as Manager of an orchestra because he thought his calmness in emotional crises was an asset, but he now realised that this calmness was a defence against his own feelings, and that as a result he had lost his creativeness. In Session 6 he spoke of being 'over-emotional' about an unfavourable review, but then said that being upset was the price to be paid if one didn't want to be a robot all the time. In this same session he quoted, with clear understanding of its relevance to himself, the -libretto of a modern opera in which a woman who had adopted an efficient and impersonal façade discovers her own humanity. In Session 9 he came to realise the serious emotional deficiencies of his upbringing, quoting the remark of a former girl-friend: 'In your family there was a lot of care and respect, but little love.' Finally, in Session 10 he realised that his inability to cry was not a strength but another defence, and he showed this insight when he changed the libretto of the opera mentioned above to the heroine's *not* being able to cry, with the composer's approval.

The following are two of the remarks relevant to this theme that he made at follow-up: 'The idea of my therapy was to be less afraid of showing emotions. It helped to loosen up a very strict puritanical upbringing.' 'The world is changed by the strength that there is in anger.' Moreover, he still spends an hour a day working on his feelings.

The Librarian who Sought Suffering

As described in Chapter 1, the climax of this patient's therapy occurred in Sessions 13 and 14, when she realised that she had 'a monster of violent anger within her' – a clear example of emotional freeing.

The whole gestalt of this patient's follow-up is of emotional freeing in her life in general. One of the principal pieces of evidence for this comes from the freeing of her creativeness. Amongst her original complaints, which she described in her application form, was an inability to make her writing very creative: 'I like writing poetry, but it is almost always frustratingly bad or derivative, and usually I am too blocked up to try at all.' We have in our possession concrete evidence of the fact that this blockage was dissolved, in the form of the moving poem quoted on p. 68, the theme of which was her new-found ability to spread her wings.

This ability to write more creatively persisted throughout the follow-up period. Towards the end of her follow-up interview she was asked to mention any theme not yet touched on, to which she said, 'writing'. The interviewer's account continues: 'She had had to write a 15,000 word dissertation for a diploma. She feels that she is now very good with the written word and that it is one of her principal ways of expressing herself.'

The Car Battery Man

At the first follow-up (1½ years), the patient described feeling much freer than before – his future wife had said that there had been a great change in him. At the final follow-up (nearly 8 years) he described a freeing both of his aggression and his sexuality, using the phrase 'good rows and good sex'. As with the Conductor, the rows involved physical violence, which was apparently deliberately provoked by his wife. However, after the birth of his child the intensity of both the aggression and the sexuality was mitigated: 'Now when the relation is on a steady footing the sexual side hasn't a lot of importance.' We found this situation very difficult to evaluate.

However, the gestalt of his follow-up interview also gave direct evidence of emotional freeing. In Chapter 27 we will illustrate this with some of his remarks about the relation with his wife. Here, we can illustrate it with what he said about her pregnancy and the birth of their son: 'When people talk about children, they talk about the negative side of it, changing nappies and so on. Nobody ever tells you what a fantastic experience it is. It's wonderful, because I saw my wife through all the pregnancy. I was actually there when the birth was happening – then they had to cut her and I didn't want to see that. Afterwards it was fantastic. I was delighted. A big kid. When I looked into his cot, his eyes opened and then closed again, so if you can say you have a bond with somebody, it was made at that particular second.'

The Sculptress with Nightmares

This patient showed a marked freeing of her creativeness, which of course was central to her professional life. At the final follow-up (5½ years) she said that her latest work was the best she had ever done.

The Betrayed Son

Here the main evidence comes from his getting a job as craftsman instructor, which fulfilled a long-held ambition to express his creativeness through his hands.

The Mountain Tarn Girl

She said that she 'fell madly in love' with her current man-friend, with whom she described an intense, passionate, and rewarding relation (for details please see Chapter 27). She has also experienced a freeing of her creativeness, having found artistic hobbies in which she is deeply involved.

The Allergic Receptionist

This was the only other patient who showed evidence of major emotional freeing (score 1.75). At the end of therapy she described a general increase in her ability to express herself; and all the evidence made clear that this had persisted at final follow-up, where she said, 'Now I can tell anybody what I think. I am me, I am answerable to nobody.' (This remark shows that the criterion of emotional freeing often overlaps with that of 'being oneself', which will be considered in Chapter 25.) In addition she was now going to evening classes in pottery, which she made clear was an important expression of her creativity.

Discussion

Emotional freeing is perhaps the most essential and certainly the most all-embracing aim of dynamic psychotherapy, and although in many cases it was not specifically mentioned in our criteria it was always present by implication. It obviously correlates with several other criteria, such as 'being oneself' (as mentioned above), 'emotional closeness', and the ability to express anger constructively. If a statistician were to carry out a factor analysis of our criteria, emotional freeing would probably emerge as the principal component. Since in fact it is the criterion that best distinguishes the patients with the highest scores, it seems that the computer of our clinical judgment, so to speak, had been half-consciously programmed to give this criterion special emphasis.

24

Resolution of maladaptive behaviour patterns

Introduction

This is the criterion that ranks third in importance for characterising the best results, being fulfilled in 6 of the 7 patients who scored 2.0 or more for outcome, and in only 2 of the rest of the sample. (As mentioned in Chapter 22, 'emotional closeness' was a very slightly better criterion, but this will be considered in Chapter 27 under the heading of 'relations with the opposite sex'.) In order to make clear what we mean by maladaptive behaviour patterns and their resolution we will consider two strikingly contrasting patients, the Victimised Telephonist and the Librarian who Sought Suffering.

The Victimised Telephonist, illustrating the 'compulsion to repeat'

This patient had allowed herself to be exploited by her parents in her upbringing, had always avoided anger and leant over backwards to please, and she described an extremely one-sided relation with her much older, married man-friend, in which she did all the emotional giving. This commonly encountered pattern seems to start as an attempt to gain love, which is unsuccessful, and ends as a defence against anger about not receiving it, resulting in a vicious circle. In her case it was used as the focus for therapy.

As was discussed in Chapter 3, the empirical definition of 'resolution' is that a maladaptive or inappropriate reaction should be replaced by the corresponding appropriate reaction; which in this case means the ability to express her needs and stand up for herself in a constructive way.

During her 12 sessions she appeared to make remarkable progress in these areas: for instance she refused to sacrifice her own pleasure unnecessarily for her mother; she expressed resentment to a boy-friend because she felt she was being used by him; she stated exactly what she wanted from this same boy-friend over practical issues; and she dealt effectively with a woman neighbour who had been annoying her. (More details will be given in Chapter 30, under the heading of constructive self-assertion.) This major improvement was maintained at 5-month follow-up. However, at 2-year follow-up she reported having taken up with another married man by whom she felt used; and at nearly 4-year follow-up she had quite voluntarily got herself into an utterly self-destructive situation, which consisted of being unable to refuse to marry a man whom she didn't like and who neglected her, with the aim of helping him get to England from behind the Iron Curtain.

The following are some highly condensed passages from her follow-up interview:

INT (FO): How long have you known your husband?
PT: One year and 7 months. In 7 months I got three letters from him. Well really it is the same story if you look at my case history – I was giving everything without getting anything back.
INT: When did you realise that you didn't want to marry him?
PT: When he met me at the airport, instead of kissing me, he didn't take any interest in me. This horrible feeling came over me. I was just trapped.
INT: Why trapped? Surely you could have left?
PT: I couldn't. I was illegally in his house. There was no way I could go.
INT: What would have happened if you had gone to a hotel, or taken the first airplane to London?
PT: I couldn't. When you are there and all his relatives are there, how could I get out? I suppose I didn't want to create a big scene. I had discussions with him for 5 nights. I told him I didn't love him any more, and after that he started to fuss over me like a little boy, running around, and I didn't know how to get out. I think it is basically because I am not ruthless enough. I didn't have enough courage. It was like a blank all over my head. I remember my therapist telling me that part of my trouble was not making my feelings known or demanding enough. I don't like to hurt other people. I hurt myself instead. . . .
INT: In spite of your awareness of always putting yourself in the victim position, you still do it. Why can that be?
PT: I think it belongs to my childhood. My parents. . . I was taking responsibility for them. My mother needs to be looked after, and I have never really communicated with my father.
INT: But what I am most impressed by is that these two characteristics of 'needing help' and 'not being able to communicate' are contained in your description of your husband.
PT: Now that you say that, it's funny. *He reminded me of my father.* It was very strange.
INT: In what way?
PT: Father was often shouting. When I was with my husband he couldn't talk to me as I am doing with you. He would raise his voice and shout, so I felt I couldn't leave him in just the same way. And the other thing was that he didn't seem to be interested in me as a woman or a person, the same as my father towards my mother.
INT: So why should you look for such a man?
PT: I don't really know why. Security, familiarity. . . It's funny that I always seem to like horrible people.

This story illustrates the extraordinary power of what Freud called the 'compulsion to repeat', which in many of Davanloo's case histories seems to represent partly a defence against powerful aggressive feelings, and partly a form of self-punishment for them, driven by a highly pathological superego. However, it is a power that is not invincible, as is illustrated by the next patient.

The Librarian who Sought Suffering, illustrating the resolution of a maladaptive pattern

This was a patient to whom the epithet 'masochistic' could be applied in both the figurative sense of deliberately seeking situations that caused her suffering, and the more literal sense of getting sexual pleasure from being ill-treated. For instance, at initial assessment she described a previous relation with a man in which she had discovered, to her horror, how much she enjoyed being forced into sex; when she felt excluded she would go out into the street with the fantasy of being raped, murdered, or run over; she actively promoted her husband's affair with another woman; and her sexual fantasies included being used sexually by a number of men whom she didn't know.

Where possible the definition of 'resolution' needs to make use of psychodynamic knowledge about the inner mechanisms involved – in this case the above-mentioned theory of masochism as a defence against, and punishment for, heavily guilt-laden aggression. The clearly indicated criteria of resolution then become that the patient should become in touch with her aggression and be able to use it constructively without guilt, and – in consequence – masochistic phenomena should disappear and be replaced by more gentle sexuality.

The patient met these criteria in full. As reported in Chapters 1 and 8, she came to realise during therapy that she had 'a monster of violent anger' within her, and that she both loved and hated her parents. At follow-up it was clear that she was able to assert herself constructively with her husband – whom she asked to leave – and also in her life outside. As far as masochism is concerned, the following are two condensed passages from the account of the follow-up interview:

> She is at present involved with a very sweet man named Shaun and she feels that she has got over the problem of violence and sex. She likes herself better and doesn't treat herself like that any more. She said, 'Sex is nice when you want it.' The trouble with her husband was that he liked in some way to rape her occasionally and always tried to exercise power over her. In her sexual relations since her marriage broke up there have been none of these power games, except for one man who 'made her feel like a panel of knobs'. [We may make the crucial comment here that she broke with this man very quickly, in marked contrast to her previous pattern – and also in contrast to what happened in the case of the Victimised Telephonist.]

The following is a passage relevant to the issue of guilt: 'I asked her about the incident in her childhood where her brother was near to drowning. She laughed and said, "I have forgiven myself for that. I don't think about it any more. It certainly doesn't bother me".'

Thus all the criteria described above seem to be fulfilled.

The other patients with favourable outcome

The Nurse Mourning her Fiancé

Here the maladaptive pattern was entirely conscious: before she came to therapy she had deliberately broken off a relation with a man for fear – if she became deeply involved with him – of being subjected to yet another loss; and early in the follow-up period she had shown similar behaviour, deliberately provoking rows in order to end the relationship. Clearly this pattern was highly self-destructive, and the obvious criterion that she needs to fulfil is that she should allow herself to risk becoming involved with a man, and should go on to form a rewarding relationship with him. The evidence is unequivocal that this criterion was fulfilled. For details please see Chapter 1. Further discussion is given in Chapter 27.

The Pacifist Conductor

Here the resolution of maladaptive patterns was really no different from the improvements already reported under the heading of emotional freeing: his resumption of conducting after a 5-year withdrawal; and his giving up the defensive mechanism of getting other people to express emotions for him while he remained calm, which was replaced by the ability to express effective and constructive anger.

The Car Battery Man

When he came to therapy he had shown a repetitive pattern of staying only a short time in each of his jobs because of his inability either to restrain, or to express effectively, his anger with bosses. At the final follow-up (nearly 8 years) he had kept his last job for 4½ years. He said that although there was still some residual anxiety in his relation with bosses, he could now argue with them and get his own way.

In addition he had shown a pattern with women which was similar to that of the Nurse Mourning her Fiancé, consisting of blowing small incidents up out of proportion in order to have an excuse to break with them. This also was resolved: during therapy he began the process of committing himself to the girl whom he subsequently married; and at follow-up he described being able to quarrel and make up in a way that did not destroy the relationship.

The Sculptress with Nightmares

When she first came to us she showed three highly maladaptive behaviour patterns: excessive drinking and histrionic behaviour, as ways of coping with stress; and an extraordinary degree of promiscuity, each relation starting passionately, as if it was going to be the 'real thing,' and then coming to an abrupt end within 1 or 2 weeks. The criteria are therefore that she should be able to cope with stress in an active, realistic, and effective way, without either excessive drinking or histrionic behaviour; and to form a close and lasting relation with a man in which both partners are committed to one another. Of these criteria, the first was largely fulfilled, but the second was not (see Chapter 7 for details). Her problem over commitment was still being expressed through her choice of partner.

Like the Victimised Telephonist, at follow-up she showed clear insight into another unresolved maladaptive pattern, expressing the compulsion to repeat. Below is an extract from the follow-up interview:

PT: My father was a little Frenchman, a god in his shop [ladies' dresses, before the restaurant]. I think I was competing with the ladies, doing things to get his attention. He was working so hard he didn't give me much attention. He is still a very handsome man. I wanted to gain his favour because he didn't give me enough attention.
INT: But in your relations with men you often find yourself in situations where getting attention is difficult.

PT: Yes, I went to choose the same thing recently. The man can't give attention at all. He seemed to be so generous, but I filtered off what I didn't want to see.

The Mountain Tarn Girl

Here the maladaptive pattern was to become involved over and over again in triangular situations. Obviously such situations are a natural hazard of relations between the sexes, but in her case the evidence was strong that triangular relations were something that she was actively seeking, whether consciously or not. At initial assessment we counted at least six: e.g. she had twice transferred her affections from a boy-friend to one of his male friends, she had apparently pushed another boy-friend into a relation with one of her female friends, and she had had more than one affair with married men, one of which was still current. She said of this last relation, 'It is necessarily clandestine. I fear involvement with anyone else.' She showed insight into the fact that this pattern was a problem to her by writing in her questionnaire, under the heading of 'How do you expect treatment to help you?', 'Perhaps to find a reason for my use of affairs'.

At 5½-year follow-up she had had one disastrous relation ending in another triangle – the man went off with one of her friends – and this was followed by a brief period of promiscuity; but she finally settled with her current man-friend, with whom she had been for 4 years. Here the relation was full of companionship, shared interests, and enjoyable sex, but the problem was that he himself felt unable to make a final commitment to her – so, as in the case of the Sculptress, we meet the apparent expression of problems of commitment through choice of partner.

Of the seven 'best' patients, only the Betrayed Son failed to show maladaptive patterns of this kind, so that in his case the criterion is not relevant.

Resolution of maladaptive patterns in the rest of the sample

Only 2 of the other 17 patients fulfilled this criterion.

The Concert-goer

This patient's basic anxiety was apparently about competition with other males. In consequence he tried to avoid competitive and group situations; and he remained in relation to a much older, married woman with the collusion of her crippled husband – a situation of 'no contest'.

At the final follow-up (nearly 6 years), although he was still in this same triangular situation, he said that his anxiety in the presence of other men and in group situations was much reduced. He now took part in competitive leisure activities, and he felt much less threatened by male authority-figures and was able to assert himself with them.

This represents a distinct improvement, but since he was only now beginning to consider parting from his woman-friend, his ability to compete for a woman in reality had not yet been put to the test.

The Secretary in a State of Nirvana

Her original problem emerged with the utmost clarity as a preoccupation with everyone else's needs at the expense of her own, which was now breaking down into depression masking intense resentment. At initial assessment we overlooked a second problem similar to that shown by the Librarian and the Victimised Telephonist, namely a tendency to form relations with exceedingly difficult and inconsiderate men. One of these was her current boy-friend, who she said never lifted a finger to help her, and another was her boss. Her application for therapy had been precipitated by extreme stress caused by having to cope both with this boss and also with her workmates in general, who according to her statement were all in a state of potential or actual breakdown.

At 4-year follow-up she described the change in her: 'I used to try and please everybody except myself. I have become more selfish. I am infinitely better at standing up for myself at work and also with my parents. Now I go home when I want to, not out of a sense of duty.' She was still working for the same difficult man but was coping with him much better than before.

This was a very clear and insightful statement of the replacement of an inappropriate by an appropriate reaction, but further examination of her situation revealed many reservations. When she was asked for a specific example of acting 'more selfishly' she was unable to give one. Moreover, she made absolutely clear that work was the only area where she was able to allow herself to be emotionally involved – in particular to feel angry and assert herself – and that her whole life-style was one of 'nirvana' and emotional withdrawal. This lack of involvement included her feelings about her current man-friend, with whom it seemed that the main factors in his favour were that there was no question of commitment, and that the relation 'made no demands on her at all'.

Conclusion

Neurotic behaviour patterns such as these have the reputation of being extremely resistant even to long-term psychotherapy, and it is encouraging that so many of them should have been resolved by the relatively brief interventions with which this book is concerned.

25

The ability to 'be oneself'

Introduction

This criterion overlaps with emotional freeing and self-assertion, but some patients made direct references to it, while others showed changes for which the 'ability to be themselves' seemed the obvious and specific description. The scores of '+' extend further down Table 22.1 than they do for emotional freeing, and are more frequent below the line than for resolution of maladaptive patterns, so that the line of demarcation between scores of '+' and '0' tends to fall between the intermediate and poor results rather than between the best and intermediate. Indeed, perhaps the clearest statement of a change in this area came from one of the intermediate patients, as described below.

The Allergic Receptionist (score for outcome 1.75)

Many people say the sessions have altered me completely. I have become far more decisive.... Now I can tell anybody what I think. I can do what I like, when I like, how I like. I am *me*. I am not answerable to anybody, apart from people I might affect. I have made decisions about the things that I want when I want them. I go and ask people what they think on some occasions, but then I decide for myself. If I disagree with what is being said, I say so.

Evidence from the seven 'best' patients

Of these seven patients, the Nurse Mourning her Fiancé and Conductor were put in touch with the whole range of their hitherto blocked-off feelings, which obviously means that they became able to 'be themselves' in every area of their lives. Details have already been given in Chapter 1 for the former patient and Chapter 23 for the latter, and there is nothing further to add here. The Car Battery Man is also omitted since he apparently did not suffer from a problem in this area. However, the other four patients provided specific evidence on this issue, as follows.

The Librarian who Sought Suffering

In her initial application form she had made one of the clearest statements of a problem over being herself, in the words: 'I have no one inside me who can tell me who I am.'

She was followed up by the Individual Team, who made an extremely careful formulation before seeing her. Two criteria laid down were: 'the ability to relate to people in general in a way that she feels is her true self', and 'the ability to be alone'.

The following are extracts from the account of her follow-up interview:

> Nowadays she enjoys the difference between her life before therapy and her life now, since it is no longer run by somebody else's precepts.
>
> She supposes that she is something of a perennial student, but previously she had never really done what she wanted, and she feels she is now catching up in her 30s on the experience that she has missed in her 20s.
>
> As far as being alone is concerned, 2 years ago her husband, from whom she is separated, took the children for Christmas. She had rather dreaded the thought of being on her own, but in fact she had a marvellous time and enjoyed it immensely. She was able to write, listen to music, and dance, and she felt very much that she was *herself* in a way that she had never achieved before.

The Sculptress with Nightmares

At initial assessment this patient described what was clearly a defence against facing her true self, consisting of hectic over-activity: 'I feel all right as long as I keep rushing around to friends and to the pub.'

Part of the account of Session 27 – the session in which the patient described her purification by the 'white witch' – reads as follows: 'She feels she has changed now, and everyone feels she is different. She feels slowed down, calmer, more contained. It's a very good feeling.'

The following is from the account of the 3-month follow-up: 'One of the striking things, she said, is that she doesn't need to show off any more. She can be quiet and pleasant with other people and finds that they still accept her even though she doesn't have to act all the time.'

However, at the 5½-year follow-up she made clear in a very honest and insightful way that this tendency to put on an act was still present, though she could control it: 'I always wanted to be shocking, to impress people all the time. I wanted to be the centre of attention. I am not totally off that still. I would say, God, Violette, you are doing it again, stop it. I don't like what I found out about myself, that that bit of me can still bubble up. But now I am using my excess energy in a more positive way. I think the sculptures I have been doing lately are the best ones of my life.'

The Betrayed Son

The following is an extract from the therapist's account of Session 3, where there was a graphic and moving description of the patient's awareness of a need to be himself, which included being creative with his hands:

> He said that as far back as he could remember he had had an image of a house with two rooms. One room would be where he expressed himself, full of pictures, modelling clay, and so on, a kind of studio where he could really let go and be himself. There would be a door connecting this room with his other room. This would be far more formally and plushly decorated. He would entertain his friends in this second room, and then once he got to know them he would open the door and show them the first room and see what their reaction was.

In Session 20 he said that he was still looking for a way of life that 'isn't a complete rejection of everything everybody else wants for him, but is also something of him'.

In Session 27 he said that he was now determined to make decisions on what *he* wanted, and not on his mother's ideas, his wife's, his boss's, or the therapist's.

At follow-up it was clear that he had achieved this goal, since he had given up his work as manager of a chain of delicatessen shops, which he had never liked, and, having gone through a training, had become a craftsman instructor in a rehabilitation centre.

The Girl and the Mountain Tarn

In this patient the issue of being herself was very complicated and became the principal issue dealt with in her therapy. Like the Librarian, she was followed up by the Individual Team, who made a very detailed formulation of her problems. Moreover, in spite of the fact that – in accordance with research policy – they were only allowed access to the material available at initial assessment, they were able to forecast the main focus of therapy with much greater accuracy than had been possible in the original clinical situation. Part of their formulation reads as follows:

> We think she suffers from great anxiety and anger about her identity, with the problem of whether she can express her true personality or whether she has to adopt some different role imposed on her from outside in order to be acceptable. The main causes of this seem to be that her father both wanted her to be a boy, and also encouraged her artistic talents; while her mother discouraged both her artistic side and the use of her intelligence. The patient's first hysterical attack occurred when she was faced with the decision of whether to follow what her mother or her father wanted for her.

At 5½-year follow-up there was considerable evidence that much of this problem had been solved. She had found work and hobbies which made use of both her intelligence and her artistic interests, and had tackled them in a most creative way, carrying out her own research.

She said of herself in general, 'I feel more like how I think I am'. She also said that she doesn't need to put on an act any more, but can 'put it on or take it off like clothes'. However, at the follow-up interview she gave the impression of having to be constantly entertaining, 'talking at a tremendous rate and using a whole range of catchy phrases and anecdotes', so perhaps this problem was not solved completely.

Evidence from the rest of the sample

In addition to the Allergic Receptionist, described above, three others of the patients with intermediate scores (including those who adopted false solutions) fulfilled this criterion.

The Mother or Teenage Daughter

As her pseudonym implies, this patient's situation was of a kind likely to lead to great confusion of her sense of identity, since she had become a mother at 18 and at 26 was still living at home with her parents and her 8-year-old son, for whom her own mother had virtually taken over the mothering role. Her conflict seemed to be between staying at home and being looked after, while at the same time feeling cooped up, and giving up this easy life in order to attain her longed-for independence.

During therapy she became able, for the first time in her life, to bring about a genuine dialogue with her parents about her problems and theirs, which produced a major shift in her relation with them (details will be given in Chapter 30, under the heading of constructive self-assertion). However, it is not certain that this persisted at follow-up. On the other hand, a crucial change that was found at follow-up was that she had finally been able to leave home and live her own life.

The Hypomanic Advertising Executive

In early sessions the therapist brought out that the patient adopted the role of 'an amiable clot' and avoided all forms of aggression throughout his life; and also that he was unable to be himself in the presence of his powerful mother, who tried to keep him as a little boy, and by whom he felt swamped and engulfed.

In Session 21 he spoke of wanting to 'throw off the fetters', and take his own decisions. At 5-year follow-up this seemed to have been very much fulfilled. He spoke of his pathological tie to his mother in most forceful terms, ending by saying 'now the link is broken and things are just pleasant between us'. As far as work was concerned, so far from being amiable and lacking confidence, he was now leader of a team training other executives, and was apparently doing very well – though how much his glowing account of this was tinged by a hypomanic state was impossible to judge.

The Secretary in a State of Nirvana

When she first came she suffered from a preoccupation with everybody else's needs at the expense of her own. This seemed to change very early in therapy, and in Session 4 – after a violent break with her boy-friend – she described having passed a very pleasant week-end on her own, feeling free and using the time doing exactly what she wanted.

In Session 8 she reported an incident with her parents similar to that described above in the case of the Mother or Teenage Daughter. She had at last spoken her mind to them, and this had resulted in the first meaningful dialogue with them that she had ever had in her life (again, more details will be given in Chapter 30).

At 4-year follow-up the patient's *statements* seemed to indicate that these improvements in her ability to be herself had been maintained: 'I used to try and please everybody except myself. I have become more selfish. I am infinitely better at standing up for myself at work and also with my parents. Now I go home when I want to, not out of a sense of duty.' These statements are very difficult to evaluate in face of the powerful opposite evidence that she was in a state of 'nirvana', coping with relationships by a general emotional withdrawal.

Conclusion

The above material makes clear that the criterion of being oneself can be taken on several different levels. At the most superficial level, the Mother or Teenage Daughter achieved the criterion *geographically* in the sense of leaving home and thus escaping from the situation that caused confusion in her sense of identity; but it is by no means certain that this resulted in much inner change. At a deeper level, several of the above patients changed from either having to put on an act for other people, or from feeling compelled to conform to other people's view of them, on the one hand, to being able to be more natural or to pursue what they wanted for themselves, on the other. And finally, at the deepest level, several patients found aspects of their personality which had never previously seen the light of day, typified by the Conductor who was put in touch with all his buried emotional life, and by the Librarian, who found the ability to express herself in an entirely new way when she was alone.

The capacity to be oneself is probably the most subtle and least objective of all the criteria discussed here. It has only rarely been mentioned in criteria laid down in advance of follow-up; and in a sense, like emotional freeing, this may be because it seems to be too general, for it needs to be applied to the great majority of neurotic patients and goes without saying; and yet the patients described here have demonstrated that it can often be highly specific and can figure prominently in the over-all judgment of psychodynamic change.

26

Symptoms

Recovery from symptoms is often regarded as one of the least significant types of change, since in many cases it may be the manifestation of a false solution. In the past, these false solutions led to one of the many difficulties and disappointments experienced by Freud and his followers, who found that symptoms regularly disappeared early in therapy as a result of 'transference cure' or 'flight into health'. In the former mechanism, the patient loses symptoms because of the support and symbolic love provided by the analytical situation, only to relapse immediately at mention of termination; in the latter the symptoms probably disappear as a result of repression, brought about by anxiety at the threat of having the underlying conflict uncovered, only to recur at some time during the follow-up period. Moreover many neurotic symptoms, particularly depression, are self-limiting and sometimes remit permanently, with treatment or without, by a mechanism that is essentially unknown. In the present series something of this kind happened in the case of the Rebellious Script Writer, where no light whatsoever was thrown on the meaning of her symptom of obsessional preoccupation with lesbianism, which just disappeared as mysteriously as it came.

As a result of all these observations, many dynamically oriented therapists make the distinction between 'symptomatic change' and 'dynamic change' in such a way as to imply that these two types of change are entirely separate, whereas of course *symptomatic recovery represents an essential criterion for dynamic recovery in every patient.* It is possible to have symptomatic recovery without dynamic recovery, but it is not possible to make a judgment of dynamic recovery unless symptomatic recovery is present also. Therefore, as long as the evidence for false solutions is carefully examined, we regard symptomatic changes as no less important than any of the other criteria considered in these pages.

Like the ability to 'be oneself', recovery from symptoms is found extensively among the intermediate as well as the best results. Details are summarised in Table 26.1.

Discussion

It needs to be emphasised that the judgments of symptomatic change have been made in isolation, i.e. quite independently of other changes that the patient may have shown, and without the help of any psychodynamic thinking. With this in mind, the most important observation that can be made from the table is as follows. Whereas there are 7 patients (29%) who score 2.0 or more for outcome on dynamic criteria, there are perhaps 15 who would be rated as at least 'improved' on purely symptomatic criteria. The proportion 15/24 is 62.5%, so that even this small sample conforms to Eysenck's thesis that no matter what treatment patients are given, or if they have no treatment at all, roughly two thirds will be rated as symptomatically improved after 2 years (see Eysenck, 1952, 1960). On the other hand, if the improvements in the present series are examined carefully, some of those in patients lying towards the middle of the table become highly suspect. The three clearest examples are as follows:

1 The Advertising Executive said he had recovered from his impotence, but this kind of recovery had proved to be evanescent on two previous occasions, and moreover at follow-up he was clearly hypomanic.
2 The Nirvana Secretary showed overwhelming evidence of having achieved her symptomatic recovery at the price of severe emotional withdrawal.
3 The Self-driving Physicist no longer suffered from a chronic anxiety state, but this had been replaced by compulsive anxiety – in his own words, 'I feel I must run at 100 mph even if it's only necessary to run at 50 mph'.

These observations underline the importance of judging outcome in the patient as a whole, making the maximum use of psychodynamic insight. Only if this is done can Eysenck's figures be truly evaluated.

The other interesting observation is the presence of some degree of residual symptoms in certain patients who otherwise were recovered or at least very much improved. This applies to the two male patients suffering from phobic symptoms.

At initial assessment the Car Battery Man suffered from a feeling of panic, with the fear that he would faint, in every kind of enclosed public place, most of which kinds of situation he would avoid. He was unable to travel by Underground, there were certain clubs that he was unable to enter, and he could not go to a concert unless he could sit near an aisle. At final follow-up he still suffered from anxiety in the same situations, but now it was sufficiently improved for him to be able to control it and to behave in such a way that it was reduced to a minimum. As an example he was now able to travel by Underground as long as he stood near the door, so that he knew he could get out at the next station.

The Betrayed Son suffered from very similar symptoms: sudden attacks of fear that something terrible was going to happen to him, leading to feelings of panic, which came on him in the middle of a crowded room, often forcing him to leave. These symptoms also sometimes came on when he was alone. His working life was considerably affected. At follow-up he said that he still suffered from similar symptoms occasionally, but it was clear that they were much less severe and no longer interfered with his life. He gave as an example that when he was talking to some colleagues about coming for follow-up, he suddenly began to sweat profusely and to feel 'drained'. However, he said he knew the cause was anxiety about the forthcoming interview, and he was therefore able to 'talk himself through it'.

There were a number of patients in the Individual Series who similarly appeared to be recovered except for residual symptoms, including some who had had long-term therapy at several times a week, and one who had had a 5-year analysis at five times a week on the couch. Neurotic symptoms – and particularly phobias – are often mysterious phenomena; and the possibility needs to be considered that their persistence may be due to some self-perpetuating mechanism, rather than to

Table 26.1 Symptomatic changes

Patient (Score for outcome)	Initial symptoms and duration	State at follow-up
Nurse Mourning her Fiancé (3.75)	Depression (lack of interest, loss of feeling), 18/12	Recovered
Pacifist Conductor (3.0)	Unable to sleep before 3 a.m.	Recovered
	Nocturnal eating, with anxiety	Still present, no longer anxious
	Depression/elation (all the above for 4 years)	Recovered
	Asthma from age 2	Unchanged (found to be allergic to dust)
Librarian who Sought Suffering (2.875)	Recurrent depression (wish for death), 18 years	Recovered
Car Battery Man (2.75)	Acute anxiety attack 2 years ago	No recurrence
	Claustrophobia in crowded places, 2 years	Improved
Sculptress with Nightmares (2.75)	Depression (crying, early waking)	Much improved
	Problem drinking	Recovered
	Rhinitis	Recovered
	Eczema (all the above for 2 years)	Much improved
Betrayed Son (2.25)	Headaches, chest pain, etc. with hypochondriacal anxiety	Unchanged
	Fear of collapsing in a crowded room or when alone	Recovered
	Depression (moody, irritable) (all the above for 2 years)	Improved
Mountain Tarn Girl (2.0)	Histrionic outbursts, 7 years	Much improved
		Recovered
Rebellious Script Writer (1.75)	Obsessional preoccupation with lesbianism, 6/12	Recovered
	Phobia of flying (some years)	Unchanged
Allergic Receptionist (1.75)	Depression, mood swings (lifelong)	Recovered
	Dizziness, fainting, headaches	Recovered (?due to diet) except dysmenorrhoea
	dysmenorrhoea (some months)	
Concert-goer in an Acute Panic (1.625)	Recent severe panic attack	No recurrence
	Anxiety with other males (many years)	Much improved
Mother or Teenage Daughter (1.5)	Mood swings	Much improved
	Recurrent physical symptoms (both for some years)	Much improved

Patient	Symptoms	Outcome
Hypomanic Advertising Executive (1.375)	Impotence, 6/12	Recovered (hypomanic)
Secretary in a State of Nirvana (1.0)	Depression (lethargy, insomnia, lack of concentration) 2 years	Recovered
Self-driving Physicist (1.0)	Constant anxiety, 2 years	Replaced by self-driving
	Impotence, 2 years	Recovered
Acting-out Accounts Clerk (0.5)	Claustrophobic anxiety (social gatherings, public transport), 6 years	Slightly improved
Actress with Elocution Problems (0.25)	Voice difficulty in dramatic passages, many years	Unchanged
	Lifelong recurrent depression (emptiness, lack of meaning)	Recovered
Miner's Daughter (0.25)	Severe claustrophobic social anxiety with blushing, 3 years	Still present but controllable
	Severe histrionic outbursts, 15/12	Still present potentially but controllable
Anorexic Museum Assistant (0.0)	Depression with early waking, 2 years	Slightly improved but still unable to cope
Psychiatric Nurse with Attacks of Rage (0.0)	Manifold physical symptoms, 2 years	Unchanged
	Amenorrhoea, 2½ years	Highly irregular periods
	Depression (exhaustion, insomnia), 10/12	Unchanged
Girl with Eye Problems (−0.5)	Inability to focus her eyes (some years)	Unchanged
Borderline Graduate Clerk (−1.0)	Depression, crying attacks (lifelong)	Unchanged
	Tension, headaches, gastrointestinal symptoms (many years)	Unchanged
Robot Man (−1.0)	Derealisation, 13 years	Somewhat improved
Victimised Telephonist (−1.0)	Depression, 7 years	Unchanged
	Physical symptoms, back pain (some years)	Unchanged
Acutely Suicidal Receptionist (no score)	Depression, 18/12	Suicide

a failure to deal thoroughly with the underlying conflicts. However, Davanloo (personal communication) states categorically that his aim is always *total resolution* – which means that no trace of the original disturbances, including symptoms, remains – and moreover that in the majority of his patients this is in fact achieved. One of the main characteristics of Davanloo's therapy is that, under persistent challenge to the defences, the patient reaches the direct experience of every kind of hitherto unconscious feeling. The reason for the common persistence of symptoms in other forms of therapy may therefore lie in the possibility that the experience of feelings is insufficiently direct and intense, or insufficiently comprehensive. This remains one of the deficiencies of those forms of therapy, obviously including the form considered here, which rely for their effectiveness on interpretations alone.

27

Relations with the opposite sex

I Clinical material

Introduction

The quality of intimate relations is perhaps the most searching test of an individual's mental health and adjustment, and it is this area that has always received the greatest weight in our judgments of outcome.

Here there are three criteria which will be considered together: commitment, emotional closeness, and 'relation free from serious reservations'. Obviously, if either of the first two is not fulfilled the third will not be either, and therefore it will not need to be mentioned specifically. Of the three, perhaps the most interesting is *commitment*, with special reference to the anxiety it causes and the various devices that patients find for avoiding it.

At a follow-up interview it is extremely difficult to assess the true quality of a patient's relation with his or her partner, and often the final judgment can only come from the over-all gestalt that the patient conveys. For this reason we will often quote relatively long passages, where possible in the patient's words, which may help readers to draw their own conclusions.

Clinical material

The Nurse Mourning her Fiancé

This was the only patient in the series who fulfilled all three of these criteria for certain.

When she first came she suffered from a major resistance against committing herself to any new relation, the reason being that she had been so seriously wounded by the sudden deaths of three people to whom she had been deeply attached in the past: first her mother, then her father, and finally her fiancé. The nature of her anxiety was thus both obvious and entirely conscious. Before she came to therapy she had, quite deliberately, parted from a man when she felt she was becoming too deeply involved; during therapy and at 8-month follow-up her only male friend was homosexual; and in the early follow-up period she had brought the relation with another man to an end by deliberately provoking quarrels with him. Her own graphic description of the decision to risk a further commitment has already been given in Chapter 1.

Of all the criteria, the evidence on emotional closeness is the most difficult to obtain, and in the case of this patient we could wish that we had more detail. Nevertheless she made clear that she felt the relation with her husband, including the sexual relation, was very satisfactory to her, and this was confirmed by the whole gestalt that she conveyed. Two important pieces of evidence, already presented in Chapter 1, were that she was able to share her deep feelings about her stepmother's illness with him, and that in her description she was not idealising the relation, since she described being able to quarrel with him and make it up without any residue of resentment.

As far as the third criterion is concerned, we were unable to find any reservations concerning her relation with her husband whatsoever.

For full details please see Chapter 1.

The Pacifist Conductor

Before he came to therapy this patient had formed a relation with an Indian girl who was later to become his wife. The relation was very strangely chequered, and the feelings that he expressed throughout the entire period of his contact with us were extraordinarily – and most openly and honestly – ambivalent.

During therapy serious quarrels developed between them, involving physical violence on both sides. Some of these were concerned with her wish for him to marry her to solve her problem over a work permit, which indeed he had promised to do, but which he must have felt as an unreasonable demand. At 6-month follow-up he spoke in an extremely negative way about her, saying that he wanted to get rid of her but couldn't do so because she had nowhere to go, and the only solution would be to kill her. It was here, also, that he said that he felt she deliberately provoked him into violence, and that this was something that she needed. At the same time he made the remark: 'Sex is always satisfactory and often gentle – in our relation we seem to oscillate between physical violence and physical intimacy.'

At final follow-up (6½ years) they were married. He now gave the impression of trying to play down his feelings by being humorous, while at the same time apparently revealing an emotional commitment of considerable depth. Thus their marriage had partly fulfilled the purpose of enabling her to get a work permit, but he then made clear that he now feels much closer to her. One of the important factors in this was the profoundly emotional experience of his year's stay in India, which had resulted in a new-found understanding of Indian people and their language, and a very warm relation with her family, particularly her mother; 'I feel I have adopted a mother, even though we couldn't speak together. There is an intuitive understanding between us.' Of his wife he said, 'I realised how it feels to live in a very different culture. I think it has made our relationship *even stronger,* because I understand how difficult it was for her to live here.'

On the other hand, when asked about the question of having children, he spoke of the relation needing to be 'consummated' by children, and he then went on to say that 'it would mean having a kind of commitment to this marriage' – as if he was still doubtful about committing himself finally.

As far as violence was concerned, he said: 'It is gradually improving. It seldom happens now. It used to be pretty awful – it's got less and less like that. But I don't think it's because I thought I must control myself. The relationship has moved on without any effort on my part.'

All the above made clear that his relation with his wife contained much that was positive, but left us with possible reservations about its true quality and his final commitment to her (the '+' sign for commitment in Table 22.1 was the result of giving him the benefit of the doubt).

The Librarian who Sought Suffering

This patient's maladapative pattern of masochistic relations with men, and its resolution, has already been described in Chapter 24. Here we need to consider only the quality of her relations with men at final follow-up.

She said that now she is very nervous of intellectual men, and she has had two long-lasting relations with men who are by a long way her intellectual and social .inferiors. When she was asked about the question of marriage to the second of these men she said, 'Well, we are almost living together, but I can't commit myself to that level of involvement, and nor can he. He is very dear to me and I wouldn't like to lose him. If we did stop being close I would like to be friends with him. He is very loving and tender and not possessive.'

Thus there is little doubt that she fulfils the criterion of emotional closeness, but she seems to be avoiding a final commitment by choosing men with whom this is out of the question. The nature of her anxiety in this area is unclear.

The Car Battery Man

At initial assessment this patient described having been seriously let down by his first girl-friend. In order to avoid further commitment he had then adopted a maladaptive pattern in relation to women, which consisted of blowing up small incidents out of proportion in order to have an excuse to leave. This pattern and its progressive resolution, ending in his marriage, have been described in Chapter 24.

At the second follow-up (nearly 3 years) he spoke of his wife as follows: 'I had absolutely no intention of getting married when I first met her, and not for a long time after. Finally she confronted me with what I was going to do. I took a week to think about it but then I decided we'd get married. From this point everything took off.'

'I sometimes fool myself that I'd be happier with some other girl, like one I see walking down the street. But I've met a good cross-section of women and none of them would I have taken on as a wife. When I get home I know I have found the right one. She's fiery. She doesn't let me get my own way – that's a good thing, I like it. The number of times she's packed her bags and been ready to go! But next day or even an hour later she settles down and it's all right again.'

At the final follow-up (nearly 8 years) he described the following: it turned out that his wife had a violent temper and thought nothing of attacking him with her fists – 'There was so much vengeance and anger behind it. . . . She is pretty unique, that's why I married her. She can be ultra-nice but also ultra-nasty – the extremes are pretty fantastic, but the middle of the road is the good part. What it brought out in me was that I started to lose my temper for very little reason. It became a way of life.' The main cause of her anger was her jealousy of one of his male friends in particular – whom he still wanted to go out with, seemingly to a not unreasonable degree. He had finally got as far as going to a solicitor, but in the end had decided to see his marriage through. 'I don't give up so easily. I wanted a stable relation and a happy marriage, and I didn't want to go back to the single life. I have seen so many friends who wanted to do so – I was the opposite.' He thus gave strong evidence of true commitment.

A further cause of their quarrels was that whereas he wanted to have children, she didn't. He described events on the evening on which he came back from the solicitor: 'I went home and said, "I've seen a solicitor and I've had enough of this situation". She cried and said she was pregnant. It was a very nice evening. I cancelled the solicitor and it's really been fine ever since.' Since the baby was born, he said, 'It's a different way of life and things have been much pleasanter.'

As far as the sexual side of his marriage was concerned, he spoke of 'good rows and good sex' before her pregnancy, but ended by saying, 'Now, when the relationship is on a pretty steady footing, the sexual side hasn't a lot of importance.'

As mentioned in the full account of the follow-up, this remark is very difficult to evaluate. Does it simply represent a passing phase in the relationship, does it mean that violence is a necessary preliminary to enjoyable sex, does it mean that their closeness is bought at the price of some degree of emotional withdrawal? There is room for many different opinions. It made us uneasy, which is why we did not give a '+' sign for 'free from serious reservations', in Table 22.1, but this may well be unnecessarily conservative.

We have quoted much of the material in full, because the final conclusion must depend on the over-all gestalt conveyed to the reader, who then must quite unavoidably make a value judgment on the evidence. Apart from the reservations mentioned above, his description seems to be of a deep and genuine commitment between two people able to express their emotions freely; and the criteria of commitment and emotional closeness seem completely fulfilled. The marriage has indeed been exceedingly stormy, but there is no evidence that the violence has any neurotic or pathological quality, and the view could be taken that it is within normal limits.

The Sculptress with Nightmares

Before her marriage this patient had had a series of passionate and stormy affairs, several of them with disturbed men, and had had four engagements, all of which she herself brought to an end. At the age of 30 she married a man in complete contrast to the others, since he was rather Victorian and inhibited, and seemed to offer her security and stability. Their marriage finally broke up because of his sterility and his unsympathetic attitude to her desperate wish to have children. It is clear that he drifted away from her and began to neglect her. One of the men with whom she took up after this was someone who she knew would be going away for 6 months in a few months' time – which did in fact result in the break-up of the relationship. Since then she embarked on a series of increasingly short-lived affairs – during therapy each relation seemed to last no more than a fortnight. Thus her history suggested few problems over 'emotional closeness' – though we may question its true depth – but a severe problem over 'commitment'.

The evidence that this problem continued to be expressed by her choice of partner is overwhelming and has already been presented in Chapter 7.

Moreover, she was able to link her choice of men to the relation with her father, as described in Chapter 24.

The Betrayed Son

This patient's problems, and the background to them, bore many similarities to those of the Car Battery Man, but his relation to the opposite sex turned out very differently. When he first came to us he was already married, but we had little information on which to judge the quality of his relation with his wife. We only knew that in their early relation sex had been highly satisfactory, but that since then there had been a falling off, which had at least partly been caused by his physical symptoms. During therapy he worked through a considerable degree of hostility towards his wife, which was linked to hostility against his mother after the birth of his younger brother.

At the 4-year follow-up there seemed to have been a considerable deterioration in the marital relation. He spoke of their being more able to say what they felt to each other, but said that this did not necessarily make them any closer. The most unsatisfactory aspect of their relation was that they were both expressing hostility to each other in indirect ways. They need to renovate their current flat in order to get the maximum price for it, and he is putting this off – one of his complaints about her was that she was too materialistic. In order to put pressure on him she has been withholding sex from him. Both these forms of behaviour seem to be highly destructive and lead to no resolution of the situation. Here there is a marked contrast from the Car Battery Man, in whose case the mutual hostility seems to have been present on the basis of a fundamentally good relation, and in the end was satisfactorily resolved.

It was on the information in this 4-year follow-up that the final assessment was made. It was very difficult to judge the relation between the patient and his wife. They were obviously going through a major crisis, and only the future would show whether it eventually became resolved or whether it would lead to further deterioration. One thing was certain, that the criterion of 'the relation free from serious reservations' could not possibly be said to be fulfilled.

In fact there is subsequent information which indicates deterioration rather than resolution. Both partners were seen (separately) by one of the present authors (DM), with the aim of assessing them for marital treatment. The patient's main complaint at this time was depression caused by his feeling that his wife did not support him at times of stress. He now said that if he could go back to the beginning and meet his wife again he was not sure that he would want to marry her.

When she herself was seen, it was possible to link her unwillingness to support him with the situation in her upbringing: in which she both failed to get support from her father during his lifetime, and, after his death, had to sacrifice her own teenage freedom in order to give support to her mother. The account of the interview continues: 'I felt we had achieved an important piece of insight, and therefore I was much taken aback when she refused flatly to involve herself in treatment. There was something so final about this that I felt thoroughly rejected and very annoyed with her, and the interview came to a rather abrupt halt.'

Thus in her relation to the Clinic she also behaved in what seemed to be a thoroughly destructive and self-destructive fashion, and if this was typical, then her husband can hardly be criticised for his doubts about having married her. Moreover, as we wrote in the full account of this patient, it is very difficult to assess a follow-up result when the patient originally came to us having made an unsatisfactory marriage, and the situation has not yet been resolved.

The Mountain Tarn Girl

As described in Chapter 24, under the heading of 'maladaptive patterns', this patient repeatedly formed relationships with men which began, or ended, in 'triangles'. This was a quite different pattern from that shown by the Sculptress and did not obviously express a problem over commitment.

At 5½-year follow-up she had been together for 5 years with a man named Howard. The following are some extracts from the account of the follow-up interview, which seem to describe an almost ideal relationship:

> From the beginning they fell madly in love, just like adolescents. She describes him as a 'superb man'. He has had steady and harmonious sexual relationships since he was 15 and doesn't have to prove anything to himself. She feels the commitment is total. Sex with him is fine. In this area they are on an equal footing. They can talk about sex with ease. . . He has taught her about his intellectual and artistic interests and she has taught him about hers.

Thus it was clear that there was no problem whatsoever over emotional closeness.

However, the relationship is subject to certain limitations. Their homes are hundreds of miles apart and they can only live together for half the year; he clearly has a need to 'wander' and is intending to spend a year in a solitary expedition to the jungles of South America; and he gave direct evidence of a problem over commitment, saying that he did not want to have children because he 'cannot commit himself like that for 18 years'.

Of course one cannot consciously choose the person with whom one falls in love, and if one's partner turns out to have certain kinds of problem it does not necessarily express any problem of one's own. Therefore the question of whether or not this patient herself has a fear of commitment must remain open. In any case, their relation is clearly so deep and rewarding that it may be ultra-conservative to judge the problem of commitment as a serious reservation. In the end we did give the patient a score of 0 under the heading of 'freedom from reservations' in Table 22.1, but the decision was certainly marginal.

It is also important to note that this patient had clearly not resolved her intensely ambivalent relation with her father, since she suffered from 'a knotted gut for days afterwards' each time she visited him.

The Rebellious Script Writer

In recent years there had been two contrasting men in this patient's life. The first was a man named Dick with whom she had been living for the past 7 years, who was steady and reliable, with whom she got on very well, but whose life principle seemed to be the avoidance of any kind of difficult feeling. The second was Colin, who was passionate and impulsive, by whom she felt liberated, but whom she did not really like and with whom she could not imagine settling down. When she had finally broken with Colin he had suffered a depressive breakdown, and this had precipitated her application for treatment. During therapy it emerged that in her upbringing she had never been able to be rebellious, and that one of her impulses was to *cause trouble* in her close relationships.

At follow-up she had settled for the relationship with Dick, which seemed to be little changed. They get on very well and there is no doubt that she finds the relationship highly rewarding. Yet we may raise the question of whether it is being used to avoid the more impulsive, instinctual side of her nature. It was this that caused us to score '0' under the heading of 'freedom from reservations'.

The Allergic Receptionist

When this patient came to the Clinic she suffered from a clear-cut problem over commitment: 'As soon as I write a man's name in my address book I lose interest in him. In therapy she manifested a similar problem, at times becoming clearly involved in the transference relation – but, when this was pointed out, immediately denying any involvement whatsoever. There was strong evidence that this was based on a very powerful unresolved attachment to her father, who had seriously disappointed her by leaving home when she was 17.

At 5-year follow-up, when she was 27, she said that she would like to get married but had not yet met any man with whom she would want to settle down. Her current relationship seems highly Oedipal. Her man-friend is very much older and married, with grown-up children, and commitment with him is obviously impossible. An additional detail is that he has a grand-daughter with the same name as the patient's. She gave the impression of considerable closeness in the relation with him, and of deep involvement on his part but not on hers. She ended her description by saying, 'I don't see it lasting indefinitely. When the end comes, it comes.' Thus she was given a score of '+' for closeness, but '0' for commitment.

The Concert-goer in an Acute Panic

At initial assessment this patient was in an even more strikingly Oedipal situation than that just described for the Allergic Receptionist. His woman-friend, Ruth, was nearly old enough to be his mother. He spent much of his time at her house, where her crippled husband colluded with their relationship. He said at that time that he did not envisage the relationship lasting for more than about another year.

He was precipitated into coming for therapy by a catastrophic panic, which had resulted from a basically trivial incident of rivalry involving Ruth and another man. This suggested that the 'no-contest' situation with Ruth and her husband was being used as a defence against very severe anxieties about competing with a man for a woman.

Contrary to all expectation, at follow-up (nearly 6 years) he and Ruth were still together, and only now – at her gentle insistence – was he contemplating leaving her and starting to look for someone else. It was clear that the relation was highly rewarding to both partners, sexually and in every other way, and there was no doubt that the criterion of *emotional closeness* was completely fulfilled. The problem of course was that both partners were agreed that it could not lead to a final commitment, so that this criterion was not fulfilled. The question of how much pathology was locked up in the relation with Ruth can only be answered by knowing how the patient fared if he tried to commit himself to another woman, and particularly if he had to face competition in doing so.

The Mother or Teenage Daughter

One of this patient's major problems was a conflict between a need to be looked after and a need for independence, and a second problem was a repetitive pattern of inappropriate choice of men. The most obvious case of this latter was demonstrated by the very disturbed man whom she married, who she said had more or less raped her at the age of 17 and had made her pregnant. They were later divorced and he ended up by committing suicide in prison.

During therapy she had a boy-friend, Stephen, with whom the relation was at times very warm and close, as was clear from many details (see Session 10, p. 131), but which eventually broke up because of his infidelity.

The follow-up (nearly 4 years) was brought about by a re-referral from her GP, who wrote that she 'has been having serious difficulties in her relations with men'. She is now 30 and has had a number of relations, all of which have been unsatisfactory. She said at interview that she needed help to find out why she always chooses the wrong man. One of these relations, with a boss, had lasted for 3 years. She described him as physically very gentle, but 'chauvinistic', taking her for granted, and making her feel inferior. She said that she sought out men who bossed her around because they took responsibility and decisions for her, but on the other hand she was afraid of commitment because this threatened her independence. Thus the original conflict between dependence and independence still seemed to be in operation, and was now preventing her from committing herself to a man.

It is clear that in her relation with Stephen, mentioned above, she was potentially capable of emotional closeness, but she does not seem to be attaining it currently. The criterion of commitment is obviously not fulfilled.

The Hypomanic Advertising Executive

This patient was precipitated into impotence when his wife, after 2 years of pretending, finally told him that he had never succeeded in giving her an orgasm. Their subsequent relation consisted of similar long periods of emotional dishonesty, punctuated by moments of frankness which apparently brought about a major improvement in their relation. There seemed no doubt that at these moments the two partners were capable of considerable emotional closeness, and their commitment to each other was never in question. Thus the first two criteria, emotional closeness and commitment, were probably fulfilled (his entry under 'commitment' in Table 22.1 was left blank because there was no evidence for a problem in this area at any time).

At 5-year follow-up he claimed a further recent major improvement in the relation with his wife, which had followed his being shown how to give her an orgasm by stimulating her clitoris. Unfortunately he had claimed similar improvements, which had proved to be evanescent, on two previous occasions. Moreover, there was considerable evidence at this follow-up that he was in a hypomanic state, so that it was impossible to know the degree to which he was being over-optimistic. Thus the third criterion, 'relation free from serious reservations', could not be said to be fulfilled.

The Secretary in a State of Nirvana

As described under the heading of 'maladaptive patterns', this patient suffered from a tendency to gravitate towards men who overtly ill-treated her or at least showed extreme lack of consideration for her. When she first came to us she wrote in her application form, 'I have been involved in some very nasty situations with men from which I found it very difficult to extricate myself.' She had previously had a 4-year relation with a married man who suffered from violent attacks of temper; she said that her current boy-friend expected that she should always be around to cook and clean for him and attend to his needs, and created a scene if she came home late; and she described her boss as a difficult man who put a ridiculously excessive work-load on her. Nevertheless she wrote that sexual relations with her boy-friend 'are and always have been very good'. The type of man that he was seems illustrated by the following two incidents which took place during therapy: she described how he had behaved at a wedding reception, starting sulky, getting drunk, going out and coming back announcing that he had 'been sick all over the garden and would like to be sick over everyone here'. About a week later she said that he had again got drunk and had started shouting and cursing at her. He eventually left saying that he hated her, had never really liked her, and never wanted to see her again.

At 4-year follow-up she said that this man was 'probably schizophrenic', but at the same time she said that the relation with him had possessed 'depth and intensity', and that there were no sexual problems; and she added that she had had no relation possessing such qualities since then.

Shortly after the end of therapy she took up with a married man with whom she has been ever since. She described a relation with many positive features: 'We can communicate at an intellectual level. He is a nice person, very intelligent, very supportive and very biased in my favour over my difficulties at work.' So far there might have seemed evidence that her maladaptive pattern with men had been truly resolved. However, she also said the following: 'The relation is very stable, because there is no question of its progressing to anything different. It's limited and therefore it's easy to live with. It makes no demands on me at all.' She said that when it comes to an end, it would be she who ends it. And, of her sexual relations since the break-up with her previous boy-friend, she said, 'it has been like a switch turned off'.

Her whole attitude to life was one of detachment, and it seemed evident that she had solved her problem in relation to men by emotional withdrawal. The final judgment can only be that she fulfils neither the criterion of emotional closeness nor that of commitment.

The Self-Driving Physicist

When he first came to us his whole life was permeated by a sense of inadequacy, both in his relation to women and in his comparison of himself with other men. His first girl-friend had helped his self-confidence, but when she left him it had precipitated him into impotence. He now said that he felt at ease with ugly women, but if he tried to speak to a pretty woman he 'just wanted to dig a hole and bury himself'. One of the main problems in his background was the utter sterility of his parents' marriage.

At 5-year follow-up he still sought people who helped to boost his confidence, which included his current girl-friend. This relation shows serious limitations. She likes physical contact but is not interested in sex. He said he is no longer impotent and wishes he could have more sex with her, but he likes her in other ways and does not want to leave her. Two years ago they planned to get married, but at the last moment he became very frightened and cancelled the arrangements.

The intensity of his wish for closeness, and yet his inability to achieve it, is illustrated by the following remarks: 'Sometimes I have the feeling that I could melt inside a woman's arms. I just want to let her hold me, but I cannot cope with this wish any more than I could before.'

He later spoke of his girl-friend as follows: 'She is trying to build her life around me and organise things for me; but I cannot allow her to put restrictions on my life, and I feel she will leave me because of this, as happened with all my other girl-friends. I won't listen to them, won't marry them, won't build homes for them. I see marriage as a death.' This is a quintessential statement of a problem over commitment.

The Acting-out Accounts Clerk

At initial assessment this young woman of 22 had had two superficial relations with men, both of whom seem to have used her. The most recent had made her pregnant and then left for Canada.

The problem of fear of commitment was clearly shown in the transference, since she opened the first session with three communications about avoiding or terminating relationships, and then admitted that she had almost decided not to come; and finally, after repeated acting out over appointments, she terminated prematurely. In addition she had previously left treatment with three successive hypnotists.

At follow-up (3¾ years) she told how she had gone over to Canada to see the boy-friend mentioned above, but that he had started ignoring her there. Back in England, she took up with another young man who, as she knew, did not want a deep relationship, but he left her because her phobic symptoms interfered with their going out together.

Thus her pattern of superficial and unsatisfactory relations with men, together with fear of commitment, has continued.

The Actress with Elocution Problems

This woman of 33 wrote in her application form that she had never been able to establish a satisfactory relation with a man: 'I seem to attract emotional parasites. Those I am not interested in flock to me. Those I am interested in sometimes begin to like me, but then I seem to handle it quite wrongly and it doesn't work. I become terribly afraid, lose my objectivity, and I become obsessed and quite unable to act naturally.' 'In any emotional involvement I am full of fear and doubt – this ends it, painfully.' 'Dates are generally with men I am not interested in, which can give rise to problems if *they* are.'

She thus gave strong evidence of severe difficulties over both emotional closeness and commitment.

There was a 3-year gap between her first and second consultations, during which she became engaged, and she got married in the middle of her therapy.

Her commitment to her husband was not in question, but the quality of their relation in terms of emotional closeness seemed to leave a great deal to be desired. Although she said that she had married him because he was 'nice, reliable, the very opposite of my father', at the first follow-up she said that though he and she are quite good companions, he doesn't understand her and makes no attempt to do so, with the result that she rejects his sexual overtures. At the final follow-up

(4 years) she gave the impression that her husband was extremely obsessional and withdrawn, and she described his activity as 'work, work, work', with little left over for her. The sexual relation remains unsatisfactory.

The Miner's Daughter Mourning her Baby

Before she came to therapy this patient had had a close and warm relation with a young man, and it seems that emotional closeness was not a problem to her. This man made her pregnant, which had led to her having an abortion. He behaved in a highly ambivalent way towards her and she eventually left him. She said at follow-up, 'We would have gone on to destroy each other.'

When seen for follow-up she had had a relation with two further men. The first was married, and she had deliberately become pregnant by him, giving birth to her daughter, Ellen. She stopped the sexual relation because this man's wife became pregnant, but he continues to visit. She broke with the second man because she became bored with him.

Since then she has devoted her whole life to Ellen and has withdrawn from relations with men. She herself made the judgment, which seems accurate: 'I can't help thinking that I have never been able to make a reasonable relation with a man.'

The Anorexic Museum Assistant

When she first came to us her relation to men had consisted of one very brief affair only, and during the whole of her therapy and the 1-year follow-up period she lived an exceedingly isolated life, was hardly able to allow herself any pleasure, and had no relations with men at all. It was at this point that her therapeutic result was scored.

She was then referred for psychoanalysis, which lasted 3½ years. Although she showed other improvements towards the end of this period of her treatment, there was still no improvement in her problems with men.

(At the final follow-up, 9½ years after the termination of her brief therapy, she had a warm and close relation with a man with whom she was contemplating marriage, but whether or not her brief therapy made any contribution to this is impossible to assess.)

The Psychiatric Nurse with Attacks of Rage

Throughout almost the whole of our contact with this patient she had a relationship with a young man called James, and there were no doubts either of her commitment to him, or of her ability to achieve a considerable degree of emotional closeness with him. However, one of her patterns consisted of leaning over backwards to please and allowing herself to be exploited. This had started in her adolescence when she felt compelled to do the housework in order to please her parents, much of whose energy was directed towards her crippled younger sister who needed constant attention. With James she continued this pattern of allowing herself to be exploited, and at 4-year follow-up the result had been an uncontrollable explosion of pent-up resentment in which she smashed up one of his most valued possessions – the consequence of which was that he broke with her. Since then she has had no relations with men. She said at follow-up that she would cook for women but would never allow herself to cook for a man.

Thus her problems in relation to men clearly remained unresolved.

The Girl with Eye Problems

It became clear early in therapy that this patient was borderline or psychotic, and it is very difficult indeed to get a picture of her relation with her husband. After her initial assessment interview her husband was interviewed by a (woman) social worker, who made the judgment that he was frightened of all kinds of feeling or of any disagreement, that there was no emotional communication between the two partners, and that he 'seemed to be exactly the sort of man to have a non-marriage with'. The patient, on the other hand, wrote, 'I have a full and happy marriage', and under the heading of 'things enjoyed most', wrote, 'the first 2 or 3 years of marriage, setting up home'. During therapy it emerged that she could only reach a climax in sexual intercourse 'if my husband is aware of my rather dim sight', a strange communication for which a possible explanation is given in the account of her therapy (see pp. 179–80).

At final follow-up (nearly 7 years) she said of her relation with her husband, 'It's fine, we enjoy each other very much'. Indeed, it did appear that they have a good deal of companionship. However, her next remark was, 'He is rather untouched by what goes on', and it seems that the lack of communication continues. There has also been a falling off in their sexual relation, and her own sexuality remains as strange as before. They are certainly committed to each other, but of course this was never a problem, and the criterion of emotional closeness cannot be regarded as being fulfilled.

The Borderline Graduate Clerk

This 28-year-old patient wrote in his original application form: 'With girls I like, inevitably I feel I'm in love and become very tense. Usually I do nothing about it.' His pattern was to fall in love with a girl from a distance and have many fantasies about her; but if he did manage to take her out he would 'freeze' inside and find himself unable to make any contact with her. His longest relationship with a girl had lasted only a few weeks.

At 5½-year follow-up he said that he had always been afraid of any intense situation, and that if he got into any close relationship he would become 'swamped'. This problem had arisen in a recent relation with a girl which had lasted a year, and had led to its coming to an end. He said: 'Now I am even more afraid of being swamped than ever before. I suppose it's a false generalisation that other girls might be just as domineeering, but that's what I feel – perhaps it's men that are caring.' 'I've lost my libido. I can't have sexual fantasies any more because I doubt the possibility of having a caring woman.' He now lives an isolated life in a bed-sitting room and seems to have largely given up human relationships.

The Robot Man

When he first came to us most of his relations with girls had been superficial; but there had also been one girl who meant more than this, and who had caused an exacerbation of symptoms when she moved away and left him.

At 5-year follow-up he had also had a few superficial relationships. He said several times that if he stayed any length of time with anyone he got 'confused' and needed to withdraw. He also said that it was unlikely that he would get married. It seems therefore that commitment was a serious problem for him, and that his capacity for emotional closeness was strictly limited.

The Victimised Telephonist

When she first came to us this 33-year-old patient had had a 7-year relationship with a much older, married, man with whom she had fallen in love. Within the limits of his being unwilling to leave his wife, there was a considerable degree of commitment on both sides – he bought a flat for her and took her with him on business trips. There seemed little doubt of her capacity for emotional closeness, but it was clear that this was a very one-sided relation in which she did all the emotional giving. The moment she began to make demands on him he broke with her.

Moreover, careful enquiry revealed that commitment was a serious problem for her. Other men had asked her out, but she never wanted to get involved with them and usually decided after a short time that she didn't like them. She said that she had been put off the whole idea of marriage by the constant quarrelling between her parents. It is thus almost certainly significant that her only long-term relation had been to a man with whom final commitment was impossible.

At follow-up (3¾ years) she had got herself into a most disastrous situation by marrying a man whom she didn't love and who neglected her, with the aim of helping him to leave Poland. This has already been described in detail in Chapter 24. She said that even if he manages to get to England she does not want to live with him, and she feels that the marriage will end in divorce.

28

Relations with the opposite sex

II Problems of commitment

How necessary is commitment?

Throughout this work we have made the tacit assumption that final commitment to a partner of the opposite sex is a desirable end. We fully realise that this is a view of an issue where many opinions are possible, and that it is not self-evident in western society towards the end of the 20th century. However, it does seem reasonably certain that people should not suffer from *anxieties* about commitment which prevent them from having the choice of whether to commit themselves or not. The majority of patients described below did not fulfil this criterion, even after their therapy, and we therefore make no apology for regarding the therapeutic results in their case as incomplete.

Problems of commitment

Perhaps the most interesting aspect of the evidence presented in Chapter 24 is the variety of mechanisms that these patients used – whether consciously or unconsciously – for the purpose of avoiding commitment, and the even wider variety of anxieties that these mechanisms expressed. One mechanism for avoiding commitment, of course, is to form superficial or short-lasting relations, so that problems of emotional closeness are often involved as well. The details are summarised in Table 28.1.

Comments on Table 28.1

The table shows that 17 of the 24 patients (71%) suffered from problems of commitment, and that in only 3 (12%) – the Nurse Mourning her Fiancé, Car Battery Man, and Actress with Elocution Problems (who married between her first and second initial assessment interviews) – were these fully resolved at follow-up.

Although the mechanisms adopted by these patients for avoiding commitment were very varied, they can be classified into two broad categories: deliberate avoidance of commitment, and forming relations in which final commitment is impossible.

Table 28.1 Problems of commitment

Patient	Way of avoiding commitment	Nature of anxiety
Nurse Mourning her Fiancé	Breaking off relation; provoking quarrels*	Further loss
Pacifist Conductor	'Can't imagine a relation without an end-point'* Avoiding having children	?Loss of independence
Librarian who Sought Suffering	Intellectually inferior men	?
Car Battery Man	Leaving girls on the slightest pretext*	Being let down again
Sculptress with Nightmares	Short-lived relations*; men who can't commit themselves	?Attachment to her father
Mountain Tarn Girl	Partner has fear of commitment	(Possibly only her partner's problem)
Allergic Receptionist	Loss of interest when committed; relation with much older, married man	?Attachment to her father
Concert-goer in Acute Panic	Attachment to much older, married woman	Competition with other men ?Attachment to his mother
Mother or Teenage Daughter	Consciously avoids commitment	Loss of independence
Secretary in a State of Nirvana	Very limited relation with married man	Emotional demands
Self-driving Physicist	Consciously refuses commitment	Repeating his parents' marriage
Actress with Elocution Problems	If she is not interested they flock to her; if interested she handles it wrongly*	?Fear of being controlled
Miner's Daughter Mourning her Baby	If a man is interested in her she 'overnight' loses interest in him	Fear of being deprived like her mother
Anorexic Museum Assistant	Withdrawn life	Cannot allow herself pleasure
Robot Man	Superficial relations; becomes 'confused' if stays too long	?Intense ambivalence
Borderline Graduate Clerk	In love from a distance; later, isolated life	Fear of being 'swamped'
Victimised Telephonist	Attachment to much older, married man; marries a man who neglects her	Self-punishment; repeating her parents' marriage

*Resolved at follow-up.

Deliberate avoidance of commitment, or termination of the relation if commitment is threatened

The Nurse Mourning her Fiancé broke off one relation when she was afraid she was becoming too involved, and in the follow-up period she brought another relation to an end for the same reason by deliberately provoking quarrels. Similarly the Car Battery Man broke off relations with girls on minor pretexts. The Mother or Teenage Daughter and the Robot Man kept their relations superficial. The Physicist stated his position unequivocally: 'I won't listen to them, won't marry them, won't build homes for them. I regard marriage as a death.' The Allergic Receptionist said: 'I lose interest as soon as I enter a man's name in my address book.' At follow-up the Museum Assistant and Graduate Clerk lived an entirely withdrawn life and avoided relations with the opposite sex altogether (the Museum Assistant succeeded in breaking this pattern after her analysis). Two borderline patients showed manifest and intense anxiety if they felt they were getting too close: the Robot Man described becoming 'confused' if he stayed in a relation for any length of time, and the Graduate Clerk spoke of 'freezing inside', with a fear of being 'swamped'.

(In addition, one of the female patients spoke of ensuring that 'it was always *she* who caused the heartbreaks', but we have lost the reference to this and have been unable to find it again.)

Forming relations in which final commitment is impossible

Four patients had long-standing relations with partners who were much older and already married (the Allergic Receptionist, Concert-goer, Nirvana Secretary, and Victimised Telephonist). The Sculptress, and to a lesser extent the Mountain Tarn Girl, formed relations with partners who themselves suffered from problems over commitment. The Librarian took up with men who were by a long way her social and intellectual inferiors; and the Victimised Telephonist finally allowed herself to be pushed into the situation of marrying a man whom she didn't love and who neglected her, in order to help him get out from behind the Iron Curtain.

The anxieties preventing commitment

The inferred anxieties were very varied and some patients suffered from more than one. They can be classified as follows.

Two patients were afraid of further loss: the Nurse Mourning her Fiancé because of three previous traumatic bereavements; the Car Battery Man because of having been jilted by his first girl-friend. Two women patients (the Sculptress and Allergic Receptionist) were probably unwilling to give up their highly ambivalent attachments to their fathers, and one male patient (the Concert-goer) his attachment to his mother. Two patients (the Physicist and Victimised Telephonist) were afraid of repeating their parents' disastrous relation; two women patients (the Victimised Telephonist and Museum Assistant) suffered from what seemed to be deep-seated superego pathology, resulting in either a deliberate seeking of suffering at the hands of a man, or an inability to allow pleasure in the form of a relation with a man. The Nirvana Secretary was afraid of the emotional demands of close relations; while two much more disturbed patients (the Robot Man and Graduate Clerk) were probably afraid of intense ambivalent feelings. At initial assessment the Concert-goer had been terrified at becoming involved in a competitive situation; and finally the Mother or Teenage Daughter and the Actress with Elocution Problems feared the loss of their independence.

Problems of commitment and emotional closeness in another series

It is interesting to compare this series of brief psychotherapy patients treated by trainees with the Individual Series which was first described in Chapter 2 and has been mentioned many times since. This consisted of 84 patients treated with individual psychotherapy of any length by therapists of all degrees of experience, and included 8 of the patients in the present series.

Of the 84, only 12 (14%) could be regarded at follow-up as having fully achieved both commitment and emotional closeness, while 49 (58%) unequivocally failed to achieve either.

The mechanisms for avoiding commitment in this series were as follows:

1 withdrawal from any attempt to form relations with the opposite sex at all (18 patients);
2 the deliberate avoidance of commitment (8 patients);
3 some form of 'splitting', e.g. only unattainable partners are desirable, attainable partners are not, or the impossibility of combining love and sex in the same relationship (5 patients);
4 the formation of relationships in which commitment is impossible (4 patients).

One of the above patients explicitly described a mechanism similar to that used by the Nurse Mourning her Fiancé and the Car Battery Man: blowing up incidents out of all proportion in order to have an excuse for breaking off, because she was beginning to feel panic that the man was getting too close to her.

Finally it is worth quoting remarks made at follow-up by two further patients from this series, which epitomise in a dramatic way some of the issues of commitment which we have been discussing.

The first was made by a woman patient who achieved a remarkable piece of insight about her murderous feelings towards the members of her family, in a therapy which she terminated after four sessions, feeling that she had got what she was seeking. At follow-up she and her partner were in a position remarkably similar to that of the Mountain Tarn Girl; and for her, all problems were resolved except one:

In the last 2 years he has said, 'Why don't we get married?' But this is one of my *scars*. As soon as there's a threat of total commitment, I'm like a bat out of hell. We each have our own home, we aren't a drain on each other, he works abroad a lot, it suits both of us. It may be immature, it seems to be taking the highlights, we aren't sharing the nitty-gritty with each other, but it has worked well. We are better pals and have a more fruitful relation than many of my married friends. He's been divorced and has got scars too... I've been lucky to come to terms with it all, but I still panic at the mention of marriage. I can't bear the idea of being *owned*. Some things can't change. I've had to accept this.

Thus her anxiety seems to be the same as that of the Mother or Teenage Daughter – though probably much more deep-seated – namely loss of independence.

The second patient was a young woman who had a 5-year analysis at five times a week from an American psychiatrist in psychoanalytic training (the therapist who treated the Borderline Graduate Clerk) which illustrates equally dramatically the *resolution* of a problem of commitment:

My husband, Colin, is a rare person. There's something transparent and trustworthy about him. This is what made it possible to try and have a permanent relation together, as distinct from the bisexual squiffs that I used to get entangled with. I remember saying to one of those horrid little men that I was going to leave him for Colin, because I could see the possibility of a future with Colin. We both wanted to have a home and marriage.

This is a tribute to a gifted therapist and a highly successful analysis. But it must be clear by now that though such statements are found from time to time, they are not found often enough whether therapy be brief or long-term. As has been touched on many times in previous chapters, all our follow-up work has illustrated that a truly satisfactory relation with the opposite sex is one of the most difficult to achieve of all kinds of therapeutic aim.

29

Problems of aggression and self-assertion

I General

Introduction: maladaptive and adaptive forms of aggression

The main issues in this area may be illustrated particularly clearly by excerpts from the follow-up of three patients from the Individual Series.

A male patient, when asked what happened when he had disagreements with people, replied: 'I get upset. I don't say what I really think. I've never had the confidence to shout at anybody. I'm afraid of what they'll do to me back. If someone is moving his head in front of me in a theatre I get irritated but I wouldn't say anything.'

A second male patient described a state in which his fantasies were full of violence and he was losing his temper with everybody, which had caused serious problems at work. In addition, some kind of vicious circle had been set up between him and his 5-year-old daughter: 'When I demanded affection, she would say "Yuk" if I kissed her. I said, "If you do that again I'll slap you very hard". She did it again, and I slapped her hard on the face. I gave her, not exactly a hiding, but I smacked her bottom too. Since then, she has always dutifully said, "I love you, Daddy".'

The Determined Mother

The third example comes from the 5-year follow-up of a woman who entered psychotherapy at the age of 28. In her application form she had written of herself, 'I am quiet and always trying to please', and her initial interviewer wrote: 'I felt no aggressive elements in her. She seemed to be all pleasantries and agreement and trying to please me.' (It is worth remembering these two quotations when reading the follow-up material, for anyone may be excused for doubting that we are describing the same person.)

This is a further example of a successful brief therapy not included in the present series, since she was treated in 27 sessions by a trainee under the supervision of another consultant.

As in the case of the Psychiatric Nurse with Attacks of Rage, a process of freeing was set off in her by her father's death, an event which in her case occurred 2 days after her last therapeutic session. At follow-up she spoke of this as follows: 'When my father died I thought, sod it, it's no good pleasing everybody. It doesn't matter a damn whether they like me or not. If they like me they like me. If they don't, hard luck. If I disagree I say so. I'm not worried about the repercussions.'

Her younger child, Grant, now aged 7, had been in and out of hospital with a possible serious diagnosis. Recently she had taken him to hospital for yet another biopsy: 'In the old days I would have laughed at anybody who told me I could cope. There was a young woman doctor there who lifted him out of the cot to take him down for his test. I know that 2 years earlier I would have just let him go and would have felt cross and upset. But this time I said, "You can't go without me". I had the confidence to think, he's *my* child, you're not going to take him away, and I'm going to say it. They let me go with him. In fact I developed a very good relation with the staff in the hospital.'

Grant had had a period of severe tantrums at the age of 3. 'I thought I was going to strangle him. He was absolutely impossible. But after a time I thought to myself that I'll either kill him or else I must do something about it. We evolved a system: after a lot of warnings he'd be sent up to his room and made to stay there until the storm had passed, sometimes as much as an hour. Then he'd come to the top of the stairs and call me, but his voice would still be sobbing, and I wouldn't let him come down till he could speak to me normally. Then *I* needed to cuddle him as much as *he* needed to cuddle me. Eventually his tantrums stopped. Now he's a delightful little boy, a real poppet.'

The concept of constructive self-assertion

In civilised society anger and aggression serve the important function of enabling us to defend ourselves and those close to us, to stand up for our rights, and to prevent other people from imposing on us; and there are two broad classes of disturbance in this function, which are illustrated by the first two patients respectively. In the first patient there was too little aggression, in the second too much. Both states are ultimately destructive to the individuals themselves and to the people around them. The first patient will be unable to stand up for his rights and will allow other people to take advantage of him, while unexpressed, accumulating resentment may well spoil his close relations in one way or another (as indeed happened with the Psychiatric Nurse with Attacks of Rage). The second patient will antagonise everyone around him, and though he may succeed in cowing his daughter into submission, he is hardly likely to create a genuinely warm relation with her.

The third patient illustrates an intermediate state, which has the following characteristics:

1 She is in touch with the full intensity of her aggressive feelings.
2 These are not out of proportion to the situation that arouses them.
3 They can be controlled, channelled, and used in an effective and realistic way.
4 When they have served their purpose they are over and done with and leave no unexpressed residue, and, most important of all:
5 In the end the situation is greatly improved, and often *everybody* is happier – including the people against whom the aggression was directed.

This final characteristic is illustrated by the good relation which the patient achieved with the staff at the hospital, and both the short-term and long-term warmth that developed between herself and her son. This is therefore what we mean by the concept of *constructive self-assertion,* the attainment of which – in those patients in whom the expression of aggressive feelings is disturbed – should be one of the main aims of all forms of dynamic psychotherapy.

Constructive self-assertion in the present series

Interestingly, all 24 of these patients suffered from problems of aggression when they first came to us, so that for each the criterion of constructive self-assertion formed an essential element in an ideal therapeutic result. Moreover, and perhaps surprisingly, this criterion was at least partly fulfilled *during therapy* in a very high proportion (18 out of 24, 75%), and at follow-up it was still at least partly fulfilled in more patients than any other (14 out of 24, 58%). The reasons for this are discussed in detail at the end of Chapter 30.

These patients can therefore be divided into three categories:

1 Those who discovered constructive self-asssertion, mostly during therapy, and who maintained this position at follow-up (14 patients).
2 Those who discovered constructive self-asssertion during therapy but later relapsed – including the patient who committed sucide. The others were: the Mother or Teenage Daughter, the Psychiatric Nurse with Attacks of Rage, and the Victimised Telephonist.
3 Those who failed to fulfil the criterion at any time (6 patients).

The detailed evidence is presented in the next chapter.

30

Problems of aggression and self-assertion

II Clinical material

This clinical material consists largely of a series of fascinating stories, many of the details of which have not been given before. The use of constructive self-assertion is illustrated many times and quite unmistakably – as indeed is the failure to use it.

The Nurse Mourning her Fiancé (criterion fulfilled)

The freeing of this patient's aggression occurred quite dramatically in the later part of her therapy, and it was clear that this had persisted at follow-up. Many details have already been given in Chapters 1, 8, and 23.

The Pacifist Conductor (criterion fulfilled)

This patient was brought up in a home in which his pacifist father conveyed the message that showing anger was forbidden because it was 'the first step on the path to war'. During therapy he was freed from the shackles of this message remarkably quickly. In Session 11 he reported the following incident.

He was offered a job conducting an opera while the regular conductor was on holiday. He asked his boss if he could take some leave that was owed to him in order to fulfil this task, and the boss refused. The therapist's account continues: 'In the end he shouted at the boss in public, telling him that he was going to take his leave as from Monday, and handed in his resignation. His heart was beating fast, he was incoherent with rage, and he allowed himself to show his anger in a way that had never happened before. He said he is intent on taking this temporary job and there is no way that he can be diverted from it.'

In the next session: 'He said he had been allowed to do what he wanted without having to resign from his job. He would never have been able to do this without making his feelings so clear. He was extremely pleased about it and said that his self-confidence was ever increasing.'

The move back to conducting was of quite vital importance to the patient's whole emotional and professional life, and this incident illustrates *par excellence* the function of anger in overcoming obstructions to a person's legitimate self-interest, in a way that ultimately is of benefit to everyone.

At follow-up the patient made clear that the ability to assert himself had persisted, and he described another of the characteristics of constructive anger, namely the absence of an unexpressed residue which so often bedevils relationships: 'I find it easier to be angry – and then it just passes.'

Here we need to add an important reservation. This discovery of aggression was accompanied by repeated episodes of violence against his Indian girl-friend, later to be his wife. It is very difficult to evaluate this, since it seems that she deliberately provoked it in him and he felt it was something that she needed: 'I see a glow of satisfaction in her eyes.' At final follow-up he said that he felt much closer to her and that these episodes had been considerably mitigated, though it was clear that they still occurred from time to time.

The Librarian who Sought Suffering (criterion fulfilled)

When this patient first came to us she was hardly capable of expressing anger, which was forbidden in her childhood, and her principal mechanism for dealing with anger was to turn it against herself in the form of masochism. During therapy she came to realise, through an experience in the transference, that she had 'a monster of violent anger within her'.

At follow-up she said that the masochistic phenomena had entirely disappeared. The main area where we possess evidence of her being able to assert herself was the relation with her husband. The final rift between them had occurred after a complicated series of events which ended with his hitting her, accusing her of deliberately provoking him. She was sure that this was not true and that all she was doing was trying to help, and she refused to accept his accusation. She began to realise some of her husband's less favourable characteristics, e.g. that he was 'grotesquely sexist' and was extremely disrespectful to her. She reflected, 'How can I be married to this man?' and asked him to leave, which he did.

The Car Battery Man (criterion fulfilled)

In the Tavistock Clinic's application form, sent to patients when they first apply for treatment, there is a section asking for their job history, which allows space for five jobs. This patient wrote: 'I would need a full page for this question.' The reason behind this was that he repeatedly left jobs because of intense resentment which developed against bosses.

At his penultimate follow-up (nearly 3 years) he described an incident with a boss which has all the characteristics of constructive self-assertion. He put in a claim for expenses, but was told that he could not be paid till the end of the next month, which would have meant a delay of 7 weeks. He confronted the boss about this, and they argued heatedly for about an hour, not mincing their words with each other. Eventually the boss admitted that the system was out of date, and lent the patient the money. The two of them have got on well with each other since.

At the final follow-up (nearly 8 years) he told of the situation with his wife described in Chapter 27 under the heading of relations with the opposite sex. Apparently she became physically violent when they quarrelled, and he used to hit her back. 'It became a way of life.' At the same time these rows had some of the characteristics of constructive anger, since he used the phrase 'good rows and good sex', implying that when they had got their anger off their chest there was no residue and they could make love passionately.

The problems of evaluating this situation have already been discussed in Chapter 27.

The Betrayed Son (criterion fulfilled at work, not at home)

In Session 11 the patient reported the following: in most previous years he had worked throughout the Christmas period, but this year he thought he would 'do himself a good turn'. Instead of letting people assume that he would do the same as usual, he arranged the staff's holidays and stated definitely that he was not going to work over Christmas – he was going to spend the time with his family and enjoy himself. The therapist's account continues: 'He commented that it was very strange, he couldn't have imagined himself doing this a few months ago. He was afraid his boss and colleagues would protest and he would cave in. In fact he had to do some persuasion, but to his surprise it all worked out without too much conflict.'

In Session 19 he described another change towards the ability to express healthy aggression – though he also said that his wife didn't like it and felt that he was becoming unbearable to live with. 'He said that now he has short, furious outbursts of temper, and he no longer conceals his anger with her as he used to. He used to keep his anger inside and would brood and sulk at length. Now it comes out in a short outburst and is gone almost as quickly as it came.'

At the final follow-up he had retained his ability for constructive self-assertion outside the home, for he said that he is able to express his opinions and not to 'let things stew'. However, as described under the heading of relations with the opposite sex, a vicious circle of indirectly expressed aggression developed between him and his wife, and in this relation the criterion of constructive self-assertion was now clearly not fulfilled.

The Sculptress with Nightmares (criterion fulfilled)

One of this patient's problems was that she tended to behave in a histrionic, inappropriate, and ineffective way in situations where self-assertion was required. However, already by Session 19 she had found her ability to be assertive effectively in a quite different way. She had lost her temper with a woman who had put up some posters in the patient's section of an exhibition, and had made her take them down. She said that she had never lost her temper in this way in a work situation before.

At the final follow-up she described an incident in which her previous self-destructive pattern had begun to reassert itself, but which she had then been able to convert into constructive and effective behaviour. For details please see Chapter 7.

The Mountain Tarn Girl (criterion fulfilled)

This patient used to be terrified of her own attacks of temper, in which she became histrionic and verbally and physically violent. As described in Chapters 1 and 10, an incident of this kind occurred immediately after one of her therapeutic sessions.

At follow-up she said that this pattern no longer occurred, and she described an incident in which – like the Sculptress above – she had been able to control her potential inappropriate reaction and convert it into constructive and effective behaviour. She was on holiday with her man-friend and sleeping in the car. He was exceedingly restless, which kept waking her up, and she began to feel frantic, with the fear that she was going to become violent. Instead of this, she woke him up and spoke to him about it, as a result of which they changed places and the situation was resolved.

The Rebellious Script Writer (criterion not fulfilled)

This patient's main problem was a conflict between her wish for safety on the one hand, and her need to express her rebelliousness and passionate feelings on the other. This conflict was expressed in her life by her relation with two men, one of whom (Dick) represented safety, and the other (Colin) represented instinctuality. It was clear that in the end she had settled for safety, though the relation was also highly rewarding to her.

At follow-up the interviewer made a sustained attempt to get her to describe how she dealt with disagreements between herself and Dick, but she was quite unable to describe any situation in which disagreement had happened. Her final statement was: 'I am the sort of person who would probably avoid a row or a difference of opinion with anybody, because I don't know how I could cope with it.'

The Allergic Receptionist (criterion fulfilled)

At her final follow-up she described several instances of self-assertion, two of which were as follows:

> The biggest change for the better was to get out of living in my eccentric grandmother's flat, which I did immediately after finishing therapy. I told the Council, 'If you don't give me accommodation you'll have to pay for more psychotherapy, so it's more convenient for you to do so.'
>
> They came and saw my room, which had a piano in it, six mattresses, 15 Turkish carpets and many other things. They found my larder was in the fuse cupboard – they could hardly believe it. They offered me a super flat. My grandmother said, 'She is not going to move to that flat.' My mother said she would pay the rent, because she knew of the good use I'd made of the therapy that I'd had. Grandmother was absolutely furious. 'How do you expect to live?' When I was living with her and I went out in the evening, grandmother would phone my mother saying, 'Pauline is 10 minutes late. What shall I do?'... I went to the new flat, taking some of the carpets with me. When you are desperate and you don't have any money, you have to do what you can....
>
> In the new flat the tenants down below were Saudi Arabians. As you know, with them women don't have any rights. I was woken up at 3 in the morning with the husband playing the guitar. I complained. They said, 'So you have to move out. You are a simple female.' So one Sunday afternoon I said to a neighbour, 'Will you please come up and say if I'm unreasonable?' So we jumped on the floor, and the husband came up and threatened us and said we had caused his wife's miscarriage. We went to court and I won.

She eventually managed to move to a new flat.

It was after describing all this that she made the remarks quoted in Chapter 25 under the heading of being oneself: 'It has all brought about a totally altered pattern of living. Now I can tell anybody what I think. I can do what I like, when I like, how I like, and I am not answerable to anybody.'

The Concert-goer in an Acute Panic (criterion fulfilled)

One of this patient's problems was extreme hostility to male authority figures, which spoiled his relation with them and made it difficult for him to cooperate with them. In his final session he described a mitigation of these feelings; as a result of which he had been able to ask for, and to be given, better accommodation in his place of work.

At final follow-up the evidence in this area was more mixed. The interviewer wrote: 'There were a number of complicated and rather convincing circumstances which he put forward as having contributed to his having made rather less progress at work than he might otherwise have hoped. It seemed, however, that at least in the last year or two he had been more assertive, and had recently been rewarded with – albeit somewhat overdue – promotion.'

The Mother or Teenage Daughter (criterion at first fulfilled, with later relapse)

The important moment of this patient's initial interview occurred when she reached the insight: 'perhaps I want to tell the lot of them to go to hell', referring to her family, with whom she was living.

Much of the work of therapy centred around the problem of speaking up for herself and making her needs known, and she made very considerable progress in this area. This was typified by Session 10, the first after a month's break for Christmas, in which she reported the following.

There was an incident in which she was let down by her boy-friend. Her reaction was first to throw a tantrum at home, which consisted of kicking the doors and screaming; but she followed this by having a constructive discussion with him about their relation, which ended in a rewarding sexual experience.

Not long afterwards the following occurred, which is described here in the therapist's words: 'For the first time that she remembers she went to her father for a cuddle, and burst into tears. This provoked a discussion between her and her parents of why she needed to come here, and how she felt they hadn't given her all sorts of care, and how awful she'd felt when she'd been sent away from home in her childhood. She was able to tell them many things that they had never confronted together, particularly how she felt that her mother had always stopped anger being expressed in the home. It emerged that her mother had experienced an enormous number of rows in her own family; and her mother said that perhaps she had erred in smoothing over situations too much – the first time that this had ever been admitted openly. Her parents told her that they felt she had always bottled things up, and perhaps she had been pushed out by her sister's depressive illness, just as she now felt pushed out by the presence of her son. She obviously found it a huge relief to be able to admit this with them. She said it became a bit of a family joke afterwards, and they would constantly rush up and cuddle her; and she said, rather charmingly as well as triumphantly, that she almost wished she hadn't said anything as it had provoked such demonstrations of affection and such care.'

However, at final follow-up (nearly 4 years) most of this progress seemed to have been lost. She said, 'I express anger in outbursts, in the wrong way', and she described throwing a tantrum about having failed to find a boy-friend whom she had arranged to meet. In addition, she had clearly not come to terms with her angry feelings towards her son, and she was afraid of losing her temper with him and becoming violent.

The Hypomanic Advertising Executive (criterion fulfilled)

At his initial assessment this patient told the psychologist who tested him that he 'wanted to be aggressive but didn't know how'.

During therapy he showed considerable evidence of improvements in this area. In Session 21 he reported having stood up to his father for the first time, by being sarcastic to him, and he was 'surprised to find how powerful this was'. Similarly, he said in Session 25 that 'he is being much more effective at work and feels very gratified by this, trying to reverse the impotent image'.

At follow-up he spoke of being able to be 'gloriously angry' with his wife. This phrase suggests a non-destructive form of anger, but he was not asked for a specific example. In his current work, which consists of being head of a team training other executives, he claimed to be extremely effective and very highly esteemed. Obviously such a position requires a considerable degree of constructive self-assertion. However, because he was clearly in a hypomanic state at follow-up, there is no means of knowing to what degree some of his statements were exaggerated.

The Psychiatric Nurse with Attacks of Rage (criterion not fulfilled)

This patient's problem of handling her anger runs through her whole story from beginning to end. Up to the age of 11 she described herself as having had a violent temper, always screaming and throwing things. At this age she made a conscious decision to control herself, but as a result she seems to have lost her ability to express any feelings at all. Not only this, but she developed a pattern of bending over backwards to please, with accumulating unexpressed resentment underneath.

The immediate cause of her application for treatment was an outburst of rage, after severe provocation, against the disturbed teenagers in her care – the first time she had lost her temper since before she became an adolescent herself. This had in fact been non-destructive (except for a pile of plates which she swept to the floor) and effective, and in her it produced an extreme feeling of liberation: 'After this incident I felt so powerful – I wouldn't have minded if there were a hundred of you young bastards, I could deal with you.' However, when she applied for treatment one of her complaints was still 'inability to channel anger'.

As described in Chapter 16, the patient's compliant defence against her anger did not come up in her therapy; but nevertheless during this time there was a marked improvement in her ability to assert herself. The most dramatic manifestation of this, which has all the hallmarks of constructive self-assertion, occurred at an interview for a course at London University. The interviewers challenged her application on two grounds, that her academic record was not good enough, and that the subjects in which she had specialised were not relevant. She fiercely contested both points, maintaining that she had the ability to go through the course and succeed. The final result was that she received a letter from them in which, although they did not offer her a place that year, they made plain that they would do so in the next year if she cared to apply; and they ended by complimenting her highly on her handling of the interviews.

In her 4-year follow-up she seemed to have maintained her ability to assert herself at work, but – as already described – she destroyed her relation with her boy-friend of long standing by having an attack of rage in which she smashed up one of his valued possessions.

It was at this point that the result was scored, but by now there is subsequent information. When she was followed up 2 years later she seemed to have relapsed. She was clearly functioning below her potential at work, had refused promotion, and was now leaving her career without knowing what else she would do. She thus finally cannot score positively for self-assertion even outside her intimate relationships.

The Secretary in a State of Nirvana (criterion partly fulfilled)

The manifest patterns concerning aggression and self-assertion with which the patient presented were an inability to put her own needs forward, and a preoccupation with everyone else's needs rather than her own; and a tendency to gravitate towards men who ill treated her, which included her current boy-friend and her boss. The usual interpretation of patterns of this kind is that the patient is full of anger, but both defends herself against it and gets other people to punish her for it.

During therapy there were two major moments of breakthrough of her anger. In Session 3 she reported a terrific row with her boy-friend, who walked out on her (which we did not regard as a disaster); and in Session 8 she reported the following sequence of events with her parents, which bears some resemblance to the incident between the Mother or Teenage Daughter and her parents described above. It is told here in the therapist's words:

> She said that just after I [the therapist] went on holiday she had become quite depressed. Her father had commented that when next she visited he hoped that she would be more cheerful and less moody. She felt very angry at this, and had subsequently phoned her mother saying that if her father felt that about her she wouldn't come home, since it was obvious that they were not prepared to accept her as she really felt. In fact when she did go home she had a serious talk with her parents, telling them about the break-up with her boy-friend and saying that that was why she had felt depresssed. It was the first time that she had ever talked to her parents in a meaningful way, and she said that she had been able to reveal her true feelings – both depression and anger – to them because of her therapy.

In the next session she reported having changed her compliant and altruistic pattern at work by demanding overtime pay.

In her last session there was major confirmation that this improvement had persisted. The following incident is told in the therapist's words:

> As an example of how things had changed with her boss, she told me that this morning she had overslept and gone into work late. When she arrived a client was waiting to see her, and her boss had had to try and deal with the client in her absence. Her boss had been absolutely furious, saying that he had wasted a whole hour of his time, and where on earth had she been? In the past, the patient said, she would have felt very guilty; but this morning her retort was that she had often had to spend hours of her time dealing with her boss's problems, and she now thanked him for returning the favour! Later he sent her a note apologising for his behaviour. She smiled at me as she said this, and I found myself smiling back at her, feeling glad for her sake and somehow sad that it was our last session at the same time.

At follow-up the patient showed clear insight into her original pattern and said that she was far better at standing up for herself both at work and with her parents. However, she also made the remark, 'Apart from work, I don't find any anger. In other relationships I don't feel there is any sort of connection with anger.'

The Self-driving Physicist (criterion fulfilled)

When this patient first came he suffered from a severe inability to assert himself. For instance, he said he is never praised at work but always criticised, and he would like to attack back but feels 'like somebody with a gun containing one bullet against somebody with an automatic with a a full magazine'. In the early stages of therapy he replied to an interpretation about anger with his father in the past by saying, 'I was never violent. I preferred to smash *things*.'

During therapy he began to respond to work on his anger. As examples, in Session 12 he reported 'feeling great' because he had had an argument with his current girl-friend and had been able to express himself in this kind of situation for the first time in his life. In Session 22 he reported having threatened some friends who were criticising a girl in a pub, with the words, 'Shut your mouth or I'll do something I'll regret'.

At follow-up he had made remarkable progress in the area of self-assertion. At work he was now in charge of 80 men and was able to get very high productiveness out of them, which gave his boss great satisfaction. This was not just trying to please, since he was able to disagree with his boss where necessary and bring him round to his own point of view.

The reservation in the assessment of the therapeutic result was that these changes showed an extreme compulsive quality. Nevertheless the improvement in his ability to assert himself was marked and undeniable.

The Acting-out Accounts Clerk (criterion not fulfilled)

This patient's original complaint was claustrophobia, and one of her main problems concerned the inability to deal with anger. In situations that made her angry she was unable to express anything, and she then took her anger out on herself when alone, e.g. by banging her head against the wall.

The events of therapy illustrate with great clarity the emergence of insight about the sources of her anger and the defence mechanisms that she used against it – unfortunately with only minor therapeutic effects. She spoke of being afraid of what would happen if she lost control, and of wanting to swear and shout at her mother, and indeed she had a moment of speaking her mind to her mother over the phone. This led to another moment of apparently crucial insight: that perhaps her claustrophobic anxiety in the presence of other people was due to her impulse to say something really hurtful to them. Later she admitted to murderous thoughts against both her woman boss and her parents.

This apparent progress was illusory. In the final session she mentioned (in passing) that a few days ago she had made a suicidal gesture with tablets after having a tremendous row with her woman boss. Thus a moment of liberation of her anger was followed once more by turning her destructive impulses against herself.

At follow-up she was still able to some degree to speak her mind to her mother, and her claustrophobic anxiety was somewhat improved; but in other situations the original pathological ways of dealing with anger had reasserted themselves. As described in Chapter 15, she had expressed anger against one boy-friend by 'smoking and smoking and smoking and getting a headache', and against another by going home and 'smashing the door and screaming and yelling'.

The Actress with Elocution Problems (criterion fulfilled)

In her application form this patient wrote, 'I used to be direct with people, but it drove them away.'

At the first follow-up (1 year) she gave a clear description of the conversion of the above kind of inappropriate aggression into constructive self-assertion – in one area at any rate. She said that she got on much better with her husband's parents. Her father-in-law was a difficult man but now she 'gave as good as she got' and this had greatly improved their relation. She also said that therapy had put her more in touch with her anger, which made her less afraid of it in general, so that she felt freer with people and less anxious about having to please them.

The Miner's Daughter Mourning her Baby (criterion partly fulfilled)

This patient suffered from a severe problem over anger. At initial assessment she described having become overwhelmed with feelings of hatred for the boy-friend who had mde her pregnant, so severe that she felt she was near to doing him physical harm, together with fears of killing people in a motor accident. This had culminated in an extremely violent hysterical attack, in which she 'seemed to go berserk' and started screaming uncontrollably, with the feeling that she was going mad. Since then she has suffered from other violent attacks in which she may tear at the wallpaper or bang her head on the wall. These inappropriate ways of expressing anger were accompanied by difficulty in asserting herself in everyday situations.

In Session 14 she mentioned a small amount of progress over the issue of self-assertion: she was able to modify her behaviour so that things could be more on her terms, e.g. by deliberately withholding altruistic actions so that she would not be taken for granted.

At follow-up she had not suffered from any further hysterical attacks. She said that now she was able to blame things on other people, which she had never been able to do before. When asked for an example, she said, 'Now I am quite critical. I found out that doctors aren't always right.' She went on to say that her daughter, Ellen, was under an ENT Clinic, but they never examined her properly nor took any action. She then discovered that Ellen was going deaf. She got her visited by a second doctor, who said that she needed an operation. She refused to go back to the original Clinic and insisted, and was granted, that Ellen should be operated on at another hospital.

She now added, however, that if this had been for herself rather than her daughter, she felt she would not have been able to do it. This was confirmed by her having failed to lodge an appeal with the local Council, which she was entitled to do, about a grant which had been refused. 'I am not very aggressive really. I have always found it works better to be nice.'

The Anorexic Museum Assistant (criterion not fulfilled)

During her therapy, at 1-year follow-up, and throughout most of her subsequent analysis, this patient led an extremely isolated, withdrawn life, so that she largely avoided situations in which she was required to assert herself.

The Girl with Eye Problems (criterion not fulfilled)

This patient suffered from attacks of violence from an early age, in one of which (at age 10) she cut her bedroom curtains into pieces with a pair of scissors. This was the night before she was due to be sent away for a 6-week holiday, probably because she was being difficult at home.

At initial assessment she said that she has violent quarrels with her husband in which she shouts abuse, and in a recent incident she hurled a chair at him. The reason for this last incident was not at all clear, and indeed there were a number of episodes of intense feeling – anger, depression, or weeping – for which she could give no cause. The psychologist wrote of her Rorschach: 'The quality of intense anger which came through in her voice was carried over into her percepts, nearly all of which were of violent, destructive forces or damaged objects.'

At follow-up (nearly 7 years) she contradicted herself over her attacks of violence. She said first that the last time anything like this had happened was about 4 years ago, when her elder son was 1 year old. He had fallen downstairs and she had started screaming and shouting at her husband. She denied that it had been her husband's fault. Later she said that during a recent attack of depression she had hit her husband on a number of occasions. She was unable to give any reason for this, and at another point she said: 'They are *bodily* emotions, not really *my* emotions. My body cries and my body throws things.' Thus the theme of not being able to account for her intense feelings was continued into the follow-up period.

The Borderline Graduate Clerk (deterioration)

When he first came to us this patient suffered from a severe problem of suppressed hostility against people of both sexes. With bosses he was 'always swallowing his anger', and with women he experienced intense feelings of inner rage, which frightened him.

At follow-up he had become a student again, and he was living an almost completely isolated life, so that he had avoided his problems with both sexes. Moreover, he now not only denied angry feelings but denied that he had ever had them.

The Robot Man (criterion partly fulfilled)

Like the Psychiatric Nurse, the main event in this patient's early psychic life was that at the age of 13 he made a conscious effort to control his violent behaviour, which had resulted in general inhibition and a form of derealisation.

During therapy he described a 'good row' with his father, which resulted in their getting on better together. At follow-up he had also been able to assert himself effectively at work.

The Victimised Telephonist (major improvement followed by complete relapse)

In the present series there were three women patients – the Librarian who Sought Suffering, the Secretary in a State of Nirvana, and the present patient – who showed a pattern of actively getting themselves into situations in which they were ill-treated. As was described in connection with the Nirvana Secretary, this pattern usually seems to represent a way of dealing with anger by turning it against the self, while serving the purpose of self-punishment for the anger at the same time. The natural consequence is a total inability to be self-assertive.

As far as this problem was concerned, the Victimised Telephonist's life fell into three phases: before she came to therapy, during therapy, and at final follow-up.

The reason for her seeking treatment was a state of depression which came on when she was abandoned by her married man-friend. She was quite unaware of any anger with him, and this had to be brought out at initial interview by a series of confrontations. It became clear that, like the Psychiatric Nurse and several other patients in this series, she had adopted a pattern of bending over backwards to please since an early age. Reading between the lines, it seems that her man-friend left her at the point at which she began for the first time to move away from this position and make demands on him.

During therapy, which consisted of only 12 sessions, there were a series of incidents in which she showed a remarkable capacity to be constructively self-assertive. Already in Session 3 the following had occurred, here reported in the therapist's words: 'She spent last week at Eastbourne watching the tennis. On the Saturday, when she phoned home, she discovered that her mother had been admitted to hospital for a lung infection. This is part of a chronic illness which recurs from time to time. Clearly the expectation was that she would leave the tournament and go home (a journey which would have taken almost a whole day). However, she was enjoying herself, and she thought of our discussions and felt that to leave would be pleasing only to her parents and not necessary. She then called a friend near home and made arrangements for flowers to be sent to her mother, and she also called a neighbour of her parents and left a phone number where she could be reached in an emergency. As things turned out her mother was discharged from hospital after 2 days and the patient feels she made the right decision.'

Obviously the reader must make his or her own judgment of this, but to us it seems that it has all the charactersitics of healthy, concerned, responsible, and realistic behaviour: she refused to be panicked into complying automatically with her parents' wishes and sacrificing her own enjoyment; she showed her concern for her mother by sending flowers; and she awaited events and made all possible arrangements to reverse her decision if the need should arise. Taking into account her previous pattern of compulsive compliance, this was entirely out of character and seemed to indicate a major advance.

There were three other incidents of constructive self-assertion reported in her short therapy, which for brevity we will omit.

These events raised our hopes that she would show a major and permanent character change, but this was not to be. Her final position has already been described in Chapter 24 under the heading of maladaptive patterns. The relevant aspect of this is that she fell in love with a man behind the Iron Curtain and became engaged to him, but that when she visited him subsequently he started ignoring her. She felt unable either to protest or to walk out, apparently because she was afraid of what his relatives might think, and she has ended up by marrying him even though she no longer loves him, in order to help him get to England.

The Acutely Suicidal Receptionist (suicide)

This patient had only 9 sessions before she committed suicide. At initial assessment she had given clear evidence of a pattern of allowing herself to be put upon and exploited; yet already in Session 2 she reported having been able to move away from this position. Again we report it in the therapist's words: 'She said that when she went to her sister's she made an important discovery. For the first time she had been able to ask things for herself instead of always being the giver. She was not bossy or demanding but just able to ask.' Thus, extraordinarily enough, even this patient gave therapeutic effects in the area of self-assertion at the very beginning of her therapy, before everything was nullified by the final catastrophe.

31

Problems of aggression and self-assertion

III Discussion

Comparison between problems of aggression and problems with the opposite sex

There were three main similarities between these two areas, as follows:

1 At initial assessment 100% of our sample suffered from problems in both areas.
2 Although many patients showed major advances in these two areas, very few can be said to have solved their problems in either area *completely*. Complete resolution in *both* areas occurred only in the Nurse Mourning her Fiancé. In problems of aggression there was probably complete resolution also in the Librarian, and perhaps surprisingly the Allergic Receptionist (whose outcome was only scored as 1.75). The other '+' scores for problems of aggression were subject to reservations of various kinds, such as the residual violence in the Conductor and Car Battery Man, the temporary relapse into inappropriate aggression in the Sculptress, the compulsive quality of the achievement shown by the Self-driving Physicist, and the inability even to acknowledge anger in close relations in the Nirvana Secretary.
3 In spite of these reservations, just as in relations with the opposite sex, many of the improvements shown in the area of aggression were extremely worthwhile, and – as we have stated many times in connection with other types of improvement – in some cases they resulted in a major transformation of the patient's life. This was particularly true of the Conductor, who most effectively used constructive self-assertion in the furtherance of his career; the Car Battery Man, who was enabled to stay in jobs instead of repeatedly leaving because he had fallen out with bosses; and perhaps also the Hypomanic Advertising Executive, who achieved a highly effective and responsible position at work.

Classification of problems over aggression

Among these patients there were seven broad categories of maladaptive mechanisms for dealing with aggression, which cover most of those likely to be encountered in psychotherapeutic practice. Some patients showed more than one. They are listed below roughly in ascending order of the directness with which aggression was expressed. An asterisk marks those patients in whom the problem was at least partly resolved at follow-up.

1 General inhibition of aggressive feelings

The Nurse Mourning her Fiancé (since bereavement)*, Pacifist Conductor (lifelong, a consequence of pacifist upbringing)*, Rebellious Scriptwriter (inability to rebel at home, repeated in choice of partner), Hypomanic Advertising Executive (role of 'amiable clot')*, Psychiatric Nurse (inhibition resulting from conscious control at the age of 11), Anorexic Museum Assistant (lifelong), Robot Man (inhibition resulting from conscious control at the age of 13)*, Graduate Clerk (emotional withdrawal at follow-up).

2 Over-compliance, excessive altruism

The Betrayed Son (always working during the Christmas holiday)*, Nirvana Secretary (attends to other people's needs at work and home)*, Victimised Telephonist (exploited at home, one-sided relation with man-friend), Suicidal Receptionist (exploited at home).

3 Masochism, self-directed aggression, taking the position of victim

The Librarian (masochistic sexuality, promoting her husband's affair)*, Nirvana Secretary (gravitates towards difficult and demanding men, whom she cannot cope with)*, Acting-out Accounts Clerk ('used' by men), Victimised Telephonist (unable to refuse to marry a man whom she didn't love).

4 Inner feelings of violence that cannot be expressed

The Allergic Receptionist (apparently undirected)*, Mother or Teenage Daughter (against family), Self-driving Physicist (against father – 'I prefer to smash *things*')*, Miner's Daughter (against the boy-friend who made her pregnant), Graduate Clerk (against male authority).

5 Indirect and destructive ways of expressing aggression

Betrayed Son (against wife by putting off decorating their flat, at follow-up).

6 Histrionic behaviour, tantrums

Sculptress (in response to stress at work and in relations with men)*, Mountain Tarn Girl (hysterical attacks)*, Mother or Teenage Daughter ('I express anger in outbursts, in the wrong way'), Acting-out Accounts Clerk ('smashed the door and screamed and yelled'), Miner's Daughter ('seemed to go berserk and screamed uncontrollably'), Girl with Eye Problems (smashed chair but did not know why).

7 Inappropriate or uncontrolled aggressive behaviour, verbal or physical, directed against people

Pacifist Conductor (violence against wife), Car Battery Man (violence against wife), Concert-goer (reacts aggressively with bosses, damaging his career)*, Psychiatric Nurse (violent tempers against family in early life, smashed boyfriend's possession at follow-up), Actress (antagonises people)*, Robot Man (violent tempers in early life)*.

Side by side with the above classification, there were three patients who at follow-up were able to use aggression or self-assertion constructively in certain situations but not in others. Thus the Betrayed Son was able to be constructively assertive at work but was behaving destructively with his wife; the Nirvana Secretary said she could experience anger at work but not in close relations; and the Miner's Daughter was able to be assertive on her daughter's behalf but not on her own. These cases illustrate that aggression tends to be more difficult to express the 'nearer to home', so to speak, the situation is in which it is required.

The causes of problems over aggression

These are shown, as far as the evidence allows, in Table 31.1.

Comments on Table 31.1

It needs to be said, of course, that there is nothing very remarkable in any of the features shown in this table, particularly in the fact of finding a number of patients who were angry with one or both parents. However, it is perhaps worthy of note that the main event leading to problems of aggression in the childhood of five patients was the birth (followed in one case by the death) of a younger sibling; that no fewer than six patients (25%) were brought up in homes where the messsage was conveyed that any form of aggression was unacceptable, and that in four of these the parents were in a sense 'too good' for their children's welfare (pacifist, understanding, or altruistic); and finally that two patients lost a large part of their capacity for feelings of all kinds in their childhood after making a conscious decision to control their own violent behaviour. Thus the main feature illustrated by the table is the ever-recurring nature of emotional problems in western society.

Improvements that occurred during therapy

It is a remarkable observation that some kind of important improvement occurred during the course of therapy in almost every patient in this series, though not all of these withstood the test of time. In no area was this more true than in problems of self-assertion, which seem to represent the type of disturbance that gives way more quickly and easily than any other under the impact of psychotherapy. The Nurse Mourning her Fiancé and Pacifist Conductor are the best examples. This whole subject will be considered in detail in the next chapter.

'Subjective' and 'objective' evidence

The central problem in assessing therapeutic results is how to make the evidence as objective as possible without causing it to become clinically meaningless. Of

Table 31.1 Causes of problems over aggression

Patient	Main cause
Nurse Mourning Fiancé	Loss of all feeling in response to traumatic bereavement
Pacifist Conductor	Impossibility of anger at home due to pacifist upbringing
Librarian who sought Suffering	Guilt-laden jealousy of younger brother
Car Battery Man	Competitiveness with his father
Betrayed Son	Anger with his father, who let him down
Sculptress with Nightmares	Anger with her father, who disappointed and exploited her
Mountain Tarn Girl	Caught between pleasing her father or her mother; required by her mother to control herself
Rebellious Script Writer	Impossibility of rebelliousness at home
Allergic Receptionist	Anger with her father, who deserted her
Concert-goer in an Acute Panic	Highly ambivalent feelings about his father, with whom he also had a very good relation
Mother or Teenage Daughter	Loss of care due to becoming a mother; impossibility of anger at home
Hypomanic Advertising Executive	Jealousy of his younger brother; domination by his mother; parents too understanding
Nirvana Secretary	Childhood deprivation, altruistic parents leading to impossibility of anger at home
Self-driving Physicist	Emotionally empty home life; constant quarrelling between parents
Acting-out Accounts Clerk	Anger with her mother's constant criticism
Actress with Elocution Problems	Anger about both parents' domination; physical abuse by her father
Miner's Daughter	Altruistic, idealising parents; impossibility of anger at home
Anorexic Museum Assistant	?Birth and death of younger sister
Psychiatric Nurse with Attacks of Rage	Excluded by her sisters; need to control violent temper
Girl with Eye Problems	?No true contact with parents
Borderline Graduate Clerk	Jealousy of younger brother; rejection by his mother
Robot Man	Need to control violent temper
Victimised Telephonist	Leaning over backwards to please; impossibility of anger at home
Suicidal Receptionist	Exceedingly disturbed background, demented father, alcoholic mother

course hardly any of our evidence is truly objective, since almost all of it depends on *reports* from patients; but, apart from this, much of the evidence is extremely compelling. This applies particularly to constructive self-assertion, when not only has the assertion been effective, but in addition there is hard evidence of a marked improvement in the relation with the people against whom the assertion was directed, derived from the latter's actual behaviour. Striking examples are provided by the Car Battery Man who, after an hour's argument, succeeded in getting his boss to admit that the firm's system was out of date and to lend him the money he needed; the Nirvana Secretary, who answered her boss back in the most caustic terms and got him to apologise; and the Psychiatric Nurse, who vigorously defended her academic record with her interviewers, and ended by receiving not only the offer of a place at University next year, but also their congratulations on her handling of the interview. Finally, in a slightly different kind of situation, the Conductor's new-found assertive and creative personality caused two composers to ask him to conduct their works for them.

Unless all these patients have been telling completely fabricated stories, which is hardly probable, this kind of evidence is surely as acceptable as could be desired by anyone looking for objective truth.

Part Four

Research Results

32

Therapeutic effects during therapy

In Part Four we will consider the scientific results that have emerged from this work. We begin with evidence from therapeutic effects which occurred during the course of therapy, a subject which has an important bearing on the question of the validity of psychotherapy.

The evidence, which is very extensive, is summarised below. Where there had been improvement during therapy, but at follow-up the patient was found to have relapsed in this area, the entry is marked with '†'.

The Nurse Mourning her Fiancé

Main problem: She had lost all feeling, particularly grief and anger, after her traumatic bereavement 4 years ago.
Session 1: She began to cry for the first time in 4 years during the session, and the crying became uncontrollable immediately afterwards, but she was not in touch with the cause of her grief.
21: She expressed open anger ('shaking with rage') against a bus conductress who had behaved callously to an old lady.
26: She was so angry with a girl at school who had answered her back that she swore at her and wanted to hit her.
27: She was let down by a friend and cried – i.e. she was now able to be in touch with the cause of her grief.
31: She said she feels 'different'. She now knows when she is upset. She was able to cry with a bereaved girl and the grief was for herself as well as for the girl.

The Pacifist Conductor

Main problems: As a result of his pacifist upbringing he had been quite unable to feel or express anger all his life; 5 years ago he had given up his creative life by ceasing to be a conductor and becoming manager of an orchestra.
5: He received an offer to conduct, and was happy to accept. He said, 'The rusty parts of me have got going.'
6: He was able to experience anger, and wrote an angry letter to a paper about an unfavourable review.
10: The first time he had conducted professionally for 5 years.

11: He had a row with his boss in public – he was 'incoherent with rage' in a way that had never happened before in his life. The effects were entirely beneficial. Two composers asked him to conduct their works for them.

12: He took over as conductor of an opera and the composer was well pleased with his interpretation of the music.

15: He said he is 'much more tolerant' of himself, e.g. about his symptom of eating in the middle of the night.

The Librarian who Sought Suffering

Main problem: Since her childhood she had been quite unable to feel anger or jealousy. She had coped with these two feelings by turning them against herself, e.g. by masochistic fantasies and by actively promoting her husband's affair with another woman.

26: She had been openly angry with her husband who had phoned to say that he was staying with his girl-friend.

28: She had got so angry with her husband and his girl-friend that she had tried to push them both out of the door.

30 (last session): She said she can 'forgive herself more easily'. Even her attitude to money has changed. She used to put up a big fight against buying anything for herself, but now she and her husband decided quite naturally that she should have some new clothes.

During her therapy there was extensive evidence of an ability to express herself better in writing. Formerly, she said, she used to lean on her husband's creativeness. In the last session, number 30, she brought up the moving poem quoted on p. 68, the theme of which was that she was emerging into the light and beginning to spread her wings.

The Car Battery Man

Main problems: He suffered from a recurrent problem of anger with bosses, which resulted in his either leaving jobs or behaving in such a way that he was fired. He also suffered from a mixture of claustrophobia and agoraphobia. He showed a pattern of short-lived relations with girls in which he couldn't commit himself. He lacked confidence in the presence of other men.

9: His boss handed over the keys to his (the boss's) car and told him to fetch it. The patient said he wasn't a messenger boy and handed the keys back. He kept the job.

18: He lost his temper and shouted on two occasions with girl-friends. This has not happened for years and he is glad he has been able to do it.

24: He was able to recognise that a policeman friend wasn't as self-confident as he had thought, and gave the friend advice. 'It was a strange experience.'

25: He became panicky when on a long-distance car journey. He then shouted at another driver who blocked his road, the driver shouted back, and he felt better and was able to drive again.

26: He went on a training course. There were many occasions on which he had to speak in front of people, be in crowded places etc. In particular he had to attend a meeting in a small room with 25 other people, at the end of which a friend said he (the friend) 'wouldn't have been able to stay there a moment longer'. The patient experienced anxiety but was able to overcome it.

On this course he was chosen to present a subject and managed very well – previously if he made one mistake his effort would collapse. He was the only one to get a prize.

In this same session he reported being able to contemplate commitment to his current girl-friend (in fact he married her 7 months after the end of therapy).

28: He had argued with a colleague and got his point across. He felt very satisfied, and to his great surprise they were friends afterwards.

He saw that a customer, the boss of a firm, was quite anxious. He felt proud of being able to recognise that there were weaknesses in other men.

The Sculptress with Nightmares

Main problems: Depression, drinking, over-activity, very short-lived relations with men, loss of creativeness, histrionic behaviour in response to stress.

14: For the first time for many years she had not been devastated by rejection by a man.

19: On two occasions she lost her temper effectively with other women at work. This has never happened before.

24: She is working creatively and not drinking nearly so much. Her ex-husband says that her recent sculptures are the best she has ever done. According to her mother, she is much more understanding and aware of what she is doing.

26: After a seemingly endless series of affairs lasting 1 or 2 weeks, she took up with a new man on a long-term basis (follow-up showed that the relation lasted for 5 years).

27: Everybody says she is different. 'She feels slowed down, calmer, more contained – it's a very good feeling.'

The Betrayed Son

11: He has been asserting himself in an entirely new way. He refused to be on duty at Christmas, and it had caused no trouble.

19: He no longer conceals his feelings with his wife. He has short, furious outbursts of anger which are gone almost as quickly as they came, and he feels better for it.

29: He resolved an attack of anxiety by confronting his boss about his future and giving in his notice.

30: He said he had been taking decisions about his future that would have been impossible a year ago.

The Mountain Tarn Girl

13: For the first time for a very long time she saw that 'she could exist, that she had some autonomy, that it wasn't all hopeless'.

20: She had been accepted for a new, good job. Taking this job was the first time that she had ever made a decision on her own, without support from someone else.

The Rebellious Script Writer

None.

The Allergic Receptionist

9: She said that her body felt more coordinated, and this had enabled her to take driving lessons.

21: She said she feels 'much happier deep down inside'.

22: She said she is more decisive and able to see things for what they are. She knows better what she wants.

The Concert-goer in an Acute Panic

26 (last session): He said he is less angry with authority figures. He used to be unreasonable, now he is more calm. He used to refuse to listen to men in a superior position – now he is more tolerant and has achieved things he couldn't have before. The other day he asked for and got an improvement in his working conditions. He said he *had* improved and it didn't matter whether or not the therapist agreed. The proof is that not only has he noticed changes, but other people have too.

The Mother or Teenage Daughter

10: She was angry with her boy-friend. After first throwing a tantrum she had a frank discussion with him about their relation, which was quite new for her†.

On a later occasion they had made love in a satisfying way that had not happened before†.

For the first time she asked her father for a cuddle, which he had given her. This ended in an open discussion about her problems in relation to her family, with the result that they treated her with much greater consideration from then on†.

The Hypomanic Advertising Executive

10: He reported having been more forceful sexually with his wife than ever before, 'which they had both enjoyed'.

19: For the first time in his life he openly criticised his mother for putting his father down.

21: He used his sarcasm with his father for the first time and was surprised to find how effective it was.

25: He said he is trying to 'reverse the impotent image' at work, and has found himself being much more effective.

The Secretary in a State of Nirvana

She had been quite unable to express aggression or assert her own needs, either at work or with her parents.

3: She had a tremendous row with her seemingly unpleasant and inconsiderate boy-friend for the first time in her life†.

4: Her boy-friend has not contacted her and she has experienced great relief and has been able to take great pleasure in doing just what she wants to.

8: After her father had criticised her for being moody and depressed, she went home and had a long talk with her parents about her current dificulties – 'the first time she had talked to her parents in a meaningful way'. She attributed her ability to do this to her therapy.

11: She used to think that people were doing her a favour by employing her, but now she realises that she puts a lot into her work and that it ought to be acknowledged. She has asked for overtime pay.

29 (last session): She answered her boss back in forceful terms and got him to apologise.

The Self-driving Physicist

At initial assessment he had described feeling powerless, as if he had a gun with one bullet in it against someone with an automatic.

12: 'I had an argument with my girl-friend and felt able to express myself, and after that I felt great. I felt I did not need her any more. Before, I always tried to be nice with people, but now I think I have to say what I want. A friend let me down last week and I told him off, saying I did not like the idea of going out with him.'

He had also stood up for the first time against his mother, but not against his father.

22: He had asserted himself successfully against a male friend with the words, 'Shut your mouth or I'll do something I'll regret'. This involved protecting a girl against his friend's criticism – a triangular type of situation in which he would previously have been quite incapable of being effective.

23: After some important work on Oedipal problems in the transference in Session 22, he said, 'A lot of things are happening in a better way, and it is all related to last session, in which I understood a lot of things.' He has been symptomatically much better, shaking much less. He feels less tense and more able to communicate with other people. This was illustrated by its effect on his boss, who had said to him, 'Now you are one of us', and had taken him by the arm. 'We went out together and I felt that was great.'

The Acting-out Accounts Clerk

10: She mentioned feeling less tense with her mother. She agreed that this was because she had been able to express some of her anger to her mother.

The Actress with Elocution Problems

None.

The Miner's Daughter Mourning her Baby

10: She said she was now able to modify her behaviour in such a way as to cause things to be more on her terms.

22 (last session): She said she was better than when she started. She felt she had been understood and had sorted out some things that were bothering her. There is no record of what these were.

The Anorexic Museum Assistant

After two initial assessment interviews: She had her first menstrual period for 2½ years.

10: She said she was able to go home when *she* wanted to, and not just to please her parents. She was able to relate to them much better than before.

The Psychiatric Nurse with Attacks of Rage

Main problems: An inability to deal with anger and self-assertion, irregular periods.

9: She revealed that, ever since her initial interview, she has started having regular menstrual periods for the first time since they began 9 years ago.

15: She had been extremely effective at an interview for a course at London University. She vigorously defended her academic record and ended up by being offered a place next year and being congratulated on her handling of the interview†.

The Girl with Eye Problems

None.

The Borderline Graduate Clerk

15: He reported a number of improvements that had appeared during the Christmas break: he had got through a probation period at work; he was getting more pleasure out of playing the piano; authority figures seemed less threatening; he had managed to get on quite well with an uncle whom he disliked; and his father had asked him for help over something†. (These improvements did not stand up during further therapy and he became paranoid again.)

The Robot Man

During therapy he asserted himself effectively with his father. He described this as a 'good row' and said the two of them were getting on better since then.

The Victimised Telephonist

Main problem: Leaning over backwards to please and being unable to demand her rights.

3: She realistically refused to sacrifice her own pleasure because her mother had been admitted to hospital. Her mother was discharged after 2 days.

5: She had gone out with a new boy-friend – the first time she had gone out with a man by whom she was attracted since the break-up with her married lover 18 months before.

6: She had been able to express resentment to this same boy-friend because she felt she was being used†.

11: She had stated exactly what she wanted from her boy-friend in their business venture; she had dealt effectively with a woman neighbour who had been annoying her; she is now thinking more clearly – formerly her thoughts had been muddled and slowed; she had invited a woman out and is now more involved with people than at any time during the past 7 years†. (None of these improvements persisted at final follow-up).

The Acutely Suicidal Receptionist

Main problems: Allowing herself to be exploited, being unable to say what it was that she wanted for herself.
2: For the first time she was able to ask for things for herself from her sister – 'not bossy or demanding, just able to ask'†.
6: Her sister invited her out and she was able to say she didn't want to go†.

Comment

The foregoing shows the remarkable variety of improvements, many of which were still present at follow-up many years later, that occurred in these 24 patients in the period during which they were being treated. If these patients had not been treated and had been observed for equal periods of time, it seems very difficult to believe that anything like a comparable degree of change could possibly have taken place.

This whole subject will be considered in detail in the next chapter.

33

Can the improvements be attributed to therapy?

Introduction: the nature of the evidence

If we wish to draw conclusions about the effectiveness of psychotherapy from this kind of study, we are at a serious disadvantage because of the lack of a control sample. Consequently we can never be sure that any changes that are found would not have occurred without treatment, as a result of such factors as normal maturation, the effects of life experience, and the spontaneous remission of symptoms.

Nevertheless there are two main ways of obtaining quite strong evidence suggesting that the changes were in fact due to therapy.

The first is entirely circumstantial and occurs when disturbances of long duration (which we may represent by a months) improve during the course of therapy of brief duration (represented by b months). Obviously, the higher the value of the ratio $a:b$ (the duration ratio) the less likely it is that the improvements 'just happened' to occur while the patient was coincidentally having therapy. As mentioned at the end of Chapter 32, this kind of evidence suggests strongly that the improvements were due to therapy, but it says nothing about what the therapeutic factors were, and particularly about whether or not these were specific to dynamic psychotherapy.

However, evidence on this second issue can be obtained more directly if the improvements followed immediately after, or a short time after, particular therapeutic events. In order to be convincing the events should contain one or more of the following features, all of which of course must be *psychodynamically relevant* to the changes that occurred:

1 interpretations to which there was a clear-cut response;
2 fresh insight;
3 a changed attitude to the expression of feelings;
4 the breakthrough of previously unconscious feelings, or
5 a direct statement by the patient that the changes have been made possible by therapy.

The evidence is further strengthened if clinical experience confirms that similar changes occur in response to similar events in other patients.

The present series provides a great deal of evidence of these kinds, and – since the validity of dynamic psychotherapy is always being questioned – the material presented here is the most important from a scientific point of view in the whole study.

We will now consider in detail those patients in whom evidence of this kind can be obtained.

Patients in whom the improvements persisted at follow-up

The Nurse Mourning her Fiancé

Evidence from the duration ratio

She had been completely out of touch with feelings of all kinds, particularly grief and anger, since the death of her fiancé 4 years before. She started to cry in the first therapeutic session and her tears became uncontrollable immediately afterwards. As in all these patients, we have to count the beginning of therapy not as the first session but the initial assessment, in which much dynamic work was always done. Since in her case the initial assessment consisted of two interviews some weeks before the start of therapy, this means that a disturbance of *4 years'* duration began to be resolved in *three therapeutic contacts* during *5 weeks*.

Work preceding the freeing of grief

At initial assessment she started very resistant, trying to deny the importance of facing her feelings, and the interviewing psychologist succeeded in bringing home to her the fact that this denial was the basic cause of her depression. The psychologist also led her to fresh insight about the immediate precipitating cause for her depression, which had not been her fiancé's death but the bereavement of a girl in the school where she worked. Towards the end of the first session she spontaneously reached the further insight that one of her defences was to concentrate on irrelevances in order to keep painful thoughts at bay, and it was at this point that she started to become tearful.

This already striking evidence is reinforced by the clinical observation – which is really also everyday knowledge – that an essential factor in recovering from bereavement is the ability to experience grief to the full and pass through it.

Work preceding the freeing of anger and the lifting of depression

The therapist made a determined search for ambivalent feelings against the three people in the patient's life who had died, namely her mother, her father, and her fiancé. The patient admitted to quarrels with her mother in her teens, but no actual ambivalent feelings towards her fiancé were uncovered (extraordinarily enough, her relation with her father played no part in therapy). Nevertheless, on three occasions during therapy she reported a mitigation in her depression after a session in which important work was done on her anger. The clearest example of this occurred in Session 17: after a number of sessions in which the therapist had exerted pressure towards aggressive feelings, the patient now said that she had been trying to recall incidents when she had been angry. She described a number of these and then said that recently she had been less depressed.

In Session 19 she told a dream which led to her admitting highly guilt-laden death wishes against her grandmother, and in the next session she again reported an improvement in her depression.

The freeing of her aggression was most strikingly illustrated two sessions later (in Session 21) in which she reported the moment of extreme anger with the bus conductress.

In Session 24 she described an incident in which her friend, Derek, had failed to arrive to meet her, and she had been afraid that something terrible had happened to him. The therapist made the link between this fear and aggressive feelings by bringing out that the patient had nearly quarrelled with Derek the day before.

Again, two sessions later (in Session 26), she said that she had been much more aggressive recently, and she described having been effectively angry with a girl at the school who had answered her back.

The Pacifist Conductor

Work preceding the freeing of aggression

It has been mentioned many times that one of the principal themes of the therapist's interpretations early in therapy consisted of the patient's defences against aggressive impulses, together with the anxiety that these feelings might get out of control. The defences that were brought into the open included: becoming paralysed in a situation of anger (Session 3), remaining calm while other people lost control (Sessions 3 and 4), and feeling as if he were another person looking at himself (Session 4). In Session 5 there was a clear response to the interpretation that 'he could watch with satisfaction the emotional turmoil in other people as a part of himself that was being acted out by them'.

Evidence from the duration ratio

The first freeing of his anger was reported in the next session (number 6). This meant that a *lifelong* disturbance in a man of 30 began to be relieved after seven therapeutic contacts (including the initial interview) during the course of 4 months. The major discovery of constructive self-assertion was reported at 5 months, in Session 11.

Changed attitude to feelings

From early in his therapy there was extensive evidence of an entirely new and accepting attitude to the experience and expression of feelings. The details have been listed in Chapter 23 under the heading of emotional freeing.

The Librarian who Sought Suffering

Work on defences against anger and jealousy preceding improvement in depression, reduction in masochistic impulses, and freeing of aggression

Much of the early part of therapy was concerned with work on the patient's masochistic defence against anger and jealousy, one of the manifestations of which was her active promotion of an affair between her husband and his girl-friend Denise.

In Session 13 she reported a dream transparently expressing murderous feelings towards her husband, Denise, and younger siblings. There also emerged open anger with the therapist because of the latter's small stature, which resembled that of the patient's sister. Between this session and the next the patient phoned the therapist saying how angry she was at having the current triangular situation linked with her upbringing, but that now 'everything had fallen into place' – i.e. she had reached a major piece of insight about the nature of her problems. In the next session (number 14) she specified the nature of this insight by saying that she now realised that she had 'a monster of violent anger within her', and she also said that she felt very much less depressed.

In the later part of therapy (Sessions 26 and 28), instead of trying to promote her husband's affair, she reported having expressed open anger with both him and Denise.

We do not know when her overtly masochistic fantasies began to weaken, but we do know that at follow-up she reported that they had disappeared.

However, we can appeal to evidence from other cases. Davanloo has shown time and again in videotaped interviews presented at international symposia, that when a patient presents with masochistic pathology, violent impulses will be found underneath, and that when these are brought to the surface the masochistic phenomena disappear.

The Car Battery Man

Work on anger and paranoid projection preceding the freeing of aggression and the reduction of phobic symptoms

One of the climaxes of therapy came in Session 23, when the patient spoke of paranoid feelings in a crowded pub, which forced him to move to another relatively empty pub in which there was a 'cosy warm atmosphere'. The therapist linked this with the loss of the warm atmosphere in the patient's childhood caused by the birth of his sister, and then interpreted 'paranoid projection' of the patient's own anger, linking this with the anger that the patient must have felt against his mother in his childhood. There was a major response, with the patient openly admitting with intensity that formerly he had experienced paranoid feelings about the therapist, whom he had never trusted.

This was followed by the freeing of aggression both in the transference and in the patient's outside life.

In the next session (number 24) he became quite aggressive with the therapist, expressing his anger about not receiving advice. In Session 25 he reported having overcome an attack of phobic symptoms by shouting at another driver; and in Session 26 he reported a major improvement in his confidence and a marked reduction in his claustrophobic symptoms, both of which had become apparent while he was on a training course.

In Session 28 he reported having argued with a colleague, got his point across, and being surprised that he and the colleague remained friends.

Work on hostility against women accompanying his ability to contemplate committing himself to his girl-friend

In Session 26 he expressed a great deal of hostility towards women, but he then reported that he had both discussed his weaknesses openly with his girl-friend and could now talk about their future together. This was the girl whom he eventually married. Formerly his pattern had been just to 'use' women without becoming in any way deeply involved with them.

The Sculptress with Nightmares

In this patient the evidence is less convincing because there was a gap of a number of sessions between relevant therapeutic work and the appearance of therapeutic effects.

Work on anger preceding the discovery of constructive aggression

In the two initial assessment interviews the therapist brought out very clearly the intense anger experienced by the women in the family as a result of the father's behaviour over the restaurant. The patient said, 'Yes we are angry, and we can still be very nasty to him.' In Session 4 there emerged the devastating effect that her father had had on her sister Sylvie. In Session 5 the patient reported a violent row with her father over the phone on this same subject – almost certainly the first time she had ever spoken openly to him about her feelings.

Session 7 marked the beginning of a series of five nightmares, mostly involving sadistic impulses towards animals. In Session 8 she described how someone had told her that when she spoke about her father she sounded so angry that it was frightening. Also in this session, in response to an interpretation involving projection of aggression, she remembered having tried to stab her sister with a knife. In Session 12 she admitted to impulses to kick pregnant women in the belly. In Session 13 she spoke of anger with her *parents,* for the first time including her mother in her anger.

In Session 19 she reported having on two occasions lost her temper effectively with other women at work, something that had never happened before.

Work on Oedipal problems preceding improvements in her problems with men

In Session 10 she admitted to envy of her mother's fertility and jealousy of her mother's relation with her father.

In Session 14, she reported that for the first time she had not been devastated by finding herself the loser in a triangular situation involving a man and another woman.

This was followed by several sessions of productive work on guilt both about erotic feelings towards her father and successful rivalry with her mother.

In Session 26 she reported having taken up with a new man with whom she in fact stayed for 5 years.

The Betrayed Son

Work on aggression preceding the freeing of anger and self-assertion

In Session 3 the therapist interpreted that the patient was resentful against both his wife and the new baby for being the centre of attention, linking this with the birth of the patient's brother. The patient responded with a highly positive unconscious transference communication.

In Session 8 the patient confirmed and intensified the above interpretation by saying that recently he had experienced recurrent fantasies of his baby dying or his wife bleeding to death.

In Session 9 he admitted that the tension between his wife and mother had made him angry with both of them.

In Session 10 he admitted that he felt tense and angry and wanted to lash out at everyone.

In Session 11 he reported having changed his pattern at work by refusing to be on duty over Christmas.

From Session 11 onwards there was much work on the patient's conflicting feelings about his father and men in general, including the therapist. This involved a great deal of anger, particularly about the feeling that he was being 'kept down' by them, which came to a head in Session 18.

In Session 19 he reported an entirely new pattern of the expression of anger with his wife: short furious outbursts which were gone as quickly as they came, leaving him feeling the better for them.

In Session 29 he reported having resolved an anxiety attack by having a confrontation with his boss, and – though seething with anger – quietly but firmly giving in his notice.

Work on 'being himself'

The patient's deeply felt need to be himself was a recurrent theme which first appeared in Sessions 3 and 4. In Session 21 he reached an important piece of fresh insight on this theme, spontaneously resolving a situation in the transference: he said he had the feeling that all the therapist wanted for him was that he should become a successful businessman, but he now realised that it was his wife and his parents who really had this attitude.

In Session 27 he said that he was now determined to take decisions on his own ideas and not those of anybody else.

The Hypomanic Advertising Executive

Work on hostility against both men and women preceding the freeing of self-assertion

From the outset the most prominent theme of therapy was the patient's extreme hostility towards women, which the therapist linked with his anger with his mother, and in addition hostility towards men. It emerged that his sexual fantasies involved violent and humiliating attacks on both men and women. Side by side with this, the therapist brought out his passive defences in real life, which consisted of behaving like an 'amiable clot'.

In Session 10 he reported having been far more sexually forceful with his wife than ever before, which they had both enjoyed.

In Session 12 he reported a mitigation of the violence of his sexual fantasies towards women.

In Session 18 he shut his eyes and described fantasies of sadistic sexual attacks on the therapist, saying what a relief it was to be able to tell her this.

In Session 19 he said that his Managing Director thought him a fool. An interpretation of projection led to his admitting that he thought the Managing Director a fool. In this session he described having for the first time openly criticised his mother for putting his father down.

In Session 22 he spoke of 'tremendous locked-up anger' with his mother – 'a lack of respect, that's what it is, it's terrible to say that, I feel as though a thunder-clap has happened.'

In Session 25 he spoke of trying to 'reverse the impotent image' at work, and finding himself far more effective.

At follow-up there was considerable evidence for greater effectiveness with men, though the evidence for the same in relation to women was much more confused and uncertain.

The Self-driving Physicist

Work preceding the freeing of self-assertion

Two of the main themes that developed in the first 11 sessions were his need for advice from the (male) therapist, which was interpreted as his need for the love that he didn't get from his father; and his need to be nice to everyone as a defence against expressing his angry and competitive feelings, for fear of being rejected. This latter came out very clearly in Session 11.

In Session 12 he reported 'feeling great' after having both had an argument with his girl-friend and having expressed anger to a male friend who had let him down.

Between Sessions 11 and 22 there was much work in Oedipal problems, especially in the transference, with the patient becoming acutely aware of his guilt about rivalry with his father for his mother.

In Session 22 he reported dealing angrily with some male friends who were criti-cising a girl by whom he felt attracted.

Additional evidence from improvements that did not persist at follow-up

The patients considered so far in this chapter are those in whom the improvements that appeared during therapy were still present at follow-up. There were also a number of patients who showed improvements that clearly followed relevant therapeutic events but did not persist at follow-up. This evidence of course is much less impressive, and yet it does suggest that potential therapeutic factors were present. The most striking examples are as below.

The Mother or Teenage Daughter

Work on aggression, and clarification of the family situation, preceding the patient's ability to have an open discussion with people close to her

One of the main themes of therapy consisted of her inability to express her anger or ask for her needs to be met. This emerged already in the initial interview, in which she reached the fresh insight: 'Perhaps I want to tell the lot of them [her family] to go to hell.' In an early session she spoke of 'not having had a good argument for years', adding that her mother always tried to keep the peace.

It was in Session 10 that she reported a series of therapeutic effects. In one, she had felt of her boy-friend, who had let her down, that 'she wanted to rip him apart', but she had then had a highly constructive discussion with him about their relation. In another, she had confronted her parents for the first time about the situation in the home, the effects of which had been rewarding in the extreme.

Unfortunately at final follow-up she seems to have largely relapsed.

The Secretary in a State of Nirvana

Work on the altruistic defence preceding the freeing of anger and self-assertion

This patient's pattern had also been to suppress all feelings of anger or expression of her own needs, and to adopt an altruistic pattern instead, which had clearly arisen from her inability to criticise her altruistic parents. The interpretation of this defence and the exposure of the underlying feelings constituted the main focus of her therapy.

Already in the initial assessment interview she responded to interpretations on this focus by expressing some of her buried resentment against her parents.

In Session 2 she reported abominable behaviour on the part of her boy-friend, and the therapist interpreted her feeling that she had no right to expect anything for herself, and linked this with her upbringing. In the next session (number 3) she reported having had a terrific row with him, and in Session 4 she said she was feeling much less depressed and had taken pleasure in doing exactly what *she* wanted. In this session she described many incidents in which her mother had not had time for her, and the therapist pointed out her defence of making excuses for her mother, and how angry and resentful she must be underneath.

In Session 7 she admitted anger with her boy-friend, but said she had never been able to let him know about these feelings. The therapist linked this once more with her feelings about her parents, at which she nodded.

It was in the next session (number 8) that she reported having become angry with her parents after an incident in which her father had criticised her for being moody. She had most effectively confronted them and had a long and fruitful discussion with them about her current difficulties. She said that it was because of therapy that she had been able to do this.

In Session 10 she allowed herself some of her hitherto denied feelings about her parents by saying that she was 'sick to death' of her father's sanctimoniousness and her mother's good works. It was in this session that she said that she used to think that people were doing her a favour by employing her, but now she realised how much she put in to her work, and she has asked for overtime pay.

In the final session (number 29) she reported having abandoned her submissive and self-sacrificing position in relation to her boss and having answered him back in the most effective manner, getting him to apologise.

The position at follow-up

This was uncertain. The patient said that she was able to be 'far more selfish' both with her parents and at work. However, she was – surprisingly – unable to give concrete examples of this; she spoke of being unable to find any anger in close relations; and her whole life-style was one of emotional withdrawal.

The Anorexic Museum Assistant

Work on anxieties about womanhood preceding an improvement in menstrual problems

This patient was seen for two initial assessment interviews, after the second of which she reported having had her first menstrual period for 2½ years.

The work done in these interviews was clearly highly relevant, since it involved bringing out a pattern in a series of traumatic events throughout her life, namely that something went wrong every time she took a step in the direction of growing into a woman.

The Psychiatric Nurse with Attacks of Rage

Work in the initial interview preceding an improvement in menstrual problems

After her single initial assessment interview this patient began to have *regular* periods for the first time since they had begun 9 years before. The interview was highly dynamic, the main theme that was brought to light being her wish to experience and use all her feelings and impulses to the full. It is interesting that her menstrual disorder was probably partly caused by physiological factors, since she had been diagnosed as suffering from mild adrenogenital syndrome (an excess of male hormones).

The position at follow-up

Although she continued to menstruate, her periods were highly irregular and often painful.

Work on anger and competitiveness preceding the discovery of constructive self-assertion

In the early stages of therapy much work was done on her defences against both her anger and her competitiveness in relation to other women, including the therapist. Her anxiety seemed to consist mainly of the fear of damaging people, which was linked with her damaged sister, who had taken so much attention away from her.

The apparent response to this work came in Sessions 8 and 9, when the patient reported an 'incredible week' in which she had been extremely effective in a number of areas. In this session she also became openly competitive with the therapist. However, it now appeared that this was the result of a hypomanic state, and in Session 10 she was quite severely depressed, which had probably been precipitated by a visit home in which she had seen that her sister's condition had deteriorated. In Session 15 she again became competitive with the therapist, talking about 'counter-transference' and laughing at her when she didn't know what to answer.

In Session 17 she reported having argued robustly and effectively with her interviewers at London University, and in this session the therapist suddenly suggested that she and the patient should change places. One of the effects of this was that the patient was able to feel much more 'on the same level' as her therapist and less intimidated by her.

In Session 18 she reported having been highly commended by her interviewers at London University.

In Session 19 she reported having attended a conference at the Tavistock and handled the situation extremely well, feeling 'on the same level' as the staff there.

In these later sessions there was no evidence of her being in any way hypomanic.

The position at final follow-up

This ability to be constructively self-assertive was not maintained. She gave up her work without knowing what else she would do; and her inappropriate expression of anger destroyed the relation with her boy-friend.

The Victimised Telephonist

Work on the patient's defences against anger preceding the discovery of enlightened self-interest and constructive self-assertion

In the initial interview some intensive work was done on the patient's anger with her much older (Greek) man-friend, linked with deprivation in her childhood, and her lifelong defence of trying to please. She ended by saying that 'there were a lot of things deep down which needed to come out, like being angry. That night [when her man-friend broke with her] I did throw a glass at the wall. Perhaps I should have smashed everything in the house.'

In Session 1 she half-denied her anger, and then said 'it was a pity the Turks missed a few Greeks in the troubles in Cyprus'.

In Session 2 she recollected incidents involving lack of care on the part of her man-friend, and the therapist linked this with her childhood.

It was in Session 3 that she reported abandoning her altruistic position in relation to her mother's admission to hospital, and replacing it by enlightened self-interest.

Unfortunately, at final follow-up she had relapsed totally into her original pattern of taking the position of victim.

The Acutely Suicidal Receptionist

Work on anger with parents preceding the ability to ask things for herself

Even this patient showed the beginning of therapeutic effects following work on her anger in her early contacts with the Clinic.

Thus in the initial interview she was enabled to speak with considerable anger about her parents and their lack of care; and the psychologist who gave her projection tests (during four subsequent interviews) wrote that 'she was able to bring into awareness her anger against both her parents, and to face the fact that this was of an intense and overwhelming quality'.

In Session 1, in response to interpretations mentioning defence, anxiety, and underlying feeling, she spoke with great anger of her mother's drunkenness, hitting the arm of the chair to emphasise her feelings.

It was in Session 2 that she reported being able for the first time to ask for things for herself.

Comment

Perhaps the clearest evidence is provided by the two patients with the highest scores for outcome: the Nurse Mourning her Fiancé, who began to be put in touch with her grief in the first therapeutic session; and the Pacifist Conductor, whose *lifelong* inhibition of feeling began to be transformed after seven therapeutic contacts over the course of 4 months. Both these patients spoke with appreciation of the therapist's accepting attitude, which enabled them to feel safe to express what they really felt.

Rather surprisingly, almost equally strong evidence is provided by the two patients with menstrual problems: the Psychiatric Nurse with Attacks of Rage, who began to have regular periods *for the first time since her menarche 9 years previously* after a single interview; and the Anorexic Museum Assistant, who had her first period for 2 ½ years after two interviews.

Two patients whose relations with the opposite sex had been superficial and ephemeral formed long-lasting or permanent relations during their therapy. The Sculptress changed from having a seemingly interminable series of affairs lasting 1 or 2 weeks to forming a relation which lasted for 5 years; the Car Battery Man, who said that formerly he always just 'used' women, began the process of committing himself to the girl who later became his wife.

A very interesting phenomenon, also reported by two patients, was the ability *for the first time in their life* to speak openly to other people – mainly parents – about problems and needs in the relationship. The Mother or Teenage Daughter reported in Session 10 having had a frank discussion first with her boy-friend and then with her parents. The latter discussion was extremely productive and resulted in her parents' acknowledging, also for the first time, that aggression had never been allowed in the home; that this was due to her mother's experience of violence in her own upbringing; and that the patient had always had reason to feel pushed out in the family, first by her sister's depressive illness and later by the presence of her son.

The Secretary in a State of Nirvana reported in Session 8 that she had had a most effective confrontation with her parents after her father had criticised her for being moody on her last visit home. This also was extremely productive, and she was able to have a frank discussion with them about her current difficulties in relation to her boy-friend.

We could suggest that one of the main factors making this possible was the whole atmosphere of a form of therapy in which the expression of true feelings represents a fundamental principle.

Much the same applies to constructive self-assertion, the widespread improvement in which represents one of the most striking observations emerging from the present study. Here one factor preceding the improvement was often dynamic work on problems of aggression, with the use of the two therapeutic triangles; but in addition the atmosphere of therapy must inevitably have conveyed the message that aggressive feelings are acceptable, which quite probably resulted in a form of de-conditioning to the patient's anxiety in this area. Indeed, the ease with which such improvements occur may well provide evidence to support the effectiveness of assertive training as used in behaviour therapy.

Conclusion

At the end of Chapter 32 we concluded that some kinds of factors in therapy were responsible for the observed improvements. The evidence presented in this chapter strongly suggests that these factors consisted mainly of bringing hitherto unconscious feelings to the surface, which is generally accepted as the essential and specific factor in all forms of dynamic psychotherapy.

34

Selection criteria

Introduction

We may start by recapitulating the previous conclusions on selection criteria and the use that was made of these in selecting patients in the present series.

In *The Frontier of Brief Psychotherapy* (Malan, 1976a) the evidence provided on this important subject by the 46 patients from Balint's Workshop was very carefully reviewed. Four main criteria were formulated (p. 256), and these were used in the selection of patients in the present study – an example of the influence of research on clinical practice.

Once the obviously unsuitable patients have been excluded (see Chapter 2 of the present book), the ideal situation indicating a favourable prognosis appeared to be as follows:

1 The clinical team is able to understand the psychodynamics and on this basis to formulate what seems to be a feasible focus.
2 The patient has responded to interpretations relevant to this focus.
3 The patient's motivation appears adequate.
4 Possible dangers of giving interpretative brief psychotherapy have been considered, and they can either be discounted or foreseen and overcome.

In a properly designed *scientific* study, evidence would be best obtained by comparing a sample of apparently suitable patients who fulfilled the criteria, with a control sample who did not fulfil them and were thought to be unsuitable. However, since Malan's Workshop was purely clinical rather than scientific, and was designed to provide both a service to the community and an important experience for the trainees, no attempt was made to create such a control sample; and patients were selected who appeared to fulfil the criteria to a reasonable degree. However, there were certain exceptions to this, which arose in two ways: from clinical experiments and clinical mistakes. As a consequence of this, some 'control' patients were provided, and the data therefore became more valuable scientifically; but the way in which conclusions may be drawn from it needs careful discussion.

We must bear in mind first of all the kind of hypothesis that is under test. This is essentially that, statistically speaking, these criteria are *necessary conditions* to success – the practice of psychotherapy seems altogether too uncertain to lead to the hope of finding *necessary and sufficient* conditions. This means that:

1 The hypothesis is confirmed by (a) patients who *fulfilled the criteria* and gave a *good result,* and (b) patients who *did not fulfil the criteria* and gave a *poor result.*
2 The hypothesis is contradicted by patients who did *not* fulfil the criteria and gave a *good* result.
3 Finally, because the hypothesis only involves the necessary condition, it can tolerate a certain number of patients who *fulfilled* the criteria and gave a *poor* result, provided their proportion is not too large.

This means that the hypothesis is most strongly tested only by patients *who did not fulfil the criteria,* and that amongst these the ratio of good results to poor results needs to be as small as possible, ideally zero.

Each of these criteria will now be discussed, though in a slightly different order.

The evidence on the four criteria

Criterion 1: An understanding of the psychodynamics leading to the formulation of a focus

There were only two patients who did not fulfil this criterion – the first the result of an experiment and the second the result of a mistake.

The first was the Rebellious Script Writer, where we had no idea of the meaning of her original complaint, an obsessional preoccupation with the word 'lesbianism'. We took her on because this symptom seemed to be associated with a recent traumatic event, namely the break-up of her relation with a man, which was followed by his depressive breakdown; and we thought that her feelings about this might provide a focus. In fact this issue did not feature in her therapy at all, and though she lost her symptom we did not understand why. The final result was a false solution of a kind that she might well have adopted without therapy, with little evidence for any significant degree of true resolution.

The second patient was the Girl with Eye Problems, where again we had no idea whatsoever of the psychopathology, and after six exploratory sessions discovered that she was borderline or psychotic. No focus was formulated, and at follow-up she was judged to be marginally worse.

Thus both these patients suggest that a failure to understand the psychopathology at initial assessment is an unfavourable sign.

Criterion 4: Dangers

Mention of the Girl with Eye Problems leads us at once into a discussion of dangers, since at initial assessment the possibility that this patient was psychotic was not even considered. The same applies to the Robot Man. Here the patient's main symptom was a form of derealisation following on a conscious attempt to control his outbursts of temper at the age of 11, the psychodynamics of which were obvious; but it failed to occur to anyone that derealisation might be a premonitory symptom of psychosis. This patient also was regarded as worse at follow-up, since his psychosis was now becoming manifest.

The third psychotic or borderline patient was the Graduate Clerk. Here therapy was extremely intense, brilliantly conducted, and apparently highly effective. Yet at follow-up the patient had taken one of the paths characteristic of such patients: he had given up hope and was in a state of almost complete emotional withdrawal.

Thus all three of these borderline or psychotic patients received negative scores at final follow-up. This suggests that trying to give brief therapy to such patients is a mistake. However, we must remember that this conclusion may apply more certainly to trainees than to experienced therapists. Balint's series provides one example of an excellent result in 29 sessions with a psychotic patient (the Stationery Manufacturer), where the therapist was Balint himself (see Malan, 1976a); and one fair result in 58 sessions in another (the Paranoid Engineer), where the therapist (it now can be revealed) was one of the present authors (DM) (see Malan, 1963 and 1976b).

Finally, of course, we must mention the most serious mistake of all, which was made in the case of the Acutely Suicidal Receptionist. It needs to be noted in our defence that we recognised to the full the ominous significance of her exceedingly disturbed family history; that we carefully considered the danger of suicide, but took at face value her statement that it was against her religion; that we referred her for extended psychological testing, which proved reassuring; and that we offered her 40 rather than the usual 30 sessions. The factor that was not properly taken into account was that she was living alone and had very little support (during therapy she went to stay with her sister, but such an arrangement could not last indefinitely and it caused almost as many problems as it solved).

This clinical story remains as a warning to anyone practising psychotherapy of any kind and brief psychotherapy in particular.

An important additional danger in this patient was her *intense need for regression,* which was a major factor leading to the disastrous final outcome. A similar strong need was also a feature in the Miner's Daughter Mourning her Baby (score 0.25), who repeatedly mentioned her wish for an all-caring partner who would be all things for her at all times. At follow-up it was quite clear that her regressive need had caused her to be *unable to mourn her therapist within the time limit that she had been set* – 'It was wrong to be abandoned when I wasn't ready.' The same may well apply to the Self-driving Physicist, whose final session was full of almost agonising pain about the loss of his therapist, and whose poor outcome was scored at 1.0. We should add that the Girl with Eye Problems said at follow-up that she felt 'let down' by the termination of her therapy.

This problem has been recognised from the earliest days of brief psychotherapy, but a patient's capacity to mourn is very difficult to assess, and in the first two of these patients the danger was not properly foreseen.

Thus our evidence strongly reinforces the principle, which is obvious enough but often insufficiently emphasised, that a proper consideration of the dangers of brief psychotherapy is an essential part of the process of initial assessment.

Criterion 3: Motivation

Here we must remember the research finding – see *Toward the Validation of Dynamic Psychotherapy*, (Malan, 1976b), Chapter 10 – that it is motivation after therapy has got under way that matters rather than motivation during the initial assessment period. This means that when we select patients we are really making a prediction of motivation in the future, which is of course somewhat speculative. The precarious nature of such implied predictions is illustrated by six patients.

The most obvious example was the Acting-out Accounts Clerk, whose apparently high motivation was entirely deceptive and was therefore misjudged. The judgment of her motivation was based on the following: after a highly dynamic initial interview she experienced a flood of fresh memories of her adolescence, about which she brought up written notes, a sign of very high motivation indeed. Nevertheless, from the very beginning of her therapy she started acting out, and in fact she missed four of her first eight appointments. Behaviour of this kind was mentioned in *A Study of Brief Psychotherapy* (Malan, 1963) as an ominous sign (p. 196), and it is not surprising that this particular patient gave a poor result, her score being 0.5.

Acting out over appointments was also a feature of the Miner's Daughter Mourning her Baby. At the end of the initial interview she had shown herself to be keen to come, and – although not yet definitely offered treatment – had brought out her work timetable in order to discuss times when she would be available. However, when the therapist was forced to cancel appointments, which happened twice, the patient began to act out. She failed to confirm an alternative time offered for Session 1; and on a number of later occasions failed to turn up, starting between Sessions 8 and 9. Her score for outcome was 0.25.

Another important observation is that both these patients opened their first session with communications about a wish to avoid involvement, which gave a clear indication that their apparently high motivation was deceptive.

The Actress with Elocution Problems was given six exploratory sessions for the purpose of seeing if she could work with the focus of mixed feelings for both her parents. During these sessions she started systematically opposing everything the therapist said; but in the sixth she accepted with enthusiasm the idea of making this opposition into the focus of her therapy, thus apparently showing a marked increase in motivation. However, from then on she became as resistant as before, repeatedly denying insight with which she had previously agreed, and it really seems that she finally succeeded in her implacable determination to defeat the therapist at all costs. Moreover, she also showed considerable acting out over appointments, even – ominously – arriving 20 minutes late for her first therapeutic session. Her very poor therapeutic result was reflected in her score of 0.25.

The Victimised Telephonist showed apparently high motivation at the end of her initial interview, as indicated by her remark, 'There are a lot of things deep down inside that I need to get off my chest, like being angry;' but as soon as therapy began her motivation became doubtful, which was symbolised by her keeping her coat on in the sessions; and of course she gave one of the worst therapeutic results in the whole sample.

The Secretary in a State of Nirvana started her therapy with high motivation and apparently made considerable progress; but she said at follow-up that later in therapy she 'began to think that she could do much better by distancing herself', and at one point she suggested stopping a month early. Her follow-up indicated a false solution by emotional withdrawal, scored at 1.0.

At the end of his initial interview the Concert-goer in an Acute Panic spoke of the important insight that he had acquired through the precipitating event, and how he had been able to make use of it, thus indicating genuine motivation. However, as soon as therapy started he went into resistance, often ruminating about irrelevant and emotionally sterile subjects; and he held back crucial information about his sexual fantasies till the last moment of the last session. His therapeutic result contained a strong element of false solution, but he did also show a number of apparently genuine therapeutic effects (score 1.625), so that in his case poor motivation did not lead to an entirely wasted therapy.

Finally, the most difficult problem in assessing the relation between motivation and outcome was presented by the Nurse Mourning her Fiancé, the patient with the highest score for outcome in the series. She might possibly be regarded as contradicting the hypothesis that poor motivation leads to poor outcome, but the situation is not as simple as this. The difficulty lies in a phenomenon discussed in *A Study of Brief Psychotherapy* (Malan, 1963, p. 186), namely that in many patients motivation clearly contains two opposite components. This is typified by the events covering her initial interview and the first two sessions: at the end of the former she decided to reject our offer of psychotherapy and to rely on anti-depressants; she then realised that this did not work and asked us to renew our offer, which of course we did; during most of Session 1 she was in a state of passivity and resistance, and yet she eventually *interpreted her resistance herself,* saying that she was concentrating on trivialities in order to stop herself from thinking painful thoughts; then, the moment she got outside the session she broke down into uncontrollable tears; she opened the next session by saying that because of this she nearly didn't come, and she dismissed her tears as 'about nothing;' yet, at final follow-up she described the feeling of relief at being able to cry, and said that she came to the second session 'for more relief'. Similar positive and negative components characterised the whole of her therapy, partic-ularly the final quarter. The truth seems to be, therefore, that she both sought relief, on the one hand, and tried to avoid her pain, on the other; and it seems clear that in the end the positive component of her motivation was sufficient to carry her through.

Our final conclusions, therefore, are that our material confirms the crucial importance of motivation, but that unfortunately the assessment of motivation at the end of the initial assessment period is very unreliable.

Criterion 2: Response to interpretation on a focal issue

This has always been regarded as virtually a *sine qua non* for the acceptance of a patient into brief psychotherapy, and the present series was no exception. The only patient who did not fulfil this criterion was the Girl with Eye Problems whose poor therapeutic result has already been mentioned, so that the hypothesis is confirmed by this single clinical mistake.

When patients are selected on the basis of response to focal interpretations, then by implication the prediction is being made that if they responded once they will continue to do so, i.e. that *they can work on this issue in dynamic psychotherapy.* Now sometimes our focus was wrong, but (unlike the similar prediction in the case of motivation) the implied prediction that they could work on some focus was almost 100% accurate, as it was in Balint's series also. In fact there seems to be one thing of which a clinician can be virtually certain in this most uncertain of all subjects: namely that *it is possible on the basis of a dynamically conducted initial interview to pick out those patients who can work focally in interpretative therapy,* an ability which would seem fairly obviously to be *necessary* to the conduct of brief psychotherapy. That it is not *sufficient* is equally obvious.

The four criteria: conclusion

We may therefore conclude that the evidence quite strongly supports the hypoth-esis that these four criteria taken together are – statistically speaking – necessary conditions to success. As before, we know they are not sufficient conditions, but the question is whether they are 'sufficiently sufficient', i.e. did they lead to a reasonable degree of success? This is the main theme of the two final chapters.

35

Further research results

Further disproof of the conservative view of brief psychotherapy

It may be remembered from Chapter 2 that according to the conservative view, only patients with superficial disturbances can be treated, only a superficial technique is appropriate, and the results themselves can only be superficial.

Types of patient treated and focus used

Now it is true that – apart from the four patients who were mistakenly selected – there were none of the remaining 20 who were seriously *psychically damaged*. However, it could not be said that any of these 20 suffered from superficial disturbances, nor that the focus dealt with in therapy was itself in any way superficial. The best examples illustrating this are perhaps the Librarian and the Sculptress. The former patient could be described as a long-standing masochistic character, and this aspect of her pathology was taken as focus; while in the latter a whole range of psychopathology was worked through, including ultimately the 'depressive position', i.e. the integration of good and evil, love and hate. In the Car Battery Man the therapist dealt effectively with the extremely primitive mechanism of paranoid projection. In all the others also the focus dealt with was the patient's central problem, and in all but the Nurse Mourning her Fiancé this included its origins in the distant past.

Transference

Another aspect of the 'superficial' technique advocated by those who hold the conservative view is that the therapist should not use transference interpretations. Here the assumed danger is that their use will inevitably intensify transference and ultimately lead to the formation of the 'transference neurosis' – a state in which the majority of a patient's life revolves around the relation with the therapist. In fact the opposite is the truth, and in most cases it is both possible and essential to deal with the transference in brief psychotherapy, and indeed to resolve it. This was conclusively demonstrated in Balint's Workshop, and it must be obvious that the same has been demonstrated by the work reported here. Once more the best example is provided by the Librarian, where the breakthrough not only occurred through the transference, but this led straight into the patient's intensely ambivalent feelings about her parents, and then to immediate therapeutic effects; and it finally left the patient with an excellent and completely non-dependent relation with her therapist throughout the whole of the follow-up period.

Therapeutic results

The view that the therapeutic results also can only be superficial was conclusively disproved in Balint's Workshop, and again this has been confirmed here. As discussed in Chapter 11, the Nurse Mourning her Fiancé showed total resolution of her problem; and six of the seven 'best' patients showed major changes in long-standing maladaptive behaviour patterns, for at least two of which the term 'character disorders' would be perfectly appropriate (the inability to express aggression in the Conductor and the masochistic phenomena in the Librarian).

Two fresh observations from the present work

Of course so far all the results described in this chapter simply represent confirmation of observations already made in Balint's Workshop. However, there are also two very important conclusions that Balint's Workshop did not reach.

The possibility of 'multi-focal' therapy

The first is as follows: *that if one chooses a highly responsive patient, then it not necessary to adhere to a single focus, or even two; but on the contrary it is possible to deal successfully and at depth with any aspect of psychopathology that emerges.*

This is best illustrated by the Sculptress, with whom the problems dealt with were exceedingly wide-ranging, as summarised in Chapter 7.

Another example is the Car Battery Man, with whom the therapist dealt not only with many aspects of the highly ambivalent relation to the father – often through the transference – but also with the patient's anger with his mother over the birth of his younger brother, his hostility to women in general, and the exceedingly primitive mechanism of paranoid projection of his aggressive feelings.

Brief therapy by trainees

The second fresh observation is the most obvious one of all and the most important from a practical point of view: namely that *the kind of brief therapy that was carried out in Balint's Workshop can be repeated successfully under supervision by trainees.*

This obviously has an important bearing on the working of therapeutic clinics and will be discussed in Chapter 37.

Part Five

The Value of the Work

36

The practical and theoretical value of the work

I For trainees, supervisors, and psychotherapists in general

Introduction

The over-all value of the work needs to be discussed from three points of view; that of trainees, and also of course supervisors and other therapists; that of psychotherapeutic clinics; and that of patients. Obviously the third is the most important both practically and ethically, and the other two depend on it. Since we are leaving this till the last, we need to say at the outset that we do believe this form of therapy to be of value to patients – a statement which we are sure will be giving away no secrets.

Trainees, supervisors, and other therapists

We can state with some confidence that this kind of work is an excellent training experience. As described in Chapters 2 and 31, patients are chosen because of *clarity of psychopathology* and *capacity to interact dynamically*. Consequently, trainees are given the opportunity to understand the principles of active dynamic psychotherapy, particularly the use of the two therapeutic triangles; to see psychopathology laid bare before their eyes; and in addition they may often experience the satisfaction of seeing early therapeutic effects, together with clear evidence of the kind of work that has produced them. Moreover pre-circulation of written reports of the sessions, together with supervision in a group setting, multiplies the experience of each therapist by a factor equal to the number of patients being treated at any one time, which may be as many as six or eight.

Looking back over these 24 therapies, we list below the many important features that have been illustrated. As will be seen, even some of the less obvious features often occurred in more than one patient, which clearly demonstrates the ever-recurring nature of human problems.

Initial assessment

Here the following are illustrated:

1 The importance of *interpretative work in initial assessment,* with the consequent ability to formulate a focus, to plan therapy, and to be sure that the patient will be able to work in dynamic psychotherapy.
2 The importance of a *full psychiatric assessment,* leading to the exclusion of patients showing certain dangers, in particular potential psychosis or suicide.
3 The fact that, after an initial assessment of this kind, realistic *therapeutic planning* is indeed possible, and predictions of the main focus of therapy are often broadly – or even entirely – correct.

Psychopathology

Here there is a long list. Below we mention only those aspects that are illustrated with unmistakable clarity.

The role of miscarried grief in depression

This was illustrated most clearly by the Nurse Mourning her Fiancé, who had become depressed because she could not face her grief. For her the process of mourning began with her tears in the very first session.

The role of buried anger in depression

This was illustrated by three patients:

1 The Nurse Mourning her Fiancé, whose depression improved on three occasions after work on anger.
2 The Librarian, who wrote on her application form, 'I want to be dead and I don't know why', and whose depression lifted after her realisation of a 'monster of violent anger within her' (Session 14).
3 The Nirvana Secretary, who arrived for Session 2 in a state of severe depression, which lifted after a terrific row with her inconsiderate boy-friend (Session 3).

The manic defence against grief

This was shown by the Nurse Mourning her Fiancé, who threw herself into hectic over-activity after his death; and by the Pacifist Conductor, who took a job as a gravedigger after his father's death and watched with satisfaction his colleagues dancing on the coffins.

The role of pent-up feelings, especially aggression, in phobic and anxiety symptoms

This was illustrated by four patients:

1 The Betrayed Son, who resolved a panic attack by confronting his boss with his grievances (Sessions 28 and 29).

2 The Car Battery Man, who realised that it was anger with people that made him claustrophobic (Session 23), and who resolved a panic attack by shouting at another driver (Session 25).
3 The Self-driving Physicist, who at follow-up described his claustrophobic symptoms as due to the feeling that he might 'explode'.
4 The Acting-out Accounts Clerk, who reached the insight that her anxiety in crowded places was caused by her wish to say something hurtful to people who got in her way (see p. 134).

The role of paranoid projection in some phobias

This was illustrated by the Car Battery Man (Session 23), who responded markedly to an interpretation linking his paranoidally tinged claustrophobic feelings in a pub to the projection of his anger about the loss of the warm atmosphere of his home, caused by the birth of his brother.

It is rare for phobic symptoms to mask paranoid phenomena, but it does happen, and it creates an important problem in differential diagnosis which needs to be borne in mind by clinicians undertaking initial assessment.

The effects of lack of aggression in the patient's upbringing

Here there were six patients:

1 The Conductor, whose parents were pacifists, which ultimately resulted in the loss of his whole emotional life, particularly his creativeness. Only when he was put in touch with his anger could these aspects of his personality be restored.
2 The Librarian, who came to realise (Session 14) that 'not even small amounts of anger' were allowed in her upbringing, and who had to be put in touch with her anger to be relieved of her severe masochistic tendencies.
3 The Rebellious Script Writer said at initial assessment that the only time that feelings had been evoked in her family was when she decided to leave home, and that she had never been 'troublesome' in any relationship. The two sides of this conflict between rebelliousness, on the one hand, and keeping the peace on the other, were very clearly expressed in her conflict over the relation with the two men in her life.
4 With the Mother or Teenage Daughter much of the initial interview was concerned with her feeling that something inside her needed to come out. This culminated in a moment of fresh insight, expressed in her intensely felt statement: 'Perhaps I want to tell the lot of them [i.e. her family] to go to hell.'

The reason why this was a problem became clear later when it emerged that her mother had been so affected by rows in her own family that she had always done her best to keep the peace at all costs (Session 10).
5 The Hypomanic Advertising Executive said that he 'had had no adolescence. My parents were so bloody understanding that I couldn't rebel' (Session 18).
6 Similarly, the Miner's Daughter Mourning her Baby spoke of her parents' altruism as 'too good for my own good. It did not prepare me for the realities of life. Their goodness hid the emptiness of their lives' (Session 5).

The all-pervading effects of a conscious decision to control aggressive impulses

This was observed in three patients:

1 The Actress with Elocution Problems, who became 'emotionally dead' after trying to control her verbal attacks on her mother in her teens (Session 16).
2 The Psychiatric Nurse with Attacks of Rage, who lost her capacity for feelings at the age of 11 as a result of trying to control her outbursts of temper against her sisters.
3 The Robot Man, who developed a symptom of derealisation at the age of 12 when he tried to control his outbursts of temper against his father.

The fear of being 'swamped' or 'engulfed' by another person

This occurred in five patients and clearly represented a fear of losing their identity because of the control exercised by other people. An interesting observation is the similar – and graphic – language used, quite independently, by several of these patients:

1 The Mountain Tarn Girl spoke of her fear of being 'swamped' by her husband, saying that she had to leave him or lose her identity.
2 The Rebellious Script Writer spoke of her relation with her man-friend, Colin, as resembling that with her controlling parents, saying that she felt she had to get out or be 'swallowed up'. She later spoke of the closeness with her mother as representing a 'stranglehold'.
3 The Hypomanic Advertising Executive (Session 13) spoke of his fear of being 'sucked in and engulfed' by his wife, which was clearly linked with his feelings about his dominating and controlling mother.
4 The Actress with Elocution Problems originally sought treatment because her mother had become extremely dominating after having a stroke, a tendency which the patient now felt had always been present beneath the surface. In Session 16 she spoke of her mother as 'only wanting her to be an extension of herself'.
5 At follow-up the Graduate Clerk said that he was afraid of being 'swamped' if he got into any close relationship with a girl. This fear, in a borderline patient, was probably of a more primitive kind than it was in the four patients above.

Feelings about the father in the male Oedipus complex

Four patients (the Car Battery Man, the Betrayed Son, the Concert-goer, and the Self-driving Physicist) illustrate the very complicated and conflicting feelings in men who have had – at least at one time – a basically good relation with their father: consisting of love, disappointment, anger, and severe and anxiety-laden competitiveness.

Triangular relations in the male Oedipus complex

Two patients illustrate the literal nature of the male Oedipus complex in terms of guilt- and anxiety-laden competition with another man for a woman:

1 The Concert-goer, who was living with a woman old enough to be his mother, and who suffered a paralysing anxiety attack when this relation seemed to be threatened by another man.
2 The Self-driving Physicist, who in Session 22 mentioned open competition between himself and his father for his mother, which also appeared manifestly in the transference with his fantasy that the psychologist was the therapist's wife.

The Oedipus complex in women

Various aspects of the female Oedipus complex, including its causes, manifestations, and intensely ambivalent and literal quality, are illustrated by five patients:

1 The Sculptress, who on the one hand was enraged with her father because of his behaviour over the restaurant (Session 5), but on the other hand found him attractive and seductive and had openly flaunted herself at him (Session 13); and in addition was still choosing men who, like him, did not give her sufficient attention.
2 The Librarian, who said that her conflicting feelings for her father originated in the fact that he had both humiliated her and behaved seductively towards her.
3 The Mountain Tarn Girl, whose father constantly disappointed her and whom she described as 'keen on any girl between the ages of 17 and 25 [which included herself], and then her mother might have thought she was the "other woman"' (Session 29).
4 The Allergic Receptionist, who re-lived her intense grief and anger about the occasion on which her father returned home to collect his furniture (Sessions 20 and 21), and who was still looking for a man who resembled him (Session 26).
5 The Anorexic Museum Assistant, who reported a dream in which her mother was dead, and she had just married her father and they were about to go upstairs to bed together (Session 11).

The effects of the birth of a younger sibling

The important contribution to psychopathology caused by the birth of a younger sibling is illustrated by six patients in the present series and also one who was ineligible:

1 The Librarian, whose brother, born when she was 3, was nearly drowned while in her care when she was 5 – nobody ever knew how much this was her fault.
2 The Car Battery Man, who showed intense paranoid feelings about the loss of the warm atmosphere in his home, which had been broken by the birth of his sister when he was 4 (Session 23).
3 The Betrayed Son, who was extremely disturbed by an interpretation about his rivalry with his 7-years-younger brother, given within the setting of the birth of his own child (Sessions 3 and 4).
4 The Hypomanic Advertising Executive, who had to have psychotherapy at the age of 9, largely because of his rivalry with his younger brother, born when the patient was 2.
5 The Anorexic Museum Assistant, one of the traumas of whose life was the birth, and death, of her baby sister, born when the patient was 10. In her childhood

this patient also nearly dropped her 8-years-younger brother into a stream (cf. the Librarian, above).

6 The Borderline Graduate Clerk, much of whose therapy was concerned with his rivalry with his 2-years-younger brother. The climax of his therapy occurred with the recollection of his mother's remark that, unlike his brother, 'no woman would ever have *you*' (Session 11); and in Session 19 he made the remark, 'I guess brother-figures are all around me.'

7 To these can be added the Divorced Mother (see Chapter 4), who in her childhood apparently made an attempt on the life of her younger brother soon after he was born.

The choice of an unsatisfactory partner as an expression of the 'compulsion to repeat'

This immensely powerful and devastating psychic mechanism is illustrated by two women, who described with clear insight how their choice of men repeated aspects of the unsatisfactory relation with their father.

1 As mentioned above, the Sculptress said at follow-up that she chose men who, like her father, did not give her sufficient attention (see Chapter 24 for details).

2 The Victimised Telephonist married a man who resembled her father both in rejecting her and in 'always shouting at her' (see Chapter 24).

3 In addition, a possible hypothesis in the case of the Girl with Eye Problems is that the main situation causing difficulty in her childhood was the lack of true emotional contact with her parents; and it seems that she unconsciously trapped herself in a similar situation through her choice of the man she married.

Masochism, and the need for partners whom people dislike or by whom they are ill treated

Although these phenomena occur in both sexes, they seem to be commoner in women, and in fact they were found only in women in the present series. Of the following six patients, the first two illustrate the part that aggression plays in the underlying pathology:

1 The Librarian married a man who liked to exercise power over her. Her overtly masochistic fantasies were resolved when she was put in touch with the intensity of her anger and jealousy.

2 Very similarly, the Divorced Mother allowed herself to be exploited and misused in many kinds of situation, including her marriage; and this also was resolved when she was put in touch with her anger and jealousy.

3 The Script Writer was sexually aroused by an impulsive man whom she didn't really like, but with whom she could express the aggression which she had been unable to express in her upbringing.

4 The Nirvana Secretary described her boy-friend as exceedingly unpleasant, and yet the sexual relation with him was highly satisfactory.

5 The Miner's Daughter Mourning her Baby suffered from almost murderous feelings towards the boy-friend who had made her pregnant, yet stayed with him and contemplated marrying him. At follow-up she made the remark, 'We would have destroyed each other.'

6 The Victimised Telephonist showed a pattern of taking the role of victim throughout her recent life; and in the end she married a man whom she didn't love and who rejected her emotionally.

Trying to be 'nice', or 'bending over backwards to please'

This defence, and the fact that it is usually both destructive to the individual and ineffective, was illustrated by five patients:

1 The Self-driving Physicist, who tried to be nice to everyone, but this never resulted in his being praised.
2 The Nirvana Secretary, who said at follow-up that formerly she 'tried to please everyone except herself', with the result that her own needs were not met.
3 The Miner's Daughter, who said at follow-up that her relation with her parents had 'always been on a nice level', with the result that she could not properly communicate with them.
4 The Psychiatric Nurse, who repeated with her boy-friend her earlier pattern of keeping the peace and allowing herself to be exploited, with the result that she eventually exploded with rage in a way that finally destroyed the relationship.
5 The Victimised Telephonist, who became imprisoned in an emotionally one-sided relationship with her man-friend, in which she could never put her own needs forward, thus repeating the pattern of her childhood.

The effects of the parents' unsatisfactory relation on the patient's attitude to marriage

1 The Self-driving Physicist, who had described the utter sterility of his parents' marriage, said at follow-up that he could never commit himself to a woman – 'I regard marriage as a death.'
2 The Victimised Telephonist said that the constant quarrelling between her parents had put her off the whole idea of marriage.

Technique

Obviously such elements of technique as the interpretation of the two therapeutic triangles, and particularly the use of transference, are illustrated almost universally throughout these therapies. Here we will pick out certain less obvious themes.

The therapist's accepting atttitude

The value of this is illustrated most clearly by the remarks that four patients made at follow-up:

1 The Nurse Mourning her Fiancé spoke with appreciation of the way in which her therapist made her feel safe by not pressing her.
2 Similarly, the Conductor spoke with appreciation of the therapist's calm acceptance of his silence in the first therapeutic session.
3 The Betrayed Son said that he valued the opportunity to react to the therapist in any way that he liked.

4 The Mountain Tarn Girl valued the calm way in which her therapist had handled the very difficult problem posed by her hysterical attack after one of her sessions (number 9).

This last is a kind of situation which almost every therapist has to learn how to handle sooner or later.

'Counter-transference'

The highly creative use that can be made of counter-transference is illustrated by Session 13 of the Librarian, in which the therapist realised that her own feeling of sleepiness was a form of withdrawal in reaction to the patient's suppressed anger. This led first to the exposure of a major source of negative transference, namely the therapist's small stature, which resembled that of the patient's younger sister, and then to a major breakthrough.

Relating the current session to events in a previous session

This is an important element in technique which it is very easy to miss. It is illustrated by three patients:

1 In Session 4 the Betrayed Son spoke of the disturbance set up in him during the week, which was eventually traced to interpretations about rivalry with his brother in the previous session.
2 In the case of the Miner's Daughter the sterility and lack of communication in Session 10 was probably due to the mention of termination in the previous session – an interpretation which the therapist missed.
3 In the case of the Borderline Graduate Clerk, the sequence of sessions beginning with number 6 illustrates the disturbed and confusing material that may result from missing a crucial interpretation, which in this case concerned the patient's violent reactions to rejection by a girl.

Flexibility: the use of non-interpretative techniques

Our own view is that such techniques are often entirely appropriate and should be used more often, and indeed – as described in the next section – the failure to use them may have serious harmful effects. We may mention the following:

1 In Session 22 of the Car Battery Man the therapist dealt with the patient's wish to be given power by the therapist, saying: 'That is not the real way to growth. The aim is that you should be able to rely on your own power.'
2 In the last session of the Miner's Daughter Mourning her Baby, the therapist pointed out some of the realities, e.g. that the patient was much valued at work, and that the all-caring mother that she was seeking was neither possible nor necessary.
3 A highly creative departure from the standard interpretative technique was used in Session 17 of the Psychiatric Nurse with Attacks of Rage. This occurred when the therapist suggested that she and the patient should change places in the treatment room. The result was that the patient was able to see her therapist as a real person, and to be less afraid of competition with her. The immediate

favourable effect was an increase in self-confidence, though the final over-all outcome in this patient's case was poor.

Harmful effects of the 'passive sounding board' technique

Here we need to emphasise a crucially important *negative* observation, namely the *resentment left in patients by elements of the 'passive sounding board' technique* inappropriately transferred to brief therapy from psychoanalysis. Five patients made this clear at follow-up:

1 Even the most successful patient, the Nurse Mourning Her Fiancé, expressed resentment that in her final sessions her therapist had not advised her about whether or not she needed further treatment – something that it would have been absolutely appropriate to discuss with her quite openly.
2 The Acting-out Accounts Clerk said with resentment that her chief memory was of her therapist 'just sitting and glaring' at her.
3 A very similar remark was made by the Miner's Daughter: 'I had a friend who had the same experience with a psychiatrist as I did. They sit and stare at you, it was absolutely awful. I remember racking my brains for something to say to start the conversation.'
4 The Actress with Elocution Problems spoke with resentment of the way in which her therapist just 'shut the door and stayed silent' – even though, once each session started, her therapy consisted of a mass of highly dynamic interaction.
5 The Nirvana Secretary spoke as follows: 'My therapist was superficially a very cold person, and I found it quite difficult to understand how such a person could begin to comprehend the problems I had; and when she made clear that she wanted me to continue coming, it was the first sign that she was a human being.'

It is very difficult to know what should be done about this, since patients almost always need to be left to choose where they are going to start. There are two possible approaches: one is to be more human, and perhaps simply explain to patients that it is necessary for the opening remarks to come from them; while the other is for the therapist to keep silent, but to be aware of patients' possible resentment and to bring it out into the open. Almost invariably it will be found to link with some rejection that they have experienced in the past.

Finally, in the case of the Suicidal Receptionist, the therapist refused to step outside the traditional interpretative role and allow the patient's sister to be seen. This made a major contribution to the failure to get the patient admitted to hospital before her desperate need for suicide could be translated into reality. Here the supervisor was to blame at least as much as the therapist; and it must be admitted that a reason for his reluctance was that he still suffered from inhibitions about making interventions of this kind, carried over from his psychoanalytic training.

A more active technique?

Although these therapies were highly active, it could be argued that an even more active technique might have given better results. The general issue here consists of therapists' failure to pursue actively certain themes which formed part of the original focus but were never brought up by the patients themselves. The following are the main examples, and it is interesting to note that each of them is concerned with the original event which caused the patient to seek treatment:

1 In the Rebellious Script Writer there were two – apparently related – issues arising from the history which the patient did not bring up. The traumatic event which seemed to represent the original precipitating factor was the fact that she had broken with her man-friend, Colin, and he had then suffered a depressive breakdown; and 6 months later she had begun to suffer from a distressing preoccupation with the word 'Lesbianism'. The therapist did not actively direct her attention to either of these issues; and we still do not know what connection there was between them, or what they meant to her.

2 In the Mother or Teenage Daughter, the patient's feelings about her original traumatic experiences of being raped at the age of 17, made pregnant, giving birth, and the consequent arrival in the family of an unwanted child, were hardly mentioned in her therapy. It seems likely that there was much buried feeling about these events, almost certainly contributing to her state of tension, and particularly to the tension in her relation with her son – a relation which remained unsatisfactory throughout the whole of the follow-up period.

3 In the Psychiatric Nurse with Attacks of Rage, the original precipitating factor leading to her request for treatment consisted of her father's death, after which she experienced an intense feeling of emotional liberation, especially of anger. It seems now that her anger must have been about the permanent loss, caused by her father's death, of her unconscious hope that one day she would find in him the father that she never had; and although our original aim was to try and consolidate her liberation, her feelings about her father – both positive and negative – were insufficiently emphasised in her therapy, and her relations with men in general continued to be bedevilled by an undercurrent of hostility.

The relative absence of these themes was of course the supervisor's fault rather than that of the therapists; and if we could have the therapies over again, the supervisor would ask that patients' attention should be actively directed towards these areas – whereas in fact his own attention was directed away from them by the actual developments between patients and therapists, which were always interesting and always clearly relevant.

Material and events of therapy

Obviously our material illustrates such universal issues as the development of resistance and transference, clear response to interpretation, the effect of interpretations linking the transference to the past, etc. Here we will pick out only some of those other aspects which are especially interesting or deserve special emphasis.

Depth of material and depth of interpretation

One of the important features illustrated by these therapies is that – with appropriately selected patients – there are few limits to the depth of material that can be used and interpreted. The following are examples:

1 The Sculptress reported dreams transparently concerned with attacks on babies in the womb, and also on women's fertility (Sessions 7 ff.), which the therapist linked with the patient's mother. This kind of material was also meaningfully interpreted in Session 24, leading to an expression of guilt about how the patient had treated her mother in childhood and adolescence.

2 Both the Car Battery Man (in the first follow-up interview) and the Borderline Graduate Clerk (Session 11) presented paranoid material, which was successfully interpreted in terms of projection, with the result that each patient became able to 'take back the aggression into himself', and paranoid feelings became mitigated.

3 Both the Nurse Mourning her Fiancé (Session 18) and the Sculptress (Session 27) gave material indicating that they were reaching the 'depressive position' – the integration of love and hate. In the former patient this was expressed in a dream in which an Arctic landscape was transformed into grass, which she reported after interpretations about a mixture of love, on the one hand, and death wishes on the other, directed towards her grandmother. In the latter patient, the integration of love and hate in her relation with her husband was expressed when she said that, in spite of all the bitterness that there had been between the two of them, each had taken away something valuable from their relation – on her side creativeness, and on his side a new capacity for passion.

Major de-repression or the re-living of past events

Obviously the de-repression of hitherto unconscious feelings was a feature of most of these therapies, but there were four particularly striking moments in which this occurred:

1 As has been quoted many times, the Librarian said that she had come to realise that she had a 'monster of violent anger within her' (Session 14).

2 The Betrayed Son re-lived the events leading up to the first precipitation of his phobic symptoms 2 years previously (Session 18).

3 The Allergic Receptionist re-lived the events of the day when her father had returned home to collect his furniture, 5 years previously (Sessions 20 and 21).

4 The Hypomanic Advertising Executive de-repressed his true feelings about his mother: 'Tremendous locked-up anger – a lack of respect, that's what it is. I feel as though a thunderclap has happened' (Session 22).

Sudden freeing of the unconscious in response to the open expression of transference feelings

This freeing is a phenomenon similar to that observed regularly in Davanloo's initial interviews, (for which he uses the term 'unlocking', see Davanloo, 1990). It seems to occur especially when the patient expresses *anger* about the therapist's *correct* interventions, which threaten major defences. It occurred, though to a lesser degree than in Davanloo's hands, in two of these 24 therapies:

1 The Librarian who Sought Suffering: between Sessions 13 and 14 the patient phoned to say that she was angry with the therapist for continually linking her present relationships to the past, 'but now everything had fallen into place' and she realised her intensely ambivalent feelings for her parents. It was in the next

session that she made the above-mentioned remark about a 'monster of violent anger within her'.

2 The Borderline Graduate Clerk: in Session 11 he spoke of his resentment about the therapist's interpretations of paranoid projection. In the rest of the session the nature of the traumatic situation in his upbringing – namely his mother's preference for his brother – became absolutely clear.

The ability to reconstruct the patient's family situation

Again, this was almost universal in these therapies, but in the following instances it was possible to make hypotheses about the pathology of the parents:

1 In the case of the Sculptress the essential observation was the destructive effect on the whole family of the father's behaviour over the restaurant. When this is put side by side with his vegetarianism, it looks as if the latter was a form of over-compensation for aggressive impulses, and that his treatment of the women in the family represented an example of the 'return of the repressed'. It was not possible to see the source of his aggression, although there was evidence for a disturbed relation with his own *father* in the fact that he was left out of his father's will.

2 At initial assessment it emerged that the Nirvana Secretary's mother had herself been seriously deprived as a child. In later life she had become deeply involved in 'good works', which probably represented giving to others what she would have wished for herself. But it is easier to do this in impersonal relations than in relations with one's own family, and the end result was the neglect of her own children.

3 In the case of the Mother or Teenage Daughter it emerged that her mother had been so affected by rows in her own upbringing that she had done her best to keep the peace at all costs in the patient's home (Session 10).

Changed view of parents resulting from therapy

It is a well known observation that either a positive or a negative description of parents may break down under therapy and reveal aspects that are quite the opposite. In the present series there were four examples in which a positive description changed to negative:

1 The Car Battery Man said he had reached the realisation that his mother, who appeared warm on the outside, was actually cold on the inside, and that his father – against whom he had expressed a great deal of resentment – was the warmer of the two (Session 22).

2 The Concert-goer's original description was of the extreme closeness between him and his father, and his prostrating grief at his father's death. This did not seem to tally with his current hostility towards male authority, and indeed a later picture emerged of his father as 'exacting, critical, and severe'.

3 The Nirvana Secretary, who originally described her parents as nobly self-sacrificing, said in Session 11: 'What really gets me is that my father is so sanctimonious', and she later said that she was 'sick to death' of the way that her mother gave up all Saturday morning is to helping at the Church.

4 The Miner's Daughter Mourning her Baby, in response to an interpretation about feeling 'bad' even before her abortion, said, 'And I always thought I had

such a nice childhood' (Session 3). She went on to reveal aspects of the sterility of her parents' marriage, which were reinforced in Session 5 by her remark quoted above, that 'their goodness hid the emptiness of their lives'. Finally, in Sessions 15 and 16 she spoke of the hidden hostility between her parents, and from her description of her father it appeared that he had been miserly and obsessionally rigid.

Patients' view of the danger of facing parents with their true feelings

This clearly links with the previous heading, the breakdown of idealisation, and it gives an indication of the kinds of buried secrets that lie hidden in some families. Three patients made very similar remarks on this subject:

1 In the later part of therapy the Betrayed Son spoke of his feelings about two contrasting aspects of his father, weakness as well as strength, and he then said, 'If we told this conversation to my father it would break him.'
2 The Rebellious Script Writer said, 'To face my mother with my true feelings would be like destruction.' These feelings were concerned with her mother's controlling and domineering behaviour after her stroke.
3 The Miner's Daughter said: 'To tell my parents of my pregnancy would have destroyed their idealisation of me and undone the sacrifice of their lives' (Session 5).

Reconciliation with a parent after therapy

This is the other side of the coin to the breakdown of idealisation and is a phenomenon which often follows a successful therapy. Here the patient's hostility has been at least partially worked through, and the parent may well have mellowed, with the result that the barriers between the two of them begin to break down. This occurred in three patients in the present series:

1 During therapy the Librarian described her father in her childhood as both seductive and humiliating to her. At follow-up she said that she had become very close to him before he died.
2 Much of the Car Battery Man's therapy was concerned with his highly ambivalent feelings about his father, from whom he was estranged. At follow-up the relation had dramatically improved, and they could now go out for a drink together and collaborate in domestic jobs.
3 The Sculptress said at follow-up that she now got on much better with the members of her family, and that she could understand some of her father's behaviour as a reaction to his own upbringing.

These three patients stand in contrast to the Mountain Tarn Girl, who at follow-up said that after visiting her father she was left with a 'knotted gut for days afterwards'.

Seven memorable remarks

Every now and then patients make remarks that epitomise some aspect of human relations in a particularly vivid and moving way. Perhaps we may end by quoting seven of these, the last two made by the patient who was probably the least well educated in the series:

1 The Pacifist Conductor quoted the remark of a previous girl-friend: 'In your family there was a lot of care and respect, but little love' (Session 9).
2 Rather similarly, at follow-up the Hypomanic Advertising Executive described his childhood as containing 'a lot of pain, a lot of seriousness, and not much laughter'.
3 The Conductor described the move away from his original pacifist position with the words, 'The world is changed by the strength that there is in anger.'
4 The Mountain Tarn Girl contrasted her husband's ineffectiveness with her own hysterical impulsiveness in the delightful epigram, 'For him it's decisions without action, while for me it's action without decisions.'
5 The Anorexic Museum Assistant gave a graphic and original description of a friend's uninhibited zest for life (unfortunately in total contrast to herself): 'I have a friend who enjoys eating, and window-shopping, and speculation, and intrigue' (Session 33).
6 The Mother or Teenage Daughter said to her boy-friend, on the subject of whether or not to go to bed together: 'You don't have to do this to oblige me, you know, and I'm not going to do it just to be obliging to you' (Session 10). (A very similar remark occurs in Charles Morgan's novel, *The Voyage*, which it is most improbable that she had read.)

And finally, (7) the same patient said, 'I want a few *nows*, I'm fed up with waiting for *laters*' (Session 10).

Conclusion

We have devoted a great deal of space to the observations presented in this chapter, because material possessing this degree of clarity is pure gold, of immense value – and not only to trainees. Ultimately much of the skill and clinical judgment of all therapists is based, consciously or unconsciously, on stored experience of this kind.

37

The practical value of the work

II For psychotherapeutic clinics

III For patients

Psychotherapeutic clinics

It is obviously a great advantage to a hard-pressed psychotherapeutic clinic to be able to siphon off certain kinds of patient who can be substantially helped in a relatively short time, rather than automatically assigning them to long-term treatment and thus blocking vacancies that would otherwise be available. It is an even greater advantage if such patients can be treated by trainees. This is particularly important because in teaching clinics it is trainees who supply the majority of the vacancies.

During the period over which the present work extended, the demand for such treatment at the Tavistock Clinic almost exactly balanced the vacancies available. This, however, reveals a very considerable limitation, namely that among the general psychotherapeutic population the proportion of patients thought to be suitable for brief therapy is small. Those treated in Malan's Workshop represented just over 4% of patients who applied for treatment at the Tavistock Clinic during this period. However, it must be remembered that Malan's Workshop was not the only source of vacancies for brief therapy, so that the over-all proportion thought to be suitable for brief therapy was considerably higher than this. (The Determined Mother, mentioned at the beginning of Chapter 29, was an example of a patient treated very successfully with brief therapy supervised by another consultant.)

There is another limitation which also must be borne in mind, namely that at its best the work is highly skilled, more so than long-term therapy, and ideally it requires a considerable degree of sophistication in the trainees. The majority of our trainees already had considerable psychotherapeutic experience, as was described in Chapter 5.

Nevertheless clinics who wish to start offering this kind of treatment should not be put off by the relative sophistication of our own trainees. Recently one of us (DM) has worked in the Royal South Hants Hospital in Southampton, where patients perforce are not nearly as carefully selected as in the present work, and where they may be offered brief therapy by *complete beginners,* under experienced supervision. He has observed some of the same types of therapeutic effect as were reported in Chapter 32 already beginning to appear even during the course of this very limited therapy – consisting of an increased ability to be free with feelings, or to be constructively assertive, in everyday life. (This included a young woman with the original complaint of an inability to assert herself, who during therapy reported a phone conversation with a Tax Inspector in which she had said: 'You've got it all wrong, and I'll trouble you not to get in touch with me again until you've got it right!'.) Of course this kind of work has not been properly evaluated, but it may be more effective than might be supposed. Certainly it is excellent experience for the trainees.

Patients

Brief therapy may indeed be good experience for trainees, but this is irrelevant if the therapeutic results are poor – no one should be interested in training therapists in ineffective methods. So the most important question is whether our work was worthwhile from the point of view of the patients.

Here we must remember that by no means all patients improve significantly, even though they may be selected with great care. In the present work, whereas 57 patients were treated, 31 were followed up; and of these 31, 24 had had no further treatment. Of these 24, perhaps 12 showed worthwhile improvements (this includes five of the patients with scores for outcome between 1.0 and 1.75 inclusive). *Quantitatively* speaking, therefore, the results cannot be described as more than moderate. (It is important to note, however, that some of the non-eligible patients also showed significant improvements – see the Divorced Mother and the Public Speaker, both described in Chapter 4.)

What about *qualitative* considerations? Perhaps it is best to start with an important limitation, namely the extreme difficulty of enabling patients to form a relation with the opposite sex free from reservations. This statement can be qualified by the following consideration: although, if this criterion is applied absolutely strictly, it is fulfilled by only one patient, there were three others who formed extremely close, rewarding, basically committed relations, namely the Conductor, Car Battery Man, and Mountain Tarn Girl. This greatly improves the over-all picture of the results.

Moreover, all seven of the 'best' cases experienced a *complete transformation* of their lives, not shown merely in symptomatic relief – though this occurred also – but in major changes in serious disturbances of behaviour or feeling. The Nurse Mourning her Fiancé and Conductor were put in touch with the whole of their lost emotional lives; the Conductor and Sculptress found their lost creativity, on which their entire professional life depended; the Nurse Mourning her Fiancé, Conductor, and Car Battery Man found the possibility of commitment to the opposite sex, hitherto avoided; the Librarian was relieved of her masochistic sexuality and her devastatingly self-destructive mechanisms for dealing with anger and jealousy; the Mountain Tarn Girl was relieved of her two main self-destructive patterns, i.e. getting perpetually involved in triangular relationships and reacting to stress with hysterical outbursts; the Sculptress was relieved of her pattern of forming a relation with a new man every 1 or 2 weeks; all of the seven, with the exception of the Betrayed Son in the relation with his wife, discovered constructive self-assertion; and all but one found the ability to 'be themselves', the exception being the Car Battery Man in whom this had never been a problem.

Even some of the less satisfactory results included major changes which also transformed the patients' lives – whatever we may think of these changes in psychodynamic terms. Thus the Allergic Receptionist made remarkable progress in being herself, asserting herself effectively, and making something of her life; the Rebellious Script Writer recovered from an extremely distressing obsessional symptom; the Concert-goer became much more able to compete without anxiety and to get on with male authority-figures without underlying hostility; the Hypomanic Advertising Executive lost his 'impotent image' and became the leader of a team at work; the Self-driving Physicist also became extremely effective at work; and the Nirvana Secretary said she was infinitely better at standing up for herself both at work and with her parents. These 6 patients bring the total whose lives were transformed to 13, i.e. just over half the sample.

In this connection it is worth quoting tributes paid by five of these patients to their therapy:

1 The Nurse Mourning her Fiancé said to her therapist in Session 27, 'You may not believe it, but I've spent the whole morning trying to convince a friend that she should see a psychiatrist, because I have been helped so much.'
2 At final follow-up the Conductor described his therapy as 'the turning point of his life'.
3 The Librarian, who had been seriously suicidal when she first came, wrote in a letter many years later that if it had not been for her therapy she might *literally* not have survived.
4 At 3-month follow-up the Sculptress – like the Conductor – described her therapy as 'the turning point of her life', and added that she now felt 'a new person, almost as if she had been reborn'.
5 The Allergic Receptionist said in Session 24 that her therapy had been 'the most important experience of her life', and in Session 27 that it had been 'the best investment she had ever made'.

Therefore, discounting total perfectionism, we cannot avoid concluding that in carefuly selected patients this kind of brief therapy by trainees can be extremely effective and very much worthwhile.

The relevance to the position of brief psychotherapy in general

As described in Chapter 35, the field of brief psychotherapy has for many years suffered from the 'hypothesis of superficiality', which may be stated succinctly as follows: only superficially ill patients can be treated by a superficial technique, with only superficial therapeutic results. This hypothesis is based on preconception and prejudice, but it dies very hard and is still widely held. It can only be countered effectively by the publication of many case histories describing in detail the types of patient, the technique used, and the long-term outcome of this type of therapy. Such was the aim of the three publications emanating from Balint's Workshop (Malan, 1963, 1976a, 1976b). The evidence led inescapably to the opposite conclusion, namely that the fearless use of a 'radical' purely interpretative technique, in certain patients with long-standing and relatively severe disturbances, can lead to therapeutic effects that are wide-ranging, deep-seated, and permanent. This conclusion has been amply confirmed in the present work, and the results are even more impressive in view of the fact that the therapists in the above studies were experienced, whereas in the present study they were trainees. Moreover in this book we have had the space to publish the clinical material in greater detail than ever before, so that the hypothesis of superficiality ought to be laid to rest for ever.

However, one word of caution is needed. The therapists in both Balint's and Malan's Workshops were working in groups, with supervision both by a leader and by each other. A major effect is that enthusiasm and discipline are maintained, and the work is prevented from degenerating into long-term therapy. Therapists on their own do not find this nearly so easy.

The present work in the context of the work of Davanloo

As was described in Chapter 2, Davanloo has developed a technique of dynamic brief psychotherapy which is not purely interpretative, but contains in addition the element of systematic *challenge* to the patient's resistance. It also involves paying extreme attention to enabling patients to experience and express their transference feelings directly. In Davanloo's hands this technique is capable of breaking through and achieving direct access to the unconscious of even the most resistant patients in a single interview. There follows therapy varying from a single session in the simplest and least resistant patients, to 40 sessions in the most difficult and most resistant, which regularly results in *total resolution* of the neurosis, confirmed at follow-up of many years. Moreover, his technique is capable of being transmitted to trainees, who have achieved some similar and spectacular results under his supervision. All these observations have been demonstrated unequivocally by videotapes, shown time and again at international symposia. Thus the effectiveness of this method can be in no doubt; it is of a different order of magnitude from that of methods that rely on interpretation alone; and in time all other methods of psychotherapy are likely to be supplanted by it.

But his technique also requires very intensive training and supervision, which ideally can only be carried out by Davanloo himself, and its dissemination throughout the world is a slow process. Until this happens there is an important place for the kind of work presented here, which can be extremely rewarding both for patients and trainee therapists – and also, of course, for the more experienced staff who supervise them.

References

Alexander F.G., and French T.M. (1946). *Psychoanalytic Therapy*. New York: Ronald Press.

Bandler B. (1948). In Oberndorf, Greenacre, and Kubie (1948), pp. 26–7.

Clementel-Jones C., and Malan D.H. (1988). Outcome of dynamic psychotherapy. *Brt. J. Psychother.*, **5**, 29–45.

Clementel-Jones C., Malan D.H., and Trauer T. (1990). A retrospective follow-up study of 84 patients treated with individual psychoanalytic psychotherapy. Outcome and predictive factors. *Br. J. Psychother.*, **6**, 363–374.

Davanloo H. (1978). *Basic Principles and Techniques in Short-term Dynamic Psychotherapy*. New York: Spectrum Publications.

Davanloo H. (1980). *Short-term Dynamic Psychotherapy*. New York: Jason Aronson.

Davanloo H. (1990). *Unlocking the Unconscious*. New York: Wiley.

Eissler K.R. (1950). The Chicago Institute of Psychoanalysis and the sixth period of the development of psychoanalytic technique. *J. Gen. Psychol.*, **42**, 103–157.

Eysenck H.J. (1952). The effects of psychotherapy, an evaluation. *J. Cons. Psychol.*, **16**, 319–324.

Eysenck H.J,. ed. (1960). *Handbook of Abnormal Psychology*. London: Pitman.

Gutmann D.L. (1980). Psychoanalysis and aging: a developmental view. In: *The Course of Life: Psychoanalytic Contributions towards Understanding Personality Development* vol. 3 (Greenspan S.I., Pollock G.H., eds) Washington: U.S. Department of Health and Human Services.

Jones E. (1946). Review of Alexander and French, *Psychoanalytic Therapy*. *Int. J. Psychoanal.*, **27**, 162.

Malan D.H. (1963). *A Study of Brief Psychotherapy*. London: Tavistock. Reprint by Plenum, New York: (1975).

Malan D.H. (1976a). *The Frontier of Brief Psychotherapy*. New York: Plenum.

Malan D.H. (1976b). *Toward the Validation of Dynamic Psychotherapy*. New York: Plenum.

Malan D.H. (1979). *Individual Psychotherapy and the Science of Psychodynamics*. London: Butterworth.

Malan D.H., Bacal H.A., Heath E.S., and Balfour F.H.G. (1968). A study of psychodynamic changes in untreated neurotic patients. I Improvements that are questionable on psychodynamic criteria. *Brt. J. Psychiat.*, **114**, 525–551.

Malan D.H., Balfour F.H.G., Hood V.G., and Shooter A.M.N. (1976). Group psychotherapy: a long-term follow-up study. *Arch. Gen. Psychiat.*, **33**, 1303–15.

Molnos A. (1984). The two triangles are four: a diagram to teach the process of dynamic brief psychotherapy. *Br. J. Psychother.*, **1**, 112–125.

Molnos A. (1986). The process of short-term dynamic psychotherapy and the four triangles. *Int. J. Short-term Psychother.*, **1**, 161–177.

Morgan Charles. *The Voyage*. Reprinted 1988 by Ballantine Books, New York.

Oberndorf C.P., Greenacre P., and Kubie L. (1948). Symposium on the evaluation of therapeutic results. *Int. J. Psycho-anal.*, **29**, 7–33.

Osimo F. (1984). Un metodo per misurare il cambiamento psicodinamico (A method for measuring psychodynamic change). *Psicoter. Sci. Umane*, **18**, 48–72.

Phillipson H. (1955). *The Object Relations Technique*. London: Tavistock.

Index